TERRORISM, HOT SPOTS AND CONFLICT-RELATED ISSUES

TERRORISM AND VIOLENCE IN ISLAMIC HISTORY AND THEOLOGICAL RESPONSES TO THE ARGUMENTS OF TERRORISTS

TERRORISM, HOT SPOTS AND CONFLICT-RELATED ISSUES

Additional books in this series can be found on Nova's website under the Series tab.

Additional e-books in this series can be found on Nova's website under the e-books tab.

TERRORISM, HOT SPOTS AND CONFLICT-RELATED ISSUES

TERRORISM AND VIOLENCE IN ISLAMIC HISTORY AND THEOLOGICAL RESPONSES TO THE ARGUMENTS OF TERRORISTS

RECEP DOGAN

Copyright © 2018 by Nova Science Publishers, Inc.

All rights reserved. No part of this book may be reproduced, stored in a retrieval system or transmitted in any form or by any means: electronic, electrostatic, magnetic, tape, mechanical photocopying, recording or otherwise without the written permission of the Publisher.

We have partnered with Copyright Clearance Center to make it easy for you to obtain permissions to reuse content from this publication. Simply navigate to this publication's page on Nova's website and locate the "Get Permission" button below the title description. This button is linked directly to the title's permission page on copyright.com. Alternatively, you can visit copyright.com and search by title, ISBN, or ISSN.

For further questions about using the service on copyright.com, please contact:
Copyright Clearance Center
Phone: +1-(978) 750-8400   Fax: +1-(978) 750-4470   E-mail: info@copyright.com.

NOTICE TO THE READER

The Publisher has taken reasonable care in the preparation of this book, but makes no expressed or implied warranty of any kind and assumes no responsibility for any errors or omissions. No liability is assumed for incidental or consequential damages in connection with or arising out of information contained in this book. The Publisher shall not be liable for any special, consequential, or exemplary damages resulting, in whole or in part, from the readers' use of, or reliance upon, this material. Any parts of this book based on government reports are so indicated and copyright is claimed for those parts to the extent applicable to compilations of such works.

Independent verification should be sought for any data, advice or recommendations contained in this book. In addition, no responsibility is assumed by the publisher for any injury and/or damage to persons or property arising from any methods, products, instructions, ideas or otherwise contained in this publication.

This publication is designed to provide accurate and authoritative information with regard to the subject matter covered herein. It is sold with the clear understanding that the Publisher is not engaged in rendering legal or any other professional services. If legal or any other expert assistance is required, the services of a competent person should be sought. FROM A DECLARATION OF PARTICIPANTS JOINTLY ADOPTED BY A COMMITTEE OF THE AMERICAN BAR ASSOCIATION AND A COMMITTEE OF PUBLISHERS.

Additional color graphics may be available in the e-book version of this book.

Library of Congress Cataloging-in-Publication Data

ISBN: 978-1-53613-924-2

Published by Nova Science Publishers, Inc. † New York

CONTENTS

Introduction		vii
Chapter 1	Religious Extremism and Terror	1
Chapter 2	Violence and Terrorism in Islamic History	39
Chapter 3	Theological Responses to the Arguments of the Extremist Groups	187
Chapter 4	An Analysis of Islam and Its Primary Sources in the Context of Violence and Terrorism	233
Chapter 5	Respect for the Sacred versus Freedom of Expression: An Analysis in the Context of De-Radicalization	271
References		291
About the Author		315
Index		317

INTRODUCTION

The history of radical interpretation of Islamic sources and thus resorting to violence "in the name of religion" goes back to the early period of Islam, emerging shortly after the death of the Noble Prophet (623 CE). Starting with the Kharijite group which emerged in the second half of the seventh century CE, there have been various radical terrorist groups appearing in the Muslim majority communities that interpreted the Qur'an and the traditions of the Noble Prophet in some extreme ways in an attempt to justify their violence and mask their evil acts. However, these groups have always remained marginal when compared to the majority of Muslims. As a matter of fact, interpreting a religion in some extreme ways and polluting its pure message is not limited to Islam. There have been many groups in many religions and faith traditions who are inclined to violence and terrorism, thus tarnishing their faith with their extremist interpretations. By inciting fear upon society, all terrorist groups and despotic rulers have tried to control the society and impose their own extreme ideas on the public.

When examining the entire course of human history, one can easily notice that terror and violence existed in very ancient times. For example, Sargon of Akkad, who was also known as Sargon the Great or "the Great King," was a Semitic Akkadian emperor famous for his conquest of the Sumerian city-states in the 24th and 23rd centuries BC. He founded the

Sargonic dynasty lasting for about a century after his death. While invading the lands, he committed many evils and left cities in ruin. Similarly, the antiquity's first military empire, the Assyrians[1] applied very brutal methods to rule people and frighten others daring to rebel. Obviously, all tyrants and terrorist groups keep resorting to violence and terror tactics in order to constrain the behaviors of people without the necessity of actively battling against them.

Terrorism may have a religious dimension, and historically speaking, this can be seen in many forms of terrorism, such as the Jewish Zealots of the first century CE and the Assassins of the Shiite-Isma'ili sect[2] from the eleventh to the thirteenth centuries.[3] The notion of a "terrorist" may at times be difficult to conceptualize because this issue tends to be confused with ideological interpretations. Unfortunately, terror "in the name of a religion" is a recurring historical phenomenon. From time to time, certain messianic movements in Christianity resorted to violence and terror to achieve their objective. Many messianic movements postulate that the End of Times will start with the second coming of Jesus. Among messianic sects, the Evangelical movement believes that Israel's ultimate victory is a precondition for the second coming of Jesus. This messianic interpretation was revived in some Christian sects when Israel achieved a victory against Arabs in the Six-Day War in 1967.

Muslims also have the notion of the awaited coming of the Messiah (Jesus) as well as Mahdi, a leader from the Noble Prophet's descendants

---

[1] The history of the Assyrian people begins with the formation of Assyria circa 2500 BC, followed by the rise of the Akkadian Empire during the 24th century BC, in the early Bronze Age period. Sargon of Akkad united all the native Akkadian-speaking Semites and the Sumerians of Mesopotamia, including the Assyrians, under his rule. After the fall of the Akkadian Empire, the Akkadians split into two nations, Assyria in the north and, much later, Babylonia in the south.

[2] The Isma'ili sect is a branch of the Shiite Islam and gets its name by accepting Isma'il ibn Ja'far as the appointed spiritual successor (*Imam*). This group sees the family of Muhammad (*Ahl al-Bayt*) as divinely chosen, infallible, and guided by God to lead the Islamic community. After the death of Muhammad ibn Isma'il in the 8th century CE, the teachings of Isma'ilism further transformed into the belief system as it is known today.

[3] Chaliand, Gerard and Arnaud Blin. *Preface, The History of Terrorism from Antiquity to Al Qaeda*, translated by Edward Schneider, Kathryn Pulver and Jesse Browner, (Los Angeles: University of California Press, 2007).

Introduction ix

who will set the things right. The enmity that fuels the violent clashes between radical Islamists or terrorist groups and the United States, the global superpower, also has a messianic dimension. They exploit the argument of "fighting" against imperialism and the west. For example, the contemporary terrorist group ISIS (also known as ISIL or IS) has a magazine named "Dabig" which represents its apocalyptic message predicting the west's defeat. Dabig is a Syrian town where Muslim armies will defeat the west according to a prophetic narration. By choosing the name Dabig for their magazine, the ISIS terrorist group uses this messianic spirit for their evil agenda.

In religious extremism and violence, the participants do not see themselves as terrorists; rather, they accept themselves as the servants of God and this illusion gives them full sanction to become instruments of the divine. According to their extremist ideology, it is insignificant to kill civilians and innocent people in the way to achieve their target; even the terrorists can sacrifice themselves for their cause. For instance, Sheikh Omar Abdel Rahman issued a religious ruling (*fatwa*), encouraging his followers for the attack on the World Trade Centre in 1993.

In Islam, the theological and political issues are not exclusive of each other. This aspect of Islam can be traced back to its early days; the Noble Prophet was the first Muslim ruler who combined both the religious and political authority in his person. The first four caliphs were pious rulers but they did not have that religious authority. Ignoring this fact, terrorist groups put their mere emphasis on the notion of caliphate, using this concept in a wrong way just to serve their extremist ideas. For this reason, we will first examine radicalism, violence and terrorism in Islamic history as well as the religious arguments the extremist groups used in an attempt to justify their brutal acts and then will provide theological responses to those arguments on the basis of primary Islamic sources.

Contemporary terrorist groups also exploit the Islamic concept of "jihad," using it in a mere military sense while purposefully ignoring its other meanings. They aim to legitimize their terrorist organizations by a call to "original" Islam or "pristine form" of Islamic belief. Toward the end of the 1970s, the radical groups resorted to violence and terror to "revive the caliphate" and unify the Muslim community. Basing their extremist ideology mainly upon the teachings of the Salafists, this ideology is the principal threat to the global community. It is within the same period that we also see radical or militant Shiite extremism emerging with the establishment of the Islamic Republic of Iran in 1979. The jihadist ideology was then used by Iran to realize its regional ambitions and also to weaken the position of the Saudis, the rival of Iran in the region. Hezbollah, literally "the Party of God," is, for instance, a Shiite terrorist group which resorts to terrorism to help Iran to actualize its targets in the region.

The jihadist terrorist groups that want to establish the so-called caliphate and Islamic State is the most extreme form of contemporary terrorism. These groups do not negotiate, but rather resort to violence to gain political power. Therefore, they are ready to "sacrifice" themselves to get their "heroic martyrdom" for the cause of their ideology. These extremist terrorist groups have hijacked the Quranic terms and used them to justify their killings of the "other" believers of the same faith in Muslim majority societies and the innocent civilians all over the world. They are, therefore, a very serious threat to the international community.

Chapter 1

RELIGIOUS EXTREMISM AND TERROR

SANCTITY OF HUMAN LIFE IN ISLAM

Human life is sacred in Islam, and it is strictly prohibited for any individual or group to take their own or someone else's life whatever the reason might be. The Holy Qur'an commanded that human life is so sacred that whoever kills a person unjustly, he or she will be punished in Hell. The Prophetic Traditions regarding the sanctity of life and the prohibition of murder and terror are very clear as well. A Muslim can, therefore, never commit murder intentionally. Whoever claims that it is permissible to kill a human being – Muslim or non-Muslim – although God has forbidden it, that person is considered as if he has declared it lawful to kill all humanity. If he acts upon this evil claim, thus killing a person unjustly, he entails the burden in the Judgment Day as if he killed all humanity. In the Qur'an, God Almighty clearly counted the evil act of killing a human being as killing all human beings:

> He who kills a soul unless it be (in legal punishment) for murder or for causing disorder and corruption on the earth will be as if he had killed

all humankind; and he who saves a life will be as if he had saved the lives of all humankind.[4]

This verse does not discriminate human beings on the basis of their color, nationality, race or religion. All humankind is equal in the sight of God; therefore, killing any one of them is like killing all.

The value of human life is, in the sight of God, greater than the value of the Ka'ba, the House of God. Indeed, one human life is worth more than the world itself. If killing one person is worse than destroying the entire world, what would be the word to describe mass killings of innocent civilians? The Noble Prophet cautioned Muslims to be very careful even in the battlefield of a just war and warned them only resort to destroying the attacking enemy combatants as a last resort. He encouraged believers to seek peace and end the war as long as it is possible. He allowed Muslims to fight enemy only when there is no any other alternative. Even while defending themselves or their land, the Noble Prophet imposed many restrictions upon Muslims to protect human life to the best of their ability.

Once in a battlefield, Usama, a Companion of the Noble Prophet, killed an enemy combatant right after he declared his faith. The Noble Prophet got very angry upon hearing this; thus, he questioned Usama about it. Usama tried to defend himself saying that the enemy soldier killed many Muslims and that he declared his faith only after he was surrounded as there was no other hope to save his life. However, the Noble Prophet did not accept his arguments and kept repeating the words, "How will you deal on the Day of Resurrection when the man you murdered (on the battlefield) comes, saying: "There is no deity but God.""[5]

Opposing to the teachings of the Noble Prophet, terrorists and bloody extremists kill civilian Muslims and non-Muslims on the basis of their barbaric doctrines. Considering the fact that Islam instructs Muslims to protect even the life of enemy combatants in the battlefield when they

---

[4] Qur'an 5: 32.
[5] Muslim, *Sahih*, Kitab al-Iman, 1: 97.

surrender or declare faith, one can imagine how evil it is to kill civilian people in places of worship, market places, schools, and so on.

All bloody terrorists are out of the fold of Islam due to their consideration of killing innocent civilians "lawful" and their committing all kinds of heinous acts of violence and terror. They make lawful what God Almighty has strictly made unlawful. For this reason, a terrorist cannot be a Muslim and a Muslim cannot be a terrorist. Terror and violence have yet been witnessed in the Muslim majority societies as a result of religious extremism and radicalism.

SIGNIFICANT PROBLEMS OF CONTEMPORARY MUSLIMS

Radicalism, religious extremism, terrorism and violence are the major issues that Muslims have long been facing. Indeed, it is the ignorance, poverty and disunity in Islamic world that fuel these problems. The use of religious language when addressing the issues of religious extremism, terrorism and violence makes it more difficult to understand. Moreover, radical groups exploit such religious concepts as jihad and caliphate to attract ignorant minds to their ranks and manipulate their religious sensitivity towards their evil agenda. Indeed, faith traditions can turn into a deadly weapon by their extremist followers as it has been witnessed in the long history of Judaism, Christianity, Hinduism, Buddhism and Islam. Radical groups put their emphasis on religious concepts in order to legitimize their violence and attract greater support from society.

Misinterpreting the Holy Qur'an with a narrow mind produces extremism and it leads people to commit terror and violence in the name of religion. Violence and terrorism are the outcome of narrow-mindedness, ignorance, prejudice and hatred. Islam, however, aims to instill love, peace, moderation and respect in the hearts of its followers. A Muslim who has a loving and caring heart cannot kill innocent people in malls, mosques, churches, synagogues, schools and other public places. Even in the battlefield of a just war he or she acts with great caution in order not to contradict Islamic teachings.

Obviously, it is beyond words to describe how evil the act is if some "Muslims" kill other believers intentionally while worshipping God in mosques. Regarding this, God Almighty says in the Qur'an:

> Whoever kills a believer intentionally, his recompense (in the Hereafter) is Hell, therein to abide; and God has utterly condemned him, excluded him from His mercy, and prepared for him a tremendous punishment.[6]

Indeed, a Muslim can lose his or her faith by denying any Quranic verse and acting against it.

Strangely enough, the so-called "Muslim" terrorists spread disorder, violence and mischief mostly in the Muslim majority world. They deem any Muslim who does not agree to their doctrines as unbeliever and worthy of killing. However, Islam clearly forbids Muslims to kill each other and if anyone contradicts this principle knowingly and kills a Muslim, he or she reverts from Islam to apostasy. The Noble Prophet warned his followers saying: "Do not turn to disbelief after me by killing one another."[7] While delivering his Last Sermon in the Farewell Pilgrimage, the Noble Prophet said that Muslims' blood, property and honor are inviolable and sacred like the sacredness of Makkah and the Ka'ba. Moreover, he warned them in that sermon not to turn to apostasy by killing each other.[8]

MISINTERPRETING RELIGIOUS CONCEPTS TO JUSTIFY TERRORISM AND VIOLENCE

Injustices done against Muslims in the Islamic world and the double standards of the west and its military engagements in some Muslim countries have given the radical groups a tremendous opportunity to justify

---

[6] Qur'an 4: 93.
[7] Bukhari, *Sahih*, Kitab al-Fitan, 6/2594.
[8] Bukhari, *Sahih*, Kitab al-Hajj, 2/620.

their anti-west war propaganda. They have exploited the Islamic notion of jihad to manipulate and recruit the ignorant minds. They have succeeded it to a certain degree for they have found local and global support in their so-called holy war against the west. Often, they target innocent people and kill many Muslim civilians in their "holy war" against the west.

Confused with the extremist groups' use of religious discourse, young Muslims have been falling victims to terrorism and joining them to "serve" Islam. Additionally, the portrayal of a negative image of Islam in the media and the governmental policies against Muslims in many western countries have kept provoking the naive Muslim youth to be radicalized, causing them to be highly reactionary. Gradually, they are becoming more and more extreme due to their hatred of the increasing "anti-Islamic" stance of the western world and their desire for revenge from it. In time, they adopt the extremists' worldview and methods of response to the problems, eventually becoming terrorists. It seems that humanity is going towards its own end if radicalism and terrorism are not adequately addressed on a global scale.

It needs to be kept in mind that all extremist terrorist groups use Islam and religious concepts to attract new members to their ranks, but all of their actions violate clear Islamic teachings. They make use of the corruption and oppression of the ruling elite to justify their killings. With this strategy, they pretend that they have "good intention" of stopping corruption and oppression through their terror tactics. Although they may confuse some ignorant minds with this strategy, they cannot change Islamic teachings. In Islam, evil is evil in all its forms and one cannot do good, righteous deeds through unlawful means. Thus, unlawful acts cannot be made lawful on the basis of having the "good" intention of warding off some evils in society. Killing civilians, committing violence and terrorism can never be excused no matter what the intention is.

It can never be deemed good if one's intention causes him or her to shed blood and commit violence. With such "good" intention, barbarism and violence cannot be declared lawful. It is prohibited in Islam to shed blood, spread fear and cause disorder in society. God Almighty states in the Qur'an:

> Among the people there is he whose conversation on (the affairs of) the present, worldly life fascinates you, and he calls on God to bear testimony to what is in his heart, yet he is most fierce in enmity. When he leaves (you) or attains authority, he rushes about the land to foment disorder and corruption therein and to ruin the sources of life and human generations. Surely, God does not love disorder and corruption. When he is told, "Be fearful of your duty to God (and so follow His commands)," vainglory seizes and thrusts him toward (greater) sin. Hell will settle the account for him – how evil a cradle indeed it is![9]

These verses clearly depict those extremist people who use pleasant words and swear on their good intentions. They intent to provoke the masses and with their lies they spread disorder in society. However, God declares disorder, corruption and ruining the sources of life and human generations as reasons of punishment in Hell. The intention is not taken into consideration when one commits such evil acts because the act and its result are evil; therefore, the intention cannot change it.

The corrupt and criminal mentality of extreme people is described in many verses of the Qur'an. However, terrorists do not deem their evil acts as violence, disorder and corruption; rather they call it jihad and/or reform. God Almighty points to such people as the ones who cause disorder and corruption:

> Because of the disorder they intend to provoke with their lies, whenever they are told (as part of the duty enjoined upon the believers to promote good and forbid evil), "Do not cause disorder and corruption on earth," they say: "Why! We indeed are the ones who set things right." Beware, they themselves are those who cause disorder and corruption but they are unaware (of what they do and ignorant of what setting things right is and what causing disorder is).[10]

---

[9] Qur'an 2: 204-206.
[10] Qur'an 2: 11-12.

These extreme people regard their evil acts as reform in society. They think that they commit these acts for the greater good of the society. By making use of religious discourse, they try to cover up their criminal, rebellious and violent acts. If Islam declares an act as evil, no one can, for whatever reason, change it. Therefore, a good intention cannot justify violence and terrorism. Killing civilians, spreading fear and corruption in society can never be named as jihad.

Extremists keep using the early Islamic period campaigns against the polytheist Arabs of the Age of Ignorance as a pretext to justify their terrorist acts against the west. This is an unacceptable method of interpretation because the Qur'an labels those who kill civilians and non-combatants as terrorists (*baghy*) and the capital punishment (*qisas*) is applied to them.

Islam sets clear guidelines with regards to what is lawful and what is unlawful. It is a main Islamic principle that lawful objectives can only be obtained through lawful means. A sacred and noble goal cannot be achieved by resorting to evil methods. For instance, a place of worship cannot be funded by robbing a bank or stealing from people. Similarly, violence, cruelty or murder is not a method to achieve justice.

Unfortunately, the extremists declare "other" Muslims as disbelievers, polytheists and innovators in religion on the basis of their false and dangerous doctrines. They try to justify their terrorism and violence with religious concepts and kill Muslims brutally. They violate the basic teaching of Islam with regards to the sanctity of Muslims' life for the Noble Prophet declared that the dignity and importance of a Muslim is greater than the Ka'ba, the house of God.[11] If human life's value is greater than the sanctity of the Ka'ba in the sight of God, it is clear that killing people brutally is a grave sin which almost equals to disbelief.

The Noble Prophet forbade certain acts clearly in order to block all the means that would lead to evil. He forbade Muslims even to point a weapon towards believers for they may kill them mistakenly and end up in Hell due

---

[11] Ibn Majah, *Sunan*, Kitab al-Fitan, 2/1297.

to this crime.[12] Additionally, pointing a weapon to a believer may provoke him to violence. In the hadith above, he linked the act of pointing a weapon to a believer to the act of Satan and warned Muslims against it. We understand from this warning that terrorists clearly represent the deeds of the devil, thus opposing to the words of the Noble Prophet. Killing civilians through suicide bombing or vehicles filled with explosives is a grave sin which is worse than the devil's evil deeds.

In Islam, committing major sins does not, however, make its perpetrator disbeliever; rather, they are considered as sinners and the door of repentance is always open to them. For example, stealing, fornication, or drinking alcohol does not make its doer an unbeliever as long as the doer does not deny the Islamic rulings about them. Similarly, oppression, injustice and corruption are major sins, but they do not make rulers unbelievers. In addition, these social problems can be fixed through appropriate methods without causing much more evils in society.

Islam established crystal clear principles and guidelines with regards to struggling against oppression, injustice or any other form of evil. Muslims are bound to Islamic guidelines when they aim to remove evil. Therefore, it is not an acceptable way to remove injustice through terrorism and violence because the terrorists kill civilians, and mostly Muslims, although the Noble Prophet forbade it strongly. Indeed, declaring Muslims as unbelievers, revolting against the state and killing innocent people is the way of the Kharijites – the first deviated sect and terrorist group in the early Islamic history.

Islam is a religion of moderation, balance and equilibrium in both faith and action. Extremists are away from this true spirit of Islam; thus, they are labeled as deviated sects.[13] Throughout the long Islamic history, there have been deviated sects that have interpreted Islam in extreme ways and killed other Muslims on the basis of their false doctrines. The Kharijite movement was the first example of extremism in Islam which committed

---

[12] Muslim, *Sahih*, Kitab al-Birr, 4/2020.
[13] Ayni, *Umdat al-Qari*, 24/84.

terror and violence in the name of religion.[14] The basis of their violence was their partial approach to the Qur'an and cherry-picking certain verses from the Holy Book and misinterpreting them. The followers of this deviant sect are called Kharijites, meaning "the ones who are outside the fold of Islam," due to their extreme beliefs.[15] They believed that a person who commits a major sin becomes a disbeliever, thus worthy of death unless he repents and mends his way. Therefore, they declared the perpetrators of major sins as unbelievers and then fought against them with the belief that it was lawful to shed their blood.[16] The mentality of the Kharijites will continue until the end of times among some people[17] and they will interpret the Qur'an in an extreme way to justify their violence and terrorism.

In order to motivate their people, extremists put their emphasis on jihad, martyrdom, religious zealotry and the feelings of heroism. Additionally, they prepare the rebels mentally by promising Paradise, beautiful wives and eternal happy life in there if they kill or be killed for their cause. By brainwashing the mentally immature youth, extremists find supporters and followers for their evil way. They act as if they are devoted Muslims by wearing religious garb and practicing some religious rituals, and yet they kill innocent people ruthlessly. It is not a dilemma to see some extremist people acting as if they are pious while committing all evil acts of terror, violence, barbarism and brutality. How is it possible for a sane person to combine two contradicting personalities in his or her own life? Thus, terrorists and extremists are pure hypocrites who play their role well to throw doubts into the mind of people about Islam and its teachings.

Extremism in the name of religion is very dangerous for it leads people to kill each other. The Noble Prophet warned Muslims saying, "Be careful of extremism in the religion because what destroyed people before you was extremism in religion."[18] Jihad is clearly distinguished from terrorism in

---

[14] Ibn Hajar, *Fath al-Bari*, 12/283.
[15] Shahristani, *al-Milalwa al-Nihal*, 114.
[16] Ibn Taymiyya, *Nubuwwat*, 222.
[17] Ibn Taymiyya, *Majmu'a al-Fatawa*, 28/495-496.
[18] Ibn Majah, *Sunan*, Kitab al-Manasik, 2/1008.

the prophetic traditions. He warned Muslims against violence and bloodshed of extremists who commit murders in the name of Islam. He predicted that extremists would recite the Qur'an and practice religious rituals but they are not Muslims due to their bloody, evil acts:

> At the end of time, there shall be people (extremists), young in age and foolish. They will speak my words to mislead people, but they will not have faith in their hearts. They leave Islam just as an arrow passes through a hunted game.[19]

The hadith clearly indicates that Islam is a religion which encompasses every aspect of life. The most important part is related to the protection of human life; therefore, if any person kills Muslims or other people, he is not considered a true Muslim even if he may practice some religious rituals and recite the Qur'an beautifully. The hadith also warns Muslims that if one does not know every aspect of Islam, he should not interpret the Qur'an and prophetic traditions because partial approach or deficient scholarship in Islamic disciplines leads the person to disbelief and extremism.

Extremism grows on the basis of ignorance and deficient scholarship. These people cherry-pick certain verses from the Qur'an and specific words from the prophetic traditions and then misinterpret them to justify their twisted ideology. In reality, every part of primary religious sources is strongly connected with each other. Therefore, if one cannot see the full picture, he or she cannot understand that part truly. Thus, one must be very careful with regards to interpreting a verse or a prophetic tradition. There are many qualifications to be a legitimate scholar to interpret the Qur'an. Some from among them are that when a scholar wants to interpret any verse from the Qur'an, he or she must know the historical occasion behind the revelation of such a verse, the relation of the verse with the verses before and after it, the relation of the verse with the chapter in which it

---

[19] Bukhari, *Sahih*, Kitab al-Istitaba al-Murtaddin, 6/2539.

appears, the relation of the verse with the entire Qur'an and the meaning of the verse according to the well-established Islamic principles.

TERRORISTS ARE NOT MUSLIMS

Terrorism is ugly in its nature and is a clear sign of disbelief in what Islam has taught. Many Quranic verses and prophetic traditions clearly reject terrorism and describe it as an act of disbelief. A Muslim cannot kill innocent people and civilians while in the fold of Islam. There is no compulsion in religion for God let people free to choose their way of life and religion; only fanatic rebels use force to convince others to their doctrines and opinions.

It should always be kept in mind that Islam is derived from the Arabic word "silm" which means peace, safety and protection. A Muslim is, therefore, the one who represents peace and security in his or her life through practicing Islam. The Noble Prophet encouraged his followers to be moderate, respectful, tolerant, merciful, loving and caring. The Arabic names "Muslim and Mu'min" used for the followers of Islam imply that the one who practices Islam is endowed with love, mercy, tranquility and respect. People are safe from him or her individually and collectively. God Almighty stated in the Qur'an that a person cannot be a real believer until he or she practices Islam in its totality:

> (Some of) the dwellers of the desert say: "We believe." Say (to them): "You have not believed. Rather, (you should) say, 'We have submitted to the rule of Islam),' for faith has not yet entered into your hearts." But, if you obey God and His Messenger, He will not hold back anything of the reward of your (good) deeds. Surely God is All-Forgiving, All-Compassionate.[20]

---

[20] Qur'an 49: 14.

This verse clearly states that wearing religious cloaks or carrying Islamic symbols does not make a person a real believer because Islam has a set of rules, belief system and moral guidelines that design one's lifestyle. Therefore, although terrorists may wear some religious garb and carry Islamic symbols, they are not true believers because with their evil acts they contradict directly with the fundamental Islamic teachings. They do not practice Islam in its totality; rather, with their partial approach and ignorance, they misinterpret it to justify their violence and terrorism. Indeed, the Noble Prophet described the Muslim as the one whom others are safe from his tongue and hand (that is, his words and actions). By practicing Islam truly, Muslims enter the door of peace and never harm others. How come that these extreme people can still claim that they are Muslims by killing people, Muslim and non-Muslim alike? There is no place in Islam for suicide bombing, killing innocent people, murder, anarchy, chaos and destruction because Islam rejects categorically all forms of extremism and terrorism.

The sanctity and dignity of human life cannot be violated even in the battle field for Islam prohibits the killing of non-combatants, such as all peaceful men and women civilians, children, elderly people and the clergy. Similarly, places of worship, buildings, crops and trees cannot be targeted in actual war. However, terrorists kill non-combatant civilians, men and women, young and old indiscriminately. Still worse is that they kill innocent people in the name of Islam and call this bloody, evil act as their "jihad." In reality, they are not believers in Islam and their evil acts have no relation with Islamic teachings.

The Noble Prophet described the real believer as the one whom people trust with regards to their lives and properties.[21] He abstains from harming his neighbors regardless of their ethnicity, nationality and faith. If a Muslim's neighbors are not safe from his evil and harm, he is not considered as a true believer.[22] If a person is untrustworthy, he does not

---

[21] Ibn Majah, *Sunan*, Kitab al-Fitan, 2:1298.
[22] Bukhari, *Sahih*, Kitab al-Adab, 5/2240.

have a true faith, thus terrorists cannot be Muslims for no one can trust them.

Engaging in acts of terrorism and violence is against the injunctions of the Qur'an and the teachings of the Noble Prophet. God Almighty will punish all terrorists in Hell. Even if thousands of terrorists come together and kill a single believer, God will punish them all in Hell. The Noble Prophet explained this in his eloquent speech: "Even if the dwellers of the heaven and earth kill a single believer together, God would cast them all in Hell."[23]

Because of the gravity of the issue, the first matter God will make His servants give an account in the Supreme Gathering is the matter of shedding blood. Those who kill people unjustly would not save themselves from Fire as the Noble Prophet stated that there is no salvation for a person who shed blood unlawfully.[24] Unfortunately, in spite of all these religious warnings, extremist "Muslims" target civilians, and mostly Muslim civilians, due to their religious and doctrinal differences and kill them ruthlessly. However, the result of their terrorism is only anarchy, chaos and loss of lives.

Terrorism and violence negate all Islamic attributes. Therefore, God Almighty will not accept the terrorists' worship no matter how devotedly they perform religious rituals. The Noble Prophet declared that God will not accept any act of worship from a person who has killed a believer.[25] Thus, terrorists will be the most unfortunate humans in the Judgment Day for they will not find anything to save themselves from the torment of Hell.

Extremists commit acts of terrorism against all people who do not agree to their ideology. They threaten the entire society. Since they weaken the stability of the state, the extremist terrorists don't deserve any concessions. The state must eliminate all individuals and groups who terrorize the society and the greater world through their violence and murders. A mercy towards terrorists is a great injustice towards all citizens.

---

[23] Tirmidhi, *Sunan*, Kitab al-Diyat, 4: 17.
[24] Bukhari, *Sahih*, Kitab al-Diyat, 6/2517.
[25] Tabarani, *Musnad al-Shamiyyin*, 2/266.

Nevertheless, if extremists stop committing the acts of terrorism, the state or the scholars can, and should, try to correct their mentality and gain them to society again. Many ignorant minds can be saved from the hands of radical groups if the scholars refute their arguments with clear evidence from the Qur'an and the Sunnah – the two primary religious sources.

The contemporary terrorists are the ones which God has promised them the curse and the worst abode:

> But those who break God's covenant after its solemn binding, and sever the bonds God commanded to be joined, and cause disorder and corruption on the earth – such are those for whom there is curse (exclusion from God's mercy), and for them there is the most evil abode.[26]

Extremists spread corruption and disorder on the earth by killing innocent people, destructing their wealth and properties; therefore, they are destined to Hell, the most evil abode. Although the Kharijites from the early Islamic period and the contemporary extremist terrorists are seemingly pious, in reality they do not have any share in Islam due to their extreme beliefs and evil acts. The Noble Prophet said, "There will be extremists you will belittle your prayers and fasting in comparison to theirs, but they will not stay in the fold of Islam just as an arrow passes through a hunted game."[27] God Almighty says in the Qur'an:

> Say: Shall We inform you who are the greatest losers in respect of their deeds? Those whose endeavor has been wasted in this world but who themselves reckon that they are doing good.[28]

Extremists believe that they do good deeds and serve Islam by killing other Muslims and causing corruption and disorder on the earth, but in reality, they are the worst losers. They will enter Hell and stay there

---

[26] Qur'an 13: 25.
[27] Bukhari, *Sahih*, Kitab al-Adab, 5/2281.
[28] Qur'an 18: 103-104.

forever because of their false beliefs and evil acts, but they do not perceive it.

The Noble Prophet predicted the extremists that will appear among Muslims from the beginning until the end of times with divine revelation and warned Muslims against them. He said, "There will be disputes and disunity among my followers. There will be people who will religiously speak good but their actions are bad. They are the most evil of the creation (for they deceive ignorant Muslims with their extreme ideas in religion). They will invite to God's Book (the Qur'an) but they don't practice it. The Companions asked the Prophet about their distinguishing feature and he said, 'Shaven heads.'"[29] The prophetic traditions give us some more idea about the physical and psychological features of the extremists that will appear among Muslims until the end of times: they will mostly be young, brainwashed, have thick beards and shaved heads; they will emerge mostly from the east and have superficial knowledge in Islam; they will not practice main Islamic principles while inviting others to the Book of God, will be meticulous in practicing certain religious rituals but will not have any share in faith; they will recite the Qur'an beautifully but will not understand it; they will speak the words of the Prophet (to deceive ignorant Muslims) and be good orators; they will be extreme and oppressive, will shed the blood of Muslims although it is prohibited; they will waylay, ransack, and plunder the wealth of the people.

CONDEMNING TERRORISM AND VIOLENCE

In the Islamic context, the vast majority of Muslim people do neither accept radical groups nor approve their violent, evil acts. As a matter of fact, radical Islamic groups are not more religious than regular Muslims who practice Islam in their daily lives. However, they pretend to be more

---

[29] Abu Dawud, *Sunan*, 4/243.

religious, and even dare to deem themselves the only "true Muslims" and legitimize the killing of "other" Muslims violently.

Unfortunately, the voice of mainstream Muslims cannot be heard adequately in the media because the media prefers to hear the voice of the minority terrorists or the preachers of hate. Although the majority of Muslim scholars and community leaders have strongly condemned violence and terrorism committed in the name of Islam, the media did not give enough space for it. Rather, those extremely dangerous terrorist leaders who are not even qualified as Islamic scholars have found more space in the media.

Radicalism and religious extremism was, for instance, strongly condemned by renowned Muslim scholars in the Amman Message in 2005. They emphasized core Islamic values of compassion, mutual respect and freedom of religion. They rejected all kinds of extremism, violence and terrorism for they are against the Islamic teachings. They also discussed some important issues such as declaring someone as apostate and the religious authority who can issue a religious ruling (*fatwa*). They came to the conclusion that in order to end the conflicts among Islamic sects, it is necessary to ban declaration of excommunication completely. This Amman Message was endorsed by many Muslim scholars. It seems that there is a great need to issue this type of messages more often by a greater number of Muslim scholars all around the world.

THE DIFFERENCE BETWEEN ENJOINING GOOD/ FORBIDDING EVIL AND TERRORISM

Enjoining good and forbidding evil is a religious duty upon every Muslim. However, no one has a right to commit violence while carrying out such a significant religious duty. Islam sets peaceful guidelines and principles to promote good and prevent evil. Without resorting to any violence or terrorism, Islam encourages its followers to reform the society and the state so that the rights of citizens are better protected. Through appropriate methods, Muslims are required to establish justice and terminate the terror and oppression.

Islam is a religion which provides a complete set of principles for every aspect of life. It has made regulations to protect society as a whole. The rights of citizens and duties of state are clearly explained and all parties are bound to abide by law. Islam never allows individuals or groups taking arms against a state, challenging its authority and declaring war against it. Such an act is considered as rebellion and the severest punishment is applied to its perpetrators. If such rebellion takes places in a Muslim society, it is the duty of the state to destroy rebellion and terrorism in a way that no one can ruin the peace and harmony of society by shedding blood. Even if the rulers do injustice, it is not permissible to revolt against the state by committing violence and terrorism because such evil acts will ruin the peace of the whole society. However, it is the duty of the citizens to seek their rights in peaceful methods, so they can protest and boycott the rulers due to their injustices. Opposing to this, an armed rebellion against the state is a civil war and an act of terrorism; therefore, it can never be called as jihad or reform movement.

In the early Islamic history, the Kharijites revolted against Caliph Ali, the ruler of Muslim society. The rebels were so punctual with regards to performing religious rituals, but they were out of the fold of Islam. This is simply because they regarded the murder of Muslims lawful and killed many Companions of the Noble Prophet in their "lofty" cause. Indeed, the Kharijites were the first terrorist group who challenged the authority of the Muslim state and killed many Muslims on the basis of their false doctrines. Their partial approach to the Qur'an and cherry-picking certain verses and then misinterpreting them caused them to be radicalized, thus committing violence against other Muslims. Unfortunately, the sick mentality and spirit of the Kharijites continues today. Each terrorist group cherry-picks certain part of the Qur'an and misinterpret it purposefully to legitimize its violence. Disconnecting verses from each other and disregarding the whole picture given in both the Qur'an and the practice of the Noble Prophet lead them to reach wrong conclusions.

Early Muslim generations after the Noble Prophet passed through some serious sedition and trials, such as the false claim of prophethood, apostasy of some tribes and their refusal to pay their prescribed purifying alms. The Kharijites benefitted from these seditions and exploited them to constitute their own extreme religious understanding. For the first time in Islamic history, they shed blood by killing many Muslims for their false doctrines, including the righteous caliphs 'Uthman and Ali. They revolted against Muslim rulers to destabilize the state and thus establish their own doctrines in society. They were against non-violent debates, dialogue, understanding each other and settling the disputes among Muslims through peaceful methods. Thus, they accused Ali, the fourth caliph of Islam, with disbelief when he accepted the arbitration to solve the conflict with Muawiya, the governor of Damascus. They organized a terrorist group and revolted against Caliph Ali in the name of "jihad." One can see how the early period and contemporary terrorists are similar to each other in extremism and misinterpreting the Qur'an because when they declared Ali and Muawiya as unbelievers, they misinterpreted the Quranic verse (which means), *"Judgment and authority rest with none but God alone."*[30] On the basis of their false doctrines and extreme religious understanding, they committed mass killings and terrorism.

The Kharijites disobeyed Muslim rulers due to their own extreme ideology, claiming that Muslim rulers were wrong and it was thus obligatory to rebel against them. Since they declared other Muslims, including the Companions of the Prophet, as disbelievers, they killed them ruthlessly and plundered their wealth and captured their womenfolk.[31] By misinterpreting the Qur'an, the Kharijites declared even the Companions of the Noble Prophet as apostates and rebelled against the Muslim state with their armed forces. It is obvious that no state – whether Muslim or non-Muslim – tolerates terrorism or armed rebellion against it. Therefore, it is a duty upon the state to fight rebellious groups to establish peace and security in society.

---

[30] Qur'an 12: 40
[31] Ibn Humam, *Fath al-Qadir*, 5/334.

Obviously, all these evil acts of rebels and terrorists stem from their extreme ideology. They challenge the authority of the state on the basis of their false interpretation. They declare the blood of other Muslims lawful disregarding the very fact that both the Word of God and the Noble Prophet prohibited it strongly.

Muslims should fight against the extreme mentality of terrorism all together and by all means, thus destroying it wherever it appears because extremists violate people's inalienable rights to life, religion, wealth and human dignity. They strike fear upon society and terrify people through violence and terror. Frightening people with regards to their lives, wealth, freedom and security is nothing but spreading disorder, mischief and corruption; therefore, Islam regards these evil acts as waging a war against God and His Messenger. It deems all these evil acts of terrorism as the gravest sin affecting the entire society; therefore, the severest punishment is established mainly for deterrence in the Qur'an:

> The recompense of those who fight against God and His Messenger and hasten about the earth causing disorder and corruption: they shall (according to the nature of their crime) either be executed, or crucified, or have their hands and feet cut off alternately, or be banished from the land. Such is their disgrace in the world, and for them is a mighty punishment in the Hereafter.[32]

It is clear that the Kharijites did not even understand the spirit and meaning of Islam no matter how meticulous they were with regards to practicing certain religious rituals. Thus, they killed many Muslims on the wrong premises and assumptions. They were out of the fold of Islam due to their violence and terrorism against other Muslims. This terrorism was, however, the result of their misunderstanding and misinterpretation of the religious texts.

In the extreme mentality of the terrorists, they consider themselves as the only true Muslims and the other Muslims as disbelievers. They don't

---

[32] Qur'an 5: 33.

negotiate or debate; rather, they just kill and incite fear upon society. They would recite the Qur'an but could not understand it. Ignorance, misunderstanding and misinterpreting the Qur'an is one of the main reasons leading some people into extremism and terrorism. It is clear that observing certain religious rituals strictly does not mean that the person is more religious or truer because Islam offers a complete set of guidelines which encompasses every aspect of life. Therefore, if one ignores some aspects while practicing others, he is not considered a true Muslim. In this regard, it is strictly forbidden in Islam, for whatever reason, to fight and resort to violence against Muslim or non-Muslim civilians. However, extremists and terrorists openly contradict it with their evil acts and violence. Furthermore, it is strongly prohibited to declare other Muslims who do not agree with someone's doctrines as disbelievers and kill them ruthlessly and plunder their wealth. A terrorist can, therefore, never be a Muslim and a Muslim can never be a terrorist.

Unfortunately, ignorance causes extremists to see themselves as the only true Muslims; thus, they deem it appropriate to force others to believe in what they believe. With this mentality they kill Muslims and non-Muslims, spread terror, plunder their wealth and property without feeling any shame and without fearing even from God. They claim that they do "jihad" while committing the worst acts of sin and crimes. In reality, they abandon the way of the Noble Prophet and follow their own twisted whims and desires.

On top of banning terror and violence strictly, the Noble Prophet also forbade Muslims to help terrorists or provide any material support to them in any way. He stated that if anyone helps terrorists in any way to kill a believer, even if with a few words, he will meet God with the statement written on his forehead "hopeless of God's mercy."[33] This prophetic tradition clearly states that it is forbidden to provide any support to terrorists whether it is economic, strategic or propaganda purposes. Therefore, it is not permissible in Islam to even utter words supporting terrorists, irrespective of whether they are in the written or oral form. So,

---

[33] Ibn Majah, *Sunan*, Kitab al-Diyat, 2: 874.

Muslims must be very careful when addressing the issue of terrorism. Particularly, Muslim scholars must explain and reveal the hypocritical face of the extremist people with evidences from the Qur'an and the Sunnah so that ignorant youth do not fall prey to them. This is an important responsibility falling upon the shoulders of the scholars as terrorists use Islam and its primary sources to justify their killings and to attract new members to their ranks. They misinterpret the Qur'an and brainwash youth with glad tidings of Paradise for killing innocent people! So, it is a Muslim scholar's duty to refute the arguments of terrorists and prevent ignorant Muslims to be manipulated by them.

In Islam, individuals and citizens cannot do armed struggle against the state even if the administrators and rulers are sinful and corrupt. This is due to the fact that correcting the mistakes and setting the things right cannot be achieved through un-Islamic methods. Citizens can seek their rights through peaceful manners but not through terrorism and violence because while seeking their rights through terrorism, they cause more injustices, corruption, turmoil and internal clashes. Thus, Islam never allows armed struggle against the state.

However, citizens can raise their voices against the state for corrective purpose and without resorting to any act of violence when they see that the rulers and administrators are corrupt and they keep violating the basic rights of citizens. For example, if the state does not allow Muslims to practice their faith, they can protest it through peaceful methods. Similarly, they can protest the state when their basic rights such as freedom of expression, owning property, raising children and making business freely are violated by the state. However, there is no room for terrorism and violence no matter what happens because the Noble Prophet clearly stated that taking up arms against Muslims is not permissible: "He who takes weapon against us (Muslims) he is not from us."[34] If armed combat against a Muslim state is considered as disbelief, the perpetrators cannot claim that they do jihad against the state to provide justice for its citizens.

---

[34] Bukhari, *Sahih*, Kitab al-Fitan, 6/2591

On the other hand, though armed combat against the state is not permissible even if it is corrupt and unjust, this does not mean that the state can continue to violate the rights of its citizens. Citizens have full license to fight against any kind of injustice, corruption and oppression through peaceful means. Indeed, it is a religious responsibility to raise the voice against the tyrants and wrong doers, so they could fix their evil acts and reform. In order to reform the state and establish justice for all citizens in society, Muslims must act in great caution. They must be very careful for they may fall into violence and terrorism while seeking justice.

Speaking the truth against the tyrants and oppressive rulers is a communal duty for the Noble Prophet said, "The best jihad is a true word uttered in the presence of the unjust ruler."[35] Enjoining good and preventing evil is a religious duty upon all Muslims and they do it through peaceful ways. Shedding blood through committing acts of terrorism is absolutely forbidden in Islam for it creates more chaos, disorder and anarchy in society. The Noble Prophet said, "There will be rulers and administrators appointed over you. You will agree with some of their acts while disagree with others. If you disapprove their evil acts and dislike them, you will be safe. However, if you approve their evil acts and follow them you will be responsible. The Noble Prophet replied negatively when his Companions asked, 'Should we fight them?'"[36] If citizens cannot remove the evils of the rulers, then they disapprove them with their tongues. If they don't feel safe when expressing the evils of the rulers, then they keep their dislike in their hearts. However, if citizens approve the injustices and evil acts of the rulers and follow them without questioning, then they will religiously be responsible for that. As a result, citizens can in no way resort to violence or terrorism in order to correct unjust rulers and corrupt administrators.

Today, extremists with a little knowledge of Islam have been misinterpreting the Qur'an and the Sunnah to receive support from ignorant youth for their evil agenda. They claim that the rulers in Islamic

---

[35] Ibn Hanbal, *Musnad*, 3/19.
[36] Muslim, *Sahih*, Kitab al-Imara, 4/417.

lands are not true Muslims; therefore, it is permissible to revolt against them. While trying to "remove" oppression, injustice and corruption, they commit much more evils. They shed blood and spread sedition and mischief. By their evil acts, they oppose the Noble Prophet and blacken the bright face of Islam.

The ignorant youth are eager to serve Islam and remove evil; however, they do not know the proper methods to struggle against it. Their ignorance to differentiate between Islamic and un-Islamic methods to establish justice causes them to fall into falsehood to the point that they kill other Muslims who do not agree with them. This is a grave mistake and it is how the Kharijites declared other Muslims and the Prophet's Companions as "unbelievers" and killed them ruthlessly. The history repeats itself as there have been many deviated extreme sects in Islamic history that have declared other Muslims as unbelievers and have killed them on the basis of their false doctrines.

Psychologically, extremists encourage each other to enjoin the good and forbid the evil. Then, they declare rulers as oppressors and the Islamic lands as the places of disbelief. After that, they want to seize a land in which they could apply the Sharia according to their own extreme interpretations. Thus, they attack cities, towns and other settlement areas and expel their inhabitants. In the way of establishing their own cities, they commit many violence and terrorism with the ultimate goal of applying the Sharia in the land. It is so funny, indeed it is so sad, that they contradict directly with the Sharia from the beginning to the end, yet they claim that they aim to apply it. It is absolutely false and ridiculous to accuse Muslims of disbelief and shed their blood and then claim that they only want to apply the Sharia because the Sharia itself strongly forbids all these evil acts the extremist terrorists have been doing.

Although the Noble Prophet forbade Muslims to kill each other or people from other faith traditions, terrorists have been killing many people, especially the Muslims, in the Middle East almost every day. He said, "Muslims are brothers, they do no wrong or injustice to each other. They do not look down upon each other... Muslims' blood, property and honor are forbidden for other Muslims."[37] Another time the Prophet clearly stated that fighting against Muslims is disbelief: "Reviling Muslims is corruption and waging war against them is disbelief."[38] The extremists have been killing innocent people almost daily and with this evil act they cannot be considered Muslims, even if they practice certain religious rituals.

PEACEFUL COEXISTENCE AND INTERFAITH HARMONY

Islam encourages its followers to be in peaceful coexistence and interfaith harmony. It rejects hatred, prejudice, disunity, enmity and using force to convert others. Prophet Muhammad, upon whom be peace and blessings, taught his followers to promote peace by respecting the beliefs of other people and encouraged Muslims to engage in interfaith dialogue with people from different faith traditions. Many envoys from various tribes, nations and faith traditions came to Medina to learn about Islam or simply to make treaty with Muslims. The Noble Prophet hosted them well in his mosque and showed great hospitality to them. The Prophet and his Companions treated them with respect.

During the time of the Noble Prophet, the rights of non-Muslims were protected very well for the Prophet established a constitutional status for all citizens. All faith groups enjoyed equal rights with regards to their life, property, belief and other important issues. The rabbis, priests, monks and other clergy preached their faith freely. The Noble Prophet guaranteed all citizens that they would never be forced to change the religion they were following. He prohibited all kinds of oppression, persecution and compulsion towards citizens because of the differences in their faith.[39] As a result, they enjoyed many rights such as equal treatment before the law. They were appointed to administrative positions if they had necessary qualifications. They preached and practiced their faith without any

---

[37] Bukhari, *Sahih*, Kitab al-Birr, 4/1986.
[38] Bukhari, *Sahih*, Kitab al-Iman, 1/27.
[39] Abu Yusuf, *Kitab al-Kharaj*, 78.

interference. Their places of worship were accepted as sacred and treated with utmost respect. He strongly prohibited launching attacks against people from different faiths and their places of worship.

Religious and ideological differences are not a reason for fight or war. Attacking mosques, churches, synagogues and other places of worship through suicide bombers and vehicles loaded with bombs is absolutely against Islam and the teachings of the Noble Prophet. In the Qur'an God says,

> "Who is greater in doing wrong than he who bars God's places of worship, so that His Name be not mentioned and invoked in them, and strives to ruin them?"[40]

In another verse God Almighty states,

> "Were it not for God's repelling some people by means of others, monasteries and churches and synagogues and mosques, where God is regularly worshipped and His name is much mentioned, would surely have been pulled down (with the result that God is no longer worshipped and the earth becomes uninhabitable)."[41]

These verses clearly indicate that the places of worship are inviolable sites and have sanctity regardless of which religion they belong to. Therefore, if anyone or any group attacks a house of worship, for whatever reason, they are not Muslims because contradicting to the clear Quranic injunctions and acting against Islamic teachings amounts to disbelief.

Islam guarantees the protection of life, property, honor and religion of all citizens equally, regardless of their nationality and faith practice. Non-Muslims have equal rights with Muslims in a Muslim state. They can practice their religion freely in a Muslim society and their places of worship are inviolable, requiring protection against all kinds of attacks. Non-Muslims can live, work and do business in a Muslim society under

---

[40] Qur'an 2: 114.
[41] Qur'an 22: 40.

full protection. Islam strongly prohibits violence against non-Muslims; therefore, if any Muslim attacks or tortures them or kidnaps them for ransom, he or she is liable to severe punishment by the state.

Although it is permissible for a group or organization to promote its ideas through peaceful methods, Islam never allows them to use force to convince others, presuming themselves to be the only true believers. It is worth to consider here the fact that Islam is a religion of peace and a Muslim is a person from whom other people feel themselves safe. Opposing to this clear fact, terrorists have been using force to convince others to their doctrines and keep killing innocent people ruthlessly in mosques, churches, synagogues, marketplaces and other public places. This is clearly against the teachings of Islam; therefore, a terrorist is destined to a humiliating punishment in both this world and the next.

Whoever claims that it is permissible to kill a non-Muslim (although God has forbidden it) he is considered as if he declared it lawful to kill all humanity.[42] If he kills a person with this belief, he entails the burden in the Judgment Day as if he killed all humanity. It is a duty upon all community to protect all citizens' lives with collective effort. Therefore, if anyone from this society intends to kill a person, the whole community must prevent it collectively and save the person from the potential murder. This is because attempting to kill a person in a society is indeed trying to kill all community. So, Muslims and non-Muslims should work together to prevent corruption, mischief, disorder and terrorism in the entire world.

The non-Muslim citizens in a Muslim country have the same rights with regards to security, property and honor. They are protected against any aggression, oppression, wrong doings and discrimination. The Muslim authorities must provide safety to all their citizens and they must be more cautious about protecting the lives of non-Muslim citizens. The Noble Prophet said, "If a Muslim kills a non-Muslim with whom there is a peace treaty (i.e., who has legal right to live in the country), God makes Paradise forbidden for him."[43]

---

[42] Al-Maturidi, Abu Mansur. *Ta'wilatAhl al-Sunna*, 3/501.
[43] Nasai, *Sunan*, Kitab al-Qasama, 8/24.

Islam guarantees to protect diplomats, envoys and foreign representatives. It is known that once the representatives of the false prophet Musaylama the Liar came to the Noble Prophet. They declared their denial of his prophethood and confessed their apostasy. They were Muslims before, but now they denied Prophet Muhammad in his own mosque and accepted Musaylama the Liar as a prophet. Yet, the Noble Prophet and his Companions treated them kindly for they were envoys.[44] Despite the apostasy of Musaylama's men, the Noble Prophet and his Companions did not kill them nor did they imprison them. The practice of the Noble Prophet (i.e., his Sunnah) shows that people who work as a diplomat, ambassador and staff in an embassy are protected and treated with respect. It is forbidden to kill them whatever the reason might be. Killing or kidnapping diplomats or attacking embassies is clearly contradictory to the Practice of the Noble Prophet. Thus, terrorists violate Islamic principles by attacking embassies and killing or kidnapping ambassadors.

The Noble Prophet always gave the full rights of non-Muslims whenever their cases were brought before him. He clearly stated that if a Muslim kills a non-Muslim unjustly, he is killed as a way of retribution,[45] and the blood money of a non-Muslim is like that of the Muslim.[46] Once a Muslim killed a person from the People of the Book and the Noble Prophet ordered capital punishment to be applied to the murderer.[47] Non-Muslim citizens in a Muslim society have equal rights with the Muslims. As long as the non-Muslims are not combatants engaging in war against Muslims, their life is protected.

In a Muslim society, Muslims cannot abuse non-Muslims; indeed, it is not permissible to violate the dignity of non-Muslims by any means. During the time of Caliph of Umar, the son of the governor of Egypt did some wrong to a non-Muslim. Thereupon, the Caliph asked the non-Muslim to get his legal right from the son of the governor as a way of

---

[44] Darimi, *Sunan*, 2/307; Nasai, *Sunan al-Kubra*, 5/205; Hakim, *Mustadrak*, 3/54.
[45] Imam Shafi'i, *al-Umm*, 7/320.
[46] Abd al-Razzaq, *Musannaf*, 10/95.
[47] Bayhaqi, *Sunan al-Kubra*, 8/30; Shaybani, *al-Mabsut*, 4/488.

retribution. The Caliph scolded the wrong-doing Muslim saying, "Since when do you regard free men as your slaves and treat them badly!"[48]

It is a religious duty upon Muslims to treat non-Muslims well and refrain from any kind of harm towards them. Even, it is forbidden for Muslims to backbite a non-Muslim.[49] Irrespective of whether they are Muslims or non-Muslims, Islamic law gives the citizens the same privilege and rights.[50] The Maliki Jurist Qarafi holds that if a Muslim violates the rights of non-Muslims even if through backbiting, he is considered as a Muslim who disobeyed God and His Messenger.[51] The Noble Prophet said, "Whoever does injustice and wrongs to a non-Muslim, I will seek his (non-Muslim's) right in the Judgment Day."[52] The Noble Prophet will be the advocate for the oppressed non-Muslim against the Muslim in the Judgment Day to establish justice. He warned Muslims about the rights of non-Muslims stating, "Whoever hurts a non-Muslim citizen, I am his opponent and to whomever I am opponent I shall overcome him in the Judgment Day."[53]

If the non-Muslim citizens are exposed to any kind of attack, the Islamic government protects its citizens by its military and security power.[54] It is the responsibility of the state to protect the lives and properties of its non-Muslim citizens paying tax to the state. During 'Umar's caliphate, Abu 'Ubayda, the commander of the Muslim armies in the Syrian region, wanted to evacuate the city of Hims in the region because the Byzantine Roman Emperor set out to recapture Hims with his vastly outnumbered forces. Abu Ubayda gathered the non-Muslim population and said: "You have paid tax and therefore Muslims defend you. Since we cannot really defend you against the Byzantine Roman army now, it is not lawful to keep the tax we have collected from you, it will thus be refunded to you." Thus, the non-Muslims got their tax back from

---

[48] Hindi, *Kanz al-Ummal*, 2/455.
[49] Ibn Abidin, *Raddal_Mukhtar*, 3/273-274.
[50] Kasani, *Badai al-Sanai*, 7/111.
[51] Qarafi, *Furuq*, 3/14.
[52] Abu Dawud, *Sunan*, Kitab al-Kharaj, 3/170.
[53] Ayni, *Umdatu al-Qari*, 15/89.
[54] Qarafi, *Furuq*, 3/15.

the Muslim ruler. However, Christian priests and Jewish rabbis went to the churches and synagogues to pray God to give the Muslim army success against the Byzantine Romans.[55] They did this because of fair treatment that they received from Muslim rulers. Probably, people from different faith traditions living under Muslim rule were treated better than the ones who were living under the rule of Byzantine Roman emperors.[56]

Peace is essential in Islam; thus, it is not permissible to wage a war against countries that are not fighting Muslims. War is a last resort to defend the land and people. Human life is a sacred trust and Islam instructs Muslims to protect it. The ideological differences are not a valid reason to declare a war against non-Muslims. Similarly, doctrinal differences among Islamic sects cannot be a valid basis to fight against each other. God Almighty says:

> O you who believe! Be upholders and standard-bearers of right for God's sake, being witnesses for (the establishment of) absolute justice. And by no means let your detestation for a people (or their detestation for you) move you to (commit the sin of) deviating from justice. Be just: this is nearer and more suited to righteousness and piety. Seek righteousness and piety and always act in reverence for God. Surely God is fully aware of all that you do.[57]

Hatred and hostility against people should not lead Muslims to resort to oppression, transgression and injustice. Indeed, God commands Muslims to treat non-Muslims kindly, do favors to them and be righteous towards them:

> God does not forbid you, as regards those who do not make war against you on account of your Religion, nor drive you away from your homes, to be kindly to them, and act towards them with equity. God surely loves the scrupulously equitable.[58]

---

[55] Abu Dawud, *Sunan*, Adab, 164.
[56] Watt, Montgomery. *Islamic Political Thought: The Basic Concepts*, p. 51.
[57] Qur'an 5: 8.
[58] Qur'an 60: 8.

In spite of all these clear religious instructions, terrorists have been killing Muslim and non-Muslim civilians. They argue that foreign armies have occupied Muslims lands, and terrorism and violence against them is thus permissible. This sick mentality is absolutely against Islamic teachings. Muslims are always required to stick to justice and always use lawful means to achieve lawful results. Murdering civilians, innocent, non-combatant people through suicide bombings or other means of destruction is absolutely forbidden in Islam even if it is done with the claim of defending the land against the foreign forces.[59] Even while fighting against the enemy combatants in a battle, Muslims cannot kill the non-combatant women, elderly people and children for the Noble Prophet prohibited it.[60]

The Noble Prophet forbade Muslims from killing rabbis, priests and other religious leaders.[61] Abu Bakr, the first caliph of Islam, instructed the Muslim army with the following order when sending it to Syria, "You will soon see religious people who secluded themselves in monasteries; do not kill them for the sake of what they secluded themselves. Do not kill old people or a woman or a child. Do not damage cities and places where people live. Do not cut trees."[62]

In Islam, the lives of non-combatants, including peaceful farmers, traders and businessmen are also to be protected during the times of war. The Companions of the Noble Prophet did not harm farmers or merchants during a battle for they are also civilians just like the elderly people and religious leaders.[63] This is because they knew very well that the sanctity of human life is superior to the sanctity of the Ka'ba. Therefore, they resorted to war only when it was the last solution to end the greater injustices and wrong doings. On the day of the conquest of Makkah, the Noble Prophet ordered the Muslim army not to harm any civilian by stating, "Whoever leaves his weapon is safe and whoever stays at his house is safe."[64] He

---

[59] Sarakhsi, *Mabsut*, 10/5-6.
[60] Bukhari, *Sahih*, Jihad, 3/1098.
[61] Ahmad ibn Hanbal, *Musnad*, 5/358; Ibn Abi Shayba, *Musannaf*, 6/484; Bayhaqi, *Sunan*. 9/85.
[62] Bayhaqi, *Sunan*. 9/90.
[63] Ibn Qayyim, *Ahkam al-Dhimma*, 1/165.
[64] Muslim, *Sahih*, Jihad, 4/1407.

wanted to conquer Makkah through peaceful manners and protect the lives of non-Muslim Makkan people.

Islam forbids damaging crops, harming the places of worship and destroying buildings. Honor and dignity of people cannot be violated even during the times of war. Thus, soldiers cannot enter the houses forcefully and harm the households in any way. During the Khaybar military expedition, the Noble Prophet warned Muslim soldiers saying, "God forbids you to enter the houses of the People of the Book without their permission, or to beat their women, or to eat their fruit."[65] The Noble Prophet also said that there is no reward of struggling for God's cause for the one who breaks into the houses forcefully and loots people (or caravans) on the road.[66]

Umar, the second caliph of Islam, always protected and advocated the rights of minority groups in Islamic lands. He often asked the non-Muslim citizens if they were happy with the Muslim rulers. Although he was deadly wounded by a criminal from the minority groups, he advised Muslims to fulfill the conditions of the contract with them before he died. He reminded Muslims that non-Muslim citizens were under the protection of God and His Messenger.[67] He instructed his governors and other officials to treat the non-Muslims kindly. During his caliphate, Umar exempted the old, disabled and weak non-Muslim citizens from paying the tax. On top of that, he helped them from the government treasury so that they could maintain their life.[68] Once, Umar saw an old Jew who was begging in the streets. He took him his home and gave him some donation and then told the officials of public treasury to take care of him and those like him.[69] When Muslims conquered Jerusalem, Caliph Umar recognized the full religious freedom in the treaty. He guaranteed security and safety for the people of Jerusalem with regards to their lives, properties and churches. He banned Muslims from demolishing the places of worship of

---

[65] Abu Dawud, *Sunan*, Kitab al-Kharaj, 3/170.
[66] Abu Dawud, *Sunan*, Kitab al-Kharaj, 3/41.
[67] Bukhari, *Sahih*, Janaiz, 1/469.
[68] Ibn Sallam, Abu Ubayda Qasim. *Kitab al-Amwal*, 57.
[69] Abu Yusuf, *Kitab al-Kharaj*, 136.

non-Muslims or forcing them to abandon their faith.[70] So, it is clear that in Islam the differences in faith and religion are not a basis for killing non-Muslims or forcing them to convert.

During the Umayyad reign, a property which belonged to the Church of Damascus was taken by a Muslim governor and joined to a mosque. Upon hearing this, Umar ibn Abd al-Aziz, the Umayyad ruler, ordered the property to be returned to the Church.[71] He instructed his governors and officials that they shall not demolish any church, synagogue or Zoroastrian temple.[72] Islamic history represents the examples of excellent treatment towards non-Muslim citizens. People from other faiths living in a Muslim society had the opportunity to practice their religion freely. Their places of worship were protected against all kinds of oppression and wrong doings. Today, Muslims and non-Muslims do not unfortunately feel safe about their life, religion or places of worship. Terrorists can attack a mosque or temple with a vehicle filled with bomb, thus killing many innocent people. Such evil conducts of bloody terrorists have been blackening the bright face of Islam.

Religious freedom is one of the fundamental principles of Islam and all non-Muslim citizens have freedom to practice their faith in an Islamic society. There is no compulsion in religion, so no one can force others to convert. God Almighty says, *"There is no compulsion in the Religion. The right way stands there clearly distinguished from the false."*[73] Terrorists assume that they are the only true Muslims and use force to convince others, including "other" Muslims, to their extreme doctrines. They kill many innocent Muslims and non-Muslims because of their differences in faith and religion.

All citizens are required to obey the law, and in turn, the state protects them and provides their citizenship rights. Disobeying the law and launching an armed struggle against the state is deemed rebellion in Islam. Although terrorists may want to reform the society and the state, they

---

[70] Tabarani, *Tarikh al-Umam wa al-Muluk*, 2/449.
[71] Baladhuri, *Futuh al-Buldan*, 201.
[72] Ibn Qayyim al-Jawziyya, *Ahkami Ahl al-Dhimma*, 3/1200.
[73] Qur'an 2: 256.

actually cause disorder, turmoil, corruption and murders while trying to achieve their objectives. In Islamic law, no one is permitted to commit terror or oppression for any reason. Rebels transgress against citizens through committing violence and terror. They are deviated from the right path for they spread mischief in society.[74]

There are always extreme people in every faith, nation and race. Muslims who live in a foreign country may experience hostility, torture and persecution. However, it is not permissible for Muslims living in an Islamic society to punish innocent people because they are from other faiths as a way of retaliation. For example, if some Muslims experience injustice, persecution or torture in the west, the Muslims in the Middle East or in any Islamic country cannot punish people from Europe or America as a way of retribution because God says in the Qur'an, *"Every soul earns only to its own account; and no soul, as bearer of burden, bears and is made to bear the burden of another."*[75] The Noble Prophet said, "No non-Muslim is punished as a penalty for the injustice of another non-Muslim."[76] In sum, it is not permissible in Islam to try to get revenge from the US citizens or European people through terrorism with the pretext of reacting against the hostility and anti-Islamic stance of certain people in the west.

SUICIDE IS FORBIDDEN IN ISLAM

Human beings are the best art of God on earth; therefore, their lives are the most sacred divine trust that needs to be protected. God Almighty states,

> "He who kills a soul unless it be (in legal punishment) for murder or for causing disorder and corruption on the earth will be as if he had killed

---

[74] Al-Kasani, *Badail al-Sanai*, 7/140
[75] Qur'an 6: 164.
[76] Abu Yusuf, *Kitab al-Kharaj*, 78.

all humankind; and he who saves a life will be as if he had saved the lives of all humankind."[77]

Unfortunately, although the Quranic injunction regarding the sanctity of life is very clear, some so-called scholars have argued that suicide bombing is permissible if there is no any other alternative to defend Muslim lands. With this kind of bizarre reasoning they have given religious verdicts (*fatwa*s), justifying suicide attacks against the citizens of occupying countries in Muslim lands. In Islam, a wrong deed and injustice cannot be corrected by another wrong action. Islam never permits suicide bombing and killing innocent people. Muslims cannot commit terror and violence for they invoke the punishment of God in the Hereafter.

Suicide is forbidden in Islam for no one has a right to terminate a sacred trust by themselves. In this regard, suicide bombing is evil for it destroys lives and properties; therefore, nothing can justify it whatever the reason or intention is. Firstly, no one has the right to terminate his or her own life. Secondly, it is strongly prohibited to kill civilians. Thirdly, it is not permissible to damage properties, buildings and other facilities. As a result, no matter what the reason or intention is, suicide bombing is forbidden in Islam and its perpetrator is liable to punishment in Hell.

Life is the greatest gift God has bestowed upon His creatures; therefore, it must be protected very well. Sometimes, people may experience bad situations or unfortunate events but this does not justify one to kill himself or herself. Prophet Muhammad, upon whom be peace and blessings, forbade suicide in many hadiths with strong expressions. He said, "Whoever terminates his life (suicide) with something, he or she will be tormented by it in the Hellfire."[78]

Islam prohibits people to kill themselves or others through suicide bombing. Therefore, it is not permissible to obey "authorities" which command people to commit suicide and kill others. Unfortunately, some terrorist leaders motivate ignorant youth to commit suicide bombing by

---

[77] Qur'an 5: 32.
[78] Bukhari, *Sahih*, Kitab al-Adab, 5/2264.

promising them martyrdom and Paradise. In Islam, there is, however, no obedience to rulers or leaders when they command people to violate human rights. Once, the Noble Prophet sent a group of people for a mission under the leadership of a Companion from the residents of Medina. When he was angry with people under his command, he ordered them to throw themselves to fire but they did not obey him. When the incident was mentioned to the Noble Prophet, he said, "If you threw yourself into fire, you would remain in it until the Judgment Day. There is no obedience to those (rulers and commanders) when they command sinful acts. Obedience is only in that which is right."[79]

Motivating ignorant youth to commit suicide and kill themselves and others is a grave sin. It is clearly against the prophetic teachings. The extremists and their leaders brainwash ignorant Muslims by promising them Paradise if they commit suicide bombing. All Muslims must know that whoever commits suicide bombing, he or she will enter the Hellfire and be tormented there forever. Any Muslim scholar or a leader who has given *fatwa* for suicide bombing will be responsible for that and God will punish them double in Hell for they have misled ignorant Muslims and caused mass murders and death of innocent people.

CONCLUSION

Violence, terrorism and suicide bombing are not methods to serve Islam. There are many Quranic verses and prophetic traditions which clearly forbid terrorism and violence. Therefore, whoever ignores these religious injunctions and misinterpret the Qur'an and the Sunnah in the favor of extremism, they are the worst people. God will punish them the severest for these deviated leaders have misled many Muslims and encouraged them to kill innocent people by promising Paradise to them.

---

[79] Muslim, *Sahih*, Kitab al-Imara, 3/1469.

They will be responsible for the blood of every murder in the Judgment Day.

Prophet Muhammad, upon whom be peace and blessings, encouraged Muslims to take action against terrorists and eliminate them for the sake of society. Whenever extremists appear and commit the acts of terrorism, it is a duty upon the state to fight them and protect people against their evils. The most effective method to eliminate extremists is refuting their religious arguments with the evidences from the Qur'an and the Sunnah. This mission can be done by the true Muslim scholars who know the Qur'an and the Sunnah well.

By using religious concepts and Islamic terminology the extremist terrorists deceive ignorant masses and receive physical and financial support from them. The masses, especially the youth, cannot distinguish what is Islamic from what is un-Islamic. If they hear some Quranic verses and some sayings of the Noble Prophet from the mouth of the extremists, they may believe them. Deceiving people with religion is more effective than any other ideology. Therefore, all Muslims must be very careful against extremists to protect their children from falling into their hands. Instructing children with the moderate and true Islamic beliefs is an effective method to eradicate extremism. Otherwise, terrorists may brainwash them and use them against humanity. The extremist terrorists who exploit religious concepts are more dangerous than others for they have powerful elements to delude ignorant minds and exploit them for their evil agendas. Their eloquent speakers are very skillful in deceiving inexperienced youth by referring to the Qur'an and the Sunnah in their speech and brainwash them to commit acts of violence and terror. Their outward appearance may seem religious but they reveal their true identity when they resort to terror and violence. They sow the seeds of hatred, enmity and disunity among Muslims.

Terrorism is like cancer in a body; if it is not removed, it spreads and destroys the whole body. Terrorists have no mercy; they kill people ruthlessly. They split community with their extreme ideology and spread disorder, corruption and terror in society. It is, therefore, a duty upon a Muslim state not to harbor, but to destroy any terrorist group so that society can enjoy tranquility and peace. It is the state's primary responsibility to develop counter-terrorism policies and maintain peace and security in society. The state(s) should eliminate the reasons and circumstances that terrorist groups use to recruit new members. Therefore, the root causes which spread terrorism all over the world should be addressed effectively instead of focusing only upon getting rid of the extremist individuals. To this end, the state should give priority to educate its citizens that neither terrorism nor violence is an Islamic method to change the society or reform the government. It should also protect the youth from falling victim to radical groups for they can easily instill their radical ideas into the young minds and exploit their emotions and inexperience. In addition, citizens need to be very cautious about the extremists to protect the young generation from falling into their hands. Similarly, moderate Muslim scholars must speak loudly and clearly against terrorism, thus playing their pivotal role with regards to protecting and maintaining peace in society. They must reveal the hypocritical face of the extremist terrorists and refute their extremist ideology with clear evidence from the Qur'an and the Sunnah so that ignorant masses do not fall prey to them. They must also contribute to the education of young minds with the moderate and true Islamic beliefs to eradicate all kinds of extremism.

Chapter 2

VIOLENCE AND TERRORISM IN ISLAMIC HISTORY

THE KHARIJITES

Introduction

The term Kharijite literally means those who went out. This term was used in the early Islamic period for the extremist sect that disobeyed and fought against the authority of Caliph Ali ibn Abu Tālib after the caliph agreed to arbitration with his rival Mu'awiya in the Battle of Siffin in 657 CE.[80] Initially, these people were together with the caliph, but then they separated from him and broke into revolt against him.[81]

The Kharijites considered themselves as the believers who "stood up" for the sake of God or the ones who "revolted" against disbelief. Later, this term started to be used for the other radical movements that disobeyed and

---

[80] Al-Shahristani, Muhammad ibn Abd al-Karim. *Al-Milal Wa'n-Nihal*, (Beirut: Dar al-Ma'rifa, 1993), 1/132.
[81] Higgins, Annie C. (2004). "Kharijites, Khawarij." In Martin, Richard C. *Encyclopedia of Islam and the Muslim World*, vol. 1. Macmillan. p. 390.

broke into revolt against the official authority through violence and insurgency.[82]

The Kharijites have some other names that describe this extremist movement from different aspects. They are, for instance, called as "Haruriyya" because they gathered together in a placed called "Harura" for the purpose of revolt against Caliph Ali.[83] Since they rejected the arbitration between Caliph Ali and his rival Mu'awiya, they are also called as "Muhakkima," literally meaning "the ones who assigned the arbitrator," due to their statement, "Judgment belongs to God alone."[84] Some Muslims called them as "Mariqa," which means "the ones who went out of the fold of Islam easily, on the basis of the following saying of the Noble Prophet:

> There will appear some people among you whose prayer will make you look down upon yours, and whose fasting will make you look down upon yours, but they will recite the Qur'an which will not go beyond their throats (they will not act on it) and they will go out of Islam as an arrow goes out through the game whereupon the archer would examine the arrowhead but see nothing, and look at the unfeathered arrow but see nothing, and look at the arrow feathers but see nothing, and finally he suspects to find something in the lower part of the arrow.[85]

Here, the Arabic word "mariqa" used in the prophetic saying is derived from the trilateral verbal root "m-r-q" which means "to go out." Thus, the verbal noun *mariqa* refers to "the ones who easily went out of the fold of Islam." The analogy of an arrow straying from its target conveys the meaning of the superficial nature of the Kharijite faith. In another version of this prophetic tradition, the Noble Prophet stated as follows:

> In the last days (of the world) there will appear young people with foolish thoughts and ideas. They will give good talks, but they will go out

---

[82] Al-Shahristani, *Al-Milal Wa'n-Nihal*, p. 132.
[83] Baghdadi, Abd al-Qāhir. *Al-Farq Bayn al-Firaq*, (Cairo: Muassasat ibn Sina, n.d.), p. 74.
[84] Baghdadi, *Al-Farq Bayn al-Firaq*, 72.
[85] Al-Bukhari, *Sahih*, Fadail al-Qur'an, 36.

of Islam as an arrow goes out of its game, their faith (is so superficial that it) will not exceed their throats.[86]

The Kharijites did not call themselves the Kharijites, but rather "the Shurat," plural of *shari*, which literally means "the sellers." They found this title from a Quranic verse that means:

> And (there is) among the people *one who sells himself* in pursuit of God's good pleasure. God is All-Pitying towards His servants (and therefore commends to them reverent piety and fear of His punishment).[87]

In this verse, God called sincere believers as the ones who sell themselves in pursuit of God's good pleasure and the Kharijites considered themselves as such.

Some scholars connect the very ideology of the Kharijites to a man named Dhul Khuwaysira, who lived in the same age with the Noble Prophet. His story is recorded in the prophetic traditions as follows:

> Abu Sa`id al-Khudrī reports: "While we were with God's Messenger (upon whom be peace and blessings) who was distributing the spoils of war, there came Dhul Khuwaysira, a man from the tribe of Bani Tamim and said, 'O God's Messenger! Do Justice.' The Noble Prophet said, 'Woe to you! Who could do justice if I did not? I would be a desperate loser if I did not do justice.' 'Umar said, 'O God's Messenger! Allow me to chop his head off.' The Prophet said, 'Leave him, for he has friends who pray and fast in such a way that you will consider your fasting negligible in comparison to theirs. They recite the Qur'an but it does not go beyond their throats (i.e., they do not act on it) and they will desert Islam as an arrow goes through a victim's body, so that the hunter, on looking at the arrow's blade, would see nothing on it; he would look at its arrowhead and see nothing: he would look at its unfeathered arrow and see nothing, and he would look at the arrow feathers and see nothing (neither meat nor blood), for the arrow has been too fast even for the

---

[86] Al-Bukhari, *Sahih*, Fadāil al-Qur'an, 36.
[87] Qur'an 2: 207.

blood and excretions to smear. The sign by which they will be recognized is that among them there will be a black man, one of whose arms will resemble a woman's breast or a lump of meat moving loosely. Those people will appear when there will be differences amongst the people.' I testify that I heard this narration from God's Messenger and I testify that Ali bin Abi Tālib fought with such people, and I was in his company. He ordered that the man (described by the Noble Prophet) should be looked for. The man was brought and I looked at him and noticed that he looked exactly as God's Messenger had described him."[88]

Hadith commentators say that the man described in the report above was Hurkus ibn Zuhayr al-Sādi and was killed in the Battle of Siffin among the Kharijite people.[89] The expression in the prophetic report above "They recite the Qur'an but it does not go beyond their throats" indicates that although the Kharijites recite the Qur'an, it does not past into their hearts, which presumably is why they strayed and rebelled.

Although the Kharijites emerged as the opposition group to Caliph Ali, later they adopted a political doctrine with regards to caliphate. They accept the caliphate of Abu Bakr, Umar, Uthman's first six years and Ali until the Arbitration Incident. They argue that any person can be elected as a caliph and need to be obeyed as long as he follows the Qur'an and the Sunnah. This sect was divided into five major groups around the end of Umayyad's rule.[90] All these groups consider Ali, Uthman, the people of the Camel,[91] the arbitrators and whomever accepted the appointment of arbitrators as "unbelievers," and therefore worthy to be killed. They also label the perpetrators of major sins as "unbelievers."[92]

---

[88] Al-Bukhari, *Sahih*, Kitab al-Manāqib, 25
[89] Al-Tabari, Abu Ja'far Muhammad ibn Jarir. *Tārikh al-Tabari*, (Cairo: Dar al-Maarif, n.d.) 4/76-79.
[90] Baghdadi, *al-Farq Bayn al-Firaq*, 49.
[91] They were those who fought against Caliph Ali in the Battle of Camel in Basra in the year of 656 CE.
[92] Baghdadi, *al-Farq Bayn al-Firaq*, 49.

The Origins of the Kharijites

The emergence of the Kharijites begins with the Battle of Siffin in 657 CE. This incident was the first civil war that followed with the murder of the third caliph 'Uthman in 656 CE. Caliph Uthman was accused of unfair policies by the new converts and was thus asked to resign from the caliphate. When he rejected their offer, the insurgents besieged his house. They tried to convince Uthman to accept his mistakes and resign from caliphate, and after failing to convince him, they broke down his door and slaughtered him.

Uthman's caliphate of twelve years is analyzed in two categories: in the first six years, there was no conflict or dispute among Muslims while in the second half of his caliphate some seditions and disputes appeared. Some unsatisfied groups criticized Caliph Uthman and his local administrators and demanded him to resign. When he rejected their request, six hundred insurgents from Egypt, Basra and Kufa came to Medina and besieged the house of the caliph. They found Caliph Uthman guilty and murdered him in his house. It was the first civil insurgency in Islamic history. They deemed the caliph as an "unbeliever" due to some of his policies and mistakes, especially on administrative issues, and killed him brutally.

Following the murder of Caliph Uthman, Ali ibn Abi Tālib was elected as the fourth Caliph of Islam. However, Mu'āwiya, the governor of Damascus and cousin of 'Uthman, refused to give his allegiance to Ali until Uthman's murderers were found and brought to justice. The situation was very critical and sensitive indeed. The insurgents were very crowded and they were still in Medina; therefore, any attempt to punish them would cause a civil war in the heart of the Islamic state. For this reason, the newly-elected Caliph Ali wanted first to settle down the seditions, conflicts and turbulences among Muslims. As the ruler of the Muslim community he had to act responsibly and very carefully.

Mu'āwiya did not initially voice his claim for the caliphate, but asked Caliph Ali to punish the murderers of Caliph Uthman. He knew very well that there was a strong public support for his demand for justice and revenge. Therefore, he made use of this opportunity to strengthen the forces he commanded as the governor of Damascus. To this end, Mu'āwiya showed to the people of Damascus the late caliph's bloody dress in which he was murdered and thus stirred them to get revenge from the insurgents. In the meantime, Caliph Ali moved the caliphate from Medina to Kufa to secure his government against the rebels, but Mu'āwiya marched towards the city of Kufa with eighty thousand soldiers to seemingly get the revenge of the late Uthman. They confronted with the army of Caliph Ali which consisted of ninety thousands soldiers. For a while, neither side put on an impressive display of military progress but later Caliph Ali gained the advantage in the fight. In the meantime, Amr ibn As, who was a political genius in the line of Mu'āwiya, suggested the soldiers to put the pages of the Qur'an on their lances, thereby forcing Caliph Ali's forces to make peace on the basis of the Qur'an as an arbitrator. This was indeed a strategic tactic from Mu'āwiya for he could see that he was about to lose the fight. Caliph Ali perceived their tactic and commanded his soldiers to continue to fight until defeating the other side, but he could not convince them to go on fighting. This was simply because the soldiers did no longer want to fight against a group who were holding the pages of the Holy Qur'an on their lances.

Eventually, the fighting ceased and the appointment of an arbitrator from each side to resolve the conflict among Muslims was accepted. Although, the role of the arbitrators was vague, the essential condition was that the Qur'an would serve as the final judge. Mu'āwiya assigned Amr ibn As, who was considered as genius in politics, as the arbitrator while Ali assigned Abu Musa al-Ash'ari for this task. These two arbitrators came together to seek a solution and decided that each would terminate the rule of the leader on their side, and then Muslims would elect their new ruler. After making the agreement, the arbitrators came to people to announce their decision. Amr ibn As asked Abu Musa al-Ash'ari, the arbitrator of Caliph Ali, to speak first. Thereupon, he explained what they agreed upon and pronounced that he terminated the rulership of Ali and Mu'āwiya. After him Amr started to speak. He presented the public with a fait accompli, saying, "As you see, Ali's friend (his arbitrator) terminated his caliphate. Therefore, I assign Mu'āwiya as the new caliph of Muslims."[93]

The treaty between Ali and Mu'āwiya was recorded in two different forms. The summary of the agreement was as follows: "This is a peace treaty between the two parties which committed themselves to adhere to the Qur'an... the sides were to judge rightly to finish the division and war among Muslims..."[94] According to the agreement, the decision was to be disseminated in seven months, thus Ali went back to Kufa and Mu'āwiya to Damascus. This agreement was not a real peace between the sides; rather, it was a temporary solution for the conflict at hand.

When the Arbitration Incident was disseminated to the public, a group from Ali's side asked Ali to give up from his decision and resume fighting against Mu'āwiya's forces. Interestingly, they previously agreed to arbitration but now demanded from Ali to renounce his decision. However, Ali did not accept their request; thus, they left him and withdrew from his camp. They declared both Ali and Mu'āwiya as "unbelievers" on the basis of the Quranic verse which means: *"There is no judgment but God's alone."*[95] They used this Quranic expression as their motto and labeled all Muslims who accepted the arbitration as *kafir*s, or "unbelievers."

It is reported that the first Kharijite who used this motto was Urwa ibn Ubayda. He came to Ali and questioned the Arbitration Incident stating, "Is there a better arbitration than God's."[96] Then, a man from the Kharijites shouted as "No judgment but God's."[97]

Upon hearing all this, Ali told them, "I had asked you to continue to fight until defeating the forces of Mu'āwiya but you rejected it openly. But now, we have made an agreement with them and we have to obey the agreement for God says: *'Fulfill the covenant of God when you have taken*

---

[93] Al-Shaybani, Abd al-Karim ibn Abd al-Wahid. *Al-Kāmil fi al-Tārikh*, (Beirut: Dar al-Kutub al-Ilmiyya, 1987), 3/208.
[94] Madelung, Wilfer. *The Succession to Muhammad, A Study of the Early Caliphate*, (Cambridge: Cambridge University Press, 1997), p. 243.
[95] Qur'an 12: 40.
[96] Al-Mubarrad, *al-Kamil*, (Cairo: al-Istiqama Publishing, 1951), 2/116.
[97] Al-Mubarrad, *al-Kamil*, 2/116.

it, [O believers], and do not break oaths after their confirmation while you have made God, over you, a witness. Indeed, God knows what you do. "[98]

The twelve thousand rebels retreated to a place called Harura and some others joined them. Ali tried to gain them back to his camp, but they insisted that he should confess his "mistake" publicly and ask for God's forgiveness for it. The rebels proceeded to a place called Nahrawan near Tigris and many more joined them. Deeming Ali and Mu'āwiya and all their followers as "unbelievers," the Kharijites began to commit brutal attacks which are very similar to the evil acts of ISIS today.

The Kharijites were so wishful to kill those Muslims who followed Ali or Mu'āwiya and all those who accepted the arbitration. In other words, the Kharijites vowed to kill any Muslims if he or she did not accept their own extreme doctrines. The following incident is a good example to understand this evil Kharijite mindset:

> Once, Abdullah ibn Habbab ibn Arat was travelling with his wife while she was mounted on a donkey. The Kharijites stopped them and started questioning them. Once they learned that he was the son of a well-known Companion, they requested him to narrate a hadith on the authority of his father. After listening to the prophetic saying from him, they asked his opinion about Abu Bakr and Umar. Thereupon, Abdullah spoke positively about them and mentioned their favors and contributions to Islam. After that they asked him about Uthman and his caliphate. Abdullah told them that he was a good ruler at both the first and second half of his caliphate. Thereafter, they asked him about Ali and the Arbitration Incident. This time, he said, "Ali knows God more than you do, and he is more pious and wiser than you are." Upon hearing this, they started to threaten him with his life. They tied his hands from back and went on their travel. In the meantime, a date dropped from a tree and one of the Kharijites took it to eat. When he put it in his mouth, the other Kharijites told him that it was not lawful to eat before paying the cost; therefore, he threw it out of his mouth immediately. As they continued their journey, they saw a pig that belonged to a Christian and one of the

---

[98] Qur'an 16: 91.

Kharijites killed it with his sword. The other Kharijites scolded him, saying that he caused a disorder in the earth by killing the animal of a Christian. They discussed the matter stating that the People of the Book who live under the rulership of Muslims would be safe and their possessions were to be protected. Thereafter, they met the owner of the pig and paid his damage so he could be content. Witnessing all these events, Abdullah ibn Habbab ibn Arat thought that those Kharijites would never commit the heinous act of killing him. He told them that he is a Muslim and did not harm them in anyway. However, they laid him down by a river and slayed him brutally in front of his pregnant wife like slaughtering an animal. Then, they turned to his wife. She screamed saying, "I am a pregnant woman. Don't you fear from God?" However, the Kharijites split her belly and slayed the woman and her baby together.[99]

This incident clearly indicates that the Kharijites have a very violent mindset which contradicts totally with the Word of God, the Practice of the Prophet and all the principles of Islam. While practicing the religious rulings of lesser importance, they violated the major tenets of Islam, such as the prohibition of killing civilians and innocent people. They would label any Muslim as an "unbeliever" if he or she does not accept their extreme doctrines and then would kill them so brutally. The following report clearly shows that they contradicted with the teachings of the Qur'an and the Sunnah in their extreme doctrines:

> Once, Abdullah ibn Shaddad visited the Noble Prophet's wife Aisha during the days when Ali was assassinated. She asked him to tell the truth regarding the Kharijites. He said that when Ali made an agreement with Mu'āwiya in accordance with the decisions of the arbitrators, eight thousand of the soldiers from among the forces of Ali separated from him and took position against him. They gathered together in a site called Harura and started blaming Ali due to the Arbitration Incident. They argued that he abandoned the Book of God by assigning a human arbitrator, claiming that the judgment authority belongs to God and no-

---

[99] Ibn Athīr, *al-Kāmil*, 3/218-219.

one else. When Ali was informed about their accusations, he summoned the most knowledgeable ones (*qurra*) on the Qur'an for a meeting. When they gathered together, he put the Qur'an in his front and said, "O Qur'an, tell people who is right." Ali told them that the Qur'an is a judge between him and them. After that he recited the Quranic verse on arbitration: "*If you fear that a breach might occur between spouses, appoint an arbiter from among his people and an arbiter from among her people. If they both want to set things right, God will bring about reconciliation between them. Assuredly, God is All-Knowing, All-Aware.*"[100] Ali then addressed people stating, "The affairs of Muslims are more important than the problem between spouses. If God commands believers to assign an arbitrator to set things right when dispute arises between spouses, it is more proper and more important to assign an arbitrator to solve the conflicts among Muslims. The Kharijites blamed me due to writing my name as Ali ibn Abi Tālib (instead of the ruler of believers) in the agreement. However, when Suhayl ibn Amr came to God's Messenger to sign the Hudaybiya Treaty, he asked the Messenger to remove the title 'the Messenger of God' from the treaty and put the name Muhammad ibn Abdullah instead. The Noble Prophet accepted his request and told me to write it as he wished." Then, Ali continued his speech stating that he only followed the Practice of the Prophet as indicated in the Qur'an, "*Assuredly you have in God's Messenger an excellent example to follow for whoever looks forward to God and the Last Day and remembers and mentions God much.*"[101] Later, Ali sent Abdullah ibn Abbas to the Kharijites to dispute them regarding their false doctrines. They debated with Ibn Abbas for three days. After the discussion, four thousand people from the Kharijites repented and joined the ranks of Ali again. Ali informed the rest of the Kharijites that they would live freely wherever they want as long as they did not waylay people and kill them. However, they continued to kill people who did not share their ideology; therefore, Caliph Ali fought against them.[102]

---

[100] Qur'an 4: 35.
[101] Qur'an 33: 21.
[102] Al-Tamimi, Abu Ya'la Ali ibn Muthanna. *Musnad al-Abu Ya'la al-Mawsili*, (Beirut: Dar al-Mamun, 1992), 1/367-370.

As it can be seen in these reports, although the Kharijites seemingly put their emphasis upon the Qur'an and the Sunnah (or Practice) of the Prophet, they openly went against them with their evil ideology and bloody crimes.

The Kharijites committed a long series of bloody attacks against Muslims who did not agree with them. Although the main issue for Caliph Ali was to deal with Mu'āwiya and his opposition, he was eventually forced to move against the Kharijites at Nahrawan in 658 CE. The rebels were greatly outnumbered by Ali's forces. At the beginning, Ali wanted to solve the problem with peaceful methods and tried to negotiate with the Kharijites. It was, however, impossible to convince them. Therefore, Ali eventually commanded his army to attack them. The rebels suffered a severe defeat, yet the remnants continued to launch guerrilla-like raids against Muslims.

Naturally, the long lasting opposition of the Kharijites weakened Ali's rule. Indeed, he had to fight against both Mu'āwiya and the Kharijites at the same time. He wished to gain the rebels back rather than fighting against them. Indeed, if he wished so, it would not be difficult for him to protect his caliphate by receiving their supports through some political tactics. For example, he would agree to their demands (and thus repent as they wished) and win them back, thus avoiding the decline of his power.

After defeating the Kharijites at Nahrawan, Ali wanted to march against Mu'āwiya and his forces in Damascus. However, his men were very tired due to the fighting against the Kharijites. He turned back to Kufa when they asked him to postpone the march.[103] Mu'āwiya became very happy when he received the news that Ali's forces got exhausted after the march against the rebels at Nahrawan, causing Ali to delay his march to Damascus. Therefore, Mu'āwiya took the advantage and wanted to take Egypt from Ali's governor. Learning Mu'āwiya's strategy, Ali asked his governor to be strong against his enemy. Although the governor promised the caliph to be loyal to him and fight against the forces of Mu'āwiya, he could not prevent Egypt from falling into Mu'āwiya's hand. Now, with the

---

[103] Tabari, *Tārikh*, 3/124.

loss of Egypt, the Islamic state was split into two parts: the reign of Mu'āwiya in Syria and Egypt and the rest of the Islamic lands under Ali's authority.

Ali had to fight not only against Mu'āwiya's forces, but also against the five Kharijite groups. Taking advantage of the wearying marches of Ali's forces, Mu'āwiya further took the control of Medina, Makka and Yemen. Ali sent new forces to take these cities back. However, a Kharijite named Abd al-Rahman ibn Amr ibn Muljam al-Muradi assassinated him while he was going to lead the Morning Prayer in Kufa Mosque. Ibn Muljam struck on the head of Ali, who was observing the fast of the holy month of Ramadan, with a poisoned sword and killed him on January 28, 661 CE.[104]

The Kharijites after Caliph Ali

The Kharijites after the death of Caliph Ali went on with their bloody attacks against Muslims who did not share their ideology. Mu'āwiya, the first of the Umayyad caliphs, had to deal with the numerous Kharijite rebellions during his reign (661–680 CE). However, he too, could not put an end to the bloody attacks of the Kharijites. Under various leaders, this extreme terrorist group went on committing violence "in the name of religion." They received support from different groups who were not satisfied with the Umayyad rule. Thus, the Kharijites survived throughout the Umayyad period (661–750 CE). They began to establish their extremist ideology after the Arbitration Incident and were divided into many subgroups that had slight differences on their ideology and methods of protest.[105] The most violent of these groups was the Azariqa. They would kill the dissidents very violently and take their wives and children as slaves and all their property as the spoils of war.

---

[104] Tabari, *Tārikh*, 6/29.
[105] Al-Mubarrad, *Al-Kāmil*, 2/179-180.

The main motive for the bloody attacks of the Kharijites against the Umayyads was related to their rule. This extremist group accused the Umayyad caliphs of misusing the state treasury by living in castles, having guards similar to the Byzantine rulers and maintaining their regime without the consent of all Muslims. All of the Kharijite splinter groups threatened the Umayyad reign; therefore, the Umayyad rulers launched strikes against them throughout their caliphate. During the reign of the Umayyad Caliph Umar ibn Abd al-Aziz (717-720), the attacks of the Kharijites diminished due to his tolerant policy towards them. However, towards the end of the Umayyad reign, the Kharijites became very aggressive and violent again.

Despite their numerous bloody attacks during the Umayyad period, the Kharijites failed to reach their aim because of the disunity among their splinter groups. The Umayyads took advantage of this and tried to eliminate them before they were reorganized. Due to the success of the Umayyads against this extreme sect, the Kharijites had to change its bloody ideology, starting to pursue its goals through political organizations and propagation in the vast Muslim majority lands from North Africa to Oman. By the ninth century, however, the Kharijites were eliminated from the central Islamic lands.

Critical Analysis for the Emergence of the Kharijites

The emergence of the contemporary terrorist groups, including especially ISIS and Al Qaeda, has led scholars to better understand the origins of violence and terrorism in Islamic history. In view of their remarkable resemblance, they have gained better insight of not only the contemporary radical terrorist groups, but also the early history of extremism, primarily the Kharijite radicalism, and reinterpreted their views of the early Islamic period extremists.

The Kharijites were the Bedouin desert tribesmen. They were thus untamed nomads roaming in the desert and enjoying complete freedom. They took part in bloody attacks against other Muslims not out of their commitment to the religion, but out of their expectation of some worldly gains, especially by seizing war booties and getting women and children as their slaves.

When Islam was introduced to this shallow Bedouin mindset, they started to read the religious texts literally and used all their energy as reaction to anything they deemed injustice in Muslim community. In other words, the violent inclinations had been imprinted in the hearts of these Kharijites before they came to the fold of Islam; thus, they exposed all their violent characteristics whenever they had an opportunity.

There is, however, too much confusion among scholars with regards to identifying the Kharijites as a politically or religiously motivated extremist group. Some scholars identify them as a rebellious religious extremist group.[106] They argue that the Kharijite ideology was purely religious as it started to be shaped after the followers of Mu'āwiya put the pages of the Qur'an on their lances in a successful attempt to stop the caliph's march against them.[107] Then, both Caliph Ali and Mu'āwiya accepted the offer of the *qurra*, those who were firmly grounded in Quranic knowledge, when they asked the Holy Qur'an to be the ultimate judge between the two sides. Most scholars, however, argue that the Kharijites had a superficial approach to the religious texts and this led to their shallow interpretation of Islam along with their rigid form of Islamic practice when compared to the overall religious practice and piety of the Noble Prophet's Companions. Although they showed apparent religious zeal, they were very political in nature and were totally different from the other theological sects appearing in Islamic history.

Here, we need to bear in mind two things that are vital in understanding the radical mindset of the Kharijites: their reactionary stance against the Arbitration Incident in the Battle of Siffin and their eventual use of the Quranic verse, *"There is no judgment authority but God's alone"* as their motto. Obviously, applying to the Qur'an to solve the conflicts among Muslims in the time of strife is an indication that this sect has some

---

[106] Wellhausen, Julius. *Die Religios-Politischen Oppositionspartein im alten Islam*, (Berlin: n.p., 1901), pp. 7-13.
[107] Wellhausen, ibid.

religious motives in the establishment of its movement. Nevertheless, it was the "free and defiant" nature of the desert-living Bedouins that heavily influenced their reactionary behavior.

The Kharijites spread the seeds of seditions and turmoil in the early Islamic community. They appeared during the major internal confrontations among Muslims and announced their doctrines in public instead of resorting to conspiracy and widespread propaganda.[108] Although the Kharijite discourse put its emphasis upon the Almighty God, the Qur'an and justice, this extremist group committed the most evil crimes and injustices against other Muslims.

The notion of piety and other religious concepts have a great political power in the Muslim community, and the Kharijites used religious concepts in their ideology in an attempt to justify their violence. For instance, it is the duty of every Muslim to do and enjoin good while avoiding and forbidding evil. Yet, the Kharijites always acted very violently in their practice of this Islamic principle, considering all "other" believers who did not agree with them as "unbelievers," deserving to be punished brutally.

In the mindset of this extremist group, there are two important notions: the religion and the Muslim community. It is a religious duty for every Muslim to put the Almighty God and His law and commands above everything else while it is a duty upon the community to obey the ruler as long as he obeys God. The religion is above all for it is the right of God upon His servants. According to their extreme doctrines, however, the Kharijites declared other Muslims who did not agree to them to be "unbelievers," and thus justified the killing of unjust rulers and the members of the Muslim community who obeyed those unjust Muslim rulers. Politics and religion were thus inseparable in the extremist ideology of the Kharijites.

These people were mostly the stern, freely roaming, desert-living Bedouins; therefore, they were very rigid to be reconciled with other Muslims. They were motivated, in their rebellion, for some social and

---

[108] Wellhausen, *Die Religios-Politischen*, p. 18.

religio-political reasons rather than mere economic concerns.[109] They used religion as a means for their political goals. They attracted many rebels to their ranks with an appealing political theory. In this regard, they put their emphasis on the purification of Islam from all kinds of false beliefs and practices, accepted the Qur'an as the constitution of the state and advocated more rights for everyone. However, they contradicted with their own ideology with all the violence and bloody attacks they carried out. Thus, they were not perceived as a group promoting human rights in practice.

The Kharijites were mostly the nomadic, defiant Arabs roaming in the vast desert and enjoying complete freedom. When they were assigned as soldiers by the Islamic state, they could not adopt to the new system. Therefore, they played a pivotal role in the rebellion against Caliph Uthman. The Kharijite revolt against the caliph was neither religious nor political; it was a mere reaction to the system of centralized control.[110] The fundamental change in the lives of the nomads was also an effective reason for their revolt in the Battle of Siffin. Their dissatisfaction with the community could indeed be traced back to the reign of Uthman rather than an abrupt rise in the Battle of Siffin.[111] Their religious extremism caused Muslim scholars to emphasize the concept of moderation in Islamic community, which refers to the vast majority of Muslims, usually known as *Ahl al-Sunna wa al-Jama'a* (the people of middle path and unity) in Muslim community.

Some scholars argue that the Kharijite formation goes back to the time of Abu Bakr, the first Caliph of Islam.[112] When the Noble Prophet passed away, some Arab tribes did not want to recognize the new ruler and refused to give the prescribed purifying alms (*zakah*) to the state. Some

---

[109] Watt, W. Montgomery. *Islam and the Integration of Society*, (London: Routledge & Kegan Paul, 1961), p. 94.
[110] Lewis, Bernard. *The Arabs in History*, (New York: Harper Torchbooks, 1966), p. 60.
[111] Fazlur Rahman, *Islam*, p. 169.
[112] Shaban, M. A. *Islamic History, A. D. 600-750 (A.H. 132): A New Interpretation*, (Cambridge: Cambridge University Press, 1971), pp. 45-46.

people from among these tribes abandoned Islam along with their revolt against the new ruler while others only rejected to pay their *zakah*. Caliph Abu Bakr waged war against all these rebellious tribes until they surrendered. He successfully suppressed all the rebellions against his rulership.

According to one theory, some Arab tribes did not take part in the revolt against Caliph Abu Bakr, thus attaining a better status in society. As a result of this, they gained much wealth and prestige. When this prestige was later threatened by Caliph Uthman, they wanted to destroy his administration. Similarly, when Caliph Ali was busy with seditions, turmoil and revolts, they decided to break from Ali's forces because they thought that he could not protect their prestige and economic status.[113] Although this theory seems logical, it is very difficult to accept it because the Kharijites were mostly the Bedouin Arabs who had little knowledge of Islam, and yet strived to be pious. Thus, they committed much violence out of their religious zealot. Economic concerns were, therefore, not the main powerful reason for their revolt.

Pious people may have a certain political stance, but politics and piety were very closely intertwined in the Kharijite mindset.[114] For the Kharijites, piety was deemed as a way to indulge in violent confrontation with the state and the greater society. They claimed to "sell" their souls and property to God in return for a place in Paradise on the basis of their shallow understanding of piety. The Kharijites and their preachers put their emphasis on the life of the Prophet as their role model when addressing public (typically in their speech and not in action).[115] This rhetoric was very appealing, especially to those tribes who deemed themselves as suffering from the very hands of the unjust rulers. The unjust rulers who appeared after the Rightly Guided Caliphs such as Hajjaj ibn Yusuf and

---

[113] Shaban, *Islamic History*, p. 76.
[114] Morony, Michael G. *Iraq after the Muslim Conquest*, (Princeton, New Jersey: Princeton University Press, 1984), p. 467.
[115] Robinson, Chase F. *Empire and Elites after the Muslim Conquest*, (Cambridge: Cambridge University Press, 2000), p. 116.

Yazid ibn Mu'āwiya offered tremendous opportunity to the Kharijites in finding support for their rebellious activities against the rulers. Principally, their calling of the discontented Muslims for holy war (*jihad*) and migration in connection with the Prophet's call for striving in the way of God and migrating for His cause (*hijra*) attracted many people to the ranks of the Kharijites.

Considering all these, the major characteristics of the Kharijites can be summarized as follows:

i. rejecting the arbitration, thus giving the judgment authority solely to God,
ii. rebellion against unjust rulers,
iii. accepting a caliph outside of the Quraysh tribe,
iv. believing that perpetrators of grave sins remain in Hell forever.[116]

In Islamic history, the Kharijites are deemed, especially by the Sunni scholars, as a negative symbol representing disobedience, violence and terror. Even today, they are seen by the vast majority of Muslims as an extreme group that violated the basic teachings of Islam. The scholars identify the Kharijites as those rebelling against the legitimate ruler accepted by the people.[117] Causing disorder, turbulences and seditions through violence and terror has turned out to be a symbol associated with the Kharijites in Islamic history. Muslim scholars have frequently cited the name of this violent group as being the historic example for the contemporary terrorist groups. Therefore, the Kharijite mentality is not a historical remnant, but rather a lasting symbol that signifies rebellion.[118]

---

[116] Salem, Elie Adib. *Political Theory and Institutions of the Khawarij*, (Baltimore: The John Hopkins Press, 1956), p. 25.
[117] Shahristani, *Al-Milal wa al-Nihal*, 132.
[118] Kenney, Jeffrey T. *Heterodoxy and Culture: The Legacy of the Khawarij in Islamic History*, PhD Dissertation, 1991, p. 81.

Reasons for the Rise of the Kharijites

Many scholars consider the Kharijites as a political movement using religious motives to achieve their political goals.[119] The second half of Uthman's caliphate witnessed some political turbulence, and he was eventually martyred by a group of Kharijite rebels. In the beginning, this rebellious Kharijite mentality was established upon political reasons during the reign of Uthman, but they emerged as a separate extremist group after the Arbitration Incident during the rule of Caliph Ali. It thus became a religious duty for them to actively fight against any ruler they deemed unjust.

Since the Kharijites considered any Muslim who did not agree to their doctrines as an "unbeliever," worthy of killing, they deemed it lawful to take their blood and properties. In this regard, they killed the Muslims, including the Noble Prophet's Companions, and captured their properties, women and children.

During the conflict between Caliph Ali and Talha, Zubayr and Aisha in the Battle of Camel, the Kharijites played the key role to instigate the war. The caliph wanted to solve the problem with those on the side of Talha, Zubayr and Aisha in a peaceful manner and through the language of diplomacy. He promised them that he would find the murderers of Uthman and punish them, telling them that he needed some time. They readily accepted this offer as they only wished for the murderers of the late caliph to be found and punished. They did not want to get involved in a fight against the caliph.

However, the Kharijites who had taken part in the murder of Caliph Uthman were now in the ranks of Caliph Ali and they did not want to be exposed as the murderers of the late caliph. Therefore, they planned to instigate a fight between the two sides in order to cover up their atrocious crimes. For this purpose, they started to shoot arrows towards the tents of the other side in secrecy during the night. Unfortunately, the crowd from among the followers of Talha, Zubayr and Aisha thought that Caliph Ali

---

[119] Goldziher, Ignaz. *Al-Aqida wa al-Shariah fi al-Islam*, (Egypt, n.d.), p. 92.

betrayed them. Therefore, they struck back and around ten thousand Muslims lost their lives in this war, which came to be known as the Battle of Camel.[120]

Mu'āwiya, the governor of Damascus, asked Caliph Ali to immediately find the murderers of Uthman and punish them. The caliph was not able to do so because the rebels were still in the city of Medina, and any attempt to punish them would cause a civil war in the heart of Islam. Thus, he promised that he would punish the murderers, but needed some time to subdue the seditions and turmoil first. However, Mu'āwiya did not accept this promise, and the two forces eventually confronted at the Battle of Siffin. After the Arbitration Incident, the Kharijites proclaimed both Caliph Ali and Mu'āwiya as "unbelievers" due to their assignment of two human arbitrators. They argued that the judgment authority belongs to God only. Thus they separated from the forces of the caliph and kept committing more violence and bloody attacks just for their political goals.

Another main reason for the violent Kharijite mentality to emerge is their superficial knowledge of Islam. The Kharijites learned only a few verses from the Qur'an without seeing the full picture or understanding the Qur'an in its totality and made use of those verses as evidence for their extremist doctrines and violent acts. Coming from the nomadic background and living in the deserts as Bedouins, it was not easy for them to debate on a scholarly basis. Therefore, they became very strict and intolerant to any other ideas. They would easily label any Muslim they disagree as unbeliever (*kafir*) although this is clearly forbidden by the Noble Prophet himself.[121] It can be said that if a person is ignorant and yet very brave, he or she can be manipulated easily and be exploited skillfully in any violent and terrorist acts. Similarly, the Kharijites were very ignorant but brave Bedouins; therefore, they "sacrificed" their lives so easily in the way of their superficial ideology. They did not know, for instance, that it was God's command to assign an arbitrator to solve problems between people, and that Caliph Ali and Mu'āwiya only followed Islamic instructions in

---

[120] Tabari, *Tārikh*, 4/508-539.
[121] Bukhari, *Sahih*, Adab, 44.

this regard.[122] For the Kharijites, everything was either white or black and people were either Muslims if they were just like them or were simply unbelievers. Since Ali did not accept their radical doctrines, he was assassinated by a follower of this extremist group.

Tribal fanaticism is yet another aspect of the extremist Kharijite movement. They were not happy with the rulership of the Quraysh; therefore, they rejected the idea that a caliph needed to be from the Quraysh tribe. Ironically, the Kharijites themselves were mostly Bedouins who travelled in groups of families called tribes. This fanatic Kharijite group was mainly from the tribes of Mudar, Tamim, Tay, Hamadan, and Bakr. It was their tribal fanaticism which was effective in their revolt first against Caliph Uthman and then against Caliph Ali. For them, the judgment authority belongs to God only,[123] but this was mainly used as a pretext to rebel against the ruler from the Quraysh tribe.

The Kharijites were mostly nomadic Bedouin tribes who were very strict with regards to their customs. They had a very harsh, rigid and intolerant character. They did not have any sort of education. It was mostly their oral traditions and tribal customs shaping their worldview. The Qur'an addresses the Bedouins with their characteristic traits in various places. One such clear Divine address is as follows:

> The Bedouin Arabs are (by nature) more stubborn in unbelief and hypocrisy (than the city-dwellers), and more liable to be unaware of the bounds prescribed by God in what He has sent down on His Messenger. God is All-Knowing (of the nature and state of His servants), All-Wise. Among the Bedouin Arabs there are such as take what they spend (as Prescribed Alms and the contributions they are called on to make in God's cause) as a fine, and wait for some misfortune to befall you; theirs will be the evil turn. God is All-Hearing, All-Knowing.[124]

---

[122] For the issue of arbitration in the Qur'an, see Chapter an-Nisa 4:35.
[123] Baghdadi, Abd al-Qāhir. *Usul al-Din*, (Beirut, 1981), p. 275.
[124] Qur'an 9: 97-98.

The harsh conditions of nomadic life of these desert living people heavily influenced their character. They always pursued their own interest and benefit in the vast desert and they became Muslim for this purpose. Because of their life style, they could not benefit from the educational atmosphere of the Noble Prophet and thus the opportunities of a civilized society. Hence, they were very harsh, rigid and ignorant.

Religious fanaticism, or being a blind follower of Islam, is a powerful reason for committing violence in the name of religion. The Kharijites became religious fanatics when their intolerant character intertwined with their superficial notion of piety. They were not open to any thought or understanding different from their own. They accepted their ideology as the only truth and all others simply as wrong. They followed their doctrines so blindly and in absolute obedience that they never felt to question their ideology whether it was in line with the teachings of the Qur'an and the Sunnah. Although they were worshippers, performing supererogatory prayers during nights and fasting during days, they never understood the true spirit, or ultimate goal, of Islam. While practicing their religious rituals, the Kharijites were in clear contradiction with Islam by committing evils and harming others through violence and terror. Having religious fanaticism, they killed many Muslims with no feeling of any remorse.

Literal reading of the Quranic verses and superficial understanding of the Sunnah acts feed religious fanaticism. The Kharijites read the Quranic verses literally without trying to understand them in their historical and logical context. Selecting just a few verses to reach a conclusion is a partial approach, and it was the case with the Kharijites to deduce their extremist doctrines from a certain part of the religious texts. They chose a few verses which can be in line with their ideology and then interpreted them literally. Thus, the other Muslims who did not read the Qur'an as they did and did not have the same view with theirs were simply "wrong" in their eyes.[125] Ibn Hazm, a Prominent Muslims scholar, states that there was no real

---

[125] Ar-Razi, Fakhr al-Din. *I'tiqadat al-Firaq al-Muslimin wa al-Mushrikin*, (Cairo: Maktaba al-Nahda al-Misriyya, 1938) pp. 46-51.

scholar among the Kharijites; therefore, they could easily accuse each other of disbelief (*takfir*) even in minor issues.[126]

Muslim society witnessed so much seditions, turmoil and upheavals after the Noble Prophet. The hypocrites living among Muslims also played significant roles to instigate the Kharijites against the rulers and other Muslims. The Noble Prophet described their characteristics in many hadiths with his prophetic vision. In one of the hadith, he portrayed them as follows:

> There would arise from my community a people who would recite the Qur'an, and your recital would seem insignificant as compared with their recital, your prayer as compared with their prayer, and your fast as compared with their fast. They would recite the Qur'an thinking that it supports them, whereas it is the evidence against them. Their prayer does not get beyond their collar bone; they would swerve through Islam just as the arrow passes through the prey.[127]

The hypocrites used every opportunity to raise enmity and disputes among Muslims. They utilized the psychology of the masses very well and manipulated them for their self-interest. They divided Muslims into camps. Since the Kharijites were mostly uneducated nomads, it was easy to delude them. Muslim historians mentioned some important personalities who were the head of the hypocrites. One of them was Abdullah ibn Saba who played significant role to split the Muslim community as the Sunni and the Shia.[128] The insurgencies that appeared after the martyrdom of Caliph Uthman was instigated and directed by this figure. He worked together with Khurkus ibn Zuhayr, who was the head of the Kharijites, plotting the revolts against Muslim rulers.

Another factor in the formation of the Kharijite movement was a group known as "qurra." They would recite the Qur'an well and act piously.

---

[126] Ibn Hazm, Abu Muhammad Ali ibn Ahmad. *Al-Fasl Fi al-Milal wa Ahwa al-Nihal*, (Cairo, 1964) 4/156.
[127] Muslim, *Sahih*, Zakat, 48.
[128] Ibn Hazm, *al-Fasl*, 4/156.

When seditions broke out, these people expressed their longing for the days of the Noble Prophet. In this regard, the Kharijites wanted to actualize this goal of turning back to the Age of Bliss on the basis of their superficial understanding. However, they were very far from understanding the real message of the Noble Prophet because they would read the Scripture literally, separating the verses from their original context and making up some extreme interpretations for them.

The Bedouins, who were freely roaming the vast desert, were against any social order, the rule of law and regulations. They lived so freely that they did not like the central authority represented by an Islamic government. Their nomadic nature played a significant role in their reactions against caliphs Uthman and Ali as well as the Umayyad rulers. These people revolted basically against the law and order.

Another reason contributing much to the Kharijite rebellion was the widespread intertribal conflicts and clashes. The Arab tribes had a long history with regards to intertribal conflicts. Each tribe was very proud of its warriors, and this culture of clash passed down to next generations. Many of these tribes had some previous disputes with the Quraysh; therefore, they did not like their leadership in administrative affairs. The Kharijite movement channeled this intertribal enmity towards the Quraysh and fought against the rulers from the Quraysh under the mask of piety.

Theological Doctrines of the Kharijites

The theological views of the Kharijite movement were not clear at the early formation of the movement. This was mainly because of the fact that there were different rebellious tribal groups and each had its own ideology. Each group would follow in the footsteps of their own leader and accept his opinions; therefore, differences among the Kharijite sects emerged in time. Nevertheless, the common points of their doctrines can easily be followed.

The main point of the Kharijite mindset was the absolute authority of the Qur'an. It was the very foundation of their aspect of Islamic belief and practice. They asserted that Muslim society must be loyal to the Qur'an in their religious and worldly affairs. They further argued that the Qur'an cannot be interpreted; rather, it must be understood literally. Ironically, for the Kharijites, there was only one truth with regards to the interpretation of the Qur'an; and it was always their own. For this reason, they misinterpreted the Quranic verse (which means), *"There is no judgment authority but God's only"*[129] as the basis for their accusation of other Muslims with disbelief (*takfir*). This verse later became their motto.

The notion of justice was another doctrine in the Kharijite ideology. They were very strict at this notion. They argued that justice among the servants of God can be only achieved by following the Qur'an. God gives judgment in the Qur'an; therefore, justice can be done only when it is judged according to the Qur'an. Although they referred to the Qur'an in their speech in order to "establish" justice among people, they committed many unjust acts and evil crimes. Thus, they only made use of the Qur'an to cover up their heinous crimes and legitimize their violence.

The notion of the caliphate or a just ruler was of great importance in the theology of this group. They claimed that there was a strong need for a just ruler to provide justice to people. For them, a caliph must be just, pious and knowledgeable. They deemed Abu Bakr and Umar just rulers. Similarly, they accepted as just only the first six years of Uthman's caliphate and Ali's caliphate until the Arbitration Incident. They accused the prominent Companions of blasphemy (*kufr*), including Aisha, Talha, Zubayr, Abu Musa al-Ash'ari and Amr ibn As.

According to this sect, a caliph can be elected from any tribe or nation. There is no condition for a caliph to be from the Quraysh. If a caliph is a Muslim and just, he can rule Muslims. A caliph must obey God in an absolute sense; otherwise, he must resign or the community kills him. Electing a caliph is not a religious obligation unless there is a need for it. If

---

[129] Qur'an 12: 40.

people treat each other justly and in a fair way, there is no need for a caliph.

The Kharijites accepted the practice of religious obligations as part of faith.[130] Thus, if a person commits a major sin or neglects the practice of any religious obligation he or she becomes an unbeliever (*kafir*). For example, they claimed that a Muslim becomes *kafir* if he or she does not perform the daily prayers or does not observe the Ramadan fast. He has to repent; otherwise, he is killed. Carrying out religious obligations and avoiding prohibitions was considered as part of faith. Therefore, they deemed the perpetrator of a major sin an unbeliever, and he or she needed to repent immediately. With this doctrine, they pronounced many Muslims as unbelievers and killed them violently. They cherry-picked and used certain Quranic verses to defend their extremist ideas, including "*Whoever (declines to confirm and) does not judge by what God has sent down, those are indeed unbelievers.*"[131] However, this verse is related to some people from the Jewish community and the beginning of this verse clearly indicates this:

> Surely We did send down the Torah, in which there was guidance and a light (to illuminate people's minds, hearts and ways of life). Thereby did the Prophets, who were fully submitted to God, judge for the Jews; and so did the masters (self-dedicated to God and educating people) and the rabbis (teachers of law), as they had been entrusted to keep and observe the part of God's Book (revealed up to their time); and they were all witnesses to its truth. (Concerning judging by God's Book and observing It, We warned them saying): Do not hold people in awe, but stand in awe of Me; and do not sell My Revelations for a trifling price. Whoever (declines to confirm and) does not judge by what God has sent down, those are indeed unbelievers.[132]

---

[130] Ash'ari, Abu al-Hasan Ali Ibn Ismail. *Maqalat al-Islamiyyin wa Ikhtilah al-Musallin*, (Cairo: Maktaba al-Nahdiyya al-Misriyya, 1950), Vol. 1, pp. 157-159.
[131] Qur'an 5: 44.
[132] Qur'an 5: 44.

As it can clearly be seen from this example, they purposefully quoted only a certain part of a verse in an attempt to support their extremist ideology without trying to understand the verses in their historical context and in the totality of the Qur'an.

Since the Kharijites saw other Muslims who do not agree with their ideology "kafir" (unbelievers), they believed that those unbelievers needed to be invited to repentance and Islam. This understanding was the basis of their understanding of "amr bi'l ma'ruf nahy an al-munkar" (doing and promoting good and avoiding and preventing evil). For this reason, they invited Caliph Ali to repentance after the Arbitration Incident. Since he did not accept their proposal, they pronounced him as "kafir" and assassinated him. Promoting good and preventing evil was "a communal obligation" in the Kharijite ideology, and they used some Quranic verses and hadiths to defend their view:

> (O Community of Muhammad!) You are the best community ever brought forth for (the good of) humankind, enjoining and actively promoting what is right and good and forbidding and trying to prevent the evil, and (this you do because) you believe in God. If only the People of the Book believed (as you do), this would be sheer good for them. Among them there are believers, but most of them are transgressors.[133]
>
> God's Messenger said, "He who amongst you sees something abominable should modify it with the help of his hand; and if he has not strength enough to do it, then he should do it with his tongue; and if he has not strength enough to do it, (even) then he should abhor it from his heart, and that is the least of faith."[134]

Unfortunately, they committed many murders, violence and terrorism in the name of promoting good and preventing evil, according to their extremist ideology, simply because of the fact that they read the religious texts literally and disconnected them from their original context.

---

[133] Qur'an 3: 110.
[134] Muslim, *Sahih*, Iman, 78.

Conclusion

The Kharijites committed brutal violence and terrorism since their first appearance in the course of Islamic history. Today, the same violence and terrorism is represented by different groups but with the same sick mentality. The Kharijites used the Qur'an and the Sunnah not only to legitimize their violence, but also to attract new recruits to their ranks. Similarly, the contemporary terrorist groups, such as ISIS and Al Qaeda, exploit religion to mask evil crimes and deceive ignorant Muslim masses. These extremist groups deem other Muslims as *kafir*s, worthy of killing. They commit the most despicable crimes in the name of religion. It is obvious that they cannot be real Muslims because what they do is exactly opposite to the spirit and teachings of Islam.

THE QARMATIANS (OR QARAMITA)

Introduction

The Qarmatians, which emerged from the Shia sect of Islam, were a political movement that appeared in the middle of the ninth century. The original name of this group is Qarāmita, but its origin is unknown. It is transliterated into the English language as Qarmatians, Qarmathians, Carmathians, and Karmathians. According to one view, the name Qarāmita (Qarmatians) is ascribed to a tribe or an un-Islamic sect.[135] Some holds that the origins of this name go back to the tribe "Bani Qarmat" (the sons of Qarmat) who lived in the region of Sawad in Yemen.[136] Some others, however, say that the name comes from the Arabic verb "qarmat," which means "to make the lines close together in writing" or "to walk with short

---

[135] Al-Makrizi, Ahmad ibn Ali. *Kitab al-Mukaffa al-Kabir*, (Riyadh, 1989), p. 599.
[136] Al-Makrizi, *Ittiaz al-Hunafa, bi Dhikri Aimma al-Khulafa*, (Cairo, 1948), vol. 1, p. 156.

steps."[137] Another view is that this name comes from the word "qarmita" in the language of Nabataeans[138] which means a red-eyed man or a bad person.[139] Qarmatism is usually ascribed to a person named Hamdan Qarmat who had red eye. Because of its founder, the sect is called as the Qarāmita (Qarmatians) in Arabic.

Isma'ili sect is a Shia group that emerged from a dispute over the succession of Ja'far al-Sadiq in 765 CE. When Ismail died, they acknowledged his son Muhammad as the seventh and last imam, whose return they await at the end of times. The Isma'iliyah is also known as Seveners because they accept only seven imams. With this doctrine they separate from all other Shia groups who believe the twelve imams. Developed in the 9th and 10th centuries under the influence of Gnosticism and Neo-Platonism, the Isma'iliyah had esoteric teachings and mystical interpretations of the Qur'an. Hamdan Qarmat's followers became known as Qarmatians after he changed Isma'iliyah doctrines to communist principles in the late 9th century.

The Qarmatians was a syncretic religious group that combined elements of Zoroastrianism with the Isma'ili Shia Islam centered in al-Hasa in Eastern Arabia, where they established a religious utopian republic in 899 CE. It is a political group which combined the elements of Shiism (Isma'ili understanding of Shiism) with Persian mysticism. According to the Isma'ili school of thought, Imam Ja'far al-Sadiq (702–765) designated his second son, Isma'il ibn Ja'far (721–755), as the heir to the Imamate (caliphate or rulership). However, Isma'il died before his father. Thus, some did not accept his death but claimed that he had gone into hiding. Others in the Isma'ili sect accepted his death and recognized his eldest son, Muhammad ibn Isma'il (746–809), as imam. The split occurred within the sect after the death of Muhammad ibn Isma'il. The majority of the group

---

[137] Glassé, Cyril. *The New Encyclopedia of Islam*. (Walnut Creek CA: Alta Mira Press, 2008), p. 369.
[138] The ancient Arab tribe who inhabited northern Arabia and the Southern Levant and lived in 37-100 CE.
[139] Al-Tabari, Abu Ja'far Muhammad ibn Jarir. *Tārikh al-Umam wa al-Muluk*, (Beirut, n.d.) 10/24.

denied his death because they recognized him as the awaited Mahdi while a small minority of them believed in his death and eventually emerged in later times as the Isma'ili Fatimid Caliphate, the precursors to all modern groups. The majority Isma'ili sect settled in Syria and had a great success in south western Iran. During this time, Ḥamdan ibn al-Ash'as converted to Isma'ili faith in 874 CE and took the name Qarmaṭ after his new faith.

A change in leadership caused a split in the movement. While the minority Isma'ilis claimed that although Imam Muhammad died, his descendant came out of hiding as the new leader. Qarmaṭ and his brother-in-law opposed this and they did not accept the imamate (caliphate or rulership) of Ubaydullah al-Mahdi. Later, Qarmaṭ became a missionary of the new Imam, Abdullah al-Mahdi Billah (873–934) and the dissident group retained the name Qarmaṭī. When Ubaydullah pronounced himself as the awaited imam, Hamdan ibn al-Ash'as, the head of the Qarmatians, rejected his claim. He continued to defend the old doctrine which predicted Muhammad ibn Isma'il as the awaited imam. With this belief, this movement separated from the Isma'ili-Shiites and became a separate religious-political movement.

The Qarmatians were an extremist movement which resorted to violence and terrorism to achieve its goals. Hamdan Qarmat, the leader of movement, argued that the properties of rich people must be shared among the poor, and with this ideology he attracted many people to his ranks in the region of modern-day Iraq. Although they seemed pious, the Qarmatians revolted against the authority of the Abbasid caliphs and killed many innocent people, especially the Sunni Muslims brutally.[140] In this regard, they attacked Makka and stole the Black Stone located in the corner of the Ka'ba and moved it to Basra. They ambushed the pilgrim caravans and persecuted the Sunni Muslim travelers for years. With regards to the Qarmatian teachings, they deemed women as common property among their followers and indulged into illicit sexual relations

---

[140] Gulen, Fethullah. "Anarşist Ruhlar ve Modern Karmatîler" (Anarchic souls and the Modern-day Qarmatians), Weekly Sermon at *herkul.org*, last modified on Nov. 1, 2004 http://www.herkul.org/kirik-testi/anarsist-ruhlar-ve-modern-karmatiler/

with them. They consumed alcohol although it is clearly prohibited in Islam. They saw other Muslims who did not agree to their ideology as unbelievers, destined to Hell.

Emergence of the Qarmatians

During the Abbasid Caliphate (750–1258 CE) some Shiite groups opposed to their authority. One of these groups was Mubarakiyya which believed in the notion of Mahdi, the awaited savior of Muslims, which is similar to the doctrine of the awaited Messiah in Christianity. According to this Shiite group, Imam Ja'far Sadiq (702-765 CE), a descendant of the Prophet, designated his second son Isma'il ibn Ja'far, for the imamate, but he passed away before his father. Thereupon, the other son, Muhammad ibn Isma'il (746-809 CE) was recognized as the imam. The followers of these two imams constituted the sect of Isma'iliyah. When Muhammad ibn Isma'il passed away, the majority of the group denied his death simply because of their argument that the awaited savior would not die. The followers of the Isma'ili sect resided in the area between Syria and Iran. In the meantime, Hamdan ibn Ash'as embraced the doctrines of Isma'iliyah and got the nickname "Qarmat" thus called as Hamdan Qarmat. He became the leader of this group and prepared southern Iraq for the coming of the Mahdi by creating a military power there.

While the power of the Abbasid caliphs kept descending, the Qarmatians grew as their military power and influence increased during the ninth and tenth centuries.[141] The Abbasid caliphs were in a position to confirm the decisions of the local rulers, legitimizing their rulership within the state. The local governors who had military power used the caliphs for their political agendas. The weakness of the caliphate caused economic and social problems to surface.[142] Some groups revolted against the Abbasid authority. Since the Abbasid state was busy to suppress the insurgents,

---

[141] Ibn Khaldun, *Kitab al-Ibar*, (Egypt, 1863), 1/216.
[142] Lewis, Bernard. *The Origins of Ismailism*, (Cambridge, 1940), 92.

Hamdan Qarmat became successful in his establishment in Kufa.[143] In other words, the political uncertainty and rebellions against the Abbasid rulership helped the Qarmatians to establish their movement firmly.

The other reason that prepared the rise of the Qarmatians was the economic conditions of the period. During the Abbasid reign, the local governors increased the tax rate on people to cover the deficit in state budget.[144] While the oligarchic group possessed huge amount of money and had better economic conditions, the revenue of the ordinary people diminished considerably. The worsening economic conditions caused people to get ready for the revolt against the state. Thus, the Qarmatians attracted the discontented public to their ranks by promising them equal revenue among all citizens.

The Qarmatians found support for their movement from different tribes and nations. Mostly, the lower class joined their ranks.[145] Their ideology spread out among various Arabic tribes.[146] Although they received greater support from the villagers, peasants and the Bedouins, they did not have much influence in the towns for a long time. This was mainly because of the fact that the ordinary people were not interested in the ideology of the Isma'iliyah sect; rather they joined them due to their economic concerns.

The belief for the End of Times (*Qiyama*) was very strong among people at the time when the Qarmatians appeared in Muslim society. Interestingly, the Zoroastrians and the Qarmatians had a common belief with regards to the emergence of Mahdi (Savior) to save their community. Both believed that Mahdi would appear soon[147] and correct the world from all kind of wrong doings and injustice. The Qarmatians put their emphasis on the notion of Mahdi in order to recruit new members to their movement.

Indeed, various religions and faith traditions had influence on the formation of the Qarmatian ideology. The dualist Persian religions,

---

[143] Markizi, *Itti'az*, 1/113.
[144] Ibn Khaldun, *Muqaddima*, 1/372.
[145] Baghdadi, *Al-Farq Bayn al-Firaq*, 232.
[146] Markizi, *Itti'az*, 1/209-210.
[147] Al-Buruni, Abu al-Rayyan. *Al-Athar al-Baqiya An al-Ghurun al-Haliya*, (Leipzig, 1923), p. 213.

Christian-Jewish traditions, Hermeticism[148] and Gnosticism[149] had considerable influence on the doctrines of the Qarmatians. They believed that good and evil is in constant fight. Accordingly, they interpreted the scripture from an esoteric perspective.

Husayin al-Ahwazi is an important personality for the emergence of the Qarmatians in Kufa.[150] He secretly preached the doctrines of the Isma'iliyah sect and attracted many followers to his ideology. By living devoutly, he got the love and respect of local people. He became famous with his humbleness, religiosity and trustfulness. During this time, Hamdan Qarmat accepted his teachings and then became the head of this movement. Hamdan sent many preachers around to convey the Qarmatian doctrines.[151] In a short time, he received a great support from the lower class of society; he was even able to collect tax from them to convey the doctrines of the Qarmatians. When reaching considerable number of followers and a certain power, Hamdan commanded his followers to emigrate to a village in Kufa to establish their own state. They built a stronghold and started living there. Then, many Qarmatians migrated there to support their state. Then, they spread out to other regions and kept building some other strongholds in those places as well. At around the end of the ninth century, the slaves revolted in Basra and this weakened the central power of the caliphate in Baghdad. Thereupon, The Qarmatians captured the city of Hajr and al-Hasa in Bahrain and then made these cities the capital of the Qarmatians.

The Qarmatians in Kufa resorted to terror and violence to achieve their goals. Although the pilgrimage to Makka (*hajj*) is one of the five pillars of Islam, they deemed it a superstition; therefore, the bloody Qarmatians

---

[148] Hermetism is a religious, philosophical, and esoteric tradition based primarily upon the writings attributed to Hermes Trismegistus. According to his theory, there is a single true theology that is present in all religions and that was given by God to man in antiquity.

[149] A prominent heretical movement of the 2nd century Christian Church, partly of pre-Christian origin. Gnostic doctrine taught that the world was created and ruled by a lesser divinity, the demiurge, and that Christ was an emissary of the remote supreme divine being, esoteric knowledge (gnosis) of whom enabled the redemption of the human spirit.

[150] Makrizi, *Mukaffa*, 590.

[151] Masudi, Husayin ibn Ali. *al-Tanbih wa al-Ishraf*, (Beirut, 1981), p. 355.

launched raids along the pilgrim routes across the Arabian Peninsula. In 906 CE, they ambushed the pilgrim caravans and killed 20,000 pilgrims violently.[152] In 930 CE, they attacked Makka and Medina, the two holy cities of Islam, and killed thousands of Muslims in both sanctuaries. They desecrated the Zamzam Well with the corpses of the pilgrims and took the Black Stone (Hajar al-Aswad) from Makka to Al-Hasa in Bahrain.[153] After this tragic attack, they asked the Abbasids to pay a huge amount of money in return for the Black Stone. The bloody massacre and desecration perpetrated by the Qarmatian terrorists in the holy lands shocked all Muslims.

The Abbasids felt humiliated due to their weakness with regards to the protection of the holy lands and the pilgrims against the Qarmatian attacks. However, they could not do anything as the Qarmatians had turned out to be an influential power in the Persian Gulf. They were controlling the coast of Oman and collecting tribute from different regions. The followers of this extremist movement became very rich in a short time. They had vast fruit and grain estates and used Ethiopian slaves to cultivate the harvest. The Qarmatians exempted their people from tax and gave loan with no interest.[154]

After showing great disrespect for the holy lands of Makka and Medina, the Qarmatians deserted Islamic belief and its pillars by assigning a Persian leader for the movement. This Persian Qarmatian leader forbade them all Islamic rulings and rituals. For instance, he forbade the five daily prayers and the implementation of Islamic law. He ordered his followers to "curse" the Prophets mentioned in the Qur'an. He also encouraged them to use foul language against the Companions of the Noble Prophet. With the influence of Zoroastrianism, he advised his followers to worship fire. He created a new religion contrary to Islamic teachings. Their hatred and

---

[152] Saunders, John J. *A History of Medieval Islam*, (Routledge, 1978), p. 130.
[153] Touati, Houari. *Islam and Travel in the Middle Ages*, (Chicago: University of Chicago Press, 2010), p. 60.
[154] For more information about the economic status, see Yitzhak Nakash, *Reaching for Power: The Shia in the Modern Arab World*, (Princeton, 2007).

insult of Islamic values weakened the power of the Qarmatians and eventually destabilized the movement.

In 976 CE, the Qarmatians were defeated by the Abbasids and lost their power. The resisting rival Arab tribes stopped tribute payments to the Qarmatians, thus their power got diminished to a local level. They lost Bahrain in 1058 CE. With the revolts of Sunni groups, the Qarmatians lost the other cities they controlled. Their reign was over with the final attack in 1067 CE by the combined forces of Sunni Muslims.[155]

Analysis of the Qarmatian Doctrines

Although there are some major division and differences among the Qarmatian groups, their basic, common doctrines will be mentioned here. This sect deemed the Person of God beyond everything, isolating Him even from the Divine attributes. They even argued that it is not proper to give a name or attribute to God. They explained the creation with an ambiguous doctrine: the first existence and the divine destiny emerged from the command of God. He thought about the possibility of creating something similar to Himself and from this thought the universe came into existence.

In their belief, the Qarmatians negate all kind of attributes of God. God is different from all else, and can therefore never be described.[156] God created the universe all at once, but He is not one of the elements of it. God is one but cannot be qualified with any number.[157] The creation of human beings is a result of their distance from God, and losing their spiritual value, they were sent down to the Earth. Their salvation is possible only with a journey opposite to the Earth; if they work hard, they can get higher ranks in the creation.

---

[155] Larsen, Curtis. *Life and Land Use on the Bahrain Islands: The Geoarchaeology of an Ancient Society*, (Chicago: University of Chicago Press, 1984), p. 65.
[156] Al-Kirmani, Ahmad. *Kitab al-Riyad*, (Beirut, 1960), pp. 214-215.
[157] Al-Razi, Abu Hatim. *Kitab al-Zinah*, (Baghdad, 1988), Vol. 2, pp. 34-35.

They believed that there was something mystical about the number seven. They argued that there were seven speakers who would enlighten humanity. The universe has seven layers and people can reach divine truth in seven steps. This group also gives importance to seven letters, seven stars and twelve zodiacal constellations under the influence of Hermeticism and Gnosticism. They even argued that the source of speech is letters and seven of them provide guidance and salvation for human beings. These letters are *kaf, waw, nun, ya, qaf, dal* and *ra* in Arabic alphabet.[158] Each letter is ascribed to the owner of specific time period. For example, the letter "kaf" is the symbol for Adam and "waw" is for Noah. They further argued that the knowledge and revelation that come from the Divine realm have continued increasingly. They said that Qaim is the owner of the seventh period and the possessor of the letter "ra." By inheriting all the previous letters, Qaim reaches to the status of divine being.

The imams were central in the Qarmatian theology. This sect was recognized with its missionaries (*dai*) who were speaking in the name of the imam to convey his teachings. They played major political roles in the development of this fanatic sect and its spreading out in the region.

The Qarmatians argued that that Islamic law should be repealed. They rejected all forms of prayers in the main Sunni Islamic tradition. They interpreted religious obligations spiritually; therefore, they did not perform any of the obligatory pillars of Islam, including the daily prayers, fasting, and pilgrimage to Makka.

The Qarmatians did not accept marriage as the lawful way for man and woman to unite; rather, they treated women as collective property and thus led the youth to go astray with their unrestraint sexual relations. They made every kind of indulgence lawful. They legitimized wine and alcoholic drinks. By creating a new faith on the basis of their extremist ideology they labeled anyone who did not follow their doctrines as being an "unbeliever" and one "destined to Hell."

---

[158] Sijistani, *Kitab al-Iftikhar*, 47-52.

According to the Qarmatian theology, there are seven periods in the world and each period is represented by a powerful prophet. In each period, there are seven imams, one coming after another. The last imam reaches to the status of the "speaker" (*natiq*) and abrogates the Sharia (religious law) of the previous ones. The last "speaker" is the owner of *Qiyama* (the Armageddon day or End of Times) who abrogates all previous religious laws. The "speakers" (*natiqs*) according to their order are Adam, Noah, Abraham, Moses, Jesus, Muhammad and Qaim al-Zaman Muhammad ibn Ismail.[159] With this belief, they clearly contradict with the Islamic teachings, thus separating from the Sunni majority Muslims.

The Qarmatians have the notion of "imamate" parallel to their understanding of prophethood. Their "imam" has the same status with a Prophet of God. In every period, seven imams come while the last of these imams starts the new period. According to their theology, Ali ibn Abi Tālib is the essence and source of the Noble Prophet. The other imams after Ali are Hasan, Husayin, Ali ibn Husayin, Muhammad ibn Ali al-Baqir, Ja'far Sadiq, and Ismail ibn Ja'far (aka Qaim al-Mahdi), whom the Qarmatians accepted as the last imam.

In Qarmatian thought, esoteric knowledge is important and it is only learned from the imams. The salvation of human beings can be achieved with the knowledge of reasons that separated them from God. This knowledge can be obtained from the prophets and imams. When the last imam comes, all knowledge that is necessary for human salvation will come to an ultimate completion.[160] There is no clear belief for the resurrection after death in the Qarmatian theology. They believed that the souls are elevated to higher ranks through their hard work and good deeds. This belief is very similar to the traditions of Judaism with regards to the Afterlife.

The Qarmatians followed only the literal meaning of the Quranic verses and ended up creating chaos, hatred and disputes among Muslims. With their extremist doctrines, they manipulated people and used them in

---

[159] Al-Nuwayri, Ahmad. *Nihaya al-Ereb Fi Funun al-Adab*, (Cairo, 1984), 27/205–206.
[160] Al-Yaman, Mansur. *Kitab al-Rushd wa al-Hidaya*, pp. 195-199.

their terrorist attacks against innocent civilians. The following incident helps us to understand the extremist mindset of the Qarmatians:

When Abu Taher ibn Hassan al-Qurmuti, the leader of the Qarmatians, attacked Makka in 906 CE with seven hundred horsemen, he massacred the pilgrims (throwing their dead bodies into the well of Zamzam), broke the door of the Ka'ba open, tore the veil covering the Ka'ba and urinated on it. Then, he removed the Black Stone and said, "I am in God and God is in me. Where is your God? I am your great God. Where are the birds of God that protected the Ka'ba against Abraha (referring to God's protection of the Ka'ba by sending swarms of birds with stones in their beaks, bombarding Abraha and his army)?"[161]

After the bloody attack and massacre they perpetrated in Makka, Muslims stopped visiting the Ka'ba and performing the pilgrimage for eight years. Muslims feared the pilgrimage journey since the Qarmatians were terrorizing pilgrims by launching raids along their routes, killing them and plundering their caravans. The heartlands of Islam were no longer safe due to the ongoing Qarmatian terrorist attacks. They committed violence and terror to send a message to the world that the end of the Islamic era was imminent, and that the seventh (and thus the final) era of history under the advent of their "Mahdi" was very near. Their "messianic belief" turned into violence and terrorism against all those who did not agree with their doctrine. They produced their own tale of bloodshed and oppression and instigated terror and violence that continued almost for a century. In theory, the Qarmatians can be considered as the first communists in history mainly because they aimed to establish a utopian state distributing all property equally among themselves. Although their ideology was dominated by "equality" and they revolted against the tyrants, they promoted lawlessness and refused to recognize human rights and values, such as respecting the sacred of others and showing respect to different ideas.

In this regard, the Qarmatians can be seen as the anarchists of their time. The contemporary Islamic scholar, education advocate and preacher

---

[161] Al-Nuwayri, *Nihaya al-Ereb*, 27/210-233.

emeritus Fethullah Gülen talks about realizing the ever-present danger of committing violence in the name of religion, having blinders on dialogue and accusing all "others" of disbelief when they do not agree with a certain ideology:

> Today, we have seen some people who behave like modern Qarmatians and Kharijites, obstructing endeavors for dialogue and understanding and disrupting the dreams of peace and friendship. They too call themselves Muslims; yet, they have attacked the religion from some esoteric approach, replacing it instead with their own passions and thrills. Some others, entrapped in bigotry, have construed the literal meaning of the Qur'an and the Hadith as the only primary essentials, sharpening their blades of hatred and hostility against other Muslims. A subgroup within them has adopted a deep esoteric understanding, considering themselves as having attained a transcendental existence, and look down on other Muslims. Still others, however, have blindly adhered to overt divine commandments with no effort whatsoever to use their mind to interpret them. They have been deprived of any proper techniques of teaching faith or of understanding others; they have no code of conduct, good morals, or respect. What all of these people have done was to start the fire of disunity and to fan the movement of tolerance. These two groups were later joined by a third: anarchist souls. The Qarmatian zeal and the Kharijite restlessness pushed some Muslims into the web of terrorists, causing them to be involved with chaos, threatening and even murdering people. Whatever the motive was, be it national or religious, some imprudent individuals were manipulated by some dark power sources. They were denied the slightest share of religion by their actions; yet they committed murders on behalf of it, and handed over their trump card to those who were already standing opposed to religion.[162]

---

[162] Gulen, Fethullah. "Three Groups Opposing Dialogue: Kharijites, Qarmatis, Anarchists" last modified on June 14, 2006. http://en.fgulen.com/recent-articles/1878-three-groups-opposing-dialogue-kharijites-karmatis-anarchists

Conclusion

The turmoil of ninth century caused the Qarmatians, a sub-branch of the Ismaili-Shia sect, to emerge. In time, the followers of this movement seized some sites in Kufa, Basra and Bahrain. They aimed to create a utopian society on the basis of distributing all property equally among the Qarmatians. However, they created fear, terror, and violence in Muslim society. They collected tribute from the Arab tribes and the caliph in Baghdad. They desecrated Makka and Medina, the two holy lands of Islam as well as the Black Stone, Ka'ba and its cover. They killed thousands of pilgrims and plundered their caravans. They deemed other Muslims who did not accept their faith as unbelievers. With this extremist ideology, they committed many evil crimes in the name of religion.

This sect is considered as the first communist or socialist group in history. This is mainly because of the fact that they shared all properties, including even their wives, created a common treasury and organized labor under civil institutions. They were very ruthless towards other Muslims. They instigated the revolt of the Zanjj in Iraq from 869-883 CE. During this rebellion, 300,000 innocent people lost their lives. This movement was known for their attacks on their opponents, especially towards Sunni Muslims. In short, the Qarmatians were a heretic sect which resorted to terror and violence in order to reach their goals.

THE ASSASSINS (HASHASHIN)

Introduction

The Assassins (or Hashashīn) were a heretical movement in Islam, branching off from the Isma'ili-Shia sect in the late 11th century. Described as a secret order led by Hassan Sabbah, the followers of the order were called in Arabic as the Hashashīn ("Smokers of hashish") since Sabbah drugged his adherents by means of "hashish" and had them commit terror and assassinations while under the influence of drug. The term "Assassins" was then applied to this medieval terror group that committed many political assassinations to create terror and fear in society. It was the Austrian historian and author Von Hammer Purgstall, who wrote a book about them and ascribed the title "Assassins" to them.

Assassination is a political weapon and it is as old as human society. However, this term specifically refers to the terrorist activities of the Assassins. The Assassins went down in history with their extreme violence and terror, posing a serious military threat to the Seljuk State with their terror tactics. Through espionage and assassins of political figures they killed many political and religious leaders, including two caliphs and a few sultans. The Assassins did not have enough war supplies or an army, relying heavily on the assassins to reach their political targets.[163] By capturing and inhabiting many unconnected mountain fortresses throughout Persia and Syria they threatened the Seljuk authority and established Nizari Isma'ili state. Nizari-Isma'ilism coincides with the Alamut period from around 1090-1256 CE. The Nizari Isma'ili state had territories scattered in different parts of Persia and Syria. It lasted 166 years until it collapsed in 1256 under the Mongol attacks.

Hasan Sabbah, the leader of this Isma'ili sect, was following a revolutionary policy against the Seljuk Turks, especially after Imam al-Muntasir, the Fatimid caliph, died in 1094 CE. There was a dispute among the followers of the Isma'ili sect with regards to the succession of al-Muntasir. At this stage, Hassan Sabbah severed his relations with the Fatimid regime and founded an independent Nizari Isma'ili mission and propaganda.

The castle at Alamut was the headquarters of this extremist Nizari-Ismaili sect. In this significant centre of intelligence gathering and mission training, the Assassins were prepared first for their missions by being drugged with hashish, and then brought into a secret garden that was full of carnal pleasures. They were told that the place was Paradise and they would return if they fulfilled their missions or were killed in this cause.

---

[163] Acosta, Benjamin. "Assassins," *Cultural Sociology of the Middle East, Asia and Africa: An Encyclopedia*, 2012.

Although the sect had extremely wicked and dangerous methods to achieve its goals, it was very well-established in the lives of its followers. They would sacrifice their lives for this cause without hesitation. The legend of this violent group was written by Marco Polo after visiting the mountain fortress of Alamut, located in north western Persia. William Tyre, the historian of the Crusades, had written about them to reveal their ideology and history.

The Assassins were very famous with their murder of some key political figures. Their philosophy and doctrines were very complex, guiding them to establish a state at Alamut. Hasan Sabbah, the founder of the Assassins, was a man who promoted the Isma'ili mission. He was a very successful propagandist for he made many converts to his ideology throughout Persia. Well-trained in the Shiite-Isma'ili doctrines, he was very effective to attract people to his mission. He acted very piously to use the influential power of religion on people. It is related that he punished himself whenever he behaved badly and rewarded himself if he acted good. This method was very effective in persuading people to accept him as a leader. In this way, he seemed so pious that he would endure great pains for his cause. Ordinary people did not have enough knowledge to question if his methods were in line with Islamic principles. In Islam, it is not permissible to harm one's self or others. However, the ignorant masses can be manipulated through misinterpretation of religious texts.

Hassan Sabbah disguised his real identity (of being an Isma'ili missionary) by performing various professions to earn his living. Concealing or disguising one's beliefs and identity is one of the main principles of the Shiite understanding. It is called *taqiyya*, or hiding real identity from others to propagate the mission safely. Interpreting religious texts from an esoteric aspect was dominant in Sabbah's propaganda. With this approach, he was able to give "new meanings" to the well-established religious norms, thus taking them out of their original contexts in an attempt to distort them. Before he started to impose his ideology on people, he had attracted them to his personality by acting very kindly, modestly, generously, piously and compassionately. He had built up reputation for probity and piety among his followers. Gradually, he gathered around him a circle of followers and then imposed his ideology on them. He was very cautious in propagating his mission; therefore, he was always ready to change the subject if people became suspicious or hostile to his doctrines. In order to allure people to his thoughts, he would first ask them some key questions and then answer them. As he gave the answers in length, he would also impose his doctrines on them. If he found a man ready to convert to the Isma'ili doctrines, he would take an oath of allegiance from him. In this oath, the new convert would pledge his loyalty to him, pay a financial contribution and promise not to reveal the secrets of the Isma'ili sect to unauthorized people. By promising them the path for salvation, Hassan Sabbah was able to attract people to his secret and yet dangerous ideology. He would impart some esoteric knowledge and doctrines by interpreting the Qur'an esoterically to his followers. The esoteric knowledge was used in the instruction of mediation techniques. This method was parallel to their Sufi ceremonies but contrary to the main principles of Islam. There were several stages to be followed while imposing the Ismai'li doctrines on the novice, depending on his aptitude and skills. The disciple had to swear a solemn oath that he would be loyal and obedient and that he would preserve the secrets of the sect even when he suffers physical torture. While imparting their doctrines, they would also suggest him that God would abandon him in this world and the next if he fails to fulfill what is expected of him. Therefore, the candidates were expected to be very serious and determined in their mission.

The Assassins were different from the other Isma'ilis living within the Fatimid state. They resorted to violence and terrorism to achieve their goals rather than engaging directly with the theological and juristic issues from their own perspective. Additionally, they adopted the Persian language instead of the widespread Arabic language use in the religious matters. This indicates that this violent group had racist tendencies in their mission. They maintained a literary tradition by elaborating their teachings in response to the changing conditions. For example, Hassan Sabbah established a library at the Alamut Castle. The other castles the Assassins were living in Persia and Syria also contained a significant collection of manuscripts and documents. In addition to their military attacks against

Sunni Muslims during the Alamut period, they also developed polemical arguments to defend their ideology. However, the state of the Assassins gradually weakened against the superior military power of the Seljuks, and especially during the Mongol invasions. With the surrender of the Alamut Castle to the Mongols in 1256 CE, the period of the Assassins came to an end. However, their ideology and doctrines survived among the minority groups in different lands.

The Assassin history can be divided into three with regards to their reign at Alamut, their teachings and their religious policies: the initial phase refers to the period from 1090-1162 when they established their independent state and consolidated their mission. The second period (1162-1210 CE) was recognized as returning to "the realm of resurrection." The last period (1210-1256 CE) was symbolized with their teachings coming from this doctrine of resurrection and their political endeavors against the Sunni world and the termination of their state by the Mongol invasions.

The Origins of the Assassins

The development of the Hashashīn sect within Shiite-Isma'ili sect is a very complex phenomenon in Islamic history. It started as a secret organization that resorted frequently to terror and violence to achieve its goals. First, it captured some cities and castles in the region and then established its own state. In spite of its temporal success, the sect had many secrets and mysteries. Although Nizari-Isma'ilism had now become the religion of the state, the secrets of the sect and its esoteric nature were never unveiled.

A split branch within the Shiite form of Islam, the Isma'ili sect was initially based in Cairo, which was the centre of the Shia Fatimids. They believed that they were the descendants of Fatima, the daughter of the Noble Prophet. Like all other Shiite groups, the Isma'ili sect regards Caliph Ali as the first imam, considering him even at the same position with the Prophets. In Shiite sects, the imam has a spiritual authority and enormous prestige. According to the Shiite creed, the imamate passes from father to son, but the imam is hidden now.

The majority of the Shiites hold that there are twelve imams. However, the Isma'ili branch of the Shiites considers Isma'il as the seventh and last imam. This dispute within the Shiites caused Hassan Sabbah to establish his own Shiite interpretation in the tenth century. As a key figure and propagandist of the sect, Sabbah attracted many men to his side and used them in his mission. He travelled extensively to promote the Isma'ili doctrines. He also sent many Isma'ili missionaries to various lands that were under the control of the Seljuks to spread Isma'ilism. They established secret organizations in many cities to proselytize their ideology and make converts into their sect. These propagandists conveyed his ideology in "secret cells." This secret cell network was very skilful to secretly place its agents anywhere in the Islamic world. The agents would in time become a trusted servant or friend of Muslim rulers or their aides. They would be perfectly disguised for long years until the order to strike arrived.

As a matter of fact, Sabbah wanted to have a decisive single revolt against the Seljuks but he did not have an army for it. Instead, the Assassins planned many rebellious attacks to destroy the Seljuks. With a large number of men under his command, Sabbah launched many attacks against the Sunni Muslims and killed many of them.

Sabbah became very famous when he captured the Castle of Alamut in 1090 CE. The castle had actually been under the Seljuk control, but he gradually infiltrated his men into it. Through his men, Sabbah gained the control of this famous castle. Under his leadership, the Assassins captured many other castles, and thus became able to dominate a vast territory.

As the name Assassins indicates clearly, they committed many murders besides propagating their ideology. In 1092 CE, Nizam al-Mulk, the famous Seljuk statesman, was attacked fatally by an agent from the Assassins. This attack is usually accepted as the first assassination carried out by the direct order of Hassan Sabbah. Nizam al-Mulk had ordered Sabbah to be arrested; therefore, Sabbah wanted to remove him out of the way. To create fear and uncertainty in society the Assassins kept committing murders of many important political figures.

Assassination as a political weapon was the main method for the Assassins to reach their political targets. They believed that assassinating one important figure to reach their goal is better than killing many people in the battle field. Through terror and violence they wanted to destroy the Seljuks which outnumbered them enormously.

Marco Polo who visited the Castle of Alamut gives an account of "the Grand Master" Hassan Sabbah's training of the Assassins. Sabbah constructed a fantastic pleasure garden at the castle. It contained wine, honey, milk and many beautiful women. This was a representation of Paradise as described in the Qur'an. The Assassins were drugged and brought unconscious into the garden. After a time, they were drugged again and brought out of the garden. They were convinced that it was Paradise and a foretaste of its joys. They were told that they would find themselves in Paradise again after they die for the cause of the Isma'ili mission. The Assassins considered death for their cause as a great honor. The mothers would encourage their sons to be killed as martyr while propagating the doctrines of Isma'ilism. They would even put on their best clothes when they heard that their sons had been killed on a mission.

The Assassins would kill the victims publicly instead of poisoning them or killing them in secret. Congregational prayers, especially the Friday prayers, were their favorite occasion to perpetuate an assassination. In order to intimidate their enemy, they never carried out their assassinations in secret. This way, they aimed to create an atmosphere of fear and terror in society with their "necessary violent public assassinations." Although this can never be legitimized in Islam, they claimed that it was their devotion to their cause which inspired their heroism.

From the historical perspective, the establishment of the Assassins goes back to the split within Isma'ilism in Cairo. Muntasir, the Fatimid caliph, designated his eldest son Nizar as the next imam, but when he died, the officers who had power and control in state affairs assigned Mustali, another son of Muntasir, to the throne. Nizar, the eldest son, did not accept this designation, and thus a brief civil war ensued. However, Nizar was defeated and then executed. The Isma'ilis in Cairo accepted Mustali as the imam but the Isma'ilis in Iran remained loyal to Nizar. Hassan Sabbah led Iranian Isma'ilis and created his own movement. Politics and national pride played a pivotal role to divide Isma'ilism into two groups. Hassan Sabbah's title was the *hujjah* (proof) which was a high rank in the Ismaili hierarchy. Eventually, Sabbah was regarded as the imam's official representative. It seems that Hassan Sabbah used the legend of the vanished imam for his own political purposes instead of declaring himself as the imam. He concealed his fatal illness until the last moment and died in 1124 CE.

Doctrines of the Assassins

The doctrines of Isma'ilism and the Assassins are very complex indeed. Isma'ili worldview consists of many different elements. For them, the Qur'an should be interpreted from an esoteric aspect. Astronomy and astrology should be understood from an esoteric perspective. In order to understand their doctrines the notion of esoteric interpretation should be known well. Another important element in Ismaili worldview is Neo-Platonism. It is a philosophical system, originated in the 3rd century CE by Plotinus, founded chiefly on Platonic doctrine and Oriental mysticism, with later influences from Christianity.[164] It holds that all existence consists of emanations from the One with whom the soul may be reunited.

The Assassins are deemed a heretical sect by the Sunni scholars because they rejected the literal meaning of the Qur'an; rather, they interpreted it from an esoteric aspect that changed the well-established Islamic principles, pillars and creed into some weird worldviews. This interpretation led them into a strange world like fictions. According to their belief, every verse, even every letter of the Qur'an has an esoteric significance. Because of this esoteric approach they were called as

---

[164] http://dictionary.reference.com/browse/neoplatonism.

"Khurufi" which means the ones who seek meaning and significance in Arabic letters. They argued that the true meaning is beyond the literal, or surface, text; the reality is in the inner meaning in the text.

The Assassins and Isma'ilis believe that God concealed the reality of His divinity in esoteric understanding. Therefore, the truth is not given or revealed to ordinary people, but it may be exposed to those who are ready to receive it. Since they clearly contradict Islamic principles and pillars, they hide these ideas from other Muslims. The concept of dissimulation (*taqiyya*) and concealing the real worldview or belief system is very important for them. They claim that they use this concept in order to be able to convey their message and succeed in it. Otherwise, they say, the hostile world may prevent them to explain their ideology. They argue that the religious rituals, such as the five daily prayers, fasting during the month of Ramadan, and pilgrimage to the house of God, are the surface meanings of the Qur'an. The reality is beyond these very acts of worship. Since this approach clearly contradicts with what the Noble Prophet practiced himself and taught his followers, they argued that these ideas should be kept secret. This is the basis of the concept of dissimulation and they frequently make use of it to protect themselves from critics. Indeed, acting in a way which is incompatible with one's real status is clearly prohibited in Islam because it is considered as hypocrisy.

The Assassins believed that the Qur'an has four levels of meaning: the first is the surface, or literal, meaning; the second is allusion, the third is the occult sense; and the fourth refers to spirituality and esoteric teachings. They argued that these four levels of meaning have different audience. The first level is for ordinary Muslims who do not know much about the reality. The second level is for the elite who can grasp the reality a bit. The third level is for "the friends of God" who are very pious and comprehend the esoteric meanings. The fourth level is intended for the Prophets, but Ali also knows all these four levels contained in the Qur'an. With this understanding, they deemed Ali on a par with the Prophets of God which is not acceptable according to Islamic principles.

The Shiite scholars use an egg as an analogy to explain the four levels of meaning in the Qur'an. The shell is surface which protects the inner side of the egg. The white is the beginning of esoteric but inside there is a deeper truth which is the yolk. The shell symbolizes the physical body of humankind, the white is their soul and the yolk is their highest principle. In this analogy, three levels are mentioned because the fourth level is beyond human comprehension; only God reveals it to His Prophets. These three levels can be comprehended by ears (surface), eyes (inside) and heart (a deeper reality). The three levels of meaning have a cosmological corresponding as well. The first level refers to the physical world and the element of earth, the second level corresponds to religion and water while the third level addresses the spirituality and air.

In the ideology of the Assassins, the universe and nature has an esoteric significance. Accordingly, there are seven planets and seven holes, or openings, on human body and so on. The numeric significance had an important place in their ideology. They argued that the universe is a puzzle but the key to understand it is in the Qur'an. However, there must be a necessary knowledge to use the key and only the Isma'ilis and the Assassins possess it.

The Arabic language and its letters contain important clues to understand the universe. For example, the Arabic expression "kun" (which means "be") is a divine command with which God created the entire universe. The Arabic letters in this command are *kaf* and *nun*. These two letters refer to all creatures that are created in pairs to multiply. In the Arabic alphabet, each letter has a numerical value. This is called "abjad" system. Accordingly, the value of letter *kaf* is 20 and the letter *nun* is 50, giving a total 70. The number 70 is directly related to the number 7. In Arabic alphabet, there are the letters of *mim* and *lam* between *kaf* and *nun*. The Arabic letters *mim* and *lam* symbolize matter and form. It also refers to the Prophet and the Imam or emanation and the return to the source.

Neo-Platonism has great influence on the Isma'ili and Hashashīn doctrines. According to the doctrine of emanation in Neo-Platonism, the One creates the world in a hierarchy of stages of manifestation, starting with the tiniest and subtlest element and ending with the material world. Since everything separated from the One, they have strong desire to return Him, the Source of All. Isma'ilis cultivated the concept of emanation and the return to the source form Neo-Platonism. The main idea in emanation is that all existence is produced by the One in a timeless act of generation. Time itself is created by the One; therefore, the universe and its creation are outside of time. The dweller of each level of the hierarchy always desires to move one level above its rank. This is also valid for human beings, for the goal of Isma'ilism is to endow humankind with the means to "unite with God."

Humankind is in between the material and celestial worlds. In other words, human nature possesses the elements of both worlds. The materialistic side draws people downwards while the spirit desires to go upwards. The animal nature is prone to the earth while human spirit wants to go heavens. Thus, animals walk on four legs with bent backs but human beings walk on two legs and upright.

According to Jewish tradition, the true name of God cannot be uttered. Similar to this idea, the Isma'ilis believe that God is unknowable; therefore, it should not be named. This is because every name consists of letters, and the letters are created things; therefore, they cannot designate the One who is beyond all conception. The influence of Jewish tradition on this Isma'ili doctrine is obvious. What's more, Imam Ali has some divine position very similar to Jesus' position in Christianity. It seems that the doctrines of Isma'ilism developed under the influence of various faith traditions.

In the worldview of the Isma'ili Assassins, the cosmic return is a cyclical process through the agency of the prophets and imams. They argue that Adam, the first Prophet, was generated by cosmic forces. Each celestial sphere exerted its influence on the creation of Adam and the Moon brought the first man into existence at the end of seven thousand years. In their assumption, there are many Adams and each of them ruled for a 1000 year. During the rule of the sixth Adam, the truth is hidden; thus, people have to follow the exoteric aspect of religion. At the end of the year 7000, or the seventh cycle, the new Adam comes and reveals the truth. This is called the Resurrection (*Qiyama*). The Assassins believe that this stage was achieved at the castle of Alamut. They argue that each cycle is 1000 years and there will be seven cycles. In the end, the whole sequence will come to end and creation will turn back to its original state.

There are seven imams in the Isma'ili doctrine. While the Prophet teaches the exoteric aspects of the religion, the Imam teaches the esoteric aspects. The imam plays a pivotal role in the Isma'ili thought for he is the way for redemption. He is considered as the door for the esoteric knowledge and the face of God on the earth. Their approach to imam is very much similar to pantheist view because the imam identifies himself with God by using statements such as "I am with You" and "I am great like You." It seems that the imam suffers from megalomania. Indeed, in Isma'ili thought, everything is part of God as it is in the pantheist view, so the divinity of imam is not surprising at all. The Imam is an illuminating light that shines in the darkness of eternity. He sends light on the souls of his followers and they reflect the light just like a mirror does.

In the perspective of the Ismaili Assassins, the followers are responsible for one another; so, they constitute a mystical brotherhood. The whole community represents a Temple of Light. The Imam is the pillar of this temple. The followers pledge the Imam their devotion and allegiance. Each imam has his own temple and all the imams together with their temples make a Grand Temple. Although the imams have different names and live in different periods of time, they represent the same mission; therefore, they are one. The divine power which belongs to imamate is therefore present in all imams. The Assassins attributed their imam some divine entity in spite of the fact that he is a mortal, ordinary human being. When he dies, a substance emanates from the corpse and passes upwards through the various heavenly spheres. Then, the purified essence descends to the earth on the surface of water or some fruit. This water or fruit is consumed by the Imam of the time and his wife and this nutrition form the embryo of the future imam. As it can be seen, these doctrines are not Islamic at all; rather, the Isma'ili Assassins' doctrines have elements from many different religions and faith traditions.

Conclusion

Human beings have possessed different religions and faith traditions throughout the history. In many cases, some people from those religions or faith traditions have resorted to violence and terrorism to intimidate others or gain them into their own ranks by force. This fanatic mindset has exposed itself repeatedly in many cultures and religions. In the case of the Assassins, they captured the well-fortified places and committed their necessary violent public assassinations to create fear and chaos in society. They accepted themselves as the only ones who have true faith, and who will thus be saved in the afterlife. Since they see all others as the infidels or unbelievers, they never hesitated to kill them. They committed numerous murders in the name of their faith. They wanted to achieve their targets by killing especially the key political figures.

The hashish drug was used to motivate these assassin addicts. After capturing the Alamut Castle, Hassan Sabbah began to expand his influence out of his stronghold to nearby towns and districts. He sent his assassins all over the place to intimidate the local populations and gain a political power. In his stronghold, Sabbah established a secret society of deadly assassins on a hierarchical structure. He was the representative of the absent imam, and he, as the Grand Headmaster, was hierarchically followed by the propagandists, the companions, and the adherents. The adherents were brainwashed and trained to become the most feared assassins, or self-sacrificing agents.[165]

Hassan Sabbah would especially drug his young followers with hashish, and then take them to a "Paradise" which was full of carnal pleasures. After getting them out of this "Paradise" for their specific mission of assassination, he would claim that he alone had the means to allow for their return. Believing that only he could return them to "the Paradise," they were fully committed to his cause and now ready to carry out his every request.[166] He used some mystical elements to motivate his

---

[165] Nowell, Charles E. "The Old Man of the Mountain" *Speculum* 22 (4), 1947.
[166] See for details, Frampton, John (1929). *The Most Noble and Famous Travels of Marco Polo*.

followers to commit violence and terror "in the name of religion." This indicates that the religion or the metaphysical elements have great influence on human nature, and if it is used by evil people, it may cause great harm in every society.

Hassan Sabbah used self-sacrificing agents as a weapon and began to order the assassination of authority figures, ranging from politicians to great generals. The Assassins were generally young adherents who had the physical strength and stamina which would be required to carry out these murders. However, physical power was not the only trait that was required to be an assassin. The character traits of being patient, cold blooded, tough, and devious were also a must for those who were to be used as an assassin. The Assassins were generally chosen among the intelligent followers because they were required to attain detailed knowledge about their enemy, their culture and native language. They were required to disguise themselves and sneak into enemy territory for long years before they perform their assassination missions, instead of simply attacking their target without making any sophistic preparations.

In pursuit of their religious and political goals, the Assassins adopted various military strategies. Assassination of the selective prominent rival figures was one of these methods. It was usually carried out in public spaces to create resounding intimidation for other possible rivals. The Assassins would adopt a warrior code where they are trained in combat, disguises, and horsemanship. They never allowed their women to be at their bastion during military campaigns for both protection and secrecy.

The Assassins were specialized in assassinating the religious authorities (especially the Sunni scholars) and political figures. They would kill them with a dagger which contained poison. They would hide their real identity to stealthily insert themselves into strategic positions. The Seljuk vizier Nizam al-Mulk was killed by an assassin dressed as a Sufi. The vizier's murder in the Seljuk court created fear and panic in the greater society. The radical and heretical sect of the Assassins killed many people in this way to achieve their goals. Instead of confronting the rivals openly, they chose to approach them secretly and kill them in public spaces unexpectedly. This is one of the methods which radical terror groups use today.

The Assassins wanted to kill Möngke Khan, the Mongol emperor. Therefore, the Mongols besieged Alamut in 1256 CE. After being crushed by the Mongols, the Assassins lost their political power forever.

THE WAHHABIS AND SALAFISTS

Introduction

Wahhabism is a movement which got its name from its founder Muhammad ibn Abd al-Wahhab, who was born among the Bani Tamim tribe in the small town of Uyayna, located close to the north of Riyadh, in the Arabian Peninsula in 1703 CE. The Wahhabi ideology is generally accepted as a radical Islamic movement[167] which combined religious ideology with political system. The literal and rigid interpretation of religious texts plays pivotal role in the development of the Wahhabi political system and its institutions. Having the political and military power, the Wahhabi ideology transformed into real social action. Relying on the support from the British, the Saud, Saudi Arabia's ruling family, founded Saudi Arabia on the basis of Wahhabi ideology. With the establishment of this state, the Wahhabi ideology became institutionalized in a political system. It created and used its own institutions and techniques to achieve its goals.

Wahhabism is a movement that claims to restore pure monotheistic worship (*tawhid*)[168] and return to the pristine form of Islam as established by the Noble Prophet. Muhammad ibn Abd al-Wahhab (1703–1792) declared that Muslims had reverted to idolatry and started a reformist movement in the region of Najd in central Arabia. He waged war against

---

[167] Dallal, A. (1993). The Origins and Objectives of Islamic Revivalist Thought, 1750-1850. *Journal of the American Oriental Society*, 113 (3), pp. 341-359.
[168] Commins, David (2006). *The Wahhabi Mission and Saudi Arabia*. I.B. Tauris, p. vi.

certain prevalent practices such as visiting shrines and tombs and venerating the deceased friends of God (*awliya*), in the name of purifying Islamic living – practices that he considered to be innovations in religion (*bid'a*).[169] He considered these practices as associating partners to God (*shirk*) and wanted to eradicate them. With the support of the British, he formed a pact with the local leader Muhammad ibn Saud.[170] The focus in this movement was on the notion of the oneness of God (*tawhid*) and destroying anything that they considered as associating partners with God. It benefitted greatly from the teachings of both the medieval theologian Ibn Taymiyya (died 1328 CE) and the early period jurist Ahmad ibn Hanbal (780–855 CE).

Wahhabism was adopted by the local Arabian tribal chief Muhammad ibn Saud in 1744, and his successors (the house of Saud) continued to maintain their politico-religious alliance with the Wahhabi sect until the eventual proclamation of the Kingdom of Saudi Arabia in 1932. Today, Muhammad ibn Abd Al-Wahhab's teachings are state-sponsored in Saudi Arabia.[171] Although it is difficult to estimate the number of the followers of Wahhabism, the movement has grown enormously beginning in the 1970s, and now has worldwide influence.

Wahhabism, with its extreme ideology, is accused of being a source of global terrorism. It is not difficult to follow the strong relations between the ideology of the modern terror groups (such as ISIS and Al Qaeda) and the Wahhabi extreme ideology as these two contemporary terrorist groups have now been labeling Muslims who disagree with their ideology as apostates[172] on the basis of the Wahhabi definition of monotheism and kill them without hesitating. Historically, it was Muhammad ibn Abd al-Wahhab who condemned all those Muslims who did not accept his radical doctrines as heretics and justified shedding their blood or using force to

---

[169] Esposito, John (2003). *The Oxford Dictionary of Islam*. Oxford: Oxford University Press, p. 333.
[170] Lacey, Robert (2009). *Inside the Kingdom: Kings, Clerics, Modernists, Terrorists, and the Struggle for Saudi Arabia*. Viking, pp. 10–11.
[171] Glasse, Cyril (2001). *The New Encyclopedia of Islam*. Alta Mira Press, p. 46.
[172] Commins, David (2006). *The Wahhabi Mission and Saudi Arabia*. I.B. Tauris, p. vi.

impose his doctrine on them.[173] He declared "holy war" (*jihad*) against other Muslims to convince them to his ideology forcefully.

Muhammad ibn Abd al-Wahhab was not a scholar who was trained at cosmopolitan centers like Cairo or Damascus; rather, he followed the tribal family tradition of religious study. Benefiting from the teachings of Ibn Taymiyya through the study circle of his grandfather and father, he developed his Wahhabi ideology and misinterpreted Islam and its sources, insisting on a rigid, literal interpretation. This led him to break with the mainstream Muslim thought. He is considered as a deviant thinker; he spent a number of years studying in some Iranian towns with the Shiite groups and exerted his efforts later in his life to destroy the traditional Sunni Islam and its existent political and social system, the Ottoman state at the time. He absorbed heretical tendencies from some of Iran's Shiite scholars as well as their extreme approaches. Therefore, his views were not the result of an innocent intellectual mistake but a purposeful attempt to satisfy his thirst for power by destroying the Ottoman Caliphate. For this reason, he labeled genuine Muslims to be infidels whose life, property and honor were deemed to be taken as the spoils of war. He used his religious knowledge to seduce ignorant nomadic Bedouins against the authority. With religious enthusiasm the ignorant zealot nomads destroyed many tombs of the Prophet's Companions and plundered many settlements and towns.

Ibn Abd al-Wahhab argued that when the Noble Prophet conveyed the message of Islam first in Makka the polytheist people denied and opposed to it strongly for it was contrary to the beliefs, customs and mentality of the polytheists. He claimed that the Noble Prophet mobilized his community first and foremost to achieve political and military success in Arabia. This view is an indication of his extremist interpretation of Islam and the life of the Noble Prophet. Prophet Muhammad, upon whom be peace and blessings, strongly prohibited killing Muslims or any other innocent people and plundering their possessions. In spite of the clear religious injunctions to this end, Ibn Abd al-Wahhab and his followers killed many Muslims and

---

[173] Glasse, Cyril (2001). *The New Encyclopedia of Islam*. Alta Mira Press, p. 46.

caused terror in society. Seemingly, the essence of the Wahhabi mission was to revive pure devotion of worship to God alone, but in reality it was a source of extremism and violence. Ibn Abd al-Wahhab travelled to many Islamic cities to stir up ignorant masses against the Ottoman Caliphate, on the basis of his religious arguments. His deficient educational formation made him stray from the mainstream Islam, thus forming a sectarian movement. Moreover, the scholars of the Wahhabi movement discouraged their followers to travel to Ottoman lands, whose inhabitants they deemed polytheists. Destroying the classical scholastic tradition made it possible for Wahhabism to attain a monopoly on religious thought and practice in most of the Najd region. By the middle of 1800s, the Wahhabi movement turned out to be a local religious culture in the region with its own doctrine, leadership, cadre of scholars and centre of learning.

Wahhabism claims to advocate pure Islam that aims to apply the Sharia law in a strict form fostering intolerance and restricting Islam's capacity for adaption to diverse and shifting circumstances.[174] This sect is indeed a political trend within Islam that has been adopted for power-sharing purposes. Its goal is to restore *tawhid* (oneness of God) with flagrant disregard for traditional disciplines and practices that have evolved through Islamic history, such as theology and jurisprudence as well as the traditions of visiting tombs and shrines of the friends of God (*awliya*).[175] This movement has a tendency toward extremism and violence to convince others to their doctrines; therefore, it is often accused of being a basis for contemporary terrorist groups.[176]

Ideologically, Wahhabism considers the rest of the Muslim world as heretical with religious innovations. Its extreme ideas found greater acceptance when an Islamic revivalist tendency appeared in Eastern Arabia and India in the late nineteenth century. Reformists published many books and other works to revise Wahhabism's reputation in the eyes of the

---

[174] Commins, David (2006). *The Wahhabi Mission and Saudi Arabia*. I.B. Tauris. p. vi.
[175] Moussalli, Ahmad (January 2009). "*Wahhabism, Salafism and Islamism: Who Is The Enemy?*" (PDF). Conflicts Forum Monograph. Retrieved on February 26, 2016.
[176] DeLong-Bas, Natana J. (2004). *Wahhabi Islam: From Revival and Reform to Global Jihad*. Oxford University Press, pp. 123–24

Muslim world. Abd al-Aziz ibn Saud, the founder of Saudi Arabia's modern kingdom, collaborated with the Wahhabi scholars to establish the kingdom integrated into global political and economic system. The US and European powers helped the kingdom to develop its reservoirs of petroleum. As a result, Wahhabism obtained a great influence far beyond the confines of its historic homeland.

Occasionally, the term Salafism is interchangeably used for Wahhabism; however, the latter refers to a more general puritanical Islamic movement that has developed independently at various times and in various places in the Islamic world.[177] Wahhabism is a more strict form of Salafism, and it was used to control the masses in Arabia. Wahhabism evolved into a political system on the basis of Islamic and tribal practices and beliefs. With the strict interpretation of religious texts, the family of Saud achieved the ruling authority with a monopoly on the legitimate use of force and legislation. In other words, the tribal groups have obtained the opportunity in exercising political authority alongside the Islamic jurists and the clergy.

The terrorist attacks launched in the US, Europe and the rest of the world, especially those starting with the 9/11 terrorist attacks, necessitate a better understanding of Wahhabism both as an ideology and as a political system. Although Wahhabism is essentially an extreme form of religious interpretation, it has eventually turned out to be a political system, inspiring the modern terror groups to establish their own Islamic state and rule the lands according to the "religious law." However, it is not easy to say that Saudi Arabia is purely Islamic; rather the tribal, cultural and social elements have important roles in its political system. However, they make use of religious sources and concepts to justify their tribal understanding and approach, presenting it as the pure form of Islam. The main idea in both Wahhabism and the contemporary terrorist groups is that their belief or understanding of religion is the only truth and others are either

---

[177] Blanchard, Christopher M. *"The Islamic Traditions of Wahhabism and Salafiyya"* (PDF). Updated January 24, 2008. Congressional Research Service. Retrieved on February 26, 2016.

unbelievers (*kafir*) or polytheists (*mushrik*); therefore, it is legitimate to wage war against them all.

The influence and quick spread of Wahhabism is closely related with its territorial ruling. Makka and Medina are the two sacred cities for all Muslims as the Ka'ba (in Makka) and the mosque and tomb of Prophet Muhammad (in Medina) are in these cities. One of the five pillars of Islam is pilgrimage to the Ka'ba, the house of God, in Makka. By ruling the holy cities, Saudi Arabia has obtained the most effective power to impose and spread its Wahhabi understanding. With the support of the British, the Saudi family has utilized the Wahhabi political system for long decades to maintain its power over oil laden region of the world. Today, it has power over one of the largest petroleum reserves in the world. Ibn Abd al-Wahhab's ideas, along with the political ambitions of the Saudi family, served to consolidate and establish the Kingdom of Saudi Arabia. Wahhabi ideology allowed the Saudi tribal family to attain political power over all of the tribes of Arabia.

In modern days, Wahhabism has become an inspiration of ideology for radical groups and this increased its ability to recruit members into its dangerous war against the west and the "infidels." Therefore, marginalized masses are attracted to Wahhabism in the name of "defending Muslim lands and Islamic belief." If the extremist doctrines and ideology of Wahhabism are not adequately refuted by moderate Muslim scholars, it will continue to expand into different parts of the world, resulting in the propagation of a more hostile religion-based political system, and it will accelerate its expansion at a global level, giving rise to a new form of contemporary terrorism.

The Origins of Wahhabism

In order to understand Wahhabism better it is necessary to know its ideology because the Wahhabi extremist ideology has the power to communicate its ideals, aims and purposes, and logical coherence among its members.[178] The ideology provides a cause for people to act in certain directions. Wahhabi ideology provides main targets for its members and mobilizes their resources and energies for it. There are some key figures from whom the Wahhabi movement has benefitted a lot to establish its ideology. In this regard, Muhammad ibn Abd al-Wahhab and Ibn Taymiyya and their way of interpreting Islam are very important to understand Wahhabism.

Muhammad ibn Abd al-Wahhab, the founder of Wahhabism, wanted to eradicate all kinds of polytheism, but such ideology has transformed the Wahhabi movement into justifying the killing of Muslims, destructing, demolishing, and promoting the turmoil. Islam and its teachings were used by Ibn Abd al-Wahhab as a deadly weapon with the support of the British in the political arena to prevent the unity of Muslims. Indeed, Colonialism has always looked for ways to enforce its power, and one of its methods is the "divide and rule" policy. This policy is very effective to dominate those countries with no balance of power for the purpose of plundering their material and immaterial wealth.

Western influences in the Middle East contributed much to the evolution of Wahhabism as an ideology and political system. The British government, for instance, held many conferences and conducted many researches with regards to occupying the Middle East and controlling its rich oil resources. In 1710, the British Colonial Office sent its spies to Islamic centers such as Egypt, Iraq, and the holy lands of Makka and Medina, to gather information that will help tear apart Muslims and dominate the Muslim territories. The spies learned Turkish, Arabic and Persian languages to better understand the people and their cultures. Some of them pretended to be Muslims to learn more about Islam from the Muslim scholars themselves. When they returned to their countries, the British Colonial Office listened to their reports to develop the colonization strategy. It is known that the office sent Mr. Hempher to the city of

---

[178] Mullins, W. A. (1972). On the concept of ideology in political science. *The American Political Science Review*, 66(2), pp. 498-510.

Baghdad in Iraq in order to create disorder between the Sunni and Shiite Muslims. The spy's mission was to identify the conflicts among Muslims and create an atmosphere of disagreement, expiation, and mistrust among them. As Ibn Abd al-Wahhab travelled in Muslim lands extensively, he met with Hempher in Basra (in today's Iraq) around 1732 CE. Hempher convinced him to the strategy which aimed to consolidate the tribes under al-Saud's rule on the basis of Wahhabi ideology. However, the people of Basra drove him out from the city because of his extreme views.[179]

Other spies were also sent to different cities in the Middle East to create disputes and dissent among the Sunni and Shia sects. They instructed each group that they represent true Islam and the others were all infidels and must therefore be destroyed. It is obvious that the colonizers could not achieve their targets in the region without the help and support of local religious and political leaders. They provided these individuals great financial support and urged them to establish various extremist groups within Islamic community.

The British colonization helped for the creation of the extreme Wahhabi group within the Sunni Muslims in the Middle East through the leadership of Muhammad ibn Abd al-Wahhab. The other name which helped Wahhabism to be established was Saud ibn Abd al-Aziz. They were provided with the required financial and other means to attract followers to the ideology and they started their mission by killing pilgrims who did not agree to their doctrines. They treated Muslims who visited the tomb of the Noble Prophet as polytheists and thus killed them and plundered their possessions. They claimed that the pilgrims were worshipping the Noble Prophet by visiting and showing respect to his grave. However, this was a downright lie since those Muslims recognized the Noble Prophet as a servant and Messenger of God. What's more, it is permissible, and even encouraged, to visit graves and pray for the dead in Islam. Thus, those Muslim pilgrims simply wanted to show their gratitude and love to their Beloved Prophet for he conveyed God's message to them and established

---

[179] Dallal, A. (1993). The Origins and Objectives of Islamic Revivalist Thought 1750-1850. *Journal of the American Oriental Society*, 113 (3), pp. 341-359.

Islam on the strongest foundations. Indeed, God Almighty commands Muslims to pray for the Prophet in the Qur'an.[180]

In the time of Ibn Abd al-Wahhab, the Middle East was undergoing a period of social, economic, and political transition. There was no central leadership–whether political or religious, which was strong enough to bind Muslims together. The disorder and uncertainty in the region was a potential resistance to the existent political and social system.[181] People were divided into classes according to their social status, wealth and tribal strength. Ibn Abd al-Wahhab noticed the dissatisfaction among the masses and interpreted the religious texts in a strict, superficial way which addressed their level of understanding. However, his interpretation was very extreme for he condemned other Muslims who disagreed with his ideology as polytheists or infidels easily. The society was in turmoil and people could be stirred up against each other on the subtle differences. For example, there were some un-Islamic customs in the region, such as the superstitious belief in visiting tombs of saintly people, making their graves like an idol to be worshipped and asking for intercession directly from them. They were enough reason for Abd al-Wahhab to wage war against those people. With the foreign influence, Ibn Abd al-Wahhab quickly became one of the "well-known and respected" Islamic scholars in the Arabian Peninsula.[182] Branding Wahhabism as the only way to be a true Muslim, he categorized people based on their creed and labeled them as believers and non-believers just like the modern-day terrorist groups.

Ibn Abd al-Wahhab travelled to Syria and other Arabic lands and wrote books on un-Islamic customs and practices prevailing especially amongst the tribal people of the 18th century Arabian Peninsula. He accused Muslims that they were worshiping the dead Prophet instead of God, and therefore vowed to fight against them. With his call to oneness of God, Ibn Abd al-Wahhab put himself in a position of religious and political authority. This was a clear method of "identification" for those who

---

[180] Qur'an 33: 56.
[181] Lewis, B. (1970). On the evolution of early Islam. *Studa Islamica*, (32), pp. 215-231.
[182] Kechichian, J. (1986). The role of the Ulama in the politics of an Islamic state: the case of Saudi Arabia. *International Journal of Middle East Studies*, 18, 55.

became members of the Wahhabi movement. Indeed, the idea of worshipping one God was not new to Muslims, but Ibn Abd al-Wahhab attached political importance to the idea by attacking some un-Islamic customs and practices in the region. Moreover, he and his followers did not accept other Muslims as the true believers unless they agreed to Wahhabi doctrines and condemned them as polytheists.[183] While the followers of Ibn Abd al-Wahhab called themselves as true believers who believed in one God (Muwahhidun) the other Muslims called them as Wahhabis.

Fighting against the religious practices they deemed as un-Islamic customs and innovations was a key principle of the Wahhabi ideology. It strongly opposes Sufism – the spiritual aspect of Islam, religious innovations, the traditions of visiting tombs and shrines of venerated individuals. It labels these practices as polytheism, unbelief in God and apostasy. With its distinct collective identity, Wahhabism spread quickly among Arabs because when a tribal community embraced an ideology, the vast majority of individuals from that community would also be forced to accept it, thus identifying themselves with it. Otherwise, they would face strict forms of pressure from the tribe. Ibn Abd al-Wahhab used some religious concepts to promote his ideas. For example, he called Muslims for strict adherence to Islamic law, or Sharia, as interpreted by Ibn Taymiyya. He often asked people to refrain from invoking dead or visiting their tombs. He called them to stop associating partners to God and opposed to construct tombs over graves.[184] He cut down trees that were respected for the historical significance and destroyed the dome built over the grave of Zayd ibn al-Khattāb in the Najd region. With these practices he wanted to give an impression that he intended to implement the Sharia.

Receiving local support from the tribal leaders in the Najd region was a unique moment in the birth of Wahhabism. He promised them that if they supported his mission (the call to the oneness of God), God would grant

---

[183] Sirriyeh, E. (1989). *Wahhabis, Unbelievers, and Problems of Exclusivism*. British Society for Middle Eastern Studies, 16(2), pp. 123-132.
[184] Karawan, I. (1992). Monarchs, Mullas, and Marshals: Islamic Regimes? *Annals AAPSS*, 524, pp. 103-119.

them the Kingdom of Najd.[185] He was conveying his message secretly at first, but later he gained a reputation of courage against un-Islamic customs and practices; therefore, many tribal people joined his ranks. For example, he rejected the birthday celebrations for the Noble Prophet because it was an innovation in the religion. The Prince Muhammad ibn Saud offered Ibn Abd al-Wahhab political and military support to defend his ideology in exchange for Abd al-Wahhab supporting the reign of the Saud Family. When Muhammad ibn Saud died in 1765, his son Abd al-Aziz became the new ruler. He continued to support Ibn Abd al-Wahhab as his father did and with their political alliance, they captured the capital city of Riyadh in 1773. Ibn Abd al-Wahhab died in 1791 but his ideology has survived as Wahhabism.

Doctrines of Wahhabism

The Qur'an and the Sunnah are the primary sources for the development of Islamic law. The Qur'an contains around 1000 verses that point to legal principles directly or indirectly. After the death of the Noble Prophet, Muslim jurists developed Islamic law by exercising their juristic opinions (*ijtihād*) on the basis of the primary Islamic sources (of the Qur'an and the Sunnah), and this enabled the dynamism of the Islamic law. They established a methodology to extract the rulings from their sources in order to address the problems of their own times; therefore, the development of Islamic jurisprudence is a result of their interpretation of the Qur'an and the Sunnah with a strict adherence to a certain methodology. Adopting various approaches in their methodology, four Sunni schools of thought have survived up until today: Ḥanafī, Malikī, Shāfi'ī and Ḥanbalī. The influence of different schools of thought tends to be based on geographic location: the Ḥanbalī school is dominant especially in Saudi Arabia, the Malikī school in North Africa, the Ḥanafī school mainly in the Indian Subcontinent, Central Asia and Turkey and the Shāfi'ī

---

[185] Philby, S. (1955). *Saudi Arabia*. London: Ernest Benn Limited.

school mainly in Indonesia and Southeast Asia. Muslims generally recognize all four schools of law; however, they are likely to assume a preference for the particular school that is dominant in their local area.

The Wahhabis follow the interpretations of Ahmad ibn Hanbal and Ibn Taymiyya, but they do not consider themselves as the strict adherents of any legal school. They just see themselves as the "true Muslims" while deeming others deviants or polytheists. They interpret the religious sources literally and follow the Islamic law strictly. The law, however, is their own way of interpretation which consists mainly of their own tribal culture, customs and local traditions. For example, they execute drug dealers although there is no clear injunction in Islam about it. Similarly, they do not allow women to drive car or work in business environment. Again, there is nothing in Islam which prohibits women from working or driving a car. Obviously, many practices which we have been observing in Saudi Arabia today are clearly related to their own culture, customs and their rigid interpretation of Islamic sources.

In Islam, there is no compulsion, but Wahhabi ideology legitimizes the use of force to convince people to their doctrines or practice the religious rituals. They deem other Muslims as polytheists associating partners with God by practicing Islam differently from their Wahhabi model. They strictly reject statues and visiting the tombs of saintly people and destruct the tombs and statues even if they are not worshipped by people. In the Qur'an, God Almighty declares, *"The truth is from your Lord, so whoever wills - let him believe; and whoever wills - let him disbelieve."*[186] People are free to believe or deny; no one has the authority to force people to believe Islam or practice it.

In Wahhabism, the religious authority or ideological leader is accepted as a judge who is capable of enforcing legislation by force. The Saudi kingdom recognizes their authority as long as they provide political support for their rule. Similarly, as long as the Saudi kingdom follows Wahhabi ideology, the scholars and religious leaders support it. Therefore,

---

[186] Qur'an 18: 29.

Wahhabism is a political system which practices and enforces the principles of ideological Wahhabi belief.

The Wahhabi movement aims to establish an Islamic community that practices the laws of God with a Muslim ruler who has authority over the people to enforce the Sharia.[187] Emerged within the Arabian tribal society, Wahhabism seeks to expand its political authority on the basis of religious references.

In Islam, there is the rule of law; the law which provides justice to everyone, regardless of their religious or ethnic background, is superior, but in the Wahhabi model, the Saud family is above the law. The long lasting Bedouin traditions and the strict tribal loyalty in the Middle East necessitated the Saudi kingdom to use its political and military force to unite people under its sovereignty. Thus, Wahhabism has its own social and educational institutions to maintain its religiously oriented ideology. Its ideology has the elements of the jurisprudence of the Hanbalī School, Ibn Taymiyya's ideas and Ibn Abd al-Wahhab's personal teachings.

Wahhabism started as an ideology to supposedly call people to the real meaning of the oneness of God (*tawhid*). However, Wahhabi understanding forces people to adhere to a very strict and literal interpretation of monotheism (*tawhid*). Wahhabism argues that Muslims must have a pure faith in the One and Only God and live this faith in practice without associating any partners with God. Therefore, they considered visiting graves, and even the tomb of the Noble Prophet, as an act of polytheism (*shirk*) in this movement. Wahhabism rejects and strongly opposes practices in which other Muslims engage, such as listening to music, doing paintings, and following schools of Islamic jurisprudence. It easily labels other Muslims as apostates or polytheists; therefore, the majority of Muslim scholars reject their extremist stance. The followers of Wahhabism call themselves as the Salafists who follow the way of the first three generations of Islam. They claim that other Muslims have been wrong by living a state of pre-Islamic paganism

---

[187] Brown, C. (2000). *Religion and state: the Muslim Approach to Politics*. First edition, New York: Columbia University Press.

(*jahiliyya*) and moving away from the way of the *salaf* (the first three generations of Islam) for over ten centuries. They accused Muslims who lived under the Ottoman Caliphate with disbelief (*kufr*) because they adopted a political system which was not known by the salaf. Yet, they saw no problem in monarchy with their king being above the law.

They claim that they are the right advocators of *tawhid*; on the other hand, they understand the Divine attributes strictly literally. For them, for instance, God literally sits on the throne and descends physically. The Lord's literal seating upon a throne and His physical descent makes them anthropomorphist. The Almighty God is, however, beyond dwelling in His created things and beings. He is beyond everything that He has created and His Person (Dhat) is separate from His creation. The Wahhabis also oppose to the practice of Muslims who ask God for things through using the deceased pious friends of God (*awliya*) as an intermediary. In this regard, they deem all Shiites who venerate certain saints as unbelievers. Indeed, accusing other Muslims with disbelief (*takfir*) is a prominent feature of the Wahhabi ideology. Because of these extreme views, the followers of Wahhabism waged a war against other Muslims and they fought against the "infidel" Ottoman Caliphate. The funny thing is that they see no problem in the support of British in their fight against the Caliphate and the Muslims. As such, Ibn Abd al-Wahhab legitimized the revolt against the state, killing many innocent people. He accused the Ottomans with unbelief, polytheism, and apostasy and launched violent military campaigns against it. Similarly, Ibn Baz (d. 1999), another Wahhabi scholar, labeled other Muslims as pagans, apostates, deviants and innovators. Obviously, this understanding provides the basis for modern terror groups in their violent attacks against Muslims.

The scholars and religious leaders are highly respected in society; therefore, the Wahhabi leaders and scholars have played a pivotal role with regards to protecting and maintaining the Wahhabi ideology in Saudi Arabia. They have always supported the state during the critical incidents such as Muslim Brotherhood's revolt in 1920 and Second Gulf War in 1991. Wahhabism deems democracy contrary to Islam and the parliament house the place of associating partners with God (*shirk*). When the US asked the Saudi regime to enforce democratic principles, the royal family has rejected any real democratic change because the scholars described democracy as unbelief, polytheism and opposing to Islamic faith. Strangely enough, the same scholars support the monarchy although the very concept of a monarch's being above the law is totally foreign to the Qur'an and the Sunnah.

Wahhabism claims to return to original Islam as practiced at the time of the Noble Prophet. It opposes all intermediaries in order to establish the real monotheism and reject the Muslims' idea of benefiting from the saints and important scholars in order to better understand the Noble Prophet and his Practice. It claims to create a community which is the living embodiment of Islamic law on earth.[188] Contrary to the spirit of this law, Wahhabism does not hesitate to use violence and political power to achieve its goals. Its followers rigorously propagate their way of understanding Islam. They struggle to abolish all customs and practices that are likely to remind them any sort of polytheism and idolatry. They are against any form of social modernity because they are deemed "innovations in religion." In the name of restoring Islam to its original purity they fight against any form of innovations. They call Muslims who do not abide by the strict canons of pure Islam as "infidels" and "unbelievers." They even teach children at the age of seven to reject their parents if they do not perform the five daily prayers in congregation within the local mosques.

Wahhabi ideology uses only a limited part of the vast tradition of thought and practice of Islamic jurisprudence. With its strict literal interpretation of Islam, it is empty of spirituality and Islamic values such as human dignity, love and compassion.[189] Wahhabism aims to establish a utopian society by imposing its interpretation of Islam upon all members of society and rejecting other variants of Islam. It promotes an authoritarian

---

[188] Bahgat, Gawdat. 2004. Saudi Arabia and the War on Terrorism. *Arab Studies Quarterly*, 26. p. 51.
[189] Doorn-Harder, Nelly Van. 2004. Progressive Muslims. On Justice, Gender and Pluralism. *Theological Studies*, 65. p. 665.

political system which could spread the entire world and force people to accept its extreme ideology.

Conclusion

Wahhabism as an ideology seeks to purify Islam of any innovations or practices that deviate from the teachings of the Noble Prophet and his Companions. This is acceptable only if it is carried out through peaceful methods and means. However, the followers of the Wahhabi movement condemn other Muslims as infidels, polytheists and apostates, and therefore worthy of killing. Wahhabism does not accept any alternative worldview; thus, it urges its followers to fight against the others all over the world until they surrender. For this reason, this ideology has been a basis of terror and violence.

In the beginning, Muhammad ibn Abd al-Wahhab perceived the moral decline of his society and denounced many popular Islamic customs and practices as idolatrous. He aimed to restore the society to the pure form of Islam as thought in the Qur'an and embodied in the life of the Prophet. Al-Saud dynasty partnered with Ibn Abd al-Wahhab to unite the divided tribes in the Arabian Desert. There has been a close relationship between the Saudi ruling family and the Wahhabi movement. With this partnership Wahhabism turned into a political movement that seeks to establish a religious government. Wahhabi ideology thus formed the basis of the laws and governmental institutions in Saudi Arabia.

Wahhabism resorted to violence and terrorism to achieve its targets. Since its emergence, Wahhabism has been in conflict with other Muslim groups because it opposes most popular Islamic religious practices such as the veneration of the deceased friends of God, the celebration of the Prophet's birthday and the spiritual teachings of Sufism. They fought against the "other Muslims because they deem the non-Wahhabi Muslims as unbelievers and polytheists.

In Islam, any form of terrorism or violence is strongly prohibited. However, the Wahhabis advocate violence under the mask of "holy war" –

which is religiously motivated violence, to legitimize their evil acts with religious concepts. In 1980, the Wahhabis encouraged people to fight against the Soviet occupation of Afghanistan, and this call received a great support throughout the Muslim world. Thousands of volunteer fighters went to Afghanistan and radical Islamic ideology spread rapidly in the region. Following the war, these fighters inspired such radical terror groups as the Taliban and al Qaeda to emerge in Muslim societies. Unfortunately, this violent ideology has attracted a great number of followers throughout the Muslim world.

The Saudi government and the wealthy Saudi families have supported the spread of Wahhabism throughout the world. This support ended up with terrorism and violence because Wahhabi ideology has been used by terror groups as it suits their political goals. Additionally, the teachings in Saudi domestic schools foster intolerance towards other Muslims as well as towards other religions. In reality, Wahhabi ideology threatens the existence of moderate Islamic beliefs and practices in the world.

TALIBAN

Introduction

The word "taliban" is derived from the Arabic word *talib*, meaning "student or seeker of knowledge," and adding the Persian plural ending "*an*" the word became Taliban, meaning "students." This extreme group is a political movement that seeks to apply their rigid understanding of religious law in Afghanistan and govern the country with it. It has been using terrorism as a method to achieve its ideological and political goals.

The Taliban extremist group originated in the early 1990s as small groups, and then it was unified with the capture of the city of Kandahar in Afghanistan in 1994. Under the leadership of Mohammed Omar, the Taliban spread throughout most of Afghanistan quickly because the public were tired of the corruption and despotism in the country. Spreading amongst the Afghan students exiled in the neighboring countries, this extremist group started as the militant insurgency in 1994. Within two years, the followers of this terrorist group established their own state "The Islamic Emirate of Afghanistan" and declared Kandahar as their capital in 1996. This state gained diplomatic recognition from three states: Pakistan, Saudi Arabia, and the United Arab Emirates. From 1996 to 2001, it controlled most of the country, enforcing a strict interpretation of Sharia in Afghanistan. However, shortly after the 9/11 terrorist attacks, the Taliban regime was overthrown by the US and its allies with the Operation Enduring Freedom in December 2001. The militants escaped to Pakistan to regroup and fight against the US and its allies.[190] Mullah Mohammed Omar was the leader and commander of the Taliban until he was killed in 2013. After his death, Mullah Akhtar Mansur was elected as his replacement, and was killed in 2015. Currently, the group is led and supported by a dozen of various militant groups in Afghanistan.[191]

The followers of this group are mostly from the Pashtun tribes, the largest ethnic group in Afghanistan.[192] While in power, the Taliban group enforced one of the strictest interpretations of religious law ever seen in the Muslim world[193] and, therefore, received a great criticism from the leading Muslim scholars. The terrorist group has been condemned internationally for its brutal treatment of many Afghan civilians, especially women.[194] The Taliban committed massacres against Afghan civilians, prevented the UN food supplies to 160,000 starving civilians, burned vast areas of fertile land and destroyed tens of thousands of homes.[195]

The Taliban received support from Al Qaeda, the Arab and Central Asian militants. Approximately, only 14,000 militants were Afghans from

---

[190] http://www.nato.int/isaf/placemats_archive/2013-08-01-ISAF-Placemat.pdf. Retrieved on March 10, 2016.

[191] Azami, Dawood (January 5, 2016). "Why are the Taliban resurgent in Afghanistan?" BBC News. Retrieved on January 5, 2016.

[192] "Pakistan and the Taliban: It's Complicated" http://www.shavemagazine.com/politics /090501/2. Retrieved on March 10, 2016.

[193] Dupree Hatch, Nancy. "Afghan Women under the Taliban" in Maley, William. *Fundamentalism Reborn? Afghanistan and the Taliban.* London: Hurst and Company, 2001, pp. 145–166.

[194] Skain, Rosemarie (2002). *The women of Afghanistan under the Taliban.* McFarland. p. 41.

[195] Rashid, Ahmed (2002). *Taliban: Islam, Oil and the New Great Game in Central Asia.* I.B. Tauris. p. 253.

among the 45,000 armed men fighting on the side of the Taliban.[196] Today, the Taliban operates in Afghanistan and northwest Pakistan, and its headquarters is near Quetta, Pakistan.[197] The followers of this terrorist group killed many civilians and are responsible for 75% of the Afghan civilian casualties in 2010, 80% in 2011, and 80% in 2012.[198]

With the influence of tribal customs and backwardness in education, the Taliban interpreted Islam very rigidly and created an innovative form of Islamic law based on Deobandi fundamentalism.[199] It represents militant insurgency on the basis of Pashtun social and cultural norms. It is alleged that the Pakistan intelligence and military provided support to the Taliban during their establishment. However, Pakistan State publicly announced that it has dropped all its support for the group after the 9/11 attacks.

Origins of the Taliban

The origin of the Taliban goes back to the Soviet invasion period in Afghanistan in 1980s. The US and Saudi Arabia provided all kind of funds to the fighters who came to Afghanistan from all over the world to fight against the Soviet invasion, and it was during this time that the Pakistani Inter-Services Intelligence trained 90,000 Afghans, including Mohammad Omar.[200] The western countries, mainly the US and the UK, gave about 20 billion dollars aid to Pakistan for training the Taliban personnel and

---

[196] "Afghanistan resistance leader feared dead in blast" http://www.telegraph.co.uk/news/worldnews/asia/afghanistan/1340244/Afghanistan-resistance-leader-feared-dead-in-blast.html London: Ahmed Rashid in the Telegraph. September 11, 2001.
[197] Gall, Carlotta. "At Border, Signs of Pakistani Role in Taliban Surge" http://www.nytimes.com/2007/01/21/world/asia/21quetta.html?_r=0 Jan. 21, 2007, New York Times.
[198] *UN: Taliban Responsible for 76% of Deaths in Afghanistan*, https://www.weeklystandard.com/blogs/taliban-responsible-76-deaths-afghanistan-un, *The Weekly Standard.* August, 10, 2010.
[199] It is a revivalist movement within Sunni Islam and centered in India, Pakistan, Afghanistan and Bangladesh. The movement was inspired by the scholar Shah Waliyyullah Dahlawi against the British rule.
[200] Price, Colin. Pakistan: A Plethora of Problems. Global Security Studies, Winter 2012, Volume 3, Issue 1, *School of Graduate and Continuing Studies in Diplomacy.* Norwich University, Northfield, VT. Retrieved on Dec. 22, 2012.

provided them with arms and ammunition for their fight against the Soviet Union.

After the failure of Soviet invasion, several Afghan political parties agreed on a peace and power-sharing agreement in 1992. This agreement resulted in the declaration of the Islamic State of Afghanistan and the appointment of an interim government for a transitional period.[201] Gulbuddin Hekmatyar, the leader of a fighting group in the country, did not recognize this agreement and, therefore, launched attacks against government forces. The Pakistani Inter-Services Intelligence provided logistic and military support to this group. On the other side, in order to gain regional hegemony Saudi Arabia and Iran provoked Afghan militias' hostility against each other. While Iran assisted the Shiite Hazara Hizbul-Wahdat forces, Saudi Arabia supported the Wahhabite Abdul Rasul Sayyaf group.[202] The conflicts between the two militias turned into a civil war; therefore, the newly established Islamic State of Afghanistan did not have time to form its governmental institutions. Although ceasefires were occasionally declared between the groups, they did not last long.

Going back to the early history of the Taliban, the group was initially known as Jamiat Ulema-e-Islam, and was running religious schools for Afghan refugees in Pakistan. Because of the chaos and uncertainty in Afghanistan, the group got an opportunity to increase its political and religious influence. The Taliban (i.e., the madrasa students) were forced to abandon their studies to answer the desperate calls of their countrymen as anarchy prevailed in their country in the early 1990s. Some local Afghan leaders had formed armed insurgents and fought against other groups. Corruption and theft were widespread in the country. Women were raped and then killed after their abuse. In the face of all this, a group of students from these madrasas decided to rise against the corrupt leaders. In the spring of 1994, Mullah Omar mobilized his followers when he heard that

---

[201] "Blood-Stained Hands, Past Atrocities in Kabul and Afghanistan's Legacy of Impunity". *Human Rights Watch*. https://www.hrw.org/report/2005/07/06/blood-stained-hands/past-atrocities-kabul-and-afghanistans-legacy-impunity
[202] Saikal, Amin (2006). *Modern Afghanistan: A History of Struggle and Survival* (1st ed.). London New York: I.B. Tauris & Co. p. 352.

the local governor near Singesar abducted two teenage girls to a camp and raped them there. Under the leadership of Mullah Omar, thirty Taliban militants killed the governor and saved the girls. With this incident, Mullah Omar started his militant movement with less than fifty madrasa students in his hometown of Kandahar.[203] The militant Taliban movement thus began in the name of bringing "security and peace" to Afghanistan.

The Taliban movement's goal was initially to stop the clashes among all rival militia and enforce Islamic law in all the lands they captured, but they ended up being bloody militants themselves. Although their uprising started with a small number of students, the Taliban soon received a large number of followers from the madrasas in Pakistan. In addition, Pakistan supported the Taliban militants to secure the land routes for trade with Central Asia.

In 1994, the Taliban captured Kandahar and the surrounding provinces. The group terminated the authority of local leaders due to their lawlessness and atrocities. With a mixture of former small-unit military commanders and madrasa teachers, Mullah Omar took control of 12 provinces within the same year.[204]

Again, in 1994, Islamic State of Afghanistan defeated the militia groups who fought to capture Kabul, the national capital. Ahmad Shah Massoud, the Defense Minister of the Islamic State of Afghanistan, invited the Taliban to join the government to bring stability to the country. He talked with the Taliban leaders to convince them about the necessity of having democratic elections to choose a future government for Afghanistan.[205] However, the Taliban rejected the offer, and Massoud returned Kabul unharmed. Although the Taliban initially suffered a devastating defeat against the government forces of the Islamic State of Afghanistan, they eventually captured Kabul in 1996 and established the

---

[203] Matinuddin, Kamal (1999). *The Taliban Phenomenon, Afghanistan 1994–1997*, Oxford University Press, pp. 25–26.
[204] Felbab-Brow, Vanda (2010). *Shooting Up: Counter insurgency and the War on Drugs*. Brookings Institution Press. p. 122.
[205] Grad, Marcela. (2009). *Massoud: An Intimate Portrait of the Legendary Afghan Leader*. Webster University Press. p. 310.

Islamic Emirate of Afghanistan.[206] The Pakistan's Inter-Services Intelligence supported the Taliban giving them financial, logistical and military support to establish a regime in Afghanistan.[207]

During 2001, the military force of an approximately 45,000 men consisting of Pakistani, Afghani and Al Qaeda militants were fighting against anti-Taliban forces in Afghanistan.[208] Many students from the Taliban madrasas in Pakistan joined them even without informing their parents. Although Iran itself supported some other militant groups in Afghanistan, it accused Pakistan of sending its air force to bomb Mazar-i Sharif in support of Taliban forces.[209] According to British Intelligence report in 2000, the Pakistan's Inter-Services Intelligence took an active role to construct training camps for both the Taliban and Al-Qaeda.[210] During the period from 1996-2001, Osama bin Laden and Ayman al-Zawahiri achieved to establish their own state within the Taliban state.[211] After the 9/11 attacks, Pakistan announced that it ended its support for the Taliban.

Ahmad Shah Massoud created the United Front (aka Northern Alliance) against the Taliban together with some other anti-Taliban leaders. However, after longstanding battles, some of these forces were defeated by the Taliban and their allies in 1998. Massoud became the only major anti-Taliban leader who was able to defend his territory against the Taliban. He wanted to bring democratic institutions to Afghanistan, and for this purpose, he signed the Women's Rights Declaration. With this

---

[206] Saikal (2006). *Modern Afghanistan: A History of Struggle and Survival* (1st ed.). London New York: I.B. Tauris & Co. p. 352.
[207] Giraldo, Jeanne K. (2007). *Terrorism Financing and State Responses: A Comparative Perspective*. Stanford University Press. p. 96.
[208] Girardet, Edward. (2011). *Killing the Cranes: A Reporter's Journey through Three Decades of War in Afghanistan*. Chelsea Green Publishing. p. 416.
[209] Constable, Pamela "Afghanistan: Arena for a New Rivalry," *Washington Post*, Sept, 1, 1998. http://pqasb.pqarchiver.com/washingtonpost/doc/408407755.html?FMT=ABS&FMTS=ABS:FT&type=current&date=Sep%2016,%201998&author=Pamela%20Constable&pub=The%20Washington%20Post&edition=&startpage=&desc=Afghanistan:%20Arena%20for%20a%20New%20Rivalry
[210] Litwak, Robert (2007). *Regime change: U.S. strategy through the prism of 9/11*. Johns Hopkins University Press. p. 309.
[211] McGrath, Kevin (2011). *Confronting Al-Qaeda*. Naval Institute Press. p. 138.

declaration he recognized the rights of women, allowing them to go to school and to work. He addressed the European Parliament in Brussels asking the international community to provide humanitarian help to the people of Afghanistan.

In early 2001, Massoud warned the world that a large-scale attack on the US soil was imminent. On September 9, 2001, just two days before the 9/11 terrorist attacks, he was the target of a suicide attack by two Arabs who pretended to be journalists and died in a helicopter taking him to a hospital. It is believed that there is a link between the assassination of Massoud and the 9/11 terrorist attacks. The terrorists killed nearly 3000 civilians in the 9/11 attacks; therefore, the US made the following demands from the Taliban:[212]

- Delivering to the US all al Qaeda leaders,
- Releasing all foreign people who were imprisoned unjustly,
- Protecting foreign journalists, diplomats and aid workers,
- Closing terrorist camps and delivering every terrorist to appropriate authorities.

The US also asked the international community to support a military campaign to overthrow the Taliban, and NATO approved it.[213] Within a month, on October 7, the US and its allies initiated a military action, bombing Taliban and Al-Qaeda-related camps to remove the Taliban from power and prevent the use of Afghanistan lands as a terrorist base of operations.[214] The Taliban lost all their strongholds but managed to escape to neighboring regions without surrendering.

The Taliban leaders have survived due to the support of the tribal groups and the drug trade in the region. What's more, the western presence

---

[212] Taken from the transcript of President Bush's address. https://web.archive.org/web/20100819021954/ http://archives.cnn.com/2001/US/09/20/gen.bush.transcript/ September 21, 2001.

[213] United Nations S.C. Res. 1368, September 12, 2001; S.C. Res. 1373, September 28, 2001.

[214] Pike, John. (2001). "Intentions of the U.S. military operation." *Globalsecurity.org*. Retrieved on March 11, 2016.

in Afghanistan gave the Taliban golden opportunity to rationalize their existence among the locals in more widely accepted terms. Additionally, the civilian deaths caused by airstrikes increased public support to the Taliban again. The terrorist group also exploited the Islamic and nationalist values to receive more support from the local people. Previously, the mass uprising against the Russians had already provided such a link between Islam and nationalism in the country. They promoted the idea that if they turn back to true Islam, it would yield to liberation from foreign invasion. However, the Taliban had not yet worked out a sophisticated view of what a genuinely Islamic system would look like.

The Taliban started to use suicide attacks as a new method of terror. They often targeted humanitarian aid workers and the doctors without borders. They targeted, for instance, health officials who worked to immunize children against polio. In 2009, they created a strong resistance in the form of a guerrilla war. This resistance received a great support from the Pashtun tribal group and local madrasas. Instead of a large scale war on the ground, the US conducted targeted killings of the terrorist Taliban leaders. Upon this, the Taliban maintained that the US and its allies invaded Afghanistan in contravention of all moral and legal norms and principles. They deemed this invasion as destroying religious, social, cultural and economic rights of the people under the notorious name "war on terror."[215]

While trying to take the control over northern and western Afghanistan, the Taliban committed dozens of massacres against civilians. These were the same type of war crimes that were committed in Bosnia Herzegovina. Afghan women were raped, and thousands of people were locked in containers and were left to suffocate. The Taliban burned orchards, crops and destroyed irrigation systems, and forced more than 100,000 people to leave their homes.[216] Some Taliban and al-Qaeda commanders started to abduct women and sell them into sex slavery in

---

[215] Brahimi, Alia. *The Taliban's Evolving Ideology*, LSE Global Governance Working Paper WP 02/2010, July 2010, p. 7.

[216] Armajani, Jon (2012). *Modern Islamist Movements: History, Religion, and Politics*. Wiley-Blackwell. p. 207.

Afghanistan and Pakistan.[217] Some women committed suicide rather than being a slave. Many of the Taliban opposed to the human trafficking operations conducted by al-Qaeda and some Taliban commanders because it was against their ideology. Nevertheless, the Taliban forbade women from being educated and required them to wear the burqa. Whenever a woman disobeyed these rulings, she was publicly beaten.[218]

Doctrines of the Taliban

Because of the social, economic and political backwardness in the country, the Taliban terrorist group received good acceptance from the Afghans who were tired of the corruption, brutality and internal conflicts.

The Taliban has made use of an extremist interpretation of Islam to get the support for their radical ideology. The ideology advocates a rigid form of the Islamic law and encourages its followers to apply it through the state. This is, indeed, an interpretation of religion that combines Pashtun tribal codes with the Islamic law.

Additionally, the Taliban benefitted from the terrorist Osama bin Laden and his extreme militant understanding.[219] The combatants fighting against the Soviet invasion as well as the members of some other radical groups who mixed with the Taliban also influenced its extremist ideology. As a result of all this, the Taliban prohibited many lawful activities for women rights, technology, paintings and photography with its rigid and tribal understanding of Islam. Men were obliged to have a beard and wear a head covering. Women were required to wear burqa and were deprived of many basic rights.

---

[217] "Lifting the Veil on Taliban Sex Slavery," *Time*, Feb. 10, 2002. http://content.time.com/time/magazine/article/0,9171,201892,00.html.
[218] Dupree Hatch, Nancy (2001). "*Afghan Women under the Taliban*" in William Maley. *Fundamentalism Reborn? Afghanistan and the Taliban*. London: Hurst and Company, pp. 145–166.
[219] Rashid, Ahmed (2002). *Taliban: Islam, Oil and the New Great Game in Central Asia*. I.B. Tauris. p. 132.

Previously, the Afghans were practicing Islam but it was tolerant. However, with the Taliban regime, their interpretation of Islam became more rigid and much less tolerant. The Taliban do not debate their doctrines with other Muslims. They are very rigid and, therefore, do not allow people to question their interpretations of Islam. In addition, they do not see the Shiites to be Muslims although their population is about 10% of Afghanistan. The Taliban argue that the Shiite beliefs were wicked and corrupt and a direct criticism of Islam itself, and therefore, they deserve to be killed. Indeed, they conducted house-to-house searches for the Shiite men, shooting them in the head or chest or suffocating them to death in shipping containers in the Hazara region.

The Taliban group strictly enforced its ideology in major cities where they had a direct control. Religious police force named after the Quranic verse that enjoins, "*Commanding the good and forbidding the evil,*" applied the Taliban rules very strictly. People were ruled by men who assumed to be following the Holy Qur'an although many of them could not even read it.

The Taliban often used the pre-Islamic Pashtun tribal codes in deciding certain social matters irrespective of whether they contradict with the Qur'an and the Sunnah. For example, they deprived women from their inheritance although the Qur'an allocates them a share; they simply kept dividing it only among the sons.

Indeed, the Taliban adopted the Deobandi form of Islam that sought to revive the Islamic interpretations and practices of early Islam and opposed the tribal and feudal structures in government during the first five years of their rule. However, since they received extensive support from the Pashtuns across the country, this changed their view from anti-nationalist to purely ethnic grounds.

Initially, the Taliban did not destroy the graves of Sufi saints or other important people as opposed to the Wahhabis. Under the Wahhabi influence, however, they started to reject any form of art reminding them of idolatry. Although Mullah Omar issued a decree that the Buddha statues at Bamyan should not be harmed, the Taliban destroyed the statues in 2001.[220] They started to show no respect to the historical art. The centuries-old Buddha statues were dynamited by the Taliban who claimed that these statues had to be destroyed with the argument that worshiping any deity other than God was unacceptable.

Since the Taliban did not have inspired-moderate scholars, the devastation and hardship of the Soviet invasion and the following period heavily influenced the Taliban ideology.[221] After the Soviet invasion, the desire of power and supremacy in Afghanistan resulted in the clash of interests among different groups and this dragged the Afghanistan into a civil war. The civil war, prevalent disputes within the society, disrupted governance, abduction, rape, rampant looting, and so on resulted in the misery of Afghanistan. The emergence of the Taliban was a result of the chaotic situation of this civil war. Madrasa students emerged in these circumstances, initially around Kandahar, and spread around the country with the aim of bringing peace to Afghanistan.

However, civil war was an employment opportunity for the Taliban (or "madrasa students") who were not educated in mathematics, science, history or geography. In such an environment, rigid radicalism was a matter of political survival. Thus, they were very strict toward those who disobeyed their imposed rules although their rules had no basis in the Qur'an or the Sunnah. Similarly, Mullah Omar, the founder of the Taliban, declared himself as the Ruler of Believers (*Amir al-Mu'minin*) with the support of the Pashtuns. He did not have scholarly learning, but became the leader of the society with this enormous tribal support. This way, the Taliban emerged as the representative of a "revived" Islamic Afghanistan.

The Taliban group does not allow politics or political parties. They don't give official salary to their men, but some food, clothes and weapons. For them, this primitive living is the pure form of Islam. With such a sick mentality, they sought to return the pristine form of Islam. However, their

---

[220] Harding, Luke (2001). "How the Buddha got his wounds" http://www.theguardian.com/books/2001/mar/03/books.guardianreview2.
[221] Rashid, *Taliban: Islam, Oil and the New Great Game in Central Asia*. p. 32.

rigid interpretation of Islam mixed with traditional tribal codes and Afghan social life resulted in more social disorder and crimes. Thus, the vast majority of Muslim scholars criticized them due to their rigid interpretation and application of Islamic law as well as their gender policies, treatment of women and questionable human rights. The scholars rejected their religious rules and extremist interpretations, declaring that they were not Islamic.

Interestingly, we now see the Taliban that once rejected to depict living images through drawing, film, or photography becoming more tolerant of television and cinema. Taliban commanders openly watch Indian soap operas featuring women dressed in revealing western attire.[222] Many of the prohibitions of the Taliban rule during the 1990s are no longer in effect. They have produced hundreds of thousands of cassettes and CDs using song to support their cause.[223] They use media technology to promote their ideology in Afghanistan. Their spokesmen have regular contact with journalists through social media and provide online reports conveying Taliban's side of the story on civilian casualties and encounters with foreign forces.

The Taliban used to apply their rules intolerantly such as whipping men who had beards shorter than their standard, lashing alcohol drinkers with rubber hoses, amputating the hands of thieves and executing murderers in front of thousands of people. However, they have relaxed their ideological strictness in time in order to receive more public support. They have also started expelling the followers who torment innocent people in order to not lose this support. Although Mullah Omar banned poppy cultivation, its production soared in areas under Taliban control, totaling more than half of the world's poppy cultivation.[224]

The Taliban group continues to burn down the schools and assassinates teachers and students with the argument that males and females are mixed.

---

[222] Rosen, Nir. "In the Lair of the Taliban," *The Sunday Times*, December 7, 2008.
[223] Giustozzi, Antonio. *Koran, Kalashnikov and Laptop: The Neo-Taliban Insurgency in Afghanistan* (London: Hurst & Co., 2007), p. 121.
[224] Erwin, Michael. "*Key Factors for the Recent Growth of the Afghan Insurgency*," CTC Sentinel, 1:9, August 2008, p. 10.

However, they don't want to be seen as a group that is totally against education and women's rights in order to include the educated Afghan population in their movement. They want to meet educational needs of Afghans according to their ideological understanding.

The Taliban used suicide bombings as a new tactic and soon it was overwhelmed with volunteers for suicide bombing operations for the sake of "martyrdom." Their suicide bombings were primarily directed towards government officials and foreign forces. However, they also killed large numbers of civilians during these bloody attacks. Suicide bombing is one of the most extreme combat tactics and the Taliban terrorist group has been relying on it. The first suicide bombing occurred against Ahmad Shah Massoud, the opponent leader, on September 9, 2001. After 2004, the suicide bombing has become an integral part of the Taliban campaign. In other words, the suicide attacks have become the Taliban's preferred strategic weapon, controlled and deployed by the military leadership against its targets.

The waistcoat filled with explosives – a suicide jacket, started to symbolize high level warriors who had been trained to conduct suicide operations. This practice and tactic is, however, totally contrary to Islamic belief and its principles as taking one's own life is strongly prohibited in Islam. The Taliban terrorist group brainwashes suicide bombers during their long training; thus, they cannot evaluate if such orders and targets comply with Islam. However, the terrorist group has been defending suicide attacks by misinterpreting Quranic passages that are related to martyrdom during a legitimate warfare. Suicide bombers use religious discourse in explaining their evil acts although they are not scholars, nor are they truly knowledgeable in religious matters. It seems that they create their own evidence by misinterpreting religious texts to legitimize their violence. In reality, the terrorists' reference to jihad, martyrdom or any other religious concepts are nothing but their purposeful misinterpretation of Islam.

In order to keep the insurgency alive the Taliban followers claim that they fight for the Afghans to free them from all the pain and hardship. They use this as a strategic narrative. They know that their success depends on paying attention to the local needs of the communities or attempting to win over the confidence of these people.[225] The Taliban group strives to interact positively with the population and advises new recruits to have good relationships with local people so that they will always be welcomed by them.

Because of the long-lasting internal conflicts which have inflicted heavy damages and huge suffering on Afghanistan, the Taliban group got a golden chance to promote its ideology over the corruption and hypocrisy of its opponents.[226] The group has made use of the ethnic polarization of a rural and segmented society under the banner of Islam. There is too much dispute over the leadership, the government, the role of women, relations with the west, and the presence of al-Qaeda largely on the Afghan soil. Nevertheless, the idea of the so-called defensive jihad played as the unifying mechanism for the Taliban.

The Taliban terrorists use the terminology of the jihad to introduce themselves as the only remaining true fighters. They claim that they fight primarily against the foreign forces and a puppet regime in Kabul. The Taliban movement has four major characteristics that are national sovereignty, military strength, the importance of jihad, and the authority of the Taliban's Islamic Emirate. However, Muslim scholars from all over the world have accused them of practicing terrorism rather than legitimate warfare. The terrorist group claims its position as resistance to both the American aggression and the Kabul-based political system for it represents American interests in violation of Afghan sovereignty. Thus, using this argument it legitimizes the use of violence as "jihad" and tries to maintain the legacy of "martyrs" for its "just cause." The terrorist group claims that jihad is obligatory for all Afghan Muslims, and whoever denies it, he or she becomes an unbeliever. The members of this movement are

---

[225] Ghani, Ashraf. "Afghanistan: Islam and Counterrevolutionary Movements," in John Esposito (ed), *Islam in Asia: Religion, Politics and Society* (New York: Oxford University Press, 1987), p. 94.
[226] Gohari, Abdul 'Ula Deobandi in M. J. *The Taliban: Ascent to Power* (Karachi: Oxford University Press, 1999), p. 126.

continuously reminded that they engage in violence simply as part of a great jihad.

Although the Taliban members are mostly ignorant of real Islam, they claim that they will establish the Islamic law on the basis of the Qur'an, the traditions of the Prophet, and the early Islamic history in order to provide Islamic justice through Taliban administrators and judges who promote good and suppress evil. The core doctrine in the Taliban ideology is obedience to the ruler as long as he obeys the Islamic law. This doctrine is a key concept to understand the Taliban and their leaders who are credited for their commitment toward implementing the Islamic law. They argue that the Taliban's success comes from maintaining unity and obedience among the followers to the ruler through the command chain leading up to their "supreme leader," or "the ruler of all believers," in their own words.

In order to obey the ruler and commanders fully the members leave their own judgments. They fulfill their tasks in full confidence to them because they believe that God works through the personality of rulers and commanders. Therefore, obedience to them is equated with obedience to the Prophet and thus to God. The commanders owed complete obedience to the ruler, so the notion of divine authority resting in the supreme leader was delegated through a command structure. However, the appointment of people in the movement for the tasks in the civilian or military commands are relatively short in order to prevent the members from the thought that the post belonged to them by right and that the movement was somehow dependent on them.

Conclusion

The Taliban is a militant terror group who has interpreted Islam in an extreme way, combining their tribal codes and customs with Islamic concepts. They have learned it from the other terror groups and have updated their strategy and ideology. Their political ideology is to apply the religious law according to their understanding in a very strict form. Because of the ignorance, poverty and continuous internal disputes, the

Afghans have been suffering from anarchy and chaos. People are searching for a way out of their problems but there is no scholarly work which can offer it because the madrasa students (Taliban) have a very long way to truly learn Islam in its authentic foundations, addressing the needs of people in a modern world. There is not a significant Afghan intellectual who can lead the ignorant people to the moderate way. Additionally, Afghanistan has been utterly isolated from the Islamic debates occurring in other parts of the Muslim world.

The terrorist group has been struggling to justify its violence, and has thus invested all its resources to show that its fight is for a just cause. Its ideology and political ideas have enabled the movement to maintain high levels of violence and motivated its followers by giving them a "moral" cover for the violent actions they commit. The commanding officers in the Taliban group are mostly ignorant with regards to Islam, yet they expect unquestioning obedience so that no one can question if their violence contradicts with the tenets of Islam. Indeed, the Taliban, or any other terrorist group, would never tolerate any criticism even if it comes from their own members.

The religious teachers (*mullahs*) have created a common identity for the Taliban on the basis of religious and cultural foundations. The identity provides a certain morality for them and encourages them to use physical force to achieve their goals. The Taliban group has been struggling to convince Afghans as a whole to accept the authority of the movement and thus support it.

The Taliban's militant insurgency has passed through five stages: the first stage was from 1990 to 1996, and it was during this time that the movement established its armed force and captured Kabul. The second stage was from 1996 to 2001. It was during this period that the Taliban established its Islamic emirate across most of Afghanistan and fought against the other militant groups in the region. During the third stage, from 2002 to 2006, Afghan government was supported internationally and therefore defeated the Taliban army and destroyed its government in late 2001. After losing its state the Taliban kept fighting international forces and the new Kabul government in small groups. During the fourth stage from 2007 to 2014, the Taliban wanted to expand its influence beyond its traditional power bases in the south and east. The insurgency is now moving toward a fifth stage during which the Taliban fights against the Kabul government, significantly reducing direct involvement of the international military forces.

After its start in 1990, the Taliban group continues to command the loyalty of thousands of Afghans to the pursuit of its political objectives. Its ideology has evolved through the involvement with its internal and external enemies during the last three decades. Its members have submitted themselves fully to the authority of the rulers and commanders. The group provides religious-moral base for its violence and punishes those who fail to support its "jihad." They declare to its members that they are engaged in a "righteous jihad" to establish an Islamic system in Afghanistan. It has unfortunately become the most effective organization in the Afghan public life.

AL QAEDA

Introduction

Contemporary terrorist groups find their religious roots in the theology of Wahhabism. Al Qaeda, the most bloody terrorist group, is known with its attack on the World Trade Centre on September 11, 2001. Al Qaeda, literally meaning "the base" or "the foundation" in Arabic, is a militant terrorist group established by Osama bin Laden, Abdullah Azzam, and several others back in 1988.[227] Its origins go back to the volunteers who fought against the Soviet invasion of Afghanistan in the 1980s. Young Muslims from around the world came to Afghanistan to volunteer in the jihad against the invading Soviets and Osama bin Laden, a 23 year old Saudi man, was one of them. He attended Abdullah Azzam's religious

---

[227] Bill Moyers Journal. "A Brief History of Al Qaeda." *PBS.com*. July 27, 2007. Retrieved on March 23, 2016. http://www.pbs.org/moyers/journal/07272007/alqaeda.html.

sermons and got the idea of jihad from him. Belonging to a wealthy family, he provided generous funding of the jihad against the Soviets.

Al Qaeda operates as a network but developed a decentralized, regional structure.[228] It consists of multinational members and has long been recognized as a terrorist group by the United Nations Security Council, the North Atlantic Treaty Organization (NATO), the European Union, the United States and many other countries. The major understanding of this terrorist group is considering all "others," including both Muslims and non-Muslims, as unbelievers, thus attacking them to achieve its goals. Indeed, labeling "others" as unbelievers and killing them violently is the common characteristic of the contemporary terrorist groups. In this regard, Al Qaeda divides the world into two camps: believers and unbelievers. Whoever does not agree with its ideology is considered as an unbeliever, and therefore worthy of murdering. The terrorist organization has carried out many attacks on civilians in many countries such as the 1998 US embassy bombings, the 9/11 attacks, and the 2002 Bali bombings. The group kills civilians on the basis that they do not agree with its ideology. They killed many Muslims and non-Muslims with this extremist mindset. They have instigated sectarian violence among Muslims for they consider other Muslims, Sufis, Shiites, and other sects as heretics, and have thus attacked their places of worship and religious gatherings. The Sadr City bombings, the Ashura massacre, the Yazidi community bombings, and the April 2007 Baghdad bombings are just a few examples from their bloody campaign against other sects.

Like other terrorist groups, al Qaeda uses suicide attacks and the simultaneous bombings of different targets to reach its goals. Its members give their pledge of loyalty to al-Qaeda leaders.[229] The terrorist group aims to eradicate all foreign influences in Muslim countries and establish a new

---

[228] Naím, Moisés. "*The Five Wars of Globalization.*" Foreign Policy (January–February 2003, issue 134), pp. 28–37.

[229] Geltzer, Joshua A. (2011). *US Counter-Terrorism Strategy and al-Qaeda: Signalling and the Terrorist World-View* (Reprint ed.). Routledge, p. 83.

caliphate ruling over the entire Muslim world.[230] They believe that a Christian–Jewish alliance aims to destroy Islam. Although the Qur'an strongly prohibits the murder of non-combatants, they religiously sanction those civilians' killings. They interpret Islam and its sources in an extreme way and aim to establish the Islamic law.[231] Since the death of Osama bin Laden in 2011, the group has been led by the Egyptian Ayman al-Zawahiri.

Organizational Structure

Although there have been numerous works and studies to understand the structural entity of al Qaeda, it is still unclear and mysterious in some ways. It is generally accepted that there are key leaders or central decision body, but there is no centralized body for executing the orders.[232] When the United States waged war on terror many regional terrorist groups have emerged using the al Qaeda name.[233] The emergence of decentralized leadership in regional terrorist groups made it difficult to understand the organizational structure of al Qaeda. Since the local militant groups use the brand al Qaeda, the terrorism experts assume that there is now no real umbrella organization for a mythical entity called al-Qaeda,[234] and that the global jihadist movement is managed and executed at every level by its leadership.

---

[230] The Future of Terrorism: What al-Qaida Really Wants." *Der Spiegel*. September 11, 2001, Retrieved on March 23, 2016. http://www.spiegel.de/international/the-future-of-terrorism-what-al-qaida-really-wants-a-369448.html.

[231] Wright, Lawrence. (2006). *The Looming Tower: Al-Qaeda and the Road to 9/11*. Knopf. p. 246.

[232] Al-Hammadi, Khalid, "The Inside Story of al-Qa'ida," Part 4, *Al-Quds al-Arabi*, March 22, 2005.

[233] "Evolution of the al-Qaeda brand name." *Asia Times*. August 13, 2004, Retrieved on March 24, 2016. http://www.atimes.com/atimes/Middle_East/FH13Ak05.html.

[234] Blitz, James (January 19, 2010). "A threat transformed." *Financial Times*. Retrieved on March 24, 2016. http://www.ft.com/cms/s/af31e344-0499-11df-8603-00144feabdc0,Authorised=false.html?siteedition=uk&_i_location=http%3A%2F%2Fwww.ft.com%2Fcms%2Fs%2F0%2Faf31e344-0499-11df-8603-00144feabdc0.html%3Fsiteedition%3Duk&_i_referer=https%3A%2F%2Fen.wikipedia.org%2Fd41d8cd98f00b204e9800998ecf8427e&classification=conditional_standard&iab=barrier-app#axzz43m3opdZp.

After the execution of bin Laden, Al Qaeda has been divided into a variety of regional movements that have little connection with one another. It is alleged that the terrorist group has an integrated network with Pakistani tribal areas and has a powerful strategic purpose. Al Qaeda is a global terrorist group which has direct affiliates in many countries such as those in Arabian Peninsula as well as in Syria, Lebanon, and Somalia.

Bin Laden was the most notable commander for this terrorist group prior to his assassination on May 1, 2011 by the US forces. After him, Ayman al-Zawahiri assumed the role of the commander.[235] There is a consulting council which consists of 20–30 people to advise the leaders. Al Qaeda uses regional leaders as an integral part of its high command. There are various committees responsible for different tasks. The military committee's task is recruiting members, finding weapons and planning attacks. The financial committee funds the terrorist group. The Fatwa committee issues religious rulings and declarations. The Sharia committee supervises and decides whether particular acts are acceptable by the Sharia. Finally, the media committee handles public relations.

Al Qaeda has the ability to provide training for regional terrorist groups. It has evolved after the 9/11 terrorist attacks and turned out to be more complicated. Once, Bin Laden and Ayman al-Zawahiri had become the focus of the world, but there was no major central organization; rather, the regional terrorist groups planned their own terror operations and looked to bin Laden for funding and assistance.[236] After Bin Laden was killed, al-Qaeda is linked together weakly. Although a large number of terrorists have been arrested, there is not much evidence that they are linked to Al Qaeda. This is, therefore, a plausible reason for the experts to doubt whether a widespread entity that met the description of al-Qaeda existed.[237]

---

[235] *"Al-Qaida Says Al-Zawahri Has Succeeded Bin Laden." The New York Times*. June 16, 2011, Retrieved on March 24, 2016. http://www.nytimes.com/aponline/2011/06/16/world/ middle east/AP-ML-Al-Qaida-Zawahri.html?_r=0.

[236] *The Power of Nightmares*, BBC Documentary. https://archive.org/details/ThePowerOf Nightmares.

[237] Gerges, Fawaz A. *The Far Enemy: Why Jihad Went Global*. Cambridge University Press, 2005.

The main strategy of al Qaeda is ironically saving all Muslims from all kind of oppression although it is them who commit all the heinous acts of violence and terror against Muslims.

The Origins of Al Qaeda

Beginning in the late 1980s al Qaeda has gone through four phases in its development: its establishment through violence and terror until 1996, its golden age until 2001, its founding of a global network until 2005, and a period of splitting and collapsing from 2005 up to today.[238] The origins of al Qaeda can be traced back to the Soviet invasion of Afghanistan. The radical militants came to Afghanistan to fight against Soviet expansionism and aggression. Pakistan's Inter-Services Intelligence supported these radical militants while Saudi Arabia provided the leading support. With the Saudi businessmen Osama bin Laden and Abdullah Yusuf Azzam's financial aid, a base was established for the militant terrorists. They gathered supplies for the construction of training camps to prepare the foreign recruits for the Afghan war. Osama Bin Laden was the major financer using his connections with the Saudi royal family.[239]

Bin Laden was born in July 1957 as a son of Saudi construction family. While studying at King Abdul Aziz University in Jeddah, Saudi Arabia, Bin Laden adopted the militant radical Islamic view. The key person who inspired him the radical views was Abdullah Yusuf Azzam. He used his personal funds to support jihadists against the Soviet invasion. In 1984, Azzam and Bin Laden established a network, called "Maktab al Khidamat" (Services Office), in the Arab world, Europe, and the United States. Throughout the war against the Soviet Union, the US perceived the jihadists as positive contributors to expel Soviet forces from Afghanistan.

---

[238] Burke, Jason and Paddy Allen. "The five ages of al-Qaida," Retrieved on September 10, 2009, http://www.theguardian.com/world/interactive/2009/sep/10/al-qaida-five-ages-terror-attacks.

[239] Gunaratna, Rohan. *Inside Al Qaeda*. Columbia University Press, 2002; Wright, Lawrance. *The Looming Tower: Al Qaeda and the Road to 9/11*. New York, Knopf, 2006. pp. 60-144.

During this period, Bin Laden and Azzam were not known with their extremist ideology against the United States. In 1988, they started to conceptualize the al Qaeda network and its ideology. The initial idea was forming a rapid reaction force which could defend Muslims whenever they were threatened or attacked. Moreover, they aimed to save Muslim countries such as Egypt and Saudi Arabia from the corrupt, pro-Western Arab leaders and establish an Islamic state. Ayman al-Zawahiri, the Egyptian confidant of Bin Laden, is another key personality who contributed to the establishment of Al Qaeda terror network. After Azzam's assassination in 1989 and Bin Laden's killing in 2011, al-Zawahiri remains the main strategist for al Qaeda today.

In 1990, Saddam's Iraqi forces invaded Kuwait, thus the US forces attacked Iraq, using Saudi Arabia as its base. Bin Laden tried to convince Saudi officials not to host the US combat troops in Saudi Arabia against an Iraqi invasion, but he could not succeed it. In 1991, 500,000 US troops were deployed to Saudi Arabia to expel Iraqi forces from Kuwait in "Operation Desert Storm" and 6,000 Air Force soldiers remained in the kingdom from 1991-2003. Bin Laden and his followers described this situation as the US occupation of the sacred Islamic lands. With his openly revealed view, Bin Laden was no longer a de facto US ally.

After the dispute with the Saudi royal family, Bin Laden settled down in Sudan and started to establish places to host and train Al Qaeda militants for "jihad" operations. He stayed in Sudan until 1996 when he was expelled by the Sudanese government under the pressure of the United States. Bin Laden and al-Zawahiri continued to establish and develop al Qaeda network to bring "Islamic regimes" to Muslim countries. They transformed Al Qaeda into a global terror organization in 1990s. Bin Laden moved to Afghanistan and established his main base of operations there from 1996-2001. During this period, Afghanistan became Al Qaeda's main base of operations. Then, on October 2001, the Taliban regime that ruled some part of Afghanistan was destroyed by Operation Enduring Freedom and the militants were driven out. Nine years after this operation, in the year 2010, the US mission aiming to destroy al Qaeda in Afghanistan was carried out by 98,000 U.S. forces and 41,000 forces from partner countries.

Throughout these years, the terrorist group continued its bloody attacks in many countries and killed many civilians, becoming a role model for the other radical terrorist groups with its 9/11 terrorist attacks. Indeed, the 9/11 attacks were part of their following five stage strategy to be realized until 2020:[240]

- A massive attack on the US soils,
- Local resistance to invading forces in Muslim lands,
- Spreading the conflicts to other countries,
- Recruiting members from other terrorist groups with al Qaeda ideology,
- Instigating a global jihad and establishing a Wahhabi caliphate.

Today, it is questioned whether al Qaeda still exists after these operations and the assassination of Bin Laden.

Doctrines of Al Qaeda

It is still disputable what al Qaeda wants and how its ideology is connected with it. It is generally accepted that al-Qaeda has the same agenda with the other political Islamist movements which is restoring Muslim dignity and establishing the Islamic law. Violence and terrorism separates terrorist groups from the Islamic movements. Al Qaeda uses terror and violence to achieve its goals. According to the leaders of this group, America's superpower imposes its cultural hegemony and global political influence on Islamic countries through overwhelming conventional military power. With this argument, radical terrorist groups keep fueling the anger of their militants and instigating them to commit bloody attacks against civilians. Moreover, they argue that the United States has attacked the Muslim world for a long time, subjugated its lands

---

[240] Atwan, Abdel Bari. *The Secret History of Al Qaeda*, University of California Press, 2006. p. 221

and dishonored its people. They claim that jihad is, therefore, every man's duty to defend their country, people and honor against the enemy.

The leaders of al Qaeda claim that the crusader spirit runs in the blood of all westerners. They argue, therefore, that the war is against the entire western world and that the conspiracy against Muslims can be stopped by this "jihad." Their first target is the secular Arab regimes which advocate western culture. Israel and the United States are Al Qaeda's next targets, but they come only after the secular Arab regimes are destroyed. Bin Laden ultimately aimed to end the US hegemony in Muslim countries so that those pro-Western regimes in the Muslim world could be collapsed, claiming that the kingdoms in the Arab world could not survive without the US support.

"Jihad" is a key concept in all terrorist movements. Although jihad has many meanings and usage in Islamic traditions, radical groups insist on interpreting it only as actual warfare. Indeed, jihad is primarily an individual's spiritual struggle against his or her own evil instincts. However, al Qaeda understands jihad only in military sense and never hesitates to declare it against other Muslims who do not agree to its doctrines. They killed many Muslims with this mindset.

The vast majority of the Muslim population is against all kinds of violence and terrorism; therefore, they are America's natural partners in the struggle against al Qaeda and similar terrorist movements. If the US separates moderate Muslims from radical ones, their fight against global terrorism will be successful. Indeed, the United States will get a great support from moderate Islamic scholars and community leaders in its fight against terrorism. In order to prevent new members from joining al Qaeda or other terrorist groups' ranks, Muslim scholars must speak loudly and clearly against terrorism and the US can benefit from it greatly.

Historically, the medieval Hanbali scholar Ibn Taymiyya (1263-1328) is an important reference for today's radical groups. In his time, the bloody Mongols were attacking the Muslim lands even after a great number of the Mongols converted to Islam. In order to justify the fight against some Muslims (Mongols in his case), Ibn Taymiyya argued that the Mongol rulers used their tribal law along with the Islamic law; they were thus apostates, and were consequently the legitimate targets of jihad. The contemporary terrorist groups use the same argument when killing other Muslims and cite Ibn Taymiyya as "an authority" for their jihad against contemporary Muslim rulers. This is because they deem these rulers apostates for they fail to impose the Islamic law exclusively.

Al Qaeda argues that Muslims were defeated by the west due to the corruption of not only the rulers, but also the Muslim masses. They maintain, therefore, that if Muslims practice Islam as it was practiced during the golden age of the Noble Prophet, they would be prosperous again. Returning to the pristine form of Islam is a key concept in the ideology of all radical groups for it sounds very attractive to the ignorant minds. They aim to unite and mobilize Muslims against the cultural and political domination of the West. In order to suppress different opinions, they condemn "other" Muslims with disbelief when they disagree with their ideology.

The jihad against the Soviet occupation of Afghanistan from 1979 to 1989 played a pivotal role to conceptualize the radical ideologies in terrorist groups. Ayman al-Zawahiri wrote prolifically to persuade Muslims to fight against all enemies. However, he was condemned by the scholars of Al-Azhar University in Egypt. Nevertheless, he became a leader of one of the Egyptian Jihad groups. Al-Zawahiri and Bin Laden worked together during the jihad against the Soviets. These two men merged their groups in 1998 and became a global terror organization threatening the United States. Today, al-Zawahiri remains Bin Laden's successor as the new leader of al Qaeda. Al-Zawahiri identified the goals of al Qaeda as creating a strong ideology and unity among Muslims and then establishing an Islamic state which can fight against the existing regimes of the Muslim world. At this stage, al Qaeda's jihad is revolutionary struggle through violence and terror against the secular Muslim regimes and the secularized Muslim elites. They seek to increase the support for their movement among Muslims by attacking the super power.

For al Qaeda, the current Arabian regimes are the real target; thus, Zawahiri wanted to encourage moderate Muslims as well in their radical cause which is fighting against these regimes in the Muslim world. In order to convince the Muslim masses to his ideology he explains his aim as "the empowerment of the true Muslims in the world theatre." In this way, he uses political and religious propaganda and action quite effectively. He argues that the Sharia is not practiced anywhere in the Muslim world; therefore, Muslims have reverted to the *Jahiliyyah* – the pre-Islamic Age of Ignorance. To return to the pure form of Islam, they argued that Muslims should establish a true Islamic State and implement the Sharia. They also need to save Muslims from the foreign influences because enemies of Islam have plotted conspiracies in the Muslim world and opposed Islam wickedly.

One of the dangerous concepts all radical groups, including al Qaeda, use is that Muslims are not true Muslims; rather, they are apostates. This approach opens the way for them to kill "other" Muslims whenever they oppose their radical ideology. Although it is strongly prohibited to kill the innocent civilians, this misinterpretation gives them a justification for it. Since al Qaeda has the Wahhabi tendency in its ideology, it condemns the Shiites for heresy. In this sick ideology, jihad against all "other" Muslims, Sunni or Shiite alike, becomes a religious obligation.

Conclusion

Al Qaeda is a global terrorist organization which seeks to launch a global war between the east and the west. It has established its organization on a global basis that is familiar with its environment and knows how to deal with the reality of situation. Al Qaeda's organizational structure can be analyzed in the following three layers:

The first layer is the central command of al-Qaeda located in Afghanistan. This layer is the core which establishes and maintains the ideology. The leaders, such as Bin Laden, al-Zawahiri, Atiyya Abdul Rahman and Abu Yahya al-Libi, have explained the ideology of this group and the core layer spread the message through media and other channels. This unit publishes the messages of al Qaeda regarding the ongoing events and declares war against those Muslim scholars who disagree with them, labeling them as terrorists.

The second layer is the regional branches that are located mostly in the Mesopotamian region, the Maghreb countries, the Arabian Peninsula, and the Horn of Africa. For instance, Al Qaeda has created close relationships with the Somalian Shabab terrorist group and the latter announced their allegiance to al-Qaeda.

The third layer can be considered as all those al-Qaeda supporters and sympathizers around the world. These individuals or local cells are not directly connected to the central leadership but rather act independently. This makes it difficult to understand the actual numbers of al Qaeda members. Although these individuals never declare their allegiance to the central body of al Qaeda, they continuously support its wars at all levels, including media, finance and military because they have sympathy to the radical ideology of al Qaeda. Unfortunately, the sympathizers of al Qaeda and other terrorist organizations are increasing significantly throughout the world.

Violence and terrorism in Islamic history goes back to the Kharijites in the 7th century. Since then, individuals with violent inclinations have developed extreme religious doctrines to justify their evil acts. One of the key concepts all terrorist groups, including al Qaeda, have used is the notion of *takfir* which can be translated as the "excommunication" of other Muslims or condemning them with disbelief due to their disagreement with the radical groups. With this extremist doctrine it becomes legal to kill other Muslims though this is strongly prohibited in Islam. Radical groups have been misinterpreting the Qur'an and the Sunnah to create a basis for their violence and terror. After deeming "other" Muslims as unbelievers or apostates, al Qaeda legitimizes killing them. In this regard, the religious scholars who disagree with them as well as those former fighters and militants who have turned against al Qaeda are killed in accordance with their evil *takfir* concept.

The development of the notion of militant jihad is a result of the erosion of religious concepts and their misinterpretation by the radical groups. Islam limits warfare for a just cause and mostly for defense.

Moreover, it strongly opposes the usage of *takfir*. However, the radical terrorist groups claim that any leader who does not implement and follow the Islamic law as they understand it is an apostate. Violent uprisings to remove rulers are strongly prohibited in Islam, but radical groups believe that it is a religious duty to wage war against rulers who refuse to implement the law. Indeed, a great part of the Islamic law can be practiced by the individual practicing Muslims without even needing a ruler. The radical groups violate the most important part of the Islamic law by killing innocent people. In Islam, civilians cannot be targeted in a war. However, al Qaeda targets anyone who lives according to democratic or secular values. This is clearly opposite to the Islamic law.

Although the support for al-Qaeda has dropped in the Muslim world, the other terrorist groups such as ISIS have taken its place and continue to receive support from radical individuals all over the world. If radicalization and terror phenomena are not addressed with truly effective methods, it will continue to persist globally. To this end, the United States and the West should work together with moderate Muslim scholars and produce authentic solutions for the problem.

AL SHABAB

Introduction

Al-Shabab, which literally means "the Youth," is an al-Qaeda-linked militant group in Somalia. It is a terrorist organization which aims to establish an Islamic State on the basis of radical interpretation of Islam. This group is also known as Harakat al-Shabab al-Mujahidin which means "the Movement of Warrior Youth." Although the African Union military campaign has weakened the group considerably in recent years, al Shabab still remains the principal threat in Somalia. This group has committed terrorism and violence mainly on targets within Somalia, but it has also carried out deadly strikes in the neighboring lands.

The terrorist group which is based in East Africa pledged allegiance to al Qaeda in 2012.[241] The group's military strength was estimated to be from 7,000 to 9,000 militants in 2014.[242] Al Shabab left major cities in Somalia in 2015. Currently, it is active in rural areas.[243] This terrorist group is an off-shoot of Islamic Courts Union which split into many smaller fractions after its defeat in 2006.[244] It continues to evolve into being extremely militant and has been inspired by the Somalian Islamic scholars who were trained in Saudi Arabia as the advocates of Wahhabism. Thus, Al Shabab is very hostile to all Sufi traditions.

Al Shabab deems itself as a group who fights against "enemies of Islam." It waged war against the Federal Government of Somalia and the African Union Mission. This group has been recognized as a terrorist organization by the US, Australia, and many other democratic countries. Al Shabab has links with Boko Haram and Al-Qaeda in Maghreb countries. The group has managed to recruit members from western countries as well.

Al Shabab has decentralized leadership structure. The leaders in local villages follow religious scholars who interpret the Qur'an and the Sunnah in a militant sense. Thus, it has adopted bloody, armed struggle against its enemies. The group was in conflict with the local moderate Muslim scholars but eliminated them in time. In 2007, al Shabab announced Sheikh Mukhtar Abdirahman Abu Zubayr as its leader. However, he was killed by the US operation in 2014. Currently, the group has some autonomous leaders, including Adan Hashi Ayrow, who is active in Mogadishu and

---

[241] "Al-Shabab joining al Qaeda, monitor group says." *CNN.* February 9, 2012. Retrieved April 4, 2016. http://edition.cnn.com/2012/02/09/world/africa/somalia-shabaab-qaeda/

[242] "Jihadist groups across globe vying for terror spotlight." *Fox News.* July 10, 2014. Retrieved April 4, 2016. http://www.foxnews.com/world/2014/07/10/world-worst-jihadist-groups-across-globe-vie-for-terror-spotlight.html

[243] "UN Points to Progress in Battling Al-Shabab in Somalia." *VOA.* January 3, 2015. Retrieved April 4, 2016. http://www.voanews.com/articleprintview/2584631.html

[244] Ali, Abdisaid M. 2008, "The Al-Shabab Al-Mujahidiin: A profile of the first Somali terrorist organization." Retrieved April 4, 2016. http://www.isn.ethz.ch/Digital-Library/Publications?v21=107785&lng=en&ord61= alphanavi&ord60=publicationdate&id=55851

central Somalia, Mukhtar Roobow, who operates mainly in the Bay and Bakool regions, and Hassan Abdillahi, who operates mainly in Lower and Middle Jubba regions in the South. Ayman al-Zawahiri, the al-Qaeda leader, has great influence on al Shabab terrorist group.

Al Shabab has members from various ethnicities, but its leadership positions are mainly occupied by the Somalians who were trained in Afghanistan and Iraq.[245] Moreover, its operational militants are primarily concerned with nationalist and clan-related affairs. The foreign members are mainly from Yemen, Sudan, the Swahili Coast, Afghanistan, Saudi Arabia, Malaysia, Pakistan, and Bangladesh.

It is speculated that al Shabab also has foreigners at the leadership level.[246] It calls international jihadists to join them in the war against the Somalian government and its Ethiopian allies. The foreigners made several suicide bombings to help this group to achieve its targets.[247] Al Shabab has attracted a large cadre of Western members.[248] In 2011, the group has attempted to recruit from the Muslim communities in the western countries and had success to a certain degree.[249] For instance, a significant number of the UK residents were trained by this group.[250] The foreign recruits played a pivotal role with regards to serving as mercenaries and as a propaganda tool for radicalization and recruitment.

---

[245] "Al Shabab tries to take control in Somalia." http://www.fpri.org/enotes/201011.shinn.somalia.html#note10

[246] "The rise of the Shabab." *The Economist*, Dec 18, 2008. Retrieved April 4, 2016. http://www.economist.com/node/12815670

[247] Duhul, Salad. (2008-10-29). "Suicide bombs kill 22 in northern Somalia, UN hit." *San Diego Union Tribune*. http://legacy.sandiegouniontribune.com/news/world/20081029-0635-af-somalia.html

[248] Kron, Josh (October 21, 2011). "African Union Peacekeepers Killed in Somalia Battle." *The New York Times*. Retrieved April 4, 2016. http://www.nytimes.com/2011/10/22/world/africa/african-union-takes-casualties-in-somalia-but-numbers-vary.html?_r=0

[249] Horowitz, Alana (July 27, 2011). "Al Qaeda Group Al Shabaab Recruited Muslim Americans: U.S. Report." *Huffington Post*. Retrieved April 4, 2016. http://www.huffingtonpost.com/2011/07/27/al-qaeda-american-recruits_n_911432.html

[250] Evans, Jonathan (September 17, 2010). "Speech delivered by Jonathan Evans, head of MI5 to the Worshipful Company of Security Professionals." *The Daily Telegraph*. Retrieved April 4, 2016. http://www.telegraph.co.uk/news/uknews/terrorism-in-the-uk/8008252/Jonathan-Evans-terrorism-speech.html

The Origins of al Shabab

The roots of al Shabab could be traced back to a group called al Salafiya al Jadid ("The New Salafists") which was established in 1970 to oppose the authoritarian socialist rule in Somalia. General Mohamed Siad Barre came to power through a military coup in 1969 and became the President of Somalia.[251] In order to defeat the coup leader, various groups were established by the opponents. The groups al Salafiya al Jadid ("The New Salafists") and then al Ittihad al Islamiya ("The Islamic Union") were established to destroy Siad Barre's oppressive dictatorship. They wanted to create an Islamic State in the Horn of Africa.[252]

In its early stage, these groups were composed primarily of young men who had studied in the Middle East. They received significant funding and support from the Wahhabi organizations in Saudi Arabia. These groups could not destroy the rule of the coup leader Siad Barre, but the warlord Mohamed Farrah Aidid overthrew him later in 1991. There was a chaos and political uncertainty from 1990-2000 in Somalia. The tribal warlords gained the control of most of the country. The Islamic Union also controlled several parts of the country and implemented the Islamic law according to their extremist interpretations. Under the leadership of Sheikh Mukhtar Robow Ali, they established the first militant jihadist training camp in Somalia in 1996.[253] Later, he became a commander in al Shabab.

---

[251] Ali, Abdisaid M. *The Al-Shabab Al-Mujahidiin – A Profile of the First Somali Terrorist Organisation*, Institut fur Strategie – Politik–Sicherheits– und Wirtschaftsberatung, June 2, 2008, available at http://www.isn.ethz.ch/isn/Digital-Library/Publications/Detail/?ots591=0 C54E3B3-1E9C-BE1E-2C24-A6A8C7060233&lng=en&id=55851

[252] Gartenstein-Ross, Daveed and Madeleine Gruen. "Understanding Al-Shabab," *CTR Vantage*, (Foundation for the Defense of Democracies), November 4, 2009, available at http://www.defenddemocracy.org/images/stories/Al-Shabaabs_Recruiting_Efforts_in_the_West.pdf

[253] Ali, Abdisaid M. *The Al-Shabab Al-Mujahidiin – A Profile of the First Somali Terrorist Organisation*, Institut fur Strategie – Politik–Sicherheits– und Wirtschaftsberatung, June 2, 2008, available at http://www.isn.ethz.ch/isn/Digital-Library/Publications/Detail/?ots591=0C54E3B3-1E9C-BE1E-2C24-A6A8C7060233&lng=en&id=55851

The Islamic Union conducted several terrorist attacks inside Ethiopia in 1996; thus, the Ethiopian military forces interfered and defeated the group and eradicated its safe heaven.[254] After this defeat the group started to operate through a network of cells. There is an allegation that the group has established its ties with al Qaeda and received some degree of training and logistical and financial support from it. In return, the group has provided protection to al Qaeda in East Africa.

In early 2000s, a small group that was dedicated to protecting al Qaeda in East Africa separated from the Islamic Union and established al Shabab terror group. Hassan Dahir Aweis was the military commander of this group. Al Shabab served as the military aspect of an emerging political force, called the Islamic Courts Union. The Sharia courts were set by the local clans to fill the gap after the collapse of the Siad Barre regime. Consequently, the Islamic courts system formed the Islamic Courts Union which played a major political role in Somalia. Hassan Dahir Aweis became the leader of one of these courts and acted as a spiritual leader. The Islamic Courts Union expanded its authority quickly throughout the southern and central parts of Somalia. This group declared "holy war" against Ethiopia; therefore, the military power of Ethiopia invaded Somalia in 2006 and drove the Islamic Courts Union from power.[255] After the invasion the leaders of this group fled to neighboring countries and the Islamic Courts Union separated itself from al Shabab.

Al Shabab is now operating independently and Sheikh Aadan Haashi 'Ayro is its commander. He divided al Shabab into three geographic operational commands, each led by a local leader. The local leaders listen to Ayro's advice but act autonomously. Al Shabab has used guerilla tactics

---

[254] Gartenstein-Ross, Daveed and Madeleine Gruen. "Understanding Al-Shabab," *CTR Vantage*, (Foundation for the Defense of Democracies), November 4, 2009, available at http://www.defenddemocracy.org/images/stories/Al-Shabaabs_Recruiting_Efforts_in_the_West.pdf.

[255] Menkhaus, "Violent Islamic Extremism." See also "Somali War Risks Turning into Regional Conflict," *Daily Nation* (of Kenya), December 27, 2006, available through World News Connection.

against its enemies and carried out political assassinations. This group has also introduced suicide attacks into Somalia.

In 2008, Ayro was killed by an American Tomahawk missile and Mukhtar Abu Zubayr took over the leadership of al Shabab. He released a message appreciating top al Qaeda leaders and their terrorist attacks. He announced a military campaign against the US, all western, and UN interests in Somalia. Al Shabab carried out many terrorist attacks on international targets in Somalia. They declared that their "holy war" would continue until all foreign troops were expelled from Somalia.

After separating from the Islamic Courts Union in 2007 al Shabab has carried out nearly 550 terrorist attacks, killing more than 1,600 and wounding over 2,100 people. The group expanded its terrorist attacks into Kenya and conducted 33 terrorist assaults there. The victims and targets of this terrorist group vary greatly, including civilians, their properties, military persons, government institutions and officers, businessmen, diplomats, journalists and the media. The foreign military bases and forces in Somalia are the targets of this group too; therefore, they have attacked military targets of various nations. They have extended their attacks to mass-casualty bombings like the terrorist attack they carried out in 2010 that killed many civilians who gathered to watch a World Cup soccer game in Kampala, Uganda. Al Shabab has used various terror tactics, such as hit and run attacks, explosive devices, assassinations and suicide bombings, and killed many civilians.

The 2006 Ethiopian invasion of Somalia has a profound effect on al Shabab to be radicalized. It played a pivotal role to recruit thousands of nationalist volunteers against Ethiopia. Al Shabab has developed its guerrilla tactics as a means of resistance against all of its enemies. The gap in the governance has given more opportunity to al Shabab to operate safely throughout Somalia. It has built many camps to train its militants. By gaining the trust of local people al Shabab is able to raise funds for its operations. After establishing ties with al Qaeda, al Shabab increased its legitimacy and resources; they changed their warfare ideology into a global war against the West. Al Qaeda affected the leadership structure of al Shabab as well as its operational strategy. They conduct suicide attacks against civilians in Somalia. They use social media and internet to recruit new members and receive support from the global terror funders.

Doctrines of al Shabab

Today, al Shabab is the most powerful terrorist group in Somalia with its well-armed and well-trained militia. It has strong political power and operates as a shadow government throughout the country. With the claim of establishing Islamic State in Somalia, al Shabab received considerable support from the south central population of the country and transformed itself into a global terrorist organization. It aims to apply a rigid form of Islamic law according to the Wahhabi understanding. In this regard, they banned music, videos, and shaving beards and punished the offenders publicly by stoning, amputations and beheadings.

Al Shabab aims to establish a caliphate according to the mindset of the Wahhabi sect in the Horn of Africa. Resorting to violence and terror, they want to create a Wahhabi stronghold in Somalia. Saudi scholars who teach Wahhabi doctrines are influential upon the members of this movement. The group emphasizes the notion of martyrdom and introduces it as the greatest and most exalted degree of jihad among its militants. It argues the God promised the martyrs marriage to 72 virgins, the right to interc with God to bring 70 family members to Heaven, and the enjoymer pleasures in Heaven. By misinterpreting religious concepts, al Sh legitimizes its terror acts and receives great support from ignorant yc Muslim masses.

After the United States designated al Shabab as a terrorist organization Sheikh Mukhtar Roobow, the spiritual leader of the group, issued a message stating that fighting against foreign forces who invaded Somalia is a religious obligation. He argued that if the US condemns them, this only increases their values in the eyes of God. With this sort of slogans, a Shabab created a strong profile among other radical groups and received financial and material support from them.

Al Shabab is a radical terrorist group who advocates turning back to the pristine form of Islam as it was practiced during the Prophet and the first four caliphs of Islam. They argue that Muslim world has deviated from the right path because there are un-Islamic states throughout the Islamic world. It is a duty upon all Muslims to establish an Islamic state and come together under the rulership of one caliph. Al Shabab is heavily influenced by the Wahhabi interpretations; thus, its doctrines are closely related with the Wahhabi ideology. They put emphasis upon strict scriptural authority of the Qur'an and the Sunnah. However, with their resorting to terror and violence they clearly contradict to the Holy Book and the Prophetic Practice. Obviously, their Islamic State set up upon the Wahhabi understanding can be described as a tribal interpretation of Islam. In other words, they try to legitimize their own violence with the Qur'an and the Sunnah.

Al Shabab established alternative ministries and regional administration within its territorial control, implementing its way of Islamic law with armed forces. Thus, it is difficult for the public to oppose their judgments. Al Shabab often establishes a local consulting body from clan elders, but the ruler is not obliged to obey their advice.

In order to be able to maintain its activities al Shabab applies tax on commercial transactions wherever it can. Although it is strongly prohibited [in] Islam, al Shabab makes money from kidnapping people and charging [high] ransoms for them. Prescribed almsgiving (*zakat*) and charity (*sadaqa*) [are a] regular revenue source for this group. They keep collecting *zakat* inside [and] outside Somalia from agricultural produce, livestock, precious metals [and] other minerals. Although the Qur'an commands believers to distribute *zakat* among eight groups of people to remove poverty from society, al Shabab distributes it only among its militants; therefore, some businessmen opposed this unjust practice. However, they have to pay it considering the heavy pressure of the armed group.

Al Shabab receives donations and charity from both Somalian and foreign sympathizers for its cause. They call this cause as "holy war in God's way" and label the reluctant people who do not want to give donations as weak Muslims and then kill them. Just like all other radical groups, "fighting" in the way of God to make His religion dominant in the world is a key concept in al Shabab's ideology. The group benefits from al Qaeda's ideology to recruit new members and uses their arguments in its war propaganda. The foreign interference in Somalia to bring peace to the region is understood as the attacks on Islam. The group labels foreign elements as African crusaders who want to spread Christianity and all falsehood in the region. They argue that the "apostates" help the foreign forces to destroy Islam; therefore, they are disgraced and will face tremendous torture in Hell. The group promotes patriotism mixed with Islamic duties and exploits religious concepts effectively.

Conclusion

Al Shabab is an extremist terrorist group threatening world peace. Its structural organization is similar to al Qaeda. It has strong leadership, technical expertise and militants from all around the world willing to die for its cause. Al Shabab controls a large part of Somalia and governs it just like the Taliban does in Afghanistan. It has borrowed many elements in its ideology and strategy from al Qaeda and the Taliban. The militants are trained and prepared by the group's administrative organization for terror attacks. Al Qaeda also trained the militants in advance on combat and guerrilla warfare tactics by taking part in a number of combat operations against the American forces. Thus, al Qaeda has a profound effect on al Shabab's structure and operational strategy. In this regard, the group carried out suicide attacks as a means to achieve its goals. Additionally, al Shabab has a close link with the training of the members of Nigeria's terrorist group Boko Haram (meaning, "Western education is unlawful"). This is because Boko Haram is also financially sponsored by al Qaeda and al Shabab.

Currently, al Shabab aims to expand its control in Somalia and desires to develop its capacity of terrorist attacks in international arena. Thus, it has threatened the West. In 2013, its militants killed over 80 people in one of the shopping malls in Nairobi, Kenya. The victims were the citizens of

France, Canada, the United States, the United Kingdom, Australia, New Zealand, and Ghana. This terrorist attack was the retribution for Kenya's military operations against the terrorist group in Somalia. It can also be understood as a global terror campaign that fits to the ideology of Bin Laden, Ayman al-Zawahiri and Abdullah Azzam. The world has become a global village and terrorism and radicalism have spread all over the world with this ongoing process. Therefore, before waging a war against any terrorist group it is a must to understand its power, command and relationships with the global terror network.

Al Shabab and other terrorist groups use religious concepts to legitimize their violence and killings; therefore, they give harm to Islam and Muslims the most. In order to receive support from Muslim population they put their emphasis upon the notion of jihad against the western imperialism and its occupations in Muslim lands. Unfortunately, many ignorant young people have joined their ranks to "serve" Islam, but they have given harm to the Muslim world the most with all their evil acts. It is clear that religion can be used as a lethal weapon in the hands of radical groups. Thus, moderate Muslim scholars must contribute to the Western world's fight against radicalism and terrorism. Similarly, the Western world must consult with Muslim leaders and scholars to develop its strategy together in its fight against extremism.

The terrorist groups usually take the advantage of weak governments and establish their violent terrorist organizations in uncontrolled regions. The advantage of al Shabab is its having control over a great part of Somalia. The official government does have neither the resources nor the capacity to pose a serious challenge to the group. This has allowed al Shabab to set up training camps in order to get better prepared for its insurgency and terrorist operations. After being exposed to brainwashing through its extreme ideology, the militants receive instruction on how to make and detonate bombs and carry out terrorist attacks. Al Shabab will maintain its capacity to train new members for further terrorist attacks unless it is successfully destroyed. However, the military success against al Shabab is not a real solution; rather, Muslim scholars must refute their exploitation of religious elements in their extremist ideology in order for them not to be able to recruit new members.

BOKO HARAM

Introduction

Boko Haram, which literally means "western education is forbidden," is a terrorist group active in Nigeria,[256] committing terrorist activities also through the neighboring countries of Niger, Chad, and Cameroon. This extremist group claims that western type of education paves way to the modern corrupt life of Nigerian politics; it is un-Islamic, and thus needs to be prohibited. The Boko (westernized) schools in Nigeria were first introduced by the British, and many religious leaders in the country opposed them for they perceived the schools as a trap to wean vulnerable youth away from Islam. They suspected that boko education would take their children away from the proper religious values that made up the society.

The group refers to itself as both "The Islamic State in West African Province" and "The Group of the People of Sunnah for Preaching and Jihad."[257] The origins of Boko Haram go back to Mohammed Yusuf, an Islamic scholar who misread and interpreted the Qur'an and the Sunnah very rigidly. In 1990s, he educated many radical young scholars in Maiduguri, the state capital of Borno in north-eastern Nigeria, and this gave roots to the movement. In 2002, Mohammed Yusuf and his followers protested the corruption of Nigerian society and aimed to establish an Islamic state where Islamic law could be practiced.[258] Since then, there has been tension and dispute between moderate and radical groups in Nigeria.

---

[256] Bureau of Counter terrorism. *Country Reports on Terrorism 2013*, The US Department of State. Retrieved on April 14, 2016. http://www.state.gov/j/ct/rls/crt/2013/224829.htm.

[257] "Is Islamic State shaping Boko Haram media" *BBC.* March 4, 2015. Retrieved April 14, 2016. http://www.bbc.com/news/world-africa-31522469.

[258] Loimeier, R. "Boko Haram: The Development of a Militant Religious Movement in Nigeria." *Africa Spectrum.* 47, pp. 2-3, 2012.

Initially, Yusuf wanted to reform society based on traditional Islamic understanding, but in time his group has turned into a radical and militant movement.[259] The terrorist group has been attacking the Nigerian civilians, Muslims and Christians alike, military troops and government officials and the foreigners in the country.

The extremist terrorist group has long become the symbol of the security crisis in the country. However, it became infamous when its followers kidnapped 200 school girls in 2014. Since 2009, the militants of this group have killed 20,000 people and displaced another 2.3 million people from their homes. It was thus considered as the world's deadliest terrorist group by the Global Terrorism Index in 2015.[260] Its attacks have become increasingly lethal. In 2009, they attacked the United Nations compound and killed over 20 civilians. It was in the same year that Yusuf and several others were arrested due to sectarian fights and clashes with the police. They were killed by the police while in custody and hundreds of his followers were jailed. The remnants of Boko Haram fled to neighboring countries to recruit and regroup. After a year, the group performed an attack on a prison and freed several hundred Boko Haram inmates. Boko Haram has killed many Muslim civilians in its "purification" campaign along with political figures, secular opposition figures, prominent clerics, and opponent preachers. In 2010, Boko Haram recruited more new members and conducted significantly more sophisticated terrorist attacks on the government. Currently, the terrorist group is commanded by Abubakar Shekau, who announced their allegiance to the ISIS (or ISIL) in 2015.

Traditionally speaking, Nigerian Muslim parents send their children to Islamic schools. It is in this context of situation that Boko Haram has rejected western civilization and aimed to eradicate its influence on people in the country. Thus, it has targeted to recruit especially those young

---

[259] Barna, Judit. *Insecurity in context: The rise of Boko Haram in Nigeria.* Policy Department, Directorate-General for External Policies, July 2014, p. 3.
[260] *Global Terrorism Index 2015* (PDF). Institute for Economics and Peace. November 2015. p. 41. Retrieved April 14, 2016. http://economicsandpeace.org/wp-content/uploads/2015/11/Global-Terrorism-Index-2015.pdf.

students sent away by their parents to travel between various religiously-trained teachers.[261] Mohammed Yusuf, the founder of Boko Haram, utilized this and built an Islamic school in Maiduguri in the state of Borno. He educated these students with radical doctrines, rejecting the West and its civilization. He misread and interpreted the Qur'an in a very strict manner, arguing that Muslims need to be purified from all false beliefs and foreign influence. He aimed to overthrow the secular Nigerian government and establish an Islamic state instead.

Indeed, the low socioeconomic circumstances have provided the golden opportunity for Boko Haram to recruit many more young militants on account of religious radicalism. Additionally, the group has achieved to attain public support due to the massive corruption in the secular government. Moreover, travelling preachers and orators have recruited numerous followers for the radical Boko Haram group. The societal and economic problems as well as the regional history are indeed the basis for radicalism in Africa. In this respect, the presence of oil, corrupt government officials, western colonization and a history of Islamic prominence need to be well understood when examining the evolution of Boko Haram into a terror organization.

It is also to be noted that fighting against corruption and despotism through militant methods is not something new in Nigeria. At the beginning of the nineteenth century, people of the region became extremely dissatisfied with the corrupt government and established a caliphate in 1804, implementing the Islamic law. Historically, the powerful Islamic caliphate governance had important reference for Nigeria's Muslims. Thus, they believe that caliphate and the Islamic law played important roles with regards to uniting Muslims and creating prosperity. Boko Haram has made full use of this historical fact to establish its movement against the corruption and western influence. It calls for "true Islam" to end the poverty and corrupt political system. It rejects the rich political elite who have been driven by their desire for more wealth.

---

[261] Goodluck, I. and J. Juliana. "Provision of Formal Education to Almajiris: Role of Libraries." *European Scientific Journal*, 8/15.

Religion is a prominent identifying feature in the lives of Nigerians, and violence between religious groups is often witnessed. Each group resorts to violence to reach its goals. Each side wants to have the control over the country's most prized natural resource. In this regard, the presence of oil reserves in Nigeria has escalated the divisions, disputes and fights. What's more, social services, public safety and education are provided at a very low level in Nigeria for the elites keep most of the revenue from the oil for themselves. In addition, high unemployment rate is the source of constant societal unrest along with massive government corruption and human rights violations. Under these conditions, Muslims see Islam as the only way to their prosperity and success, but Boko Haram and other terrorist groups have misread the Islamic sources, interpreting them very radically in an attempt to justify their violence and terrorist acts.

As a matter of fact, inspired by al Qaeda, Boko Haram has used its terror tactics, including suicide attacks, coordinated bombings of multi-locations and the release of martyrdom videos made by suicide bombers, to achieve its goals. For instance, the first terrorist group that used suicide attacks in Africa was al Qaeda, and Boko Haram has adopted its method. Actually, it has improved al Qaeda's methods over the years. To this end, it has released videos promoting the establishment of an Islamic state, thus attracting the support of other radical groups around the world.

The terrorist group has a "purification" campaign which contains political and religious elements. While fighting against the Nigerian state, the group refers to the religious concepts and claims to work towards establishing a purely Islamic state. By implementing the Islamic law, the group aims to end the poor governance as well as the sharp socio-economic inequality in Nigerian society.

Origins of Boko Haram

Boko Haram emerged in the early 2000s under the leadership of Mohammed Yusuf. The group originally consisted of Yusuf and his students, but later grew up by the participation of many unsatisfied

Nigerian people.²⁶² Mohammed Yusuf, who was a prominent Islamic scholar and preacher at the Haji Muhammadu Ndimi Mosque in Maiduguri, capital of Borno state, educated a youth group at the mosque. He was a charismatic and popular scholar. He argued that the western-type education is in obvious contradiction with the Qur'an; therefore, it should be forbidden.²⁶³ He struggled to implement the Islamic law in several northern states of Nigeria in the early 2000s. However, he could not succeed it, thus he called the youth for an "authentic" Islamist revolution.²⁶⁴

During the emergence of Boko Haram, there were many radical groups that intensely debated political Islam. They all shared a common goal which was establishing an Islamic state and implementing the Islamic law. The Boko Haram group also wanted to promote the purist vision of Islam based on the Islamic law, eradicating heretical innovations. Its main goal was the establishment of an Islamic state. Mohammed Yusuf wanted to implement the law in some northern states but failed. This failure increased the anger of young Muslims, accusing the government with deception. Then Yusuf called his followers for an "authentic Islamist revolution,"²⁶⁵ and this call attracted public attention. This way, "Boko Haram" started with the formal name of "Jama'tu Ahlis Sunna Lid-Da'awati wal-Jihad" (The group who follows the traditions of the Prophet and propagates it through jihad).²⁶⁶

The campaign for an Islamic government and strict adherence to Islamic law is a common goal among all radical groups.²⁶⁷ Revivalist movements periodically emerge in Islamic world as a reaction to secular governments. Similarly, Boko Haram has rejected secular authority and clashed with the police for this cause. It has taken radical ideas from al

---

²⁶² Walker, Andrew. *"What is Boko Haram?"* US Institute of Peace (USIP), June 2012, p. 3.
²⁶³ Crisis Group Middle East/North Africa Report N°37, *Understanding Islamism*, March 2, 2005, pp. 9-14.
²⁶⁴ Ostebo, "Islamic Militancy in Africa", *Africa Security Brief*, No. 23, November 2012, pp. 4-5.
²⁶⁵ Ostebo, ibid.
²⁶⁶ Iornongu Ker, David. *Diagnostic Review of Insurgency in Nigeria: The Cultural Dimension*, p. 130.
²⁶⁷ Falola, Toyin and Matthew M. Heaton, *A History of Nigeria* (Cambridge, 2008), p. 206.

Qaeda and other similar terrorist groups. In order to address the ills of society, corruption and bad governance, the extremist group has promoted the idea of a pure Islamic state and presented it as the true solution for people. Its members have resorted to violence and terrorism in the name of achieving this goal. Ironically, while they wanted to be good Muslims, they committed the very acts that are considered the most wicked in Islam. With all their evil acts, the group turned into a brutal organization.

At the beginning, Yusuf criticized the ruling elite without resorting to violence. In his sermons, he denounced corruption, impunity, and government failures to the general admiration of the local population. These sermons became an important source of inspiration for the group. Yusuf formed an alliance with some political figures with the expectation that he would implement Islamic law and appoint some of his followers to important governmental positions.[268] However, disappointed by the politicians, he began to direct sermons against them and labeled them as "apostates."

In 2009, the dispute between Boko Haram and the secular government increased and the group attacked police stations and headquarters as well as the officers' homes. The state security forces killed over 800 Boko Haram members and captured Yusuf. He was handed over to the police and was killed shortly thereafter at the police headquarters. After this murder, Boko Haram went underground for a year and then surfaced with attacks on police stations and military barracks to take revenge. The terrorist group expanded its attacks on critical Muslim clerics, traditional leaders, Christian people, suspected collaborators, UN agencies, and secular schools. The militants started to kill the politicians as well. The group has recruited criminals and local youth, paying them for their attacks, sometimes with a share of the spoils. They have also kidnapped important people to get large sums of ransom.

Boko Haram is a product of the problematic Nigerian demographics, history, politics and economics. The country has 36 states in six

---

[268] Olawale Albert, Isaac. "Explaining godfatherism in Nigerian politics," *African Sociological Review*, vol. 9, no. 2, 2005, pp. 95-96.

geopolitical zones. It has a diverse population with more than 250 distinct ethnic groups and over 500 languages and dialects spoken.[269] Religious diversity is similar to this ethnic diversity: the Muslims constitute about 50 percent of the population, the Christians 40 percent, and the other 10 percent practices various traditional animistic religions.[270]

Nigeria was under British colonial rule in the late 19th century. The western education was introduced in such a place where Islamic education was given for centuries with its own traditions. Thus, western education has been perceived as a threat and a symbol of British colonization. Nigeria obtained its independence from the United Kingdom in 1960, established a republic governing system. However, the 1966 military coup ended the democratic rule. Nigeria experienced civil war in 1967, resulting in about three million deaths.[271] In its independence history, Nigeria has seen military coups, short term democratic rules and dictators.

Although Nigeria is now the largest economy in Africa with the petroleum industry, agriculture and trade, the benefits of this economy go to a few Nigerians; thus, about 63 percent of the population remains in absolute poverty. This reinforces sectarian disputes and conflicts. The poverty rate was up to 70 percent in the northern region of the country where Boko Haram emerged.

Historically, Nigeria was introduced to Islam during the seventh century. Some local leaders have long attempted to implement the Islamic law in their area.[272] Some have launched an Islamic reform movement to

---

[269] Pate, Amy. *"Boko Haram: An Assessment of Strengths, Vulnerabilities, and Policy Options."* Report to the Strategic Multilayer Assessment Office, Department of Defense, and the Office of University Programs, Department of Homeland Security. College Park MD: START, January 2014.

[270] Pate, Amy. *"Boko Haram: An Assessment of Strengths, Vulnerabilities, and Policy Options."* Report to the Strategic Multilayer Assessment Office, Department of Defense, and the Office of University Programs, Department of Homeland Security. College Park MD: START, January 2014.

[271] Duruji, Moses Metumara. 2009. "Social Inequity, Democratic Transition and the Igbo Nationalism Resurgence in Nigeria." *African Journal of Political Science and International Relations*. 3:1. 54-65. http://www.academicjournals.org/article/article1379759106_Duruji.pdf.

[272] Sodiq, Yushau. 1992. "A History of Islamic Law in Nigeria: Past and Present." *Islamic Studies*. 31:1. 85-108.

remove the corrupt leaders and even declared jihad for this cause.[273] Contemporary revivalist movements often refer to these historical "jihadist struggles" to establish a caliphate which has both the political power and religious authority. Boko Haram emerged with similar arguments.

As it can easily be seen, there is no just one simple explanation for the rise of Boko Haram. However, it can be said that it is mainly the product of all these poor economic, political and social conditions in Nigeria. The situation will grow worse and the tension will escalate unless these problems are addressed effectively. Indeed, the Nigerian police brutality has also contributed a lot to the tensions. The police have killed hundreds of people every year but none of them was investigated, letting the public officials go with impunity. Nearly one thousand Boko Haram members were killed in custody only in the year 2013.

Doctrines of Boko Haram

Every movement has an ideology and identifies itself with it. Terrorist organizations develop their ideology from social realities such as oppression, poverty, disunity and injustice. Religion is a strong tool which unites individuals with each other. Radical groups often refer to such religious concepts as jihad, Sharia and an Islamic state to attract support from local people. Boko Haram is a terrorist organization which developed its ideology from Islamic concepts by misinterpreting the Qur'an and the Sunnah. They understand Islamic sources very literally and advocate a very strict adherence to their own interpretation of Islam. Moreover, they kill "other" Muslims simply because they disagree with their ideology just like the Kharijites did first in the early Islamic history.

Boko Haram strongly opposes the Western world and its education as they deem Western education as sinful, sacrilegious or ungodly, and should therefore be forbidden. They argue that in order to eliminate the influence

---

[273] Mahmud, Sakah Saidu. 2013. *Sharia or Shura: Contending Approaches to Muslim Politics in Nigeria and Senegal.* New York: Lexington Books. p. 18.

of the popular western culture, western education and interaction with the west must be forbidden. Ironically, Mohamed Yusuf, the leader of Boko Haram, enjoyed the best that Western technology offered him in the form of some exotic cars, the latest communication equipment and the best medical services. Additionally, he encouraged his followers to go abroad for medical training to be prepared for jihad against secular Nigerian state. For them, the secular governments are not Islamic and the politicians are not real Muslims. They oppose "other" Muslims, scholars and organizations and carry out assassinations if any of them criticizes them.

This terrorist group rejects science and scientific findings due to its opposition to western education. For example, they don't believe that the Earth is spherical for it is contrary to their religious understanding. It is funny that there is nothing in the Qur'an or the Sunnah supporting their argument. On the contrary, the Qur'an invites people to think, search and discover the truths in its many verses. Human intellect is an important tool to find the truth, including believing in one God. Without using human intellect and reasoning, one's belief is considered as blind imitation in Islam; therefore, the Qur'an strongly criticizes those who simply follow the steps of their ancestors without using their own intellect. Islam never opposes science; rather, it encourages people strongly to get engaged in it. Obviously, radical terrorist groups misread and misinterpret Islam. Unfortunately, ignorant young minds are not able to see their contradictions and judge them. Therefore, they are an easy target for the extremist terrorist organizations.

Boko Haram also rejects democratic governing system, aiming to establish their own caliphate. In order to reach their aim, they do not hesitate to use criminals and corrupt politicians. In reality, terrorists have strong inclinations to commit violence, but they cover that up with their use of religious concepts. They are hopeless to achieve their goals through peaceful methods, thus resorting to violence and terrorism. Boko Haram simply manipulates Nigerians' religious sensitivity. They impose their ideology on people to justify their violence. The loss of property and lives, the growing fear among public and the widespread religious sensitivity in Nigeria give Boko Haram sufficient grounds for advocating their "Islamic revivalism" as a solution. This call for religious revivalism has received great support, especially from the unsatisfied youth in Nigeria.

Having studied at the University of Medina, Saudi Arabia, and adopting the Wahhabi ideology, Mohamed Yusuf aimed to "reform" the society accordingly. His past with the Taliban prepared him for the leadership of Boko Haram. He vowed that he would not give up until establishing an "independent and just Islamic state." Throughout his life, he sought to impose the Islamic law all across the Nigerian states. He argued that Islamic state is the only solution for the massive poverty, inequality in educational and employment opportunities, governmental corruption and misuse of resources.

Conclusion

Boko Haram is a terrorist group in Nigeria with a trace of its ideological origins back to Imam Mohammed Yusuf (1970-2009). It opposes western education and culture. Yusuf preached that Western education is sinful for it is against Islamic teachings simply because western-type education came with the British colonization and with Christian missionaries. Thus, he believed that Nigeria is losing its Muslim identity to Western influence and Christianity. The elimination of all forms of Western influence and education has become a rallying cry for Boko Haram since its establishment in 2002. Yusuf further deemed all kind of sports unlawful, claiming that they lead to idol worshipping. After Yusuf, Abu Shekau emerged as the new leader of Boko Haram in 2010 and struggles to achieve their goals through violence and terrorism. In this regard, Boko Haram has carried out more than 600 terrorist attacks since 2010 and killed more than 3,800 people. This terrorist group mainly targets political and religious leaders, local churches, schools and government buildings.

Democracy was introduced to Nigeria in 1999, but it was perceived as an American product by the Muslims of northern Nigeria, where Boko Haram is very active, claiming that it would marginalize them. Boko

Haram leader Yusuf argued that employment in the Nigerian government was "haram" for Muslims because Nigeria was not an Islamic State.

The extremist group is against the secular Nigerian state and aims to destroy it, yearning for changing the secular system with a very rigid form of Islamic law. To this end, Mohammed Yusuf sought to create an Islamic State in northern Nigeria based on the model of the Taliban in Afghanistan. Although all of the twelve states in northern Nigeria have adopted the Islamic law since 2000, Yusuf criticized it as being not true form of Islamic law and accused the governors for their insincerity and for politicizing the law. Thus, he declared jihad to establish an "authentic" Islamic state in Nigeria, and if possible all over the world, through preaching his ideology. The terrorist group claims to unite Nigerian people under this Islamic state and rule them according to its religious principles. In order to actualize its goals, it has established financial, training, recruiting and logistical networks with other terrorist groups, including al Qaeda. The terrorist group has thus evolved from being a local problem to a global threat.

ISIS (OR ISIL) AND THE CALIPHATE

Introduction

The English word "caliphate" is a loanword of the Arabic term *khilāfa*, which literally means "coming after someone," thus taking his position in order to perform the legal and religious rights of the public on behalf of them.[274] It is also used in the meaning of "vicegerency"[275] and "successor"[276] in the Holy Qur'an. In Islam, Prophet Muhammad is the Seal of all Prophets,[277] and no one after him can take the place of the

---

[274] Al-Isfahani, Raghib. *Mu'jam Mufradat Alfaz al-Qur'an*, (Beirut: Dar al-Kutub al-Ilmiyya, 1997), p. 175.
[275] Qur'an 2: 30.
[276] Qur'an 35: 39.
[277] Qur'an 33: 40.

Prophet in his position as the Messenger of God. However, his position as a ruler can be represented by other Muslims for the Qur'an sates; "*O you who believe! Obey God and obey the Messenger and those from among you who are invested with authority...*"[278]

In Islamic history, the first ruler for Muslims was Prophet Muhammad, upon whom be peace and blessings, who became the head of the state for a cosmopolitan society, consisting of Jews, polytheist Arabs and Muslims. However, neither the Noble Prophet did state who would be the head of the state after his death nor the Qur'an assigned anyone for authority.[279] Choosing a ruler for Muslims is a political issue; therefore, it is left to the choice of people. After the death of the Noble Prophet, the Muslims of Makkah gathered around Abu Bakr while the Muslims of Medina around Sa'd ibn 'Ubada.[280] After long discussions Abu Bakr was elected as the first ruler of the Muslim population.[281] His title was *Khalifatu Rasul al-Allah* (Successor of the Messenger of God) which can be understood as the ruler who comes after the Noble Prophet. The first four caliphs, Abu Bakr (reigned 632–634), 'Umar (reigned 634–644), 'Uthman (reigned 644–656) and 'Ali (reigned 656–661) have been called as "The rightly guided caliphs" (*Khulafa ar-Rashidin*) by Sunni Muslims.[282] The determination of a title for the new leader was difficult for the early Muslim community. After the Noble Prophet, the Muslim community adopted two titles for Muslim rulers: the ruler of believers (*amir al-mu'minin*) and Successor of the Messenger of God (*Khalifatu Rasul al-Allah*).

Choosing a caliph in the first four personalities (namely Abu Bakr, 'Umar, 'Uthman and 'Ali) established three different selection methods: public election, designation by a previous caliph, and assigning a caliph by a council. In Islamic historical context, two different opinions emerged

---

[278] Qur'an 4: 59.
[279] Ibn Hanbal. *Musnad al-Imam Ahmad ibn Hanbal*, (Beirut: Dar al-Kutub al-'Ilmiyya, 1993), 6/63.
[280] Ibn Sa'd, Muhammad. *Kitab al-Tabaqat al-Kabir*, (London: Ta-Ha Publishers Ltd, 2012), 3/613-617.
[281] Ibn Hisham. *Sirah*, 2/657.
[282] Crone, Patricia and Martin Hinds. *God's Caliph: Religious Authority in the First Centuries of Islam*, (Cambridge and New York: Cambridge University Press, 1986), p. 5.

about choosing a leader for the early Muslim community. According to the Sunni scholars, Abu Bakr was the best candidate for Caliphate due to his seniority in Islam and his being the closest and most respected Companion of the Noble Prophet. On the other hand, the Shiites claim that 'Ali was the most suitable candidate for he was the closest relative of the Noble Prophet and he was designated as the successor by the Prophet.

Because of the political conditions of the time in Arabian Peninsula, the first four caliphs were chosen from among the Quraysh tribe. For the first time in the political history of Islam, the Kharijite sect separated from Caliph 'Ali to choose their own caliph.[283] Choosing a caliph from outside of the Quraysh bloodline became a controversial issue among Muslim scholars. There were two views on this matter. According to the first view, any person who has necessary qualifications and knows Islamic principles can be a ruler and a caliph.[284] The Kharijite and Mutazilate sects held this view. The second group, including many Sunni scholars, held that the caliph must be from the Quraysh.

Ibn Khaldun (1334-1406 CE) holds that the issues of politics and rulership are related to representing God's justice among His servants; therefore, whoever is capable of providing justice when ruling Muslims can be elected as a caliph.[285] He argues that at the gestation period of Islam, caliphs were chosen from the bloodline of Quraysh and they all tried their best to provide justice for all the citizens in the Islamic state, then it turned out to be a kingdom where obeying a caliph was accepted as if it is one of the pillars of Islamic creed.[286]

The institution of a caliphate had long been utilized by various Muslim nations throughout the Islamic history until it was abolished by the secular Turkish government in 1924. There are three views among Muslim scholars regarding the caliphate. The first view is that the caliphate is a

---

[283] Shahristani, *Al-Milal Wa'n-Nihal*, (Cairo: Maktabat al-Ḥusayn al-Tijariyah, 1948), 1/177.
[284] Ibn Ḥazm, Ali ibn Aḥmad. *Kitāb al-Fasl fi al-Milal wa-al-Ahwa' Wa'n-Nihal*, (Baghdad: Maktabat al-Muthanna, 1964), 4/89.
[285] Ibn Khaldun, *Muqaddimah*, trans. F. Rosenthal, (Princeton, NJ: Princeton University Press, 1967) 137.
[286] Ibn Khaldun, *Muqaddimah*, 155.

sacred institution; it is universal and necessary for all Muslims. The second view is that it is a political institution and was established according to the needs of Muslims. The third view is that there is no such an institution in Islam nor is there a real need for it.[287]

Mustafa Sabri Efendi (1869-1954), the last Ottoman Head of Religious Affairs (*Sheikh al-Islam*), held that caliphate is a religious and political leadership, and a caliph is a person who represents the Noble Prophet.[288] Mehmed Seyyid Bey (1873-1925), a member of the Grand National Assembly of Turkey from 1923-1925, agreed with Mustafa Sabri in the definition of caliphate, but he argues that the institution of caliphate came to an end after Ali ibn Abī Tālib, the fourth caliph of Islam. He based his argument upon a prophetic tradition: "The caliphate will last thirty years and then it will turn into kingdom."[289] He believed that the caliphate has a wise purpose but it follows the requirements of the time; therefore, it is the issue of administration and politics. He further maintained that when the Noble Prophet was on his deathbed, he did not mention anything about caliphate to his Companions, nor is it in the Qur'an.[290]

Contemporary scholar Ali Abdur Raziq holds that there is no basis for the caliphate in either the Qur'an or in prophetic traditions.[291] However, it is a fact that many Muslims are looking for a just ruler or a caliph who can unite all Muslims and end all the conflicts among them.[292] Probably, the conflicts and wars in the Muslim world have made them think this much about the notion of caliphate.

This desire for the unity of Muslims has long been exploited by many terrorist organizations in history. For example, in 1925, Taqiuddin al-Nabhani (1909–79), established the Hizb ut-Tahrir (Party of Liberation), in

---

[287] Ibn Khaldun, *Muqaddimah*, 137-196.
[288] Mustafa Sabri, *Hilafet ve Kemalizm*, (Istanbul: Arastırma Yayınları 1992), p. 73.
[289] Abu Dawud, *Sunan Abi Dawud*, Sunnah, (Beirut: Dar al-Kutub al-Ilmiyah, 2008), p. 9.
[290] Seyyid Bey, *Usul-i Fıkıh*, pp. 107-108.
[291] Liebl, Vernie. "The Caliphate," *Middle Eastern Studies*, 45 (2009), 3, pp. 373-391.
[292] START: Study of Terrorism and Response to Terrorism (College Park, MD, Program on International Policy Attitudes and University of Maryland), http://www.worldpublic opinion.org/pipa/pdf/apr07/START_Apr07_quaire.pdf.

Jordan to revitalize the institute of caliphate,[293] but he could not succeed it. In 1996, Mullah Mohammed Omar, the leader of Taliban, announced himself as the Commander of the Believers (Amir al-Mu'minin) and tried to revitalize the caliphate in his personality. His attempt was recognized by Osama bin Laden, pledging his personal loyalty to him as the legitimate ruler of the state of Afghanistan.[294] In mid-2006, Al-Qaeda declared that the Iraqi city of Ramadi was to be the capital of a new Islamic caliphate.[295] Then, ISIS, a more recently established terrorist group, declared caliphate in an area spanning Iraq and Syria and announced their leader, Abu Bakr al-Baghdadi, as their caliph.[296] Al-Baghdadi aims to resuscitate a modern version of the Abbasid caliphate that he hopes will be an apocalyptic agent to destroy the West and cleanse the Muslim world of the Shiite and Alawite apostasy.[297]

The Origins of ISIS

ISIS has its origins going back to the militant group Jama al-Tawhid wa'l-Jihad which was established by Abu Musab al-Zarqawi in 2000.[298] Initially, he fought against the Soviets in Afghanistan but then came to Jordan to fight against the monarchy there. He could not get any success in his fight against the Jordanian monarch; therefore, he moved to Afghanistan and established a militant training camp near Herat. When the US military forces invaded Afghanistan, he went to Iraq and built strong

---

[293] McQuaid, Julia V. "*The Struggle for Unity and Authority in Islam: Reviving the Caliphate?*" (Alexandria, VA: CNA Center for Strategic Studies, 2007), p. 21.

[294] Scheuer, Michael. "*The Pious Caliphate Will Start from Afghanistan*," Jamestown Global Terrorism Analysis, Vol. 2, No. 12, June 24, 2005.

[295] Fletcher, M. "How Life Returned to the Streets in a Showpiece City that Drove out Al Qaeda," UK, *London Times*, Aug. 31, 2007.

[296] Weaver, Matthew. "ISIS declares caliphate in Iraq and Syria," *The Guardian*, July 1, 2014.

[297] Celso, Anthony N. "Zarqawi's Legacy: Al Qaeda's ISIS Renegade," *Mediterranean Quarterly*, 26 (2015), pp. 21-41.

[298] Beauchamp, Zack. "ISIS, Islamic State or ISIL? What to call the group the U.S. is bombing in Iraq," *OSINT Journal Review*, September 17, 2014.

ties with the Iraqi Kurdish militant group Ansar al-Islam (Partisans of Islam).

Zarqawi led a campaign against the US military force and its other allies when they occupied Iraq in 2003. Five militant groups that were composed largely of Iraqis from the former regime, nationalists, tribal elements and many foreign fighters emerged in this campaign. They developed a militant network to expel the US occupation, destroy the Iraqi interim government and establish an Islamic state. Zarqawi used religious arguments to justify his fight against the enemies. He once expressed it clearly as follows:

> We will fight in the cause of God until His shariah prevails. The first step is to expel the enemy and establish the state of Islam. We would then go forth to reconquer the Muslim lands and restore them to the Muslim nation. I swear by God that even if the Americans had not invaded our lands together with the Jews, the Muslims would still be required not to refrain from jihad but go forth and seek the enemy until only God Almighty's shariah prevailed everywhere in the world.[299]

The insurgents led by Zarqawi not only used guerrilla tactics to achieve their targets, but also used suicide bombers targeting the Iraqi security forces, the leading political and religious figures, foreign civilian contractors, and the UN and humanitarian workers. Zarqawi also deemed the Iraqi Shiites as the enemy, naming them "the spying enemy" and fought against them. In order to get political and military support, he actively used internet for both his terror propaganda and recruiting new followers. Additionally, Zarqawi's volunteers not only posted messages from their leader, but also had some violent internet broadcasts of their militant acts like beheadings.

In 2004, Zarqawi joined al-Qaeda terrorist group which was led by Osama bin Laden. With this participation, al-Qaeda obtained a base they can attack the US soldiers. The terrorist group often emphasized the notion

---

[299] Hashim, Ahmed S. 2014, "The Islamic State: From al-Qaeda Affiliate to Caliphate" *Middle East Policy*, 11/4, 69-82.

of monotheism (*tawhid*) and the elimination of polytheism in their war propaganda. They deemed anyone who does not believe in one God as infidel (*kafir*) and, therefore, subject to excommunication and death. In order to encourage their followers in war against their enemy they put their emphasis on the so-called martyrdom (*shahada*). Zarqawi outlined the targets of al-Qaeda as defeating foreign forces in Iraq, promoting the notion of monotheism, liberating Muslims lands from infidels and establishing Caliphate to apply the Sharia rules. Zarqawi's documentaries and videos featured explosive attacks, beheadings, suicide bombings, and martyrdom statements, and all this violence and terrorist acts attracted many recruits.[300] Like any other terrorist group, Zarqawi badly needed a religious basis for his killing of Muslims; therefore, he resorted to the notion of *takfir* (accusing "other" Muslims with disbelief) and condemned, for instance, the Shiites as polytheists to justify his terror campaign against all the "other" Muslims.

Zarqawi was warned by other militant groups to stop targeting the civilians, especially the local Shiites and the churches. However, he continued to engage in mass civilian casualties arguing that they deserved to be killed for they have attacked the Sunni people and usurped their mosques and houses. In 2006, al-Qaeda created an umbrella organization to unify Sunni insurgents in Iraq. When Zarqawi was killed by the US soldiers on June 7, 2006, Abu Hamza al-Muhajir was promoted to be the representative of al-Qaeda in Iraq. After that, the terrorist group announced the establishment of the Islamic State under the leadership of Abu Omar al-Baghdadi. Most of the insurgents criticized the project of the Islamic State (IS) for they thought it was a deviation from the main task of fighting against the American occupation of Iraq.

The initial Islamic State project was a failure because the insurgents did not have the resources to rule over the territory. Interestingly, some of those insurgents allied with the United States to fight against the Islamic State organization in return for the integration of the Sunni fighters into the

---

[300] Maura Conway, "From al-Zarqawi to al-Awlaki: The Emergence and Development of an Online Radical Milieu," *CTX Journal 2*, 4 (2012): pp. 12–2.

Iraqi security services. In 2008, Islamic State (IS) was defeated and Iraq was on the path to stability and security. In 2010, Abu Umar al-Baghdadi was killed, but the notion of an Islamic State continued as an idea to be actualized among terrorist groups.

The 2010 election in Iraq was controversial; therefore, it caused sectarian tensions. Although Prime Minister Maliki did not get the majority of the votes, he formed a Shiite-dominated coalition. This act terminated the 2010 Erbil Agreement that sought consensus among all major political parties.[301] The ineffective US strategy to achieve a long-term security agreement with Maliki's government in Iraq and the withdrawal of the US combat troops in 2011 increased sectarian conflicts. Additionally, ISIS forces have expanded their control from Iraq's Syrian border to key cities in north-central Iraq. The four-year Syrian civil war has attracted thousands of foreign militants to the area and Al Qaeda's logistical network established earlier by Zarqawi was used against Assad's regime. Additionally, the ruling Islamist AKP government in Turkey facilitated safe passage for thousands of foreign fighters from all over the world to go to Syria and join the militant groups fighting against Assad regime. ISIS and al Qaeda have greatly benefitted from this opportunity.

The Rise of ISIS

Abu Bakr al-Baghdadi fought in al Qaeda's Iraqi operations. Then, he became the leader of ISIS when the US forces killed the top al Qaeda leaders in Iraq. Baghdadi expanded the group's network into Syria in 2012 when an armed insurgency has begun against Assad's regime. Like his mentor Zarqawi, Baghdadi's 2005–2009 imprisonment at Camp Bucca accelerated his religious zealotry and militant extremism.[302]

---

[301] Cordesman, Anthony and Sam Khazai, *Iraq in Crisis* (Washington DC: Center for Strategic and International Studies, 2014), csis.org/files/publication/140513_Cordesman_IraqIn Crisis_Web.pdf.
[302] Celso, Anthony N. "Zarqawi's Legacy: Al Qaeda's ISIS Renegade," *Mediterranean Quarterly*, 26 (2015), pp. 21-41.

Abu Bakr al-Baghdadi recruited his followers from all over the world for a serious battle against Assad's regime in Syria. The fight in Syria was very complex and confusing: on one side there were the Syrian regime and its internal and external supporters while on the other side there were fanatical militants as well as non-religious militant groups ranging from secular nationalists to liberal democrats.

Al-Qaeda established Jabhat al-Nusra (Al-Nusra Front) in 2012 under the leadership of Abu Muhammad al-Jawlani with the help of Syrian veterans of the Iraqi insurgency against the United States. Al-Nusra achieved success against Assad regime. Baghdadi declared that Al-Nusra had been established, financed, and supported by the Islamic State (IS); therefore, he attempted to merge Al-Nusra with ISIS. However, Abu Muhammad al-Jawlani (the leader of al-Nusra), issued a statement and denied this decision. The conflict and separation thus emerged between these two militant groups.

Al-Nusra wanted to cooperate with other insurgents to promote the goal of an Islamic state in Syria. Therefore, it contained a very large number of foreign fighters. Approximately, eleven thousand militants have migrated to Syria from Arab Gulf states, North Africa, Europe, and the Caucasus to join the terrorist group.[303] Al-Nusra fought to defeat the Syrian regime while ISIS focused on establishing its own rule over the territory; therefore, it avoided fighting against the Syrian Army. Interestingly, in May 2014, Ayman al-Zawahiri, the leader of al-Qaeda, disavowed relations with ISIS, but ordered Al-Nusra not to attack ISIS.

However, ISIS assaulted the other militant groups irrespective of whether they were Sunnis or Shiites, and this sparked major retaliation. Thousands of militants had died in battles taking place between ISIS and other rebel groups. Baghdadi's forces consolidated their position around the strategic border town of Raqqa. In order to finish the conflicts between ISIS and other al Qaeda groups, al-Zawahiri appointed an arbitrator but

---

[303] Zelin, Aaron Y. "Up to 11,000 Fighters in Syria: Steep Rise in West Europeans," *ICSR Insight*, December 17, 2013, Washington Institute, www.washingtoninstitute.org/policy-analysis/view/up-to-11000-foreign-fighters-in-syria-steep-rise-among-western-europeans.

this attempt failed for the arbitrator was killed by an ISIS suicide bomber in 2014.[304] Thereupon, Jawlani, the leader of Al-Nusra, promised a war of annihilation against ISIS forces.[305] Additionally, Al Qaeda rejected ISIS and eliminated it from its umbrella organization. However, ISIS continues to attract considerable support from radical people across the world.

ISIS started to expand its territory in Iraq by attacking the Iraqis in various cities. The links with many former Baathist insurgents have made them easily achieve their objectives. They convinced many local leaders to support ISIS. The others were targeted by suicide bombers and were frightened with the videos of their massacres. By controlling a large territory, ISIS was now able to control the access to vital needs such as water and electricity. Since Iraqi security forces were collapsed in certain places, ISIS had a chance to further advance in some Iraqi territories. ISIS controled 33 percent of Iraq and 35 percent of Syria as of 2015. Roughly, four million people from Iraq and Syria lived in the cities controlled by ISIS. It also secured control over oil production facilities around Deir Izzour by defeating opposing rebels and regime forces.[306] It continues to rely on illicit oil sales.

International militants play a key role in the ISIS offensive capability for many of them joined it from various countries. This is now the concern of many European countries; they are fearful of the consequences if those bloody militants come back to their home. There are a number of reasons for people joining ISIS from so many different countries, such as the prophecy of a final battle to destroy evil and establish an Islamic State. Opposing ISIS, many Shiite and Hezbollah militants migrated to the region

---

[304] Jocelyn, Thomas. "Al Qaeda's Chief Representative in Syria Killed in Suicide Attack," *Long War Journal*, February 23, 2014, www.longwarjournal.org/archives/2014/02/zawahiris_chief_repr.php.
[305] Roggio, Bill. "Al Nusrah Front Emir Issues Ultimatum to ISIS," *Long War Journal*, February 25, 2014, www.longwarjournal.org/archives/2014/02/al_nusrah_front_emir_1.php.
[306] Celso, Anthony N. "Zarqawi's Legacy: Al Qaeda's ISIS Renegade," *Mediterranean Quarterly*, 26 (2015), pp. 21-41.

to support Assad's regime and protect the local Shiites from the Sunni militants.[307]

Despite the US airstrikes as well as the attacks of the Shiites and the opposing Sunni groups, ISIS's position in Syria is still strong. Its forces continue to advance in Syrian lands. It is difficult to predict how long this may continue.

When ISIS forces advanced further in Iraq in May 2014, they ethnically cleansed Mosul, massacred many Yazidis, and kidnapped many women and girls to distribute them among their commanders. The ISIS issue caused the whole world to discuss where this entire violence comes from, and how it can be encountered.

According to John Esposito, most of the individuals who have joined the ranks of ISIS are not religious. He argues that well-established religious Muslims are not inclined toward radicalism. Interestingly, young ignorant minds who are willing to join ISIS keep purchasing such books as "Islam for Dummies" and "Qur'an for Dummies" to learn about Islam. Therefore, Esposito suggests that religion is not the reason for people to become extremist radicals; rather, it is the social and political problems that lead them to radicalism. Indeed, ISIS does not talk about religion in their beheading videos; rather, it talks about the moral outrage and lack of purpose in life. Additionally, ISIS pays the highest money to its militants in the region and this attracts many rebels to join it.

There are mainly two theories about the rise of ISIS: it is an American and Zionist group aiming to create chaos in the Arab world. This idea is widely shared by many local Muslims. The other theory about the rise of ISIS is that it was developed jointly by the Syrian regime and Iran, as an instrument to marginalize moderate Sunni Islam.[308] The dominant idea, however, is that ISIS is an external phenomenon and does not belong to Muslim communities.

---

[307] White, Jeffery. "Assad's Indispensable Foreign Legions," *Policy Watch* 2196, January 22, 2014, Washington Institute, www.washingtoninstitute.org/policy-analysis/view/assads-indispensable-foreign-legions.

[308] Baker, Aryn. "Is the Assad Regime in League with al-Qaeda?", *Time*, January 27, 2014, http://world.time.com/2014/01/27/syria-assad-geneva-al-qaeda/

How Does ISIS Present Itself?

Initially, ISIS separated from al-Qaeda and appeared in Iraq and Syria. This terrorist group has now its own publications, including its magazine, Dabiq, which is named after a place near Aleppo, prophesied in Islamic eschatological literature to be the location of a decisive battle between Muslims and Christians. The members of ISIS are motivated by al Qaeda leader Abu Musab al-Zarqawi's radical philosophy, tactics and strategies. In order to build credibility and establish legitimacy, ISIS has used social media and cyber technology to recruit fighters and intimidate enemies.[309]

It is different from other terrorist organizations with regards to its highly sophisticated use and understanding of social media to achieve its goals for its communication strategy aims to persuade all Muslims about their claim that battling to restore a caliphate is a religious duty on them.[310] ISIS aims to build an affinity between itself and the potential supporters through creating a shared identity. In order to achieve this, the group constructs itself as the protector of Islam while framing its enemies as evil ones who are responsible for all the crises.[311]

The terrorist group persuades the ignorant masses to join its ranks in the name of being ready for the millennial activities, or eschatological events, like that of Prophet Jesus' descend from the heavens to fight against anti-Christ (aka Dajjal) and his followers. ISIS deems itself a legitimate state, specifically one that is guided by, and properly implementing, the Islamic law. The members of ISIS believe that they provide all the services which would be necessary for an Islamic state. They introduce themselves as not only a Sharia-governed state, but also the guardian and enforcer of Islamic law. They proudly inflict torture and even execute those who deviated from Islam according to their extreme

---

[309] Shane, Scott and Ben Hubbard, 'ISIS Displaying a Deft Command of Varied Media', *New York Times*, August 31, 2014, accessed September 30, 2015, http://www.nytimes.com/2014/08/31/world/middleeast/isis-displaying-a-deft-command-ofvariedmedia.html?_r=0.
[310] Farwell, James P. "The Media Strategy of ISIS" *Survival* (56) 2015, pp. 49–55.
[311] Ingram, Haroro J. "The strategic logic of Islamic State information operations," *Australian Journal of International Affairs*, 69 (2015), pp. 729-752.

doctrinal understanding whether they are "criminals" or captured enemies. The beheadings of journalists and other brutal crimes indicate that they will not listen to anyone opposing them, irrespective of whether they are Muslims or non-Muslims.

ISIS portrays itself as the true advocate of a sovereign faith. By posting videos on the internet and by showing them in the mainstream media, the terrorist group has reached a wide range of audience all around the world. Additionally, it has actively employed Twitter, Facebook and Instagram in an attempt to influence everyone. Through internet and social media, the terrorist group aimed to create powerful images by promising people "inevitable victory" and depicting group members as fearsome warriors. Moreover, by posting videos of soldiers who eat Snickers bars and nurture kittens, ISIS wants to go for a public image that it is not only murdering "enemies," but also promoting the welfare of their people.[312] Through the active use of social media ISIS has inspired recruits from all over the world, including the US citizens and Europeans.[313] Obviously, the images of Muslims killing Muslims and other violent videos were counter-productive. Indeed, many Muslim scholars have severely criticized ISIS and labeled it not as a radical religious group, but simply as a brutal terrorist group.

There is, of course, some religious motivation in ISIS's brutality. Through its executions and armed combat ISIS regards itself as eradicating the enemies of God. Moreover, they destroy the shrines of Shiite saints in the name of taking active measures to prevent reverence being shown to anyone other than God. Ironically, the members of ISIS pay special tribute to their late leaders and inspirational figures. They show the photos of al-Zarqawi and those who have carried out suicide attacks to their fellows to encourage them to battle against infidels. They provoke these people by

---

[312] Gebeily, Maya. "How ISIL Is Gaming the World's Journalists," *Global Post*, June 25, 2014, accessed on September 30, 2015, http://www.globalpost.com/dispatch/news/regions/middle-east/iraq/140625/ISIL-ISIS-internet-twitter.
[313] Black, Ian et al., 'The Terrifying Rise of Isis', *The Guardian*, June 16, 2014, accessed on September 30, 2015, http://www.theguardian.com/world/2014/jun/16/terrifying-rise-of-isis-iraq-executions.

promising them to liberate towns from their enemies, giving them some slave girls and concubines upon their active participation in combats.

The main goal for ISIS is to establish an Islamic State with an old style caliphate ruling the entire Middle East and North Africa. To this end, announcing Baghdadi as their new "caliph" was a tactic to attract young people to their ranks. By calling themselves "the Islamic State" (IS), the terrorist organization expects greater support from Muslims in the region, What's more, they keep threatening many governments in the region, including especially Jordan, Lebanon, Israel and Saudi Arabia. ISIS wants to establish an extreme form of Islamism which is intolerant to all other Islamic sects as well as the Christians and Yazidis in the region.

ISIS is more serious about establishing a caliphate than any other radical terrorist group. The other radical terrorist groups, including al-Qaeda, have spoken about caliphate but have never taken practical steps to actualize it. ISIS is much more prone to using violence to achieve its goal and killing others who do not share their ideology. Its brutal attacks on civilians, mainly Muslims, have led even al-Qaeda to denounce ISIS.

Interestingly, an unprecedented number of women from the western world have joined ISIS for non-combatant roles, but violence is an essential part of their embraced ideology and several signs suggest that they could claim a more militant role.[314] These women have identified themselves as "immigrants" to clearly indicate their dissatisfaction with their previous life, longing for establishing a new life in a place of ideal perfection, that is, the caliphate. It is estimated that almost 10 percent of ISIS's Western participants are female members.[315] These young women are mostly aged between 16 and 24, but there are even younger teenage girls in Europe who, after being brain-washed and radicalized, wish to

---

[314] Peresin, Anita & Alberto Cervone (2015) "The Western Muhajirat of ISIS," *Studies in Conflict & Terrorism*, (38) 2015, 495-509.

[315] Sherwood, Harriet et al., "Schoolgirl Jihadis: The Female Islamists Leaving Home to Join ISIS Fighters," *The Guardian*, September 29, 2014. Available at http://www.theguardian.com/world/2014/sep/29/schoolgirl-jihadis-female-islamists-leaving-home-join-isis-iraq-syria (accessed November 9, 2015).

travel to Syria.[316] They join ISIS for a number of reasons such as finding a partner or a job, cooking or being a nurse for soldiers.[317] Another reason for these European women to join ISIS is that the growth of xenophobia and negative attitudes toward Muslim immigrants in the West boosts up their aspiration to live their religion in the territories of the Islamic State.[318] It could be said that the motivation of these women is a combination of political and personal reasons together with naive romanticism.[319]

Dabiq, ISIS's controversial magazine, attractively presents its apocalyptic message which predicts the West's defeat at the hands of this terror group. The magazine is called after the Syrian town of Dabiq which is said to be the place where Muslim armies will defeat the western forces. ISIS's propaganda tool of Dabiq focuses primarily on the caliphate, its importance and the need for the declaration of Caliphate in its issues. Indeed, many of the ISIS militants have been recruited through its sophisticated use of social media and the magazine. There are three levels in ISIS's media structure: central media units, provincial information offices and its broader membership/supporter base.[320] By means of its media units ISIS disseminates its messages through online platforms, billboards, posters and so on to shape the perceptions of its local, regional and transnational audiences.

By controlling local markets and establishing its own governmental institutions, ISIS is actively portraying itself as the only viable source of security, stability and livelihood for local people. It has established courts

---

[316] Sherwood, Harriet et al., "Schoolgirl Jihadis: The Female Islamists Leaving Home to Join ISIS Fighters," *The Guardian*, September 29, 2014. Available at http://www.theguardian.com/world/2014/sep/29/schoolgirl-jihadis-female-islamists-leaving-home-join-isis-iraq-syria (accessed November 9, 2015).

[317] Ahmed, Qanta. "Who are the Invisible Women Joining ISIS?" *Fox News*, September 19, 2014. Available at http://www.foxnews.com/opinion/2014/09/18/unveiling-invisible-women-joining-isis/ (accessed on November 9, 2015).

[318] Hoyle, Carolyn et al., *Becoming Mulan?* Institute for Strategic Dialogue, London (2015). Available at http://www.al-monitor.com/pulse/originals/2014/12/european-women-joinjihad-motives.html (accessed on November 9, 2015).

[319] Peresin, Anita & Alberto Cervone (2015) "The Western Muhajirat of ISIS," *Studies in Conflict & Terrorism*, (38) 2015, 495-509.

[320] Ingram, Haroro J. "The strategic logic of Islamic State information operations," *Australian Journal of International Affairs*, 69 (2015), pp. 729-752.

to implement the Sharia laws, collected prescribed purifying alms from Muslims, and imposed tax upon non-Muslims.

ISIS is different from al-Qaeda with regards to its ability to articulate the notion of Islamic State and its strategy for implementing it. Al-Baghdadi has created a disciplined and flexible organization. He avoids the spectacular and provocative attacks as Zarqawi did; therefore, he has achieved success in his project. The other reasons for his success are as follows:

- He has built a hierarchical organization which allows sub-organizations as long as they are loyal to the mission and guidelines established by the leader.
- He has placed those Iraqi people from the military and security force of the former Baathist regime in the top layers of his militant terrorist organization.
- He has established three councils: the consultant council, the military council, and the security and intelligence council.
- The Islamic State makes huge amount of money from the export of rich oil in the region under its control. It also taxes the population under its control.

According to al-Baghdadi, the entire people in the whole world can be classified into two categories: Muslims and *kafir*s. If anyone does not join its ranks, he or she is considered *kafir* (infidel or unbeliever) even if he or she is a Muslim. Therefore, the terrorist organization never hesitates to kill "other" Muslims to achieve its targets. For al-Baghdadi, all nations and faiths other than his own ideology are in *kufr* (disbelief), and all are being led by America, Russia, or the Jews.[321]

---

[321] Al-Baghdadi, Abu Bakr. 2014. *A Message to the Mujahidin and the Muslim Ummah in the Month of Ramadan*. Al Hayat Media Centre. http://www.gatestoneinstitute.org/documents/baghdadicaliph.Pdf.

Where Does ISIS Get Its Resources?

One of the questions many people wonder about is how the ISIS terrorist organization gets all the money and resources it has. According to the news reports, the vast majority of the money to ISIS comes from selling a huge amount of oil through illegal ways. ISIS used to produce about 80,000 barrels of oil in Iraq and Syria and it had the capability to double its product. There are some rumors that Turkey is buying the oil for its cheap price in order to destroy Assad's regime.

Although the ruling AKP government in Turkey denied its help to ISIS, some reports clearly indicated that ISIS smuggles its oil to various markets through southern part of Turkey. The other rumor was that Kurdish people buy its oil and ship it to Pakistan at a cheap price. There are even some reports accusing the Assad government of purchasing ISIS's oil.

Besides oil, ISIS gets money from other means such as getting support from external sources, demanding ransom money by kidnapping people, imposing taxes and even selling the historical artifacts and antiquities in the Mesopotamian region. Additionally, there are some wealthy individuals in Gulf countries who support ISIS in its fight against Assad. With their support to ISIS, they also aim to stop Iran's ultimate goals in the region.

It is further reported that ISIS has obtained a large number of American weapons from the Iraqi army and Syrian insurgents. The terrorist organization also smuggle weapons and other supplies through the long border between Turkey and Syria.

ISIS Is a Death Cult

ISIS (Islamic State of Iraq and Syria) has brought death and chaos to the Middle East and the greater world. Its brutal beheading of Western journalists and humanitarian aid workers was the headline in the global media in 2014. This terrorist group is also known popularly in the west by the names "Islamic State in Iraq and the Levant" (ISIL), or simply "Islamic

State" (IS), and "Daesh" in Arabic countries. Nouri al-Maliki, the Shiite head of the Iraqi government from 2006 to 2014, could not satisfy the demands of the marginalized Iraqi Sunnis; therefore, ISIS has filled the gap in the area by seizing the key north-western cities of Fallujah, Ramadi and Mosul in Iraq. Maliki's government was Shia-dominated and ISIS took maximum advantage of it among the Sunni people across Syria and Iraq to get the full support of the tribal dynamics.

During the term of the al-Maliki government, ISIS allowed the local tribal forces to govern their own state of affairs and this has greatly helped the terrorist group to grow without being recognized. By the late June 2014, ISIS – the al-Qaeda splinter group, had already occupied some territory in Iraq and Syria and then announced Abu Bakr al-Baghdadi as their leader and caliph. They have established the Islamic State (IS) so that Muslims would gather there to give their allegiance to the caliph and fight against their Muslim and non-Muslim enemies to expand their borders throughout the region.[322] Indeed, it is very surprising that after ISIS's declaration of the caliphate, many people across the world, including the western countries, have joined its ranks.

The global threat ISIS has posed is the concern of many western countries from America to Australia for the terrorist group has issued a proclamation, encouraging terrorist attacks in Western countries. Some incidents that might be connected to the terrorist organization have led the security officials to not only increase the security level, but also question the entire Muslim population in their countries. Additionally, the politicians and the media can have dramatic impact upon the public's perceptions of their fellow citizens of the Islamic faith. It is, however, the responsibility of these politicians and the media to inform the citizens with sound and accurate knowledge. While doing this, they should not polarize people, separating them into opposing groups. One of the good examples to be mentioned in this regard is the speech the former US President George W. Bush made at a mosque.

---

[322] Matthew Weaver, "Isis declares caliphate in Iraq and Syria," *The Guardian*, July 1, 2014.

In the aftermath of 9/11, incidences of hate crimes and harassment of American Muslims declined appreciably after President Bush visited a mosque, where he emphasized that America's Muslims were not responsible for the 9/11 attacks that had taken place in New York, Washington, DC, and Pennsylvania.[323] He stated that American Muslims shared the same sense of outrage and pain at the deaths of their fellow citizens as other American citizens felt on that September morning.

Former Australian Prime Minister Tony Abbott used careful language while framing ISIS as a marginal terrorist group. He wanted to distinguish Muslims in general from any terrorist group. He followed certain steps to portray Islam and Muslims in a positive light rather than seeing all Muslims as potential terrorists. In this regard, he referred to ISIS as a "death cult," rather than as an Islamic state. He stressed that many Muslims themselves have also been targets of this terrorist group, and pointed out the fact that Muslim countries are already engaged in a combat with ISIS along with Western powers. He further stressed on the words of leading Muslims who have condemned ISIS and its violence.[324]

ISIS is a marginal group addicted to human blood; hence, it is only a death cult. Any ordinary Muslim hates their evil acts and the vast majority of Muslims have openly condemned them in various platforms. For example, Fethullah Gülen, a very influential Muslim thinker and leader, deemed ISIS as a terrorist group and condemned their brutal acts in various papers, including *New York Times, Washington Post, Chicago Tribune, Wall Street Journal* and *Los Angeles Times*, on August 22, 2014:

> I deplore the brutal atrocities being committed by the ISIS terrorist group hiding behind a false religious rhetoric and join the people of conscience from around the world in calling for these perpetrators to

---

[323] Lentini, Pete. (2015), "Demonizing ISIL and Defending Muslims: Australian Muslim Citizenship and Tony Abbott's 'Death Cult' Rhetoric", *Islam and Christian–Muslim Relations*, 26:2, pp. 237-252.

[324] Lentini, Pete. (2015), "Demonizing ISIL and Defending Muslims: Australian Muslim Citizenship and Tony Abbott's 'Death Cult' Rhetoric", *Islam and Christian–Muslim Relations*, 26:2, pp. 237-252.

immediately cease their cruel and inhuman acts. Any form of attack, suppression or persecution of minorities or innocent civilians is an act that contradicts the principles of the Qur'an and the tradition of our Prophet, upon whom be peace and blessings. ISIS members are either completely ignorant of the spirit of Islam and its blessed messenger, or their actions are designed to serve their individual interests or those of their political masters. Regardless, their actions represent those of a terrorist group and they should be labeled as such and be brought to justice.[325]

Salam al-Marayati, President of the US-based Muslim Public Affairs Council, also condemned ISIS for "distorting Islam and dehumanizing Muslims by the hand of al- Baghdadi, a false prophet who has stained the sacred faith."[326]

Terrorist groups have long celebrated martyrdom, exploiting it as a recruitment tool to encourage (mostly) young men to engage in violence "to defend Islam and Muslims." Indeed, this is contrary to Islamic teachings because Islam strongly prohibits killing innocent people. In the Qur'an God Almighty says:

He who kills a soul unless it be (in legal punishment) for murder or for causing disorder and corruption on the earth will be as if he had killed all humankind; and he who saves a life will be as if he had saved the lives of all humankind.[327]

Even when Muslims have to resort to war to defend their country for a just cause, Prophet Muhammad, upon whom be peace and blessings, put many restrictions, including the following:

> Do not betray, inflict injustice, plunder, or defile the bodies; do not kill children, the elderly, or women. Do not cut down the date orchards or

---

[325] Gülen, Fethullah. *ISIS Cruelty Deserves Our Strongest Condemnation*, http://www.fethullahgulen.org/news/gulen-isis.html, accessed on February 24, 2015.

[326] Al-Marayati, S. 2014. *Islam's Theology of Life Is Stronger than ISIS' Cult of Death.* Accessed on September 15, 2015. http://religion.blogs.cnn.com/2014/09/05/islams-theology-of-life-is-strongerthan-isis-cult-of-death/.

[327] Unal, Ali. *The Qur'an*, 5: 32.

burn them; do not cut down trees that bear fruit. Do not kill sheep, cattle, or camels unless it is for food. You may come across people who have retreated into monasteries on your way; do not touch them or interfere with their worship....[328]

While committing acts of terror against civilians and innocent people, ISIS has exploited the notion of "jihad," using it in a militant sense to justify its evil crimes. Additionally, the terrorist group misinterpreted the military campaigns during the period of the Noble Prophet, the Four Righteous Caliphs and their successors by approaching them from its own extremist perspective and completely removing them from their historical contexts.[329] This radical understanding and the idea of resistance against western forces in Islamic lands have caused some young minds to join their ranks.

The violence in the Middle East or more broadly in Muslim world has some key reasons. They can be analyzed under three categories: disunity among Muslims, poverty in the area, and ignorance and educational backwardness. From the political perspective, the reasons for the violence among various groups in the Middle East are insecurity, unfulfilled demands of insurgents, disagreement and fragmentations on the basis of ethnicity and religion, and failure to deal with the underlying causes of the armed conflict.

ISIS has been gaining firm ground in Iraqi cities by manipulating religious concepts, including especially the caliphate, and by fulfilling the demands of local tribes. They have imposed tax on non-Sunni groups and tribes. They have declared other sects and ethnic groups as infidels and unbelievers, worthy of death and persecution. The sectarian bigotry is extreme and very violent within ISIS.

---

[328] Muhammad ibn Athīr, *Usd al-Ghaba* (Beirut: Dār Iḥyā' al-Turāth al-'Arabi, 1968), 2/335.
[329] Esposito, *Unholy War: Terror in the Name of Islam*, 64.

The Origins of ISIS in Islamic History and Theological Response to Their Claim

Extremist movements like ISIS are nothing new in the long history of Islam. While the roots of extremism go back to the Kharijites in the seventh century, the ISIS terrorist group displays the elements of Wahhabism, Salafism and al-Qaeda. All extreme groups in Muslim societies claim the aim of returning to the pristine form of Islam which was established by the Noble Prophet. However, there are essential contradictions between their practice and the teachings of the Prophet. Therefore, although the terrorist groups manipulated some ignorant minds and made them believe in their war propaganda, the vast majority of Muslims have always deemed them extreme and outside of the real Islamic doctrines. This is because Islam teaches its followers to respect the sacred of others. It is through this respect that humanity can breathe the peace.

Islam aims to establish healthy relations among the members of society, whatever faith traditions, cultures or ethnic groups they can come from. When the Noble Prophet migrated from Mecca to Medina in 622 CE, he signed a pact with the people of Medina, ensuring the rights of citizenship for all minority groups there.[330] This Charter of Medina constituted an agreement between the Muslim, Jewish, pagan, and Christian groups, declaring them to constitute one nation and this formed the basis of a multi-religious Islamic state in Medina.[331]

In order to promote mutual respect and friendship with different religions God commanded His Messenger to engage in interfaith dialogue with the People of Scriptures in the Qur'an:

> Say (to them, O Messenger): "O People of the Book, come to a word common between us and you, that we worship none but God, and

---

[330] Ibn Ishaaq, *Sirah al-Rasul al-Allah*, (tr: A. Guillaume, The Life of Muhammad), Oxford University Press, Karachi, 1955, pp. 231-233.
[331] Montgomery Watt, *Muhammad at Medina*, Oxford: Clarendon Press, 1956, pp. 227-228.

associate none as partner with Him, and that none of us take others for Lords, apart from God.³³²

This call, made by Islam 14 centuries ago to the People of the Book (Christians and Jews), is still valid today and it shows how various consciences, nations, religions and books can unite on one essential concept and word of truth.³³³ In line with this call the Noble Prophet visited many People of the Book, Christian churches and Jewish synagogues in order to foster mutual understanding and put an end to the inter-religious enmity and hatred.³³⁴ Similarly, a group of Christians came to Medina to learn about Islam, and during their stay, they requested permission from the Noble Prophet to perform their worship and rituals in the *masjid*, a place of worship for Muslims which is known also as a mosque.³³⁵ The Noble Prophet granted their wish and hosted them in a friendly manner. This visit resulted in a peace treaty which contained the following articles:

> Christians (living in Muslim lands) have the right to live in safety, their property will be protected, their churches will not be harmed, monasteries will not be closed and priests will not be impeded when performing their duties. Moreover, Christians will not be compelled to provide supplies for Muslims during times of war and it is not permitted to interfere with or interrupt Christian worship.³³⁶

On another occasion, at the funeral of a Jew, the Noble Prophet stood up to show his respect to people from other faiths.³³⁷ This example shows that interfaith dialogue is not limited to Arab or non-Arab people; rather, spiritual progress is possible by expanding universally and in unison, and

---

³³² Qur'an 3: 64.
³³³ Yazir, Elmalili Hamdi. *Hak Dini Kur'an Dili*, Istanbul Azim Dagitim, 2007, vol. 2, p. 1131.
³³⁴ Al-Tabarī, Abū Ja'far Muhammad ibn Jarir. *Jami al-Bayan at Ta'wil al-Qur'an*, Beirut: Ālam al-Kutub 1992, vol. 3, pp. 162-163.
³³⁵ Al-Tabarī, *Jami al-Bayan*, vol. 3, pp. 162-163.
³³⁶ Al-Tabarī, *Jami al-Bayan*, vol. 3, pp. 162-163.
³³⁷ Bukhari, *Saḥīḥ*, Iman, 50.

not by being separate from one another.[338] There is no place for repulsive manners, condemnation or rudeness in Islam when dealing with people from other faith traditions.[339]

An Alternative Approach to Destroy ISIS

In order to understand the real nature of any terrorist organization the historical, social, and political context within which they have appeared needs to be known well. Each extreme group or armed insurgency has various reasons and motives to incline towards violence. It is not an authentic approach to place all under one category because focusing only on categorization leads us to misunderstand the true nature of religious radicalism both in the past and the present. The correct question to ask is why each terrorist group feels the need to commit some of the most heinous atrocities.

Interestingly enough, most of the young people who venture overseas and join ISIS in search of militant methods "to serve Islam" come from stable domestic environments and good families. Foreign fighters in this terrorist group are drawn mainly from the Western European countries of France, Britain and Belgium. Many of these young people have joined the ranks of ISIS in search of adventure, marriage or spoils of war.

Psychologically speaking, how ordinary people become terrorists needs to be discussed and thoroughly investigated. Terrorism experts have failed to find the fundamental issues about terrorist groups, including ISIS, in their quick analysis because they could not satisfactorily answer the questions of why they do what they do, what drives them to it, and how we can dissuade them from their path of militancy and terror. Additionally, the US forces have allied with some of the insurgents in the Middle East in its fight against ISIS and this raised a question that needs to be answered: if

---

[338] Dogan, Recep. Conflict Resolution Forms in the Life of Prophet Muhammad, *The International Journal of Religion and Spirituality in Society*, vol. 4(2), 2014, pp. 9-19.
[339] Gülen, M. Fethullah. *Reflections on the Qur'ān: Commentaries on Selected Verses*, New Jersey: Tughra Books, 2012, p. 68.

these groups are terrorists, insurgents, or a mixture of both, which one can be allied and which one needs to be eliminated? It is a highly questionable strategy to rely on armed rebel groups while fighting against ISIS.

It is not enough to use only the military force to destroy ISIS or any other terrorist organization. If the question "what makes people terrorists" is not examined well, the problem will persist to continue. ISIS recruits new members by using religious language and concepts. If their arguments are not answered by Muslims scholars and their claims are not refuted theologically, the ISIS threat will escalate. In order to defeat ISIS, its cloak of religious legitimacy should be removed so that terrorists cannot hide themselves behind this religious mask and their real identity can be seen by all Muslims.

It is quite interesting that in spite of its brutality and violence, ISIS continues to attract some young people from among Muslim people all over the world. This is mainly because the terrorist organization claims to be a truly Islamic group. Although it violates even the fundamental Islamic tenets, its contradictions with Islamic faith are not addressed well and loudly by the western and/or Muslim countries. The claims of ISIS can be refuted theologically by using the primary Islamic sources (namely, the Qur'an and the traditions of the Prophet), and this will reduce the number of new recruits dramatically. When their religious mask and legitimization of murder is removed, ISIS becomes only a bunch of criminals. This will also expose how the terrorist group has distorted Islamic teachings by interpreting them wrongfully and killing Muslims with the pretext of apostasy.

The religious concepts such as *jihad* (struggling for God's cause), *tawhid* (unity of God), *takfir* (accusation of apostasy), Sharia and caliphate are interpreted in an extreme way and are exploited by all terrorists groups, including ISIS. Each term, however, needs to be understood in its religious and historical context to avoid any misunderstanding. For example, the term *tawhid* literally means oneness of God and it is one of the pillars of Islam. Islam does not force people to accept it but it provides freedom for people to choose their belief.[340] Accordingly, Islam aims to educate people in the long term in an effort for people to accept its belief system with their free will rather than forcing them or killing those who do not accept it.[341] Islam invites people to use their logic and intellect regarding their religious choices. Yet, the terrorist organization ignores the Quranic arguments and declares any individual or group who violates *tawhid* as *kafir* (unbeliever) and puts them to death.

The accusation of apostasy (*takfir*) is the declaration of a Muslims' exclusion from the Islamic community because of his or her deviation from the Islamic path. The Noble Prophet warned Muslims on this matter and ordered them not to accuse others with disbelief. For example, the Prophet said, "Any person who calls his brother as 'O unbeliever' would actually turn to be one of them. If it were so (if the person is an unbeliever as he asserted), then the unbelief of that man was confirmed, but if it was not true, then it turns back to him (to the man who condemns his faithful brother with apostasy)."[342] Although the Noble Prophet warned Muslims stating, "Insulting a Muslim is an evil action, and fighting him or her is disbelief,"[343] radical groups have ignored this type of clear religious texts, and used some others to back up their claims by disconnecting them from their actual context.

Upon examining the history of Islam, one will see that Islam does never teach Muslims to kill innocent people in the name of God. In the Qur'an and the prophetic traditions, there are many rules that invite Muslims to be "just" even when they are forced by their circumstances and conditions to fight their enemies. Islam has always favored defense over offence and advised mercy towards enemies. Moreover, the contemporary Muslim scholar Fethullah Gülen has repeatedly stated that, "A real Muslim

---

[340] Euben, Roxanne I. and Muhammad Qasim Zaman, *Princeton Readings in Islamic Thought: Texts and Contexts from al-Banna to Bin Laden*, (New Jersey: Princeton University Press 2009), 146.
[341] Sivan, Emmanuel. *Radical Islam, Medieval Theology, and Modern Politics*, (New Haven: Yale university Press 1985), p. 89.
[342] Muslim, *Saḥīḥ Muslim* (Delhi India: Adam Publishers, 1996), Iman 26.
[343] Muslim, *Saḥīḥ*, Iman, 28.

who understood Islam in every aspect could never be a terrorist."[344] He stressed on the fact that terrorism must be condemned without giving any excuse. He even labeled the suicide bombers as the companions of hellfire. However, religious extremists have hijacked Islam just like it has periodically occurred with Christianity and other religions throughout history.[345]

Although Islam strictly forbids Muslims from accusing other Muslims with disbelief (*takfir*), the terrorist groups, including ISIS, have been declaring "other" Muslims who disagree with them as unbeliever (*kafir*). For this reason, hundreds of Muslim leaders and scholars declared in the "Amman Message" that it is not permissible to declare any Muslim group as apostates.[346] However, ISIS practices its deviant doctrine of *takfir* (accusing other Muslims with disbelief) a lot, and it deems any Muslim group as apostate if they do not support its ideology. Even the terrorist organization of al-Qaeda questioned ISIS's practice of *takfir* as well as its legitimacy.

Another argument the vast majority of the terrorist organizations have been using is the concept of *jahiliyya* (ignorance). This term refers to the pre-Islamic time in Arabian Peninsula and means the state of barbarism, ignorance, immoral customs, idol worshipping and polytheism. Many Muslim scholars have produced works on this issue and warned Muslim community to be ever-vigilant in this matter; otherwise, they will return to the state of *jahiliyya* (times of ignorance) in which the strong oppresses the weak and materialism defeats spirituality.[347] However, this term is used by ISIS in the meaning of *kufr* (disbelief) and they label any individual or group who commit a sin as apostate(s). This is directly contradictory to the teachings of the Qur'an and the Noble Prophet because no one has the authority to declare other Muslims as apostates on the basis of sins,

---

[344] Saritoprak, Zeki. "Fethullah Gülen's Thoughts on State, Democracy, Politics, Terrorism," *The Muslim World*, 95 (2005), pp. 325–471.

[345] Ramsbotham, O. et al., *Contemporary Conflict Resolution: The Prevention, Management and Transformation of Deadly Conflicts* (Malden, MA: Polity Press, 2011), pp. 339-345.

[346] *The Amman Message*, (Jordan: The Royal Al-Bayt Institute for Islamic Thought, 2009), p. 17.

[347] Shepard, William E. "Sayyid Qutb's Doctrine of Jahiliyya," *International Journal of Middle East Studies*, 35 (2003): 524.

mistakes, or shortcomings. Indeed, in many verses of the Holy Book, God has promised forgiveness to believers who commit sins. For example:

> Say: "(God gives you hope): 'O My servants who have been wasteful (of their God-given opportunities and faculties) against (the good of) their own souls! Do not despair of God's Mercy. Surely God forgives all sins. He is indeed the All-Forgiving, the All-Compassionate.'"[348]

In this verse God has named sinners as "His servants" but not infidels or unbeliever. If a person was deemed as unbeliever because of his or her sins, there would not be any Muslim remaining on the earth. Therefore, such a deviant understanding is definitely against the teachings of the Qur'an and the traditions of the Noble Prophet.

Caliphate and Islamic State

With its armed combat aggression in Syria and Iraq, ISIS has had the opportunity to establish an "Islamic state." They declared Abu Bakr al-Baghdadi[349] as their Caliph (ruler) and the territory they occupied as Islamic State, starting from June 2014. They deem this success (establishing an Islamic State and declaring a Caliph) as actualizing the dream for caliphate which was abolished by the secular Turkish government back in 1924, and which has been neglected since then. The ISIS's Consultative (Shura) Council declared caliphate formally and invited all Muslims around the world to pledge their allegiance to the new caliph.

---

[348] Unal, Ali, *The Qur'an* 39: 53.
[349] Abu Bakr al-Baghdadi was born Ibrahim Awad al-Badari in Samarra, Iraq in 1971. A quiet and religious youth, he later graduated with an MA and PhD from the University of Islamic Sciences in the Adhamiya district of Baghdad. By 2005, he had been detained in Camp Bucca where he was interrogated for terrorist activities. Released in 2009, he assumed the leaderships of Al Qaeda in Iraq and then ISIL.

The military success of ISIS in occupying the territory as well as the declaration of the caliphate as a political movement have caused deep influence in the region and the world. Rebels from other militant groups have started to surrender to ISIS, and the local leaders feared to confront them, agreeing to surrender their territory to them in peaceful ways. Expanding its territories, ISIS had territorial contiguity between the lands in Syria and in Iraq.

However, its declaration of the caliphate caused dispute and division among radical terrorist groups. They argued that al-Baghdadi was not a prominent figure; therefore, he had no right to declare a caliphate. Additionally, the timing and the manner of declaring the caliphate was regarded as inappropriate. Al-Baghdadi and ISIS were annoyed by the critics coming from al-Qaeda and other militant groups. However, they defended themselves by arguing that their military success provided them both the legitimacy and the opportunity to declare the caliphate.

The weak Iraqi government was in utter shock with the rise of ISIS and its gaining power and lands within its own territory. It is now unclear if ISIS will keep control of the area it has occupied or will face internal and external challenges. As it keeps expanding its territories, ISIS may lose its increasing power and control over the area, and this can be the beginning of its collapse. One could argue that ISIS militants had military success on the ground, but they were not very effective at establishing and maintaining governmental institutions. Therefore, they will eventually collapse. The majority of Muslims deem ISIS or any other militant groups as terrorist groups who violate Islamic principles, and they suspect that these terrorist groups are supported generously by non-Islamic sources to harm Islam and Muslims. Because of this widespread negative perception, there is no chance for any terrorist group to survive for a very long time.

When one examines ISIS, he or she can easily notice that al-Baghdadi used two methods in the construction of the state: resorting to violence against all opposing groups in Syria and building and sustaining alliances with local armed groups. Additionally, ISIS provided great financial sources for the militants to join their ranks. Therefore, it may remain in the region as long as there is no any other alternative Sunni organization which can bring peace and tranquility by unifying the groups and finishing all conflicts and disputes among them. However, the prominent Sunni leaders who refused to join ISIS have either been assassinated or frightened to resist against it.

The conflicts among different groups in Iraq and Syria caused further divisions in their territories. They fought against each other over sharing the power and resources in the region. There are some militant groups who have rejected ISIS and declared their commitment to continue the struggle against it. During his presidency, the former President Obama was determined to destroy ISIS and clean the region from any terrorist groups. Since 2014, the US military power was able to stop the advance of ISIS with the help of the local Kurdish Peshmerga militants and took back some of the territories ISIS had occupied. However, if social conflicts, disunity and poverty are not eliminated in the region, it would be difficult to uproot all terrorist groups there. ISIS or any other terrorist group cannot be defeated by military means alone.

The notion of *tawhid* (oneness of God) is important in caliphate. According to this doctrine, all sovereignty belongs to God alone. However, there is a difference between the real authority and enforcing the authority. The enforcing authority is recognized by the consensus of the Muslim community and the ruler or governor practice his or her authority according to the Islamic principles such as justice and equality. For this reason, in the religion of Islam, Muslims are more important than an Islamic state because the latter exists only for the welfare of the Muslim community. There is no specific type of governing system in Islam; rather, there are criteria, principles and objectives which the state must adopt and interpret according to the conditions of the time and place. Since it is a political institution, it cannot be deemed "holy." For this reason, a ruler (caliph) must be chosen not by self-proclamation but by consensus as we see in any democratic system, and he must follow the Islamic principles during his rule.

Conclusion

In conclusion, although ISIS claims its desire of unifying Muslims under its caliphate in an attempt to mask their violence and terror, its claim directly contradicts Islamic faith and historical facts. For example, when the Ottomans declared the Sunni caliphate, the Safavids – the other Muslim Shiite community also had its own caliph; they even went to war with each other. When one examines the Islamic history, he or she will see that caliphate is a political institution. If Muslim scholars do not explain this fact clearly, the ignorant masses will continue to be radicalized by misinterpreted Islamic concepts.

ISIS and its claim of an Islamic state is in reality a criminal enterprise that aims to deceive Muslims, exploiting them for its evil agenda. ISIS does not follow Islamic principles, but simply governs through terror, torture and rape. Its brutal acts indicate that ISIS is a brutal terrorist organization which violates even the core Islamic principles. Although a great majority of the Muslim world is horrified by the ISIS terror, it does not destroy it with effective methods. Many young Muslims from all over the world continue to join the ranks of ISIS because they deem the terrorist activities justifiable. If Muslim scholars do not combat extremism and terrorism in unison and with effective methods, the problem of radicalism will remain among some Muslim groups. The scholars must refute all of the claims of ISIS with the arguments from the Qur'an, the Sunnah (traditions of the Prophet) and the Islamic history. They must speak loudly and effectively that "A Muslim cannot be a terrorist and a terrorist cannot be a Muslim." What ISIS does is absolutely against the core Islamic values because celebration of brutality, including decapitating prisoners or burning them alive, crucifying and exhibiting the victims, can never be accepted by any religion.

Chapter 3

THEOLOGICAL RESPONSES TO THE ARGUMENTS OF THE EXTREMIST GROUPS

ISLAMIC RADICALIZATION AND GLOBAL TERRORISM

Introduction

Terrorism and Islamic radicalization have become major global concerns for every citizen in this day and age. Acts of terror have been perpetrated across the borders of nations, and caused global unrest, fear, and uncertainty. People from different walks of life have become more worried about whether Islam is the source of these violent attacks, or whether it is due to the marginal groups who misinterpret it. In the light of these major concerns, we will examine the concept of terror and provide an Islamic perspective on terror on the basis of primary Islamic sources, explore radical groups' misinterpretations of Islam, look at how terrorists are perceived by the majority of Muslims, and analyze the notion of jihad in Islam as well as its misinterpretation by Islamist radicalization and extremism.

In recent years, terror groups, such as al-Qaeda and ISIS, have threatened world peace by conducting the most evil acts and murdering innocent people. There are many forms of Islamist radicalism in terrorist groups, who use varying methods to achieve their goals. Religion is the most effective instrument used as bait by the radical groups to attract new members and to use them for their evil agendas.[350]

Terrorism is defined in the Code of Federal Regulations as "the unlawful use of force and violence against persons or property to intimidate or coerce a government, the civilian population, or any segment thereof, in furtherance of political or social objectives (28 C.F.R. Section 0.85)."[351]

Radicalization, on the other hand, is defined as "a process by which an individual or group comes to adopt increasingly extreme political, social, or religious ideals and aspirations that reject or undermine the status quo or reject and/or undermine contemporary ideas and expressions of freedom of choice."[352]

According to the traditional Islamic view, religion is a pact between man and God and there can be no compulsion or force when practicing it.[353] Mainly, Muslims follow the tenets of Islam that are established by the primary sources, which are the Qur'an and the Sunnah (Prophetic Traditions), without resorting to any violence. Radical groups interpret these sources to suit their political agendas, and often resort to violence and terror to actualize their objectives.

Radical Islamist theory is built on the concept of political enforcement of religious beliefs. According to radical Islamist groups, their views are the only truth and those who do not adopt their belief are outside of the realm of Islam – an apostate, disbeliever or idolater, making the shedding

---

[350] Herriott, Peter. *Religious Fundamentalism and Social Identity* (London: Routledge, 2007).
[351] "Terrorism 2002–2005," U.S. Department of Justice Federal Bureau of Investigation, accessed June 20, 2015. https://www.fbi.gov/stats-services/publications/terrorism-2002-2005.
[352] *Definitions.net*, STANDS4 LLC, 2015. "Radicalization," http://www.definitions.net/definition/radicalization, accessed on September 26, 2015.
[353] Unal, Ali. *The Quran with Annotated Interpretation in Modern English* (New Jersey: Tughra Books, 2007), 2: 256.

of his or her blood permissible.[354] Historically, the radical Islamist approach has emerged among various Muslim groups. We will elaborate the issue with examples in this section.

In Islamic history, extremists have existed for different reasons, motivations and intentions, and they have killed many innocent people in the name of religion to justify their actions and to promote their radical ideas. For example, the Kharijites, which literally means "those who strayed from the righteous path," were an extremist group who first emerged in the late 7th century. They employed Islamic arguments and religious concepts to maximize their appeal to various segments of the greater Muslim population.[355] The Kharijites developed extreme doctrines that further set them apart from both the mainstream Sunni Muslims and the Shiite Muslims. Dividing the world into believers and nonbelievers, the Kharijites labeled any person as unbeliever (*kafir*) if he or she did not accept their radical doctrines. They did not hesitate to kill people who did not accept their doctrines unless they repented.[356]

Initially, the Kharijites supported the fourth Caliph, Ali b Abi Tālib,[357] the cousin and son-in-law of the Noble Prophet, but later rejected him when he agreed to arbitrate in 657 CE rather than continuing to fight against Mu'awiya, who was later going to be the first Caliph of the Umayyad dynasty. Misinterpreting the verse, *"The ruling authority solely belongs to God"*[358] the Kharijites announced Ali and Mu'awiya as nonbelievers[359] because they disobeyed God by acting against the Quranic verse and accepting a human arbitrator to solve the conflict among them.

---

[354] John L. Esposito, *Unholy War: Terror in the Name of Islam* (Oxford: Oxford University Press, 2003), 2.
[355] F. A. Ansary, "Combating Extremism: A Brief Overview of Saudi Arabia's Approach," *Middle East Policy* 15 (2008): 111–142.
[356] John L Esposito, *What Everyone Needs to Know about Islam*. (Oxford: Oxford University Press, 2002), 41-42.
[357] Ali was the caliph between 656 and 661 CE which was one of the hardest periods in Muslim history that coincided with the first Muslim civil war.
[358] Ünal, *Qur'an*, 12: 40.
[359] Due to appointing an arbitrator to solve the conflict Ali and Mu'awiya are deemed to be unbelievers by Kharijites as they disobeyed the Qur'anic verse "the ruling authority solely belongs to God."

After separating from Ali, the Kharijites eventually assassinated him,[360/361] established a separate community, and engaged in many brutal terror activities. On the basis of the Quranic verse (12:40), the Kharijites declared "other" Muslims to be nonbelievers and therefore deemed them worthy of death. In this way, they did not hesitate to kill Muslims, including the Prophet's Companions who supported Caliph Ali or Mu'awiya. Additionally, the Kharijites argued that people who committed major sins were subject to death unless they repented.[362] Centuries after the Kharijites, the radical Islamic understanding and extremist interpretation of Islamic sources appeared as "Salafism" in the second half of the nineteenth century.

Salafism, which defines Islamic belief in an absolutist and literalist manner, emerged with the claim of advocating the traditions of the devout ancestors.[363] The main theme in Salafism is an effort to return Muslims to the pristine fundamentals of faith. By advocating the study of texts in a more literal and traditional sense, they have adhered to the doctrines of Ibn Taymiyya (d. 1328 CE),[364] who called for a definition of Islamic belief in an absolutist and literalist manner after realizing the total decadence of the Abbasid caliphate in the thirteenth century. He issued a juristic opinion (*fatwa*), deeming the Mongol rulers as unbelievers and declared war against them on the grounds that they did not follow the Islamic law and, therefore, were not Muslim.[365] Salafism emerged as a reaction to religious innovation and focused on the restoration of Islamic doctrines to its pure

---

[360] David Cook, *Martyrdom in Islam* (Cambridge: Cambridge University Press, 2007), 54-55.
[361] Abd-al-Rahman ibn Muljam, one of the Kharijites, killed Caliph Ali during the congregational prayer in 661 CE.
[362] Esposito, *Unholy War: Terror in the Name of Islam*, 37.
[363] Gilles Kepel, *Jihad: The Trail of Political Islam* (London: I.B. Tauris, 2006), 54.
[364] Ibn Taymiyyah (1263-1328) was an Islamic scholar, theologian and logician. Ibn Taymiyyah sought the return of Sunni Islam to what he viewed as earlier interpretations of the Qur'an and the Sunnah. He is considered to have had considerable influence in contemporary Wahhabism, Salafism, and Jihadism. He is renowned for his religious ruling (*fatwa*) issued against the Muslim Mongol rulers, declaring a general jihad against them as compulsory on the grounds that they did not follow the Islamic law, and as such were not Muslim.
[365] Al-Matroudi, Abdul Hakim. *The Hanbali School of Law and Ibn Taymiyyah* (London: Routledge, 2006), p. 75.

Theological Responses to the Arguments of the Extremist Groups 191

form on the basis of the Qur'an and the Sunnah.[366] The teachings of Ibn Taymiyya and Salafism have a profound influence on the subsequent extremist groups.

Salafism turned into a political structure under the title of "Wahhabism" that emerged in the eighteenth century. Wahhabism was founded by Muhammad ibn Abd al-Wahhab (d. 1772 CE), a Hanbalī scholar, in Saudi Arabia.[367] Similar to Ibn Taymiyya, Muhammad ibn Abd al-Wahhab focused on returning to the original principles of Islam established by the Noble Prophet. He rejected certain common Muslim practices, such as visiting graves, and deemed them as religious innovation or polytheism.[368]

Wahhabism belongs to the category of radical Islamist movements that seek to return to a strict application of the Sharia while opposing both Western encroachment and the intellectual, artistic and mystical tradition of Islam itself, doing all this in the name of an early puritan Islam that they consider to have been lost by later generations.[369]

Nowadays, Wahhabism is the most important source of inspiration in Saudi Arabia, and there has been a close relation between the Saudi ruling family and the Wahhabi religious establishment.[370] Like Salafism, Wahhabism proclaims monotheism as its primary doctrine. With the claim of returning to the pristine fundamentals of faith as established by the Noble Prophet, radical Islamic understanding has become attractive for many young Muslims who live in the Western countries, especially those experiencing pressure due to their Muslim identity. This is most likely the reason why many young Muslims from Western countries have joined the ISIS terrorist group in spite of their brutal violence and crimes against all humanity.

---

[366] Esposito, John L. *The Oxford Dictionary of Islam* (Oxford: Oxford University Press, 2003), p. 275.
[367] Commins, David. *The Wahhabi Mission and Saudi Arabia* (New York: I.B. Tauris. 2006), p. VI.
[368] Delong-Bas, Natana J. *Wahhabi Islam* (Oxford: Oxford University Press, 2004), p. 17.
[369] Commins, *The Wahhabi Mission and Saudi Arabia*, p. 24.
[370] Blanchard, Christopher M. *The Islamic Traditions of Wahhabism and Salafiyya* (Washington, D.C.: Congressional Research Service, Library of Congress, 2007), p. 13.

Some young and ignorant minds in the Western countries believe that ISIS fights against infidels to protect Islam and its values; therefore, they join this group in their holy war against the West. Additionally, ISIS exploits the notion of the caliphate to convince these young minds to join their ranks for the purpose of "serving a sacred mission." On the other side, the corrupt Arab rulers and the crushing of the Arab Spring uprisings have caused some Muslims to seek alternative methods to solve the problems in the Muslim world. While seeking a solution for the problems of the Muslim world, many people found themselves in the ranks of ISIS, persecuting innocent civilians of Muslims and other faiths and committing atrocities.

Jihad in the Context of Radical Islam

Since the seventeenth century, imperialism and colonialism have represented foreign cultural instruments and structures upon the East.[371] Colonialism is defined as the policy and practice of a power in extending control over weaker people or areas. The European empires and governments aimed to design the Muslim world according to their economic, political and strategic interests, causing Muslims societies to bear negative feelings towards the West.[372] In order to protect their countries and natural resources against colonialism and its negative effects, Muslim scholars have used the notion of *jihad* as counterattack.[373] They have emphasized this notion to encourage people to defend their lands.

Radical groups have long been using the word *jihad* to only refer to their "holy war," totally disregarding its all other meanings. Today, while committing acts of terrorism against civilians and innocent people, radical terrorist groups—such as ISIS and al-Qaeda, have similarly used the notion of jihad in a mere militant sense to justify their evil crimes. Additionally,

---

[371] Fuller, Graham. *A World, Without Islam* (New York: Little, Brown and Co., 2010), p. 249.
[372] Ibid, p. 250.
[373] Kurucan, Ahmet and Mustafa Kasim Erol, *Dialogue in Islam* (London: Great Britain, 2012), p. 53.

they have misinterpreted the battles of the time of the Prophet, the Four Righteous Caliphs and their successors by removing them from their historical contexts and approaching them from their extremist perspective.[374] This extremist understanding and the idea of resisting against the Western forces in Islamic lands have caused some young minds to be radicalized.

Although such acts of violence and extremism are completely at odds with Islam's basic principles, the claims of their perpetrators have led many ill-informed Westerners to understand *jihad* as encompassing indiscriminate acts of violence in the name of Islam.[375] Many Muslims and non-Muslims are united in their condemnation of terrorism. However, a great number of scholars and the media in the West have failed to question their interpretation of Islamic concepts. Using Islamic terminology ignorantly and by propagating misconceptions, they fuel terrorism for this stance decreases the perceived gap between the marginal terrorist groups and the majority of Muslims in the minds of many western people. It also reinforces the symbiotic relationship between Islamophobia and radicalization.[376]

The impression created in the West by ISIS and al-Qaeda-style terrorism has led many Western people to new extremes of misunderstanding Islam and the concept of *jihad*. For example, American Wesleyan pastor James L. Garlow holds the view that *jihad* can be something as violent as killing those who do not believe in Islam and attacking in the name of God, including such things as kidnappings and bombings.[377]

In order to protect one's faith, person, family, property and land against aggressors, Muslims can resort to physical force; however, this is one of the many meanings of *jihad*. The other meanings of *jihad* will be

---

[374] Esposito, *Unholy War: Terror in the Name of Islam*, p. 64.
[375] Kurucan and Erol, Dialogue in Islam, p. 45.
[376] Abbas, T. "The Symbiotic Relationship between Islamophobia and Radicalisation," *Critical Studies on Terrorism* 5 (2012), pp. 345–358.
[377] Garlow, James. *A Christian's Response to Islam* (Oklahoma: River Oak Publishing, 2002), p. 15.

explained later in detail. Declaring a war against enemy can only be done by the consensus of citizens, and if individuals or some groups resort to warfare, it is considered as an act of terror.

Contemporary Islamic scholar Fethullah Gülen argues that Muslims should never approve of any terrorist activity, and that terror has no place in a quest to achieve independence or salvation as it takes the lives of innocent people.[378] Furthermore, he refers to evidence from the Qur'an to support his view:

> He who kills a soul unless it be (in legal punishment) for murder or for causing disorder and corruption on the earth will be as if he had killed all humankind; and he who saves a life will be as if he had saved the lives of all humankind.[379]

Even when the Muslim community has to resort to war to defend their country for a just cause, the Noble Prophet has also brought many limitations:

> Do not betray, inflict injustice, plunder, or defile the bodies; do not kill children, the elderly, or women. Do not cut down the date orchards or burn them; do not cut down trees that bear fruit. Do not kill sheep, cattle, or camels unless it is for food. You may come across people who have retreated into monasteries on your way; do not touch them or interfere with their worship....[380]

Gülen maintains that such commandments are the historical records that warn the heads of states against any kind of injustice, and reminds leaders that they will be taken to account on Judgment Day for their acts.[381] However, extreme groups find young minds and radicalize them to employ

---

[378] Gülen, *Toward a Global Civilization of Love and Tolerance* (New Jersey: The Light, 2006), p. 57.
[379] Ünal, *Qur'an*, 5: 32.
[380] Ibn Athīr, Muhammad. *Usd al-Ghaba* (Beirut: Dār Iḥyā' al-Turāth al-'Arabi, 1968), 2/335.
[381] Sevindi, Nevval. *Fethullah Gülen'le Global Hosgoru ve New York Sohbetleri* (Istanbul: Timas, 2002), pp. 28-29.

them for their terrorist agenda. While imposing their extreme ideas on them, they misinterpret the Qur'an and the Sunnah by their partial approach and by disconnecting religious texts from their context.

Radical groups use Islamic concepts such as *jihad* to mask their acts of violence and terror and to increase their support from the general Muslim population. This is one of the main goals of Al-Qaeda and ISIS and, in order to achieve it, they resort to terror propaganda, using terminology with which most Muslims have an emotional and spiritual connection, such as *umma* (the global Muslim community), *sharia* (Islamic legal system), or *jihad* (struggling for God's cause).[382] Social media is used as a means to disseminate their radical ideas at the global level and thereby aiding in creating new radical identities and imaginaries.[383] As such, social media can be regarded as a means of diffusion and globalization of Salafist-jihadist ideology.

Another factor radical terrorist groups utilize to attract new people is the language used by the media and politicians. Western depictions of Islam are mostly monolithic, describing Islam as a religion of violence and terror.[384] Such a description poses a threat to national security in Western countries[385] and creates a golden opportunity for radical groups to recruit Muslims who feel oppressed to their side. Due to the detrimental effect of such language used by the media and politicians, many people in the West fear Islam and its followers for they see them as a threat to their most basic values. This fear feeds Islamophobia in the West, and in return, Islamophobia fuels radicalization in the Islamic world.

Radical terrorist groups exploit the misconceptions that non-Muslims have, such as the perceived hate and fear from Islam, and build up terrorist acts within the frame of defensive posture. Nevertheless, rather than

---

[382] Antúneza, Juan Carlos and Tellidisb Ioannis, "The Power of Words: The Deficient Terminology Surrounding Islam-Related Terrorism," *Critical Studies on Terrorism* 6 (2013), pp. 118–139.
[383] Orhan, Mehmet. "Al-Qaeda: Analysis of the Emergence, Radicalism, and Violence of a Jihadist Action Group in Turkey," *Turkish Studies* 11 (2010), pp. 143-161.
[384] Antúneza and Joannis, *The Power of Words: The Deficient Terminology Surrounding Islam-Related Terrorism*, pp. 118–139.
[385] Leeuwen, Van T. *Discourse and Practice* (Oxford: Oxford University Press, 2008), pp. 53-55.

targeting the few individuals that flirt and engage with radicalism, counter-radicalization policies in the West have had the effect of targeting and victimizing entire communities, hence becoming counter-productive.[386]

An examination of primary Islamic sources shows that Muslims are forbidden to declare the excommunication of others; indeed, such an act would turn against themselves. Islamic scholar Gülen points to this issue based on the evidence from primary Islamic sources to support his arguments. For example, he cites the following prophetic tradition to deter people accusing "other" Muslims of apostasy: "Any person who calls his brother as 'O unbeliever' (has in fact done an act by which this unbelief) would turn back to one of them. If it were so (if the person is an unbeliever as he asserted), then the unbelief of the man was confirmed but if it was not true, then it turns back to him (to the man who labeled it on his brother)."[387]

The aggression of radical groups towards Muslim countries that have co-operated with Western governments attracts ignorant minds who suffered greatly from Western colonization.[388] Using their hatred against the West, they try to spread their radical ideas among the non-extremist segments of the Muslim population. The attitude in many Western countries where Muslims are perceived, and sometimes even labeled, as terrorists, is not only offensive and insulting to the majority of Muslim believers, but also a great opportunity for the radical Islamic groups to justify their terrorist activities. Additionally, this approach has caused many Muslims who live in those Western countries to become the target of attacks by non-Muslims.[389] Therefore, "Islamic terrorism" is a provocative term. Muslims reject this term as it is against the very spirit and meaning of Islam. Consequently, using such terminology is very dangerous, especially if that kind of discourse is used by the West as it reinforces the

---

[386] Antúneza and Joannis, *The Power of Words: The Deficient Terminology Surrounding Islam-Related Terrorism*, pp. 118–139.
[387] Muslim, *Saḥīḥ Muslim* (Delhi: Adam Publishers, 1996), Iman 26.
[388] Fuller, *A World Without Islam*, p. 250.
[389] Saeed, Amir. "Media, Racism and Islamophobia: The Representation of Islam and Muslims in the Media," *Sociology Compass* 2 (2007), pp. 443-463.

idea that the West is an implacable enemy of Islam. Contrary to stereotypes, Islam advocates numerous non-violent and peace-building values, and expects Muslims to abide and live by them much like Christian doctrines.[390] There have been terrorist groups in almost every religion, yet this does not justify labeling its followers as "terrorists."

Upon examining the long history of Islam, one will see that Islam does never teach Muslims to kill innocent people in the name of God. In both the Qur'an and the prophetic traditions, there are many rules that invite Muslims to be "just" even when they are forced by their circumstances and conditions to fight their enemies. The vast majority of Muslim scholars have emphasized that Islam has always favored defense over offence and has given importance to mercy even towards adversaries. Moreover, the contemporary Islamic scholar Fethullah Gülen has repeatedly stated, "A real Muslim who has understood Islam in every aspect could never be a terrorist."[391] He emphasized the fact that terrorism must be condemned without any excuses, and labeled the suicide bombers as "the companions of hellfire." However, religious extremists have hijacked Islam just like it has happened periodically in Christianity and other faith traditions throughout history.[392]

According to the US National Counterterrorism Center, in cases where the religious affiliation of terrorism casualties could be determined, Muslims suffered between 82 and 97 percent of terrorism-related fatalities over the past five years.[393] The analysis of this data manifests that it is mostly Muslims who are the victims of radical groups, and Islamic countries are significantly burdened with it.

---

[390] Antúneza and Joannis, *The Power of Words: The Deficient Terminology Surrounding Islam-Related Terrorism*, pp. 118–139.
[391] Saritoprak, Zeki. "Fethullah Gülen's Thoughts on State, Democracy, Politics, and Terrorism," *The Muslim World*, 95 (2005), pp. 325–471.
[392] Ramsbotham et al., *Contemporary Conflict Resolution: The Prevention, Management and Transformation of Deadly Conflicts* (Malden, MA: Polity Press, 2011), pp. 339-345.
[393] *Country Reports on Terrorism: Annex of Statistical Information*, NCTC (National Counterterrorism Center), accessed on June 15, 2015. http://www.nctc.gov/docs/ir-of-the-9-11-comm-act-of-2007.pdf

Radicalism is not a problem just for the religion of Islam; rather, it has emerged in many of the world's major religions and faith traditions.[394] Although radicalism and Islamism have become synonymous in contemporary usage, the former is a more conservative subset of political Islamism.[395] Simply, while Muslims follow the tenets of Islam that are established by its primary sources—the Qur'an and the Sunnah (or Prophetic Traditions)—without resorting to any violence, radical groups interpret these sources in the direction of their political agendas, and often resort to terror to actualize their objectives.

Nowadays, radical terror groups, such as ISIS, have been using the concept of *jihad* in their campaign to promote their radical approach as "fighting for God's cause." With the deceptive usage of this term, they intend not only to justify their evil deeds, but also to obtain the support of Muslims all over the world. Parallel to this, many Western authors have affiliated this concept to the meaning of "holy war."[396] With such an approach, knowingly or unknowingly, they have supported the campaign of these radical groups. Therefore, this negative Western use of the term undermines the counter-terrorist, counter-extremist and anti-radicalization efforts by accepting and reinvigorating the legitimacy that extremists ascribe to the term.[397] For example, Bernard Lewis, the renowned historian of Orientalism, does this by saying, "The overwhelming majority of classical Muslim theologians, jurists, and traditionalists understood the obligation of *jihad* in a military sense."[398]

Pointing out the primary Islamic sources that give emphasis to its various meanings, Gülen opposes this biased opinion by referring to *jihad's* meanings in different contexts. Basing his explanations on these

---

[394] Armstrong, Karen. *The Battle for God: Fundamentalism in Judaism, Christianity and Islam* (Glasgow: Harper Collins, 2001), p. 27.
[395] Fuller, *The Future of Political Islam*, p. 48.
[396] Wagemakers, Joas. "Protecting Jihad: The Sharia Council of the Minbar Al-Tawhid Wa-L-Jihad," *Middle East Policy* 18 (2011), pp. 148–162.
[397] Antúneza and Joannis, *The Power of Words: The Deficient Terminology Surrounding Islam-Related Terrorism*, pp. 118–139.
[398] Lewis, Bernard. *The Political Language of Islam* (Chicago, IL: University of Chicago Press, 1998), p. 123.

Theological Responses to the Arguments of the Extremist Groups 199

primary Islamic sources, he defines *jihad* as one's struggling against all destructive emotions such as rancor, hatred, jealousy, arrogance, pride, self-love, egotism and the evil-commanding self.[399] In Prophetic traditions, *jihad* is conceptualized in a social context; a person who works for the good of widows and the needy is like those who fight in the name of God.[400] Another form of *jihad* mentioned in prophetic traditions is speaking the truth to a despotic and tyrannical ruler's face.[401] *Jihad* also has a social and intellectual dimension in the context of exerting conscience and reason to derive a legal ruling from the sources, namely *ijtihād*.[402] Although the word *jihad* and its conjugations are repeated 34 times in the Qur'an, only four of these usages refer directly to war.[403]

Obviously, Islam is not, in any sense, a violent religion. However, the mixture of politics and radical interpretation of religion has too often resulted in violence against innocent victims.[404] Radical groups have managed to deceive some Muslim minds with the idea of the East-West or cross-crescent conflict and confrontation. In order to convince them, they have employed a conspiracy theory against the Islamic religion and way of life. Indeed, to a certain degree, they have succeeded in their manipulative war propaganda against the West, since people in Muslim countries are mostly poor peasants who have little religious knowledge.[405]

In modern times, the neo-Kharijite terrorist groups have been abusing Islamic notions, such as *takfir* (accusing someone with disbelief) and *jihad* with a manipulative approach to justify their terror and violence. A great number of Islamic scholars and the majority of Muslim believers consider ISIS as a terrorist group and their activities as crimes against all humanity.

---

[399] Fethullah Gülen, *Asrın Getirdiği Tereddütler* (Questions and Answers about Islam) (İzmir: Nil Yayınları, 1998), Vol. 3, p. 26.
[400] Bukhari, *Saḥīḥ al-Bukhari* (Riyadh: Darussalam Pub. and Distr, 1997), Nafaqat 1.
[401] Abu Dawud, *Sunan Abu Dawud* (Lahore: Sh. M. Ashraf, 1984), Malahim 17.
[402] Kurucan and Erol, *Dialogue in Islam*, p. 54.
[403] Karlığa, Bekir. "Religion, Terror, War, and the Need for Global Ethics," in *An Islamic Perspective: Terror and Suicide Attacks*, ed. Ergun Capan (New Jersey: Light, 2004), p. 39.
[404] Combs, Cindy C. *Terrorism in the Twenty-First Century* (New Jersey: Person Prentice Hall, 1997), pp. 10-18.
[405] Armstrong, *The Battle for God: Fundamentalism in Judaism, Christianity and Islam*, pp. 33-37.

Similarly, the majority of Muslims deem ISIS and other similar terrorist groups to be against Muslims in the first place because of the fact that their doctrines are completely contrary to the primary Islamic sources, and that a vast majority of their victims are civilian Muslims. The international community needs to ensure that appropriate and effective measures are taken against them, rather than adopting an ineffective and overly simplistic approach. Therefore, in order to win the battle against all extremist, terrorist groups appearing in the Muslim world, Western countries should liaise with the moderate Muslim scholars, such as Gülen – the leading contemporary Muslim scholar who have publicly condemned all terrorist attacks, including the 9/11 attacks and the terrorist attacks on French magazine Charlie Hebdo and in Paris suburbs.[406] The following paragraphs will provide some lucid examples of how Gülen publicly denounced terror, violence and Islamist radicalization, decrying turning religion into radical, political ideology and highlighting the emphasis on peace in his strong discourse condemning all terrorist activities irrespective of their nature or source.

---

[406] For some of Gülen's writings published in various papers and journals, see *Wall Street Journal* Muslims must combat the extremist cancer, accessed on April 24, 2018 http://rumiforum.blogspot.com.au/2015/08/1fethullahgulens-op-ed-wsj-muslims-must.html#axzz5DXr4Lcr1.
Muslim World Journal Fethullah Gülen on Political Islam excerpt from *Muslim World Journal*, accessed on April 24, 2018 http://www.gule nmovement.com/fethullah-gulen-on-political-islam.html#. WTcvU16vZZ0. Twitter.
Politico Europe: Muslims' unique responsibility to fight terror, accessed on April 24, 2018 https://www.politico.eu/article/muslims-unique-responsibility-in-fighting-terror-london-attack-fethullah-gulen/
Todays Zaman-Gulen calls for respect for the sacred, denounces terrorism, accessed on April 24, 2018 http://rumiforum.blogspot.com.au/2015/01/gulen-calls-for-respect-for-sacred.html#axzz3PUGSYlt3.
Rita Cosby-Muslim voices against ISIS-Fethullah Gulen's stern stance, accessed on April 24, 2018 https://www.youtube.com/watch?v=zcZUozJPRzc&feature=youtu.be.
Fethullah Gulen's Statement Condemning ISIS on 5 Dailies, accessed on April 24, 2018 http://rumiforum.blogspot.com.au/2014/09/historic-fethullah-gulens-isis-message_17.html#axzz3Dm59mg1M
Financial Times - Opinion (Op-ed) by Fethullah Gulen: Violence is not in the tradition of the Prophet, accessed on April 24, 2018 http://rumiforum.blogspot.com.au/2012/09/financial-times-opinion-by-fethullah. html#axzz5DXr4Lcr1.
The Age - A Different Jihad, Qantara - 'An Alternative to Fundamentalism. accessed on April 24, 2018 http://en.qantara.de/content/interview-with-helen-rose-ebaugh-on-the-gulen-movement-an-alternative-to-fundamentalism?wc_c=8367

Gülen deems terrorism as the greatest blow to peace, democracy, and humanity[407] and he always condemns any terrorist activity irrespective of its perpetrators, or for what purpose it is done. He issues his statements in this regard on various media platforms. After the terrorist attacks that took place in Paris, he stated:

> I strongly condemn the terrorist attacks on French magazine Charlie Hebdo and in Paris suburbs. These revolting acts of terrorism are deplorable—they serve no purpose but to bring about destruction, sorrow and grief. I reiterate my condemnation of all forms of terror regardless of its perpetrators or their stated purposes. I share my deep condolences with the victims' families, loved ones and the people of France.[408]

Gülen sees radical groups as a real threat for the entire world, and therefore openly rejects their claims on the basis of the primary Islamic sources. His statement pertaining to the ISIS terrorist group was published in *New York Times*, *Washington Post*, *Chicago Tribune*, *Wall Street Journal* and *Los Angeles Times* on August 22, 2014. In his statement, he used highly powerful language to condemn their evil acts:

> I deplore the brutal atrocities being committed by the ISIS terrorist group hiding behind a false religious rhetoric and join the people of conscience from around the world in calling for these perpetrators to immediately cease their cruel and inhuman acts. Any form of attack, suppression or persecution of minorities or innocent civilians is an act that contradicts the principles of the Qur'an and the tradition of our Prophet, upon whom be peace and blessings. ISIS members are either completely ignorant of the spirit of Islam and its blessed Messenger, or their actions are designed to serve their individual interests or those of their political masters. Regardless, their actions represent those of a

---

[407] Gülen, *Toward a Global Civilization of Love and Tolerance*, p. 87.
[408] "Fethullah Gülen's statement on Paris attacks," accessed on February 24, 2015. http://fgulen.com/ en/press/messages/47207-fethullah-gulen-statement-on-paris-attacks

terrorist group and they should be labeled as such and be brought to justice.[409]

Gülen published a strong condemnation message when the 9/11 terrorist attacks happened in the USA. He deemed the terrorist attacks as the most bloody, condemnable one, and an assault against world peace as well as against universal democratic and humanistic values.[410] He stated that those who perpetrated this atrocity can only be considered as being the most brutal people in the world.[411]

He argues that killing a human is an act that is equal in gravity to not believing in God; therefore, no one can give a *fatwa* (a legal pronouncement in Islam, issued by a religious law specialist, concerning a specific issue) to that end. In his view, Islam has always respected different ideas but some radical leaders have misinterpreted Islam and misled ignorant people. He stresses upon the true methods to attain faith and states that just as a goal must be legitimate, so must be all the means employed to reach that goal. He holds that one cannot achieve heaven by murdering another person. For Gülen, individuals or groups cannot declare war; if they do, it is considered as an act of terror. War is only declared by the consensus of citizens to defend their country against all kinds of attacks. Some terrorist groups may argue that they make a *jihad* against a dictator in their country. However, they commit more evils and violate many human rights while fighting against a dictator.

Gülen deems violence as a disease that can be observed in every corner of the world.[412] Every kind of murder is accursed no matter who commits it. Terror cannot be rationalized on any basis. Insulting Islamic concepts or values does not legitimize the killings; therefore, Muslims cannot support any terrorist activity in their heart. In order to solve this problem, Gülen suggests that scholars, political and religious leaders should organize

---

[409] Gülen, "ISIS Cruelty Deserves Our Strongest Condemnation," accessed on February 24, 2015. http://www.fethullah-gulen.org/news/gulen-isis.html.
[410] Gülen, *Toward a Global Civilization of Love and Tolerance*, p. 73.
[411] Ibid., 74.
[412] Gülen, *Kirik Testi 4 Umit Burcu* (Istanbul: Gazeteciler ve Yazarlar Vakfi, 2005), 207.

Theological Responses to the Arguments of the Extremist Groups 203

conferences, events, panels and etc. on the issue of "respect for the sacred" and promote world peace by raising awareness for the sacred.

Gülen argues that it is antithetical to the creed and conduct of a believer to say, "So-and-so was an enemy of religion, of faith, of Islam, or of the Qur'an; it is good that he was killed, for he deserved it anyway."[413] Gülen believes that life is a sacred trust and it is necessary to protect all living beings. His view on life and its value can be understood better from his following statements:

> In my lifetime, I have never deliberately and knowingly stepped on even an ant. I did not see or speak to a friend of mine for months, for breaking the backbone of a snake. I have believed in the rights of every living being, that all of them have a place in the ecosystem. I have stated that we have no right or authority to harm a living being. It is a fact that the most honorable and most sacred of all creatures is the human being. I have repeatedly stated that those who murder under these pretexts or intentions cannot enter Paradise, and cannot be considered Muslims. This is not my personal opinion. It is the voice, expression, and breath of the ethos of Islam; this belief is part of our nature.[414]

It is antithetical to the core of Islam to use various pretexts and distort religious texts to justify acts of terrorism. Gülen argues that Muslims must strongly oppose terrorism for the Qur'an equates the murder of one person to disbelief:

> Whoever kills a believer intentionally, his recompense (in the Hereafter) is Hell, therein to abide; and God has utterly condemned him, excluded him from His mercy, and prepared for him a tremendous punishment.[415]
>
> He who kills a soul unless it be (in legal punishment) for murder or for causing disorder and corruption on the earth will be as if he had killed

---

[413] Gülen, *Kirik Testi 4Umit Burcu*, 208.
[414] Ergil, Dogu. *Fethullah Gülen and The Gülen Movement in 100 Questions* (New York: Blue Dome Press, 2012), pp. 93-95.
[415] Ünal, *Qur'an*, 4: 93.

all humankind; and he who saves a life will be as if he had saved the lives of all humankind.[416]

In order to support his view, Gülen brings the statement of the famous Quranic exegete 'Abd Allah ibn 'Abbas on this verse; for him, the repentance of those who kill a believer purposefully will be denied, and they will be doomed to eternal Hell.[417] Gülen concludes that considering that the life of a human is the most honorable issue, Islam regulated many rulings to protect it against any kind of harm or violence. In the following sections, the misconception of the term *jihad* as well as the sources of violence in the Muslim world will be explained.

Jihad from Gülen's Perspective

According to Gülen, numerous Islamic concepts, including especially the notion of *jihad*, have been misunderstood either because of their being disconnected from the traditional, historical meanings or because of their willful misinterpretation or misrepresentation by some misguided Muslims or some others with a vested interest in Islam.[418] For example, Joseph Schacht, one of the most influential Orientalists of the twentieth century, misunderstood *jihad*. He argues that the basis of the Islamic attitude towards the unbelievers is the law of war; they must be converted, subjugated, or killed.[419]

In order to have a true understanding of the concept of *jihad*, however, one needs to have a better perception of its meaning(s) as an Islamic term. Derived from the Arabic trilateral root j-h-d, *jihad* literally means using one's all strength, as well as moving toward an objective with one's all

---

[416] Ibid., 5: 32.
[417] Al-Tabarī, Ibn Jarīr. *Jami al-Bayan an Ta'wil Ay al-Qur'an* (Egypt: Dār al-Ma'āri, 1954), 4/295.
[418] Ergil, *Fethullah Gülen and The Gülen Movement in 100 Questions*, p. 96.
[419] Schacht, Joseph. *An Introduction to Islamic Law* (Oxford: Oxford University Press, 1964), p. 29.

power and strength and resisting every difficulty.[420] In Islamic literature, it has been defined as "learning, teaching and implementing religious commands, enjoining good while trying to prevent evil and, most importantly, struggling against the ego's lowly, evil desires."[421] The struggling (*jihad*) can be done in the internal and/or external aspects, according to Gülen. The effort to attain one's true essence can be evaluated in the internal aspect of *jihad* while the process of enabling someone else to attain his or her essence, can be considered in the category of external *jihad*.[422] Gülen claims that the internal *jihad* is the most challenging one for it is based on overcoming all obstacles in the way of divine love and spiritual bliss.[423] Essentially, *jihad* is removing obstacles between people and faith so that they can have a free choice to adopt a way.[424]

Since *jihad* is defined by Gülen as struggling in the path of God, all efforts made to reform one's self, the family, society and people can be included in his definition. In the true sense, *jihad* is conducted against one's ego and evil desires. Believers find inner peace and vitality in struggling against the negative desires of their ego. For Gülen, there are as many roads to God as the number of His creatures, and God leads those who strive for His sake to salvation via one or more of these roads.[425] Through this inner struggling, people follow the middle and balanced way (without falling into apathy or excess) regarding their anger, intellect and lust. Therefore, Gülen asserts that the greater *jihad* is proclaiming "war" on the ego's destructive and negative emotions and thoughts (such as malice, hatred, envy, selfishness, pride, arrogance, and pomp), which prevent people from attaining spiritual perfection.

Islam aims to stop war, terror, injustice and anarchy, and thus considers war as the very last resort to end disorder, oppression, and mischief. Islam allows Muslims to fight in particular situations but it is a

---

[420] Ibn Manzur, Muhammad ibn Mukarram. *Lisan al-Arab* (Beirut: Dār Ṣādir, 2000), 3/133.
[421] Al-Jassās, Abu Bakr al-Rāzī. *Kitāb al-Aḥkām al-Qur'an* (Beirut: Dār al-Kitāb al-'Arabī, 1978), 3/208.
[422] Gülen, *Essays, Perspectives, Opinions* (New Jersey: The Light, 2006), p. 60.
[423] Ibid., p. 61
[424] Ibid., p. 62.
[425] Ibid., p. 63.

temporary solution and a final straw. Peace is, however, permanent, and essential, in Islam. The Qur'an places great emphasis on the virtue of peace[426] and does not permit anyone to respond to an evil deed with one which is worse.[427] Even in an atmosphere in which two armies have fought against each other and blood has been shed, if the enemy forgoes fighting and wants to make a treaty, then the Muslims are commanded to not react emotionally, but to accept the treaty, putting their trust in God.[428] The issue of peace is very important considering that protection of human life and upholding justice are the two essentials of Islam. God Almighty states in the Qur'an:

> O you who believe! Be upholders and standard-bearers of right for God's sake, being witnesses for (the establishment of) absolute justice. And by no means let your detestation for a people (or their detestation for you) move you to (commit the sin of) deviating from justice. Be just: this is nearer and more suited to righteousness and piety.[429]

Gülen argues that in countries where Muslims reside, some so-called religious leaders and ignorant Muslims have no power or means other than their fundamentalist interpretation of Islamic issues. They use them in order to engage people in their evil agendas and make them to serve for their own vested purposes.[430] He maintains that the sources of terrorism in the Islamic world are three fold: ignorance, disunity and poverty. It is difficult to eliminate terror once metastasized before solving these three problems in the Muslim world.

Gülen maintains that true Muslims will never allow themselves to be involved in terrorist activities. However, the current problems, especially the anti-democratic practices and human rights violations, have resulted in the foundation of various disaffected groups who are severely deprived of their rights and who have easily been manipulated and used by the terrorist

---

[426] Ünal, *Qur'an*, 4:128.
[427] Ibid., 41: 34.
[428] Gülen, *Essays, Perspectives, Opinions*, p. 176.
[429] Ünal, *Qur'an*, 5: 8.
[430] Saritoprak, *Fethullah Gülen's Thoughts on State, Democracy, Politics, Terrorism*, 325–471.

groups to achieve their goals. Moreover, these terrorist groups have based all of their efforts on destruction and the creation of fear in society and have agitated the discontented segments of society by stirring up troubles and fomenting violence.

Gülen points to how terrorist groups recruit supporters for themselves. Some evil people take advantage of the discontented youth who have lost their spirituality by using them as murderers in the pretext of their so-called Islamic goals. Indeed, killing a human is a heinous crime and as is stated in the Qur'an, killing one person is the same as killing all people; therefore, a murderer will stay in Hell for eternity. He highlights that this fundamental Islamic principle should be given a thorough emphasis in education.

"Holy War"

There is no notion of a "holy war" in Islam. It is not legitimate to declare war against any people only on the basis of their disbelief[431] for there is no compulsion in Islam. Consequently, talking about fighting or conflict is completely contrary to the basic spirit of a religion that enjoins treaties and reconciliation, not only at the time of peace, but even during times of war.[432] Gülen believes that some evil people or groups or terrorist organizations instigate ignorant people who do not know the true criteria of their religion, and who act on emotions and chauvinism to manipulate them for their wicked purposes.

It is a reality that some people living in Islamic countries are not moderate Muslims with a balanced way of thinking and sufficient knowledge of their own sources. For this reason, Gülen argues that it is not wise to blame the "other" side (West) before recognizing the problems within the Muslim societies. He argues that if one lacks sound knowledge

---

[431] Bulaç, Ali. "Jihad,"in *An Islamic Perspective: Terror and Suicide Attacks*, Ergun Capan (ed.), New Jersey: The Light, 2004, p. 56.
[432] Gülen, *Essays, Perspectives, Opinions*, p. 64.

but possesses bravery, then his blind bravery can lead such an ignorant person to insanity or evil acts of terror, which are not rectifiable. Gülen states that no period of Islam witnessed the likes of today's atrocities, the so-called *jihadist* acts committed in the name of religion—including suicide attacks that have resulted in the mass murder of innocent people.[433]

Gülen severely condemns terrorists who use vehicles loaded with bombs to kill innocent people in the name of religion. For him, this is completely against the message of the Qur'an and the tradition of the Noble Prophet and such events truly embarrass and grieve Muslims.[434] He maintains that Muslims must always act in compliance with the principles of Islam, no matter what the circumstances are, and never forget that lawful ends must only be sought through lawful means.[435] Killing innocent people is a grave sin in Islam; therefore, Imam Abu Hanifa (669–767 CE), the founder of Hanafi school of thought, ruled that it is not lawful to march upon a group of people to fight if their intention (for waging a war) is not known.[436]

Gülen argues that the Noble Prophet was a man of love and peace and that his mission was to communicate the faith as he had been enjoined by God; therefore, he visited the most hard-hearted disbelievers many times without displaying any resentment.[437] He wanted all people to enter Paradise simply by declaring that there is no deity but God.[438] However, the Prophet never forced people to accept Islam. In order to show this clearly, Gülen mentions the Prophet's conquest of Makka through peaceful means and his lenient attitude towards those relentless enemies of Islam in the city. These Makkan unbelievers had persecuted Muslims for many long

---

[433] Gülen, "Weekly Lectures," accessed February 24, 2015. http://www.herkul.org/weekly-sermons/the-grave-consequence-of-murders-committed-under-the-guise-of-religion-2/.
[434] Gülen, "Weekly Lectures," accessed February 24, 2015. http://www.herkul.org/weekly-sermons/the-grave-consequence-of-murders-committed-under-the-guise-of-religion-1/.
[435] Gülen, *Endeavor for Renewal* (New Jersey: Tugra Books, 2015), p. 147.
[436] Al-Marghinani, Abū Bakr. *Al-Hidaya* (Karachi: Darul Ishaat, 2007), 2/170-171.
[437] Gülen, *Essays, Perspectives, Opinions*, p. 176.
[438] Ibn Kathīr, Ismail Abu al-Fida. *Al-Bidāya wa'l-Nihāya* (Beirut: Dar al-Kutub al-Ilmiyya, 2003), 3/62-63.

Theological Responses to the Arguments of the Extremist Groups 209

years but were now defeated and were thus fearful of their end. Upon the conquest, the Noble Prophet gathered them and addressed them as follows:

> I say to you as (Prophet) Joseph once said to his brothers. There is no blame for the actions that you have performed before. God will forgive you, too. He is the Most Merciful of the Merciful. Go, you are all free.[439]

He forgave them all, including his bitterest enemies, and did not force them to accept Islam. He left them free to choose whatever they choose to believe. Another time, he raised his hands to pray for those who stoned him, broke his teeth, wounded his cheek, and caused his head to be covered in blood: "O God, grant guidance to my people, for they do not know!"[440]

When we examine all the evil acts of ISIS, it becomes crystal clear that there is no connection or similarity between their horrible crimes and the noble acts of Prophet Muhammad, upon whom be peace and blessings. Obviously, the terrorist groups who exploit Islamic concepts such as *jihad* to attract young minds delude people and blacken the face of Islam.

To enlighten such deluded young minds, there is an unquestionable need for moderate Muslim scholars who are able to fulfill the hope and aspirations of individuals, communities, and groups of followers alike whilst educating Muslims on respecting the members of other faiths, ethnic backgrounds and diverse cultures.[441] In this regard, Gülen and his followers displayed remarkable creativity and activism with regard to interfaith dialogue throughout the world, establishing over 50 interfaith centers in the United States alone.[442] For Gülen, Judaism, Christianity, and Islam, and even Hinduism and other world religions, accept the same Divine source

---

[439] Iraqi, Abd al-Rahim ibn al-Husayn. *Al-Mughni an Haml al-Asfar* (Beirut: Dar al-Kitab al-'Arabi, 2011), 3/179.
[440] Qadi Iyad, *Al-Shifa* (Damascus: Dar al-Wafa lil-Ṭibaʿah wa-'al-Nashr, 1972), 1/105.
[441] Dogan, Recep, "Conflict Resolution Forms in the Life of Prophet Muhammad," *The International Journal of Religion and Spirituality in Society* 4 (2014), pp. 9-19.
[442] Kayaoglu, Turan. "Constructing the Dialogue of Civilizations in World Politics: A Case of Global Islamic Activism," *Islam and Christian–Muslim Relations* 23 (2012), pp. 129-147.

for themselves, and they, along with the monotheistic religions such as Buddhism, "pursue the same universal goals."[443]

He argues that no divine religion has ever been based on conflict, whether it be the religions represented by Moses and Jesus, or the religion represented by Muhammad.[444] Gülen disagrees with Huntington who predicted the clashes among civilizations. He believes that the breeze of mutual respect and interfaith dialogue will continue to blow, and it is powerful enough to overwhelm lethal weapons, to subdue mechanized military units, and much of any other negativity that may arise.[445] He predicts that if mutual respect is represented in the best possible way, it will encourage people to come together, to foster the same basic human values enabling humankind to experience the bliss of one more spring, before seeing the end of the world.[446]

It is not hard to see that terror and Islamic radicalization threaten world peace. In order to win the war against terrorist groups, the West should utilize the opportunity of promoting moderate Islamic understanding. In this regard, Fethullah Gülen is a prominent Islamic thinker and a very effective community leader. He inspires moderate Islam to millions all over the globe. His views on terror can be summarized as follows: In true Islam, terror does not exist. A Muslim cannot kill another human being, nor could he touch an innocent person, even in time of war. Since Islam never permits any terrorist activity, Muslim scholars must be very careful on this matter, ensuring that no one gives a *fatwa* (a legal verdict) in the favor of terrorists. In this regard, a suicide bombing is absolutely forbidden in Islam; Islam does not permit it even in the event of war. Anyone who kills him/herself and other innocent people in a suicide bombing is destined to hell fire.

Islam has always respected different ideas and this must be understood before it can be appreciated in the true sense. Islam is a true faith, and on the way to attaining faith, one can never use illegitimate methods, such as

---

[443] Fethullah Gülen, *Advocate of Dialogue*, (Fairfax, VA: Fountain Press, 2000), p. 17.
[444] Gülen, *Essays, Perspectives, Opinions*, p. 256.
[445] Ibid., p. 257.
[446] Ibid., p. 258.

murdering another person, then expecting to enter heaven. The most important goal for a Muslim is to win the pleasure of God and it can never be won by killing people.

Terrorism is ugly in its nature, and it must be addressed with a great deal of consideration. Politicians and all the responsible government officials should aim to find the motivating factors for radicals and remove them; otherwise, all nations will be under threat. In order to eradicate terror once and for all, the underlying reasons behind terrorism must be discovered and addressed on a global scale.

The Major Factors for the Spread of Islam

Islam has been criticized by many scholars because it recognizes war, and even commands it in certain situations. Partial understanding of the Quranic verses and ignoring their historical context are the main reasons to misunderstand the verses dealing with the rules on war. The wars in the time of the Noble Prophet were only to defend the nascent Muslim community against the hostile world. After 15 years of severe persecution during the early period of Islam, Muslims were allowed by God to defend themselves. In other words, Islam allowed its followers to end the cruel injustice and to rescue the oppressed. The Noble Prophet wanted to establish an environment where people practice their religions freely. In this regard, he recognized Jews, Christians and polytheist Arabs as equal citizens in the Charter of Medina (aka. Medina Constitution) and this treaty was signed by all groups in Medina.

Although there is not a specific commandment in the Gospels to permit war, Western history has many examples of long, bloody wars that were waged in the name of Christianity. Indeed, Christianity was often employed by the leading western countries for the colonization of two thirds of the world's peoples and resources. Islam did not introduce war to humanity; rather, it emerged with the existence of human beings on earth. Islam – meaning peace – aims to give happiness to its followers. However, war is a reality of human history. Criminal minds and greedy people have caused many wars among nations and civilizations. If people are not trained and educated against their aggressive, evil desires, they are more likely to commit crimes and cause disorder. Since it is not possible to equip all people with good character and educate them with respect towards each other, wars will continue to be the reality of human history. Thus, rather than denying this reality, Islam recognized war and established many rulings and introduced restrictions to prevent injustice, torture and many other evil conducts, even in the state of war.

In Islam, war is the last resort to employ, and though it is not something desirable in itself, it is employed to defend the land, to prevent injustice, and to protect people and their honor. The Quranic verses on war do not encourage Muslims to attack others; rather, they allow Muslims to defend themselves on condition that it be for a just cause and that the limits set by God must never be exceeded in any state of war. Islam never permits war for motives such as occupation or plunder. In Islam, it is not permissible to force people from different faith groups to change their religions.

Some scholars and intellectuals who have prejudice about Islam hold that Islam is a religion of war which was spread by the force of the sword. This is a baseless argument because Muslims did not force people from other faith traditions to accept Islam when they conquered new lands. However, many people from various ethnic and cultural backgrounds in those new lands embraced Islam with their free will while others chose to remain with their beliefs. As a matter of fact, people's hearts must be won over before they put their lives in danger for a lofty cause. In the long history of Islam, we see many people from different cultures that embraced Islam and strived for it. There must be something in the religion itself that explains its persistence and spread. Therefore, Islam itself was the main cause for its triumph.

Islam has spread because of its religious content and values.[447] Islam's power of appeal as well as its ability to meet both the spiritual and physical needs of people is the main reason for its spread. It is also about the

---

[447] Arberry, A. J. *Aspects of Islamic Civilization*, p. 12.

tolerance Islam has shown to the people from various faith traditions, the absence of an ecclesiastic hierarchy, intellectual freedom, the equity and justice that Islam enjoins and that Muslims have striven for throughout the centuries, the ethical values Islam propagates, its inclusiveness and universalism, as well as its brother/sisterhood.[448] There are also a number of other reasons which made Islam spread so quick and wide, such as Muslim tradesmen representing Islam in the best way possible while doing business with people from other faiths in foreign lands.

Islam's creed principles are simple and rational. There is a harmony between Islamic teachings and human nature. Islam addresses every aspect of life whether it is individual, social, administrative, physical, mental or spiritual. Islamic creed is universal and compatible with the established scientific facts. The obligations Islam offers to its followers are doable in everyday life. The noted scholar Brockelman sees the religious values of Islam as the main factor for its spread[449] while Rosenthal argues that it is the religious law which was designed to cover all manifestations of life.[450]

Orientalist scholar Toynbee praises Muslim tolerance towards the People of the Book, after comparing it with the attitudes of Christians towards Muslims and Jews in their lands.[451] Another orientalist scholar, Trevor Ling, attributes the spread of Islam to the credibility of its principles, its tolerance, persuasiveness and many other attractive elements.[452] We see many Christian people from different denominations who prayed for the Muslim rulers due to their just treatment and respect to them.[453] For example, the Orthodox Christians of Byzantium openly expressed their preference for the Ottoman rulers in Istanbul to the Catholic cardinals for they recognized the freedom of religious practice, allowing the followers of different religions to perform their religious duties and rituals freely.[454] Even the Christians in Romania stated that it

---

[448] Ünal, *The Quran with Annotated Interpretation in Modern English*, Appendix 2.
[449] Brockelman, *History of the Islamic Peoples*, p. 37.
[450] Rosenthal, *Political Thought in Medieval Islam*, p. 21.
[451] Toynbee, *An Historian Approach to Religion*, p. 246.
[452] Ling, Trevor. *A History of Religion*, p. 330.
[453] Ling, *A History of Religion*, p. 331.
[454] Barth, Hans. *Le Droit du Croissant*, p. 143.

was very fortunate for the Romanian people that they lived under the government of the Turks rather than that of the Russians or Austrians; otherwise, they said, "No trace of the Romanian nation would have remained."[455] The famous Muslim historian al-Baladhuri reports:

> When Muslims heard that the Byzantine Roman emperor Heraclius massed his troops against them, they refunded the inhabitants of Hims the tribute they had taken from them, saying: "We will no longer be able to protect you. Get this back and take care of yourselves." But the people of Hims replied: "We like your rule and justice far better than the state of oppression and tyranny in which we were. We shall indeed, with your help, repulse the army of Heraclius from the city." The Jews rose, saying: "We swear by the Torah, no governor of Heraclius shall enter the city of Hims unless we are first vanquished and exhausted." After this, they all closed the gates of the city and guarded it together. The Christian and Jewish inhabitants of many other cities that were surrounded did the same thing. When, by God's help, they were defeated and the Muslims won, they opened the gates of their cities, went out with the singers and players of music, and paid tribute to them.[456]

In conclusion, Islam gives great importance to human life and deems killing a person as killing the whole humanity; similarly, it deems saving the life of one person as saving all humankind. Therefore, the purpose of war in Islam is not killing people; rather, it is done for a just cause, such as protecting people, land, human dignity and so on. Opposing the main principles of Islam, the bloody terrorist groups kill innocent people unjustly; therefore, they cannot be considered as Muslims.

In Islam, peace is essential while war is temporary. Even in warfare, Islam is ready to make peace and a treaty with the opposing side. After making a treaty with other nations, the Muslim state must remain faithful to it. The terrorist groups are, however, not open to any negotiation or

---

[455] Djevad, *Revue du Monde Musulman*, pp. 71–72.
[456] Al-Baladhuri, *Futuh al-Buldan*, trans. by P. K. Hitti and F. C. Murgotten, *Studies in History, Economics and Public Law*, (New York, Columbia University Press, 1916 and 1924), vol. I, pp. 207-211.

treaty, they just kill innocent people and, with this hostile and aggressive attitude, they oppose the very basic principles of Islam. Islam applies the strictest rules against terrorists because they employ violence and threaten public safety. Terrorist people do not understand any other language than fighting against them; therefore; the Qur'an commands believers to fight against them until they surrender.

THEOLOGICAL AND POLITICAL FOUNDATIONS OF CALIPHATE IN ISLAM

Introduction

The institution of caliphate has an honorable place among Muslims; therefore, it has been discussed by many scholars throughout Islamic history. Muslim scholars have conducted many researches about the institution of caliphate to find out whether it is based on religious or political grounds as well as its significance for Muslim nations while Western scholars considered it only as a political authority and hence constituted their views accordingly. When the Caliphate was abolished by the newly-established secular Turkish government in 1924, various views have been articulated to understand if a religious institution can be abolished by any state. Before the Noble Prophet passed away, he did not assign any person to take his position as a ruler (Caliph-successor) of the Muslim community.

There are three views among Muslim scholars regarding the institution of caliphate: the first view is that caliphate is a sacred institution, it is universal and necessary for all Muslims; the second view is that it is a political institution and was established according to the needs of Muslims; and the third view argues that there is no such institution in Islam nor is there a need for it. Considering differing views, it is imperative to examine Islamic sources to identify the nature of caliphate and whether it has theological and/or political values. This section will investigate the nature and objectives of caliphate in Islamic history and will also analyze the efforts of modern-day Muslims to revitalize it.

Caliphate in the Early Islamic History

The first ruler for Muslims in Islamic history was Prophet Muhammad, upon whom be peace and blessings. During the first 13 years of his mission in Makkah, he carried out the mission of Messengership by inviting people to the faith in one-and-only God in polytheist Makkah. It was during the last 10 years of his Messengership that the Noble Prophet took the responsibility of rulership and became the head of the state for a cosmopolite society in Medina. The community of Jews, polytheist Arabs and Muslims accepted him as their leader and ruler. During the Medinan period, the Noble Prophet performed two missions: receiving the revelations from God and conveying them to his followers and ruling the people of Medina. In short, he had the religious and political positions throughout those 10 years in Medina.

However, the Noble Prophet did not state who would be the head of the state after him nor did the Qur'an assign anyone for this position. In this regard, his beloved wife Aisha stated that the Messenger of God passed away while he did not assign anyone as the head of the state after him.[457] Similarly, 'Umar, the second Caliph, stated as to why he did not assign anyone as a ruler after him. It was simply because he did not oppose the practice of the Noble Prophet.[458] Based upon all these statements, it is logical to say that choosing a ruler for Muslims is a political issue; therefore, it is left to people to choose their rulers.

However, the election of the first caliph after the Noble Prophet was extremely important for the unity of Muslims due to the political and social conditions of the time. After the death of the Noble Prophet, Makkan

---
[457] Ibn Hanbal, *Musnad al-Imam Ahmad ibn* Hanbal, (Beirut: Dar al-Kutub al-'Ilmiyya, 1993), 6/63.
[458] Ibn Hisham, *Sirah al-Nabawiyya*, (Cairo: Dar al-Salam lil-Ṭibaʻah wa-al-Nashr wa-al-Tawziʻ wa-al-Tarjamah, 2013), 2/653.

Muslims gathered around Abu Bakr and Medinan Muslims around Sa'd ibn 'Ubada.[459] After long discussions Abu Bakr was elected as the first ruler of Muslim population.[460] His title was *Khalifatu Rasul al-Allah* (the Successor of the Messenger of God) which can be understood as "the ruler who comes after the Noble Prophet."

The first four caliphs, Abu Bakr (632–34), 'Umar (634–44), 'Uthman (644–56) and 'Ali (656–61) have been called as "the Rightly Guided Caliphs" (Khulafa al-Rashidin) by Sunni Muslims.[461] Their ruling period is considered the Golden Age of Islam when the principles of Islam were applied in every aspect of life. This ruling period of the first four caliphs lasted only 29 years (632-661 CE). However, during this period, Islam expanded swiftly, defeating the Sassanid Empire, halving and almost destroying the Byzantine Roman Empire and expanding into South Asia, Central Asia and through North Africa into the Iberian Peninsula.[462] The distribution of the ruling period of these four Caliphs is 2 years for Abu Bakr, 10 years for 'Umar (who was assassinated), 12 years for 'Uthman (who was assassinated), and five years for 'Ali (who was assassinated).

The death of the Noble Prophet caused many social and political problems to be emerged; therefore, the first Caliph Abu Bakr had to fight against apostates who did not want to recognize a new ruler and did not want to fulfill their duties towards the Islamic State. Abu Bakr successfully handled the problems during his short caliphate period and designated 'Umar as his successor in his deathbed. Muslims in the nascent Islamic community did not oppose his decision and accepted 'Umar as the second Caliph. Following his ten year-long caliphate, 'Umar was assassinated by a Persian slave in 644 CE. Before he died, he did not assign a specific person as his successor, but he had appointed a council which consisted of six people to elect the new ruler. The council chose 'Uthman ibn 'Affan as the

---

[459] Ibn Sa'd, Muhammad. *Kitab al-Tabaqat al-Kabir*, (London: Ta-Ha Publishers Ltd, 2012), 3/613-617.
[460] Ibn Hisham, *Sirah*, 2/657.
[461] Crone, Patricia and Martin Hinds, *God's Caliph: Religious Authority in the First Centuries of Islam*, (Cambridge and New York: Cambridge University Press, 1986), p. 5.
[462] Liebl, Vernie. "The Caliphate," *Middle Eastern Studies* 45 (2009), pp. 373-391.

third Caliph. Choosing a caliph in the first three personalities (Abu Bakr, 'Umar and 'Uthman) thus established three different methods: public election, designation by a previous caliph, and assigning a caliph by a council. Ali, the fourth Rightly-Guided Caliph, was also chosen by the Muslim community.

After the assassination of Caliph Ali, Mu'āwiya announced his caliphate and thereafter the Umayyad family stayed in the caliphate position for the following 90 years. The institution of caliphate then passed on to many different Islamic governments for a very long time until it was abolished by the newly-established secular Turkish Republic in 1924.

Caliphate from Theological and Political Perspectives

The Arabic word *khilāfa* (caliphate) is used in the meaning of vicegerency in the Holy Qur'an:

> Remember (when) your Lord said to the angels: "I am setting on the earth *a caliph* (vicegerent)." The angels asked: "Will you set therein one who will cause disorder and corruption on it and shed blood, while we glorify You with Your praise and declare that You alone are all-holy and to be worshipped as God and Lord." He said: "Surely I know what you do not know."[463]

> He (God) it is who has made you *caliph*s (vicegerents) on the earth. So whoever disbelieves (in ingratitude, rejecting this truth and attributing God's deeds to others than Him), his unbelief is charged against him.[464]

According to these verses, every person on earth is a caliph of God Almighty. In order to honor humankind, God has made them His vicegerents on earth. The word *khalifa* (caliph) is also used in the Holy

---

[463] Ünal, *The Quran with Annotated Interpretation in Modern English* (New Jersey: Tughra Books, 2007), 2: 30.
[464] Ünal, *Qur'an*, 35: 39.

Qur'an to indicate the honorable position of a specific person among the servants of God:

> O David! We have appointed you a *vicegerent* (*khalifa*) in the land (to rule according to Our commandments); so judge among people with the truth and do not follow personal inclination, lest it leads you astray from the path of God. Surely, those who wander astray from God's path – for them there is a severe punishment because they have forgotten the Day of Reckoning.[465]

The word *khalifa* (caliph) is also used in the meaning of successors. According to this usage in the Qur'an, each generation is the *khalifa* (caliph, or successor) of the previous one.

> He (God) it is who has brought you as *successive generations* to the earth, and has exalted some of you over others in degrees (of intelligence, capacity, and then wealth and status): thus He tries you in what He has granted you.[466]

The word *ikhtilaf*, which literally means dispute or disagreement, is also derived from the word *khilāfa* (caliphate). This word alludes to the fact that every person is different from others in regards to their thoughts, emotions, characters and worldviews:

> If your Lord had so willed (and withheld from humankind free will), He would have made all humankind one single community (with the same faith, worldview, and life-pattern). But (having free choice) they never cease to differ.[467]

In Islam, Prophet Muhammad, upon whom be peace and blessings, is the Seal of the Prophets[468] and no one takes the place of the Noble Prophet

---

[465] Ünal, *Qur'an*, 38: 26.
[466] Ünal, *Qur'an*, 6: 165.
[467] Ünal, *Qur'an*, 11: 118.
[468] Ünal, *Qur'an*, 33: 40.

in his mission of Prophethood. However, his position as a ruler can be represented by other Muslims as the Qur'an sates, "*O you who believe! Obey God and obey the Messenger and those from among you who are invested with authority...*"[469]

One of the basic principles of Islam is that only the qualified persons are to be given a job. Naturally, this principle should also valid for the selection of a caliph. Having all the necessary qualifications, Abu Bakr, for instance, was not a member of the Noble Prophet's immediate family, and was elected by the Muslims as the first Caliph, and thus the successor of the Prophet.

Considering the historical context, we can see two different opinions emerging about choosing a leader for the early Muslim community: Abu Bakr was the best candidate for the caliphate due to his seniority in Islam and being the most respected Companion of the Noble Prophet. On the other hand, the Shiites claim that Ali was the most suitable candidate for the caliphate for he was the closest relative of the Noble Prophet. This difference of opinion indicates that different attitudes appeared among Muslims on the issue of leadership after the Noble Prophet.

The determination of a title for the new leader was difficult for the Companions used the title "God's Messenger" for their leader, Noble Prophet; therefore, Muslim community adopted two new titles for Muslim rulers after the Prophet: the ruler of believers (*amir al-mu'minin*) and the deputy of God (*khalifah Allah*). The English word *caliph* is derived from this second term (*khalifah*).

Because of the political conditions of the time in Arabian Peninsula, the first four caliphs were chosen from the Quraysh tribe. For the first time in political history of Islam, the Kharijite sect (who separated from 'Ali due to the Arbitration Incident) chose their own caliph.[470] Choosing a caliph from outside of the Quraysh bloodline is a controversial issue among Muslim scholars. There are two views on this matter; according to the first view, any person who has necessary qualifications and knowledge

---

[469] Ünal, *Qur'an*, 4: 59.
[470] Shahristani, *al-Milal Wa'n-Nihal*, (Cairo: Maktabat al-Ḥusayn al-Tijariyah, 1948), 1/177.

in Islamic principles can be a ruler and a caliph.[471] The Kharijite and Mutazilite sects hold this view. The second group holds that a caliph must be from the Quraysh. This view will be discussed in detail in the next section for it is against the principles of Islam.

A marginal group in the Kharijite sect holds that Muslims do not need the institution of caliphate; rather, they apply the rules of Islam by themselves.[472] However, the majority in this group holds that caliphate is necessary for the benefit of Muslims but any Muslim who is qualified to be a ruler can be a caliph.[473] The Prominent Ash'arī scholar Abd al-Qāhir Baghdadi (1075-1153 CE) agrees with the Kharijites on this matter; he argues that any capable Muslim can be chosen as a caliph.[474]

Imam Māturīdī (d. 944 CE) who is the leading Sunni imam in Islamic creed holds that a caliph must be pious, capable to rule Muslim community in the best way and be a wise person who has the best decisions in political matters. He states that choosing a caliph must be, first and foremost, in line with Islamic principles.[475] The Ash'arī scholar Baqillānī (950-1013 CE) argues that since designation of a caliph is not determined by the religious text, it is left to the choice of Muslims.[476] Ibn Hazm (994-1064 CE), the founder of Ẓāhirī School (the sect that understands religious texts literally), holds that a caliph must be from the bloodline of the Quraysh and claims that there is a consensus on this matter.[477] However, he contradicts himself by stating that if a person can lead Muslims in prayer, he can also lead them in political matters.[478] The prominent scholar Imam Ghazālī (1058-1111 CE) has the same view as Ibn Hazm for he maintains that a caliphate

---

[471] Ibn Ḥazm, Ali ibn Aḥmad. *Kitāb al-Faṣl fī al-Milal wa-al-Ahwā' Wa'n-Nihal*, (Baghdad: Maktabat al-Muthanna, 1964), 4/89.
[472] Shahristani, *al-Milal Wa'n-Nihal*, 1/193.
[473] Al-Ash'ari, Imam Abu Hasan. *Maqalat al-Islamiyyin*, (Cairo: Maktabat al-Thaqafah al-Diniyah, 2005), 1/204.
[474] Baghdadi, Abd al-Qahir. *Usul al-Din*, (Istanbul: Matba at al-Dawlah, 1928), 275.
[475] Nasafi, Abul Mu'in Muhammad. *Tabsirat'ul Adilla*, (Ankara: Diyanet Isleri Baskanligi Yayinlari, 1993) 1/299.
[476] Baqillani, Abu Bakr Muhammad. *Kitab al-Tamhid*, (Beirut: al-Maktabah al-Sharqiyah, 1957), 178.
[477] Ibn Hazm, *Fasl*, 4/109.
[478] Ibn Hazm, *Fasl*, 4/109.

must be from the bloodline of the Quraysh.[479] The Ḥanafī scholar Sadr al-Sharia (d. 1346 CE) disagrees with them. He holds that the criterion of being from the bloodline of Quraysh to be elected as a caliph was abolished after the first four caliphs; therefore, any qualified Muslim can be elected for this position.

It is worth to mention the opinions of the famous Muslim historian Ibn Khaldun (1334-1406 CE) for he has unique opinions on the matter of caliphate. He argues that the issue of politics and caliphate is related to representing God's justice among His servants; therefore, whoever is capable of providing justice when ruling Muslims can be elected as a caliph.[480] In order to claim the rulership of Muslims, a person must possess certain qualifications according to Ibn Khaldun and these prerequisites can be summarized as follows:[481]

- The ruler or the caliph must be knowledgeable regarding Islamic Law and be capable of independent decision making.
- The caliph must be just, upright and honest person.
- The caliph must possess a strong character to carry out his political duties. He is expected to understand political affairs and maintain the welfare of the public even during the times of war.
- The caliph is expected to be healthy in all senses and limbs. He should be free from any disabilities.

When examining these conditions, it is clear that caliphate is understood as political rulership and a person can be a caliph if he has necessary qualifications to rule Muslims.

Ibn Khaldun analyzed the history of caliphate and argued that during the gestation period of Islam, caliphs were chosen from the bloodline of the Quraysh and they all tried their best to provide justice for all the

---

[479] Ghazali, Abu Hamid Muhammad. *Ihya al-Ulum al-Din*, (Lahore: Islamic Book Foundation, 1983), 2/120.
[480] Ibn Khaldun, *Muqaddimah*, trans. F. Rosenthal, (Princeton, NJ: Princeton University Press, 1967), p. 137.
[481] Ibn Khaldun, *The Muqaddimah*, pp. 158-159.

Theological Responses to the Arguments of the Extremist Groups 223

citizens in the Islamic state, then it turned out to be "a kingdom where obeying a caliph was accepted as one of the pillars of Islamic creed."[482] He argues that God did not choose a specific group or race or nations to convey His message; rather, it is incumbent upon all Muslims. A caliph is responsible to take care of political affairs; therefore, only an eligible person is to be assigned for this position.[483] With this view, he maintains that if the Quraysh cannot fulfill the conditions of caliphate, they are not assigned for this position. However, most of the Sunni scholars held the view that a caliph must be from the bloodline of the Quraysh on the basis of a specific prophetic tradition. In order to clarify the topic further from the theological perspective this hadith will be analyzed below.

Is It a Must for a Caliph to Be from the Bloodline of the Quraysh?

When the Noble Prophet passed away, he did not assign any person as a ruler in his position; therefore, the residents of Medina (Ansār literally meaning "Helpers") gathered together in a place called Thaqifatu Bani Sa'ida to choose a ruler for the Muslim community. The other main group in the Muslim community was the people of Quraysh who immigrated from Makkah to Medina together with the Noble Prophet; therefore, they were called *Muhajirun* (Emigrants). Abu Bakr and 'Umar quickly went to Thaqifatu Bani Sa'ida where Abu Bakr made his long speech including the prophetic tradition which states that a caliph must be from the bloodline of the Quraysh:

> Umar reports, "After the death of God's Messenger we were informed that the Ansar (Helpers – the residents of Medina) disagreed with us and gathered in the shed of Bani Sa'ida. I said to Abu Bakr, 'Let's go there and dispute the matter with them...' There, the speaker from the Ansar said, 'None has the right to be worshipped but God, we are God's Messenger's helpers and the majority of the Muslim army, while you, the emigrants, are a small group and some people among you came with the intention of preventing us from practicing this matter (of

---
[482] Ibid., p. 155.
[483] Ibid., pp. 195-196.

caliphate) and depriving us of it.' When the speaker had finished, I intended to speak but Abu Bakr said, 'Wait,' and then he started to give the speech: 'O Ansār! You deserve all (the qualities that you have attributed to yourselves), but this question of *caliphate* is only for the Quraysh as they are the best amongst the Arabs in relation to family lineage and home, and I am pleased to suggest that you choose either of these two men, 'Umar or Abu 'Ubayda ibn al-Jarrah...' Then one of the Ansār said, 'There should be one ruler from us and one from you.' Then there was a hue and cry among the gathering and their voices rose. Then, I ('Umar) said, 'O Abu Bakr! Hold your hand out' and I pledged allegiance to him, and then all of the emigrants gave their pledge of allegiance to him and so did the Ansār afterwards (so Abu Bakr was chosen as the first Caliph of Muslims).[484]

Upon examining this narration, one can clearly see that choosing a caliph or a ruler is a matter of administration. The problematic part here is the expression "Caliphate is only for the Quraysh as they are the best amongst the Arabs in relation to family lineage and home." Unfortunately, most of the scholars understood this expression as a prerequisite of caliphate and with this attitude, they opposed an Islamic principle for racism is abolished by the Noble Prophet and there is abundant evidence in the Qur'an and the Sunnah to prove it. God declares people equal in the Qur'an and gives them the honor only in piety:

> O humankind! Surely We have created you from a single (pair of) male and female, and made you into tribes and families so that you may know one another (and so build mutuality and co-operative relationships, not so that you may take pride in your differences of race or social rank, or breed enmities). Surely the noblest, most honorable of you in God's sight is the one best in piety, righteousness, and reverence for God. Surely God is All-Knowing, All-Aware.[485]

---

[484] Bukhari, *Sahih Bukhari*, Hudud, (Riyadh: Darussalam Pub. and Distr., 1997), 57.
[485] Ünal, *Qur'an*, 49: 13.

The Noble Prophet abolished racism with his practices and words. For example, he said, "All humankind is from Adam and Eve; an Arab has no superiority over a non-Arab nor a non-Arab has any superiority over an Arab. Also, a white has no superiority over black, nor a black has any superiority over white except by piety and good action"[486] and "If a black Abyssinian Muslim is to rule over Muslims, he should be obeyed."[487]

The Noble Prophet appointed the right people to do the right job, based on his profound prophetic judgment of them, given their skills, abilities and limitations.[488] It was not just through his words but also his actions that enabled the Noble Prophet to remove racism and discrimination so successfully and effectively. An example of this is the words of 'Umar (who was from the bloodline of the Quraysh): "Bilal (a former black slave) is our master, and was emancipated by our master Abu Bakr."[489] Also, Zayd ibn Haritha, a former slave freed by the Noble Prophet, was assigned as the commander of the Muslim army when such leading and experienced Companions as Abu Bakr, 'Umar, Ja'far ibn Abū Tālib, and Khalid ibn Walid (all from the bloodline of the Quraysh) were among the soldiers.[490]

From religious perspective, it is unacceptable that a caliph must only be from the bloodline of the Quraysh and that people from other races, cultures and nationalities cannot be assigned for this position. Now, it is imperative to explain the politic value of the statement, "Caliphate is only for the Quraysh as they are the best amongst the Arabs in relation to family lineage and home."

Makkah was the centre of Arabian Peninsula, and the Quraysh was the highly praised clan among the Arabs. Ka'ba located in Makkah gave this privilege to the Quraysh for Arabs made their annual pilgrimage to the House of God. Even in the pre-Islamic age, some rulers like Abraha, a

---

[486] Ibn Hanbal, *Musnad*, (Beirut: Mu'assasat al-Risalah, 1993), 5/441.
[487] Muslim, *Sahih Muslim*, Imarah, (Delhi India: Adam Publishers, 1996), 37.
[488] Dogan, Recep. "Conflict Resolution Forms in the Life of Prophet Muhammad" *The International Journal of Religion and Spirituality in Society*, 4 (2014), pp. 9-19.
[489] Ibn Hajar, *al-Isaba Fi Tamyiz al-Sahaba*, (Egypt: Dar Nahḍat, 1970), 1/65.
[490] Muslim, *Sahih Muslim,* Fadail Sahabah, (Beirut: Dar al-Ma'rifah, 1994), 63.

governor of San'a in Yemen, tried to change the direction of pilgrimage but did not succeed it.[491]

Considering the context of situation, there was an obvious public benefit to choose a caliph from the bloodline of the Quraysh. Knowing the sensitivity of the issue, Abu Bakr wanted to minimize the conflicts and disputes by his statement regarding the caliphate being from the bloodline of the Quraysh. In order to protect the unity of the nascent Muslim community, the first caliph was chosen from the Quraysh so that other Arab tribes would not dispute it. Naturally, the rulership after the Noble Prophet was not an easy task. As a matter of fact, many Arab tribes opposed the new ruler and did not want to pay their prescribed alms (*zakat*). However, Abu Bakr successfully defeated them and established his caliphate on strong foundations.

During the time of the Noble Prophet and the first four caliphs, the Quraysh did not have any religious privilege. The election of the first caliph was a political issue and Muslims chose Abu Bakr to prevent conflicts in Muslim society. The following incident shows the mentality of Muslims at that time. A group from Yemen came to Medina upon hearing the death of the Noble Prophet. When they visited Abu Bakr, they said, "O Quraysh, you do not have any privilege against other Arabs for God did not send His last Messenger for the benefit of a specific group."[492]

However, racial discrimination in favor of the Quraysh did actually emerge after the first four caliphs; thereafter the criterion of being from the bloodline of the Quraysh became a prerequisite of caliphate. Although the Noble Prophet did not praise himself on the basis of his ancestry, later generations did so to keep the caliphate in the hands of the Quraysh. In Islam, a job is to be given to its proper recipient who is qualified and can do it in the best way. This Islamic principle was at times violated through some racist practices. Indeed, the Noble Prophet sees such an attitude as

---

[491] Ibn Kathir, *A compilation of the Abridged Tafsir Ibn Kathir* (PDF version), (Riyadh: Darussalam, 2000), 5653.
[492] Ibn Hajar, *Isaba*, 5/91.

one of the signs of Doomsday. He said, "When the power of authority is given to unfit persons, then wait for the Hour (Doomsday.)"[493]

Caliphate in Modern Times and the Efforts to Revitalize It

After the abolition of caliphate in Turkey in 1924, some groups, including terrorist organizations, have attempted to restore this institution in modern times. As a matter of fact, there is no specific rulership in Islam for the matter is a political one, and is, therefore, changeable according to the conditions of time. This can clearly be seen in the different attitudes of the early Muslims on choosing the first four caliphs and in the varieties of political systems in Muslim states throughout the Islamic history. Therefore, caliphate, or rulership, is a socio-political phenomenon and its nature or practice is determined according to the conditions of time.

Similarly, Islam does not impose a specific legal system; rather, it has general principles, high objectives and guidelines. They are interpreted and applied according to the needs of Muslims. In the Qur'an and the Sunnah, the statements that regulate the legal aspects of Islam are very limited. This fact indicates that God has made human beings His vicegerents and has given them the authority to interpret the religious texts (including the Prophetic Traditions). Therefore, Muslim jurists are required to interpret the primary Islamic sources in line with the universal values and human rights. However, this flexibility is abused by some ignorant Muslims, and worse than that, the extremist terrorist groups have been exploiting it. For example, in mid-2006, Al-Qaeda declared that the Iraqi city of Ramadi was to be the capital of their new Islamic caliphate.[494] First of all, terrorist groups are not considered Muslims according to the majority of Muslims today. Secondly, the Noble Prophet never declared any area as Islamic state. He was chosen as the ruler of the multi-religious Medina city-state

---

[493] Bukhari, *Sahih*, 'Ilm, 2.
[494] Fletcher, M. '*How Life Returned to the Streets in a Showpiece City that Drove out Al Qaeda*', London Times, August 31, 2007, accessed on April 17, 2015, http://www.freerepublic.com/focus/f-news/1889407/posts.

having the population from various religious, ethnic and cultural backgrounds. Now, considering the historical context, it is imperative to mention briefly about the establishment of this city state where peoples' religions and values were respected.

Prophet Muhammad, upon whom be peace and blessings, immigrated to Medina in 622 CE when the unbelievers of Makkah increased their persecution. There were around 1500 Muslims, 4000 Jews and 4500 Arab unbelievers when the Prophet arrived in Medina. The presence of the conflicting Arabic tribes of Aws and Khazraj and the Jews living in Medina had long led to communal tensions within the city. Recognizing this tension and its underlying cause, the Noble Prophet prepared a pact that ensured the rights of citizenship for all groups of people living in Medina. He did not discriminate or marginalize people from different backgrounds, faiths or ethnic groups; rather, he embraced them all under the common pact.[495] It is noteworthy to mention here that political scientists today sometimes turn to the Medina constitution (aka the Charter of Medina) as a resource and model in their search for new political administrative models suited to the changing and developing world.[496] This is mainly because of the fact that the Medina constitution is a social pact that managed differences based on an agreement under principles that can be described as "natural law" which adhered to justice and equity in determining rights and duties, and which promoted common interests under a pluralist, participatory and unitary political umbrella based on lawfulness and equality before the law.[497]

During the ten year long Medinan period, the Noble Prophet never imposed Islam over the religious preferences of these people nor did he impede them in practicing their Christian or Jewish rituals.[498] It is recorded

---

[495] Ibn Kathīr, Abu'l-Fida Ismail ibn 'Umar. *Al-Bidāya Wa'n-Nihāya*, (Beirut: Daru'l-Maarif, n.d.), 3/224.
[496] Dogan, Recep. "Contributing to World Peace: An Examination of the Life of Prophet Muhammad as a Leader" *Sociology and Anthropology* 3 (2015), pp. 37-44.
[497] Kurucan, Ahmet and Mustafa Kasım Erol, *Dialogue in Islam Qur'an, Sunnah, History*, (London: Dialogue Society, 2012), p. 74.
[498] Dogan, "Contributing to World Peace: An Examination of the Life of Prophet Muhammad as a Leader" *Sociology and Anthropology* 3 (2015), pp. 37-44.

that he visited Christian churches and Jewish synagogues in order to foster understanding and to put an end to the interreligious enmity and hatred.[499]

The other important issue which refutes the violent claims of terrorist groups is the fact that the Noble Prophet was very sensitive on human life and applied strict rules to protect it even if it is in the battle field. For example, the following incident took place in a battle field:

> In one of the battles, there was a man among the army of polytheists who killed many Muslims. When he met with a Muslim soldier called Usama ibn Zayd, he fell down and Usama raised his sword to kill the soldier of the polytheists but he but declared Islam to be saved. However, Usama killed him thinking he was trying to deceive him. When the Noble Prophet was informed about the incident, he interrogated Usama so harshly. Usama tried to defend himself saying, "He killed such and such Muslims and when I attacked him he declared his Islam out of fear." However, the Noble Prophet said repeatedly, "What would you do when he comes on the Day of Judgment (and asks his right of retribution)?".[500]

Now, we will compare this report with the evil acts of ISIS who kill Muslims and non-Muslims brutally. ISIS, a terrorist group that declared caliphate in an area straddling Iraq and Syria, announced their leader, Abu Bakr al-Baghdadi as the caliph.[501] Majority of the Muslims in the world deems them as terrorists for they kill people who disagree with them in the most heinous ways such as beheading, burning in a cage, throwing from cliff and so on although Islam strongly prohibits killing people because of their differences of opinion. Therefore, their caliphate claim is not taken seriously.

The institution of caliphate does not exist since 1924 when Mustafa Kemal Ataturk, the first President of the Turkish Republic, abolished it.

---

[499] Al-Tabari, Muhammad ibn Jarir. *Jami' al-Bayan Ta'wil Ay al-Qur'an*, (Riyadh: Darussalam, 1998), pp. 162-163.
[500] Muslim, *Saḥīḥ*, Iman, 185.
[501] Tran, Mark and Matthew Weaver, Isis declares caliphate in Iraq and Syria, *The Guardian*, June 30, 2014, accessed April 17, 2015, http://www.theguardian.com/world/2014/jun/30/isis-announces-islamic-caliphate-iraq-syria.

Contemporary scholar Ali Abd al-Raziq justifies this act by claiming that there is no basis for the caliphate either in the Qur'an or in the Prophetic traditions.[502] However, it is a fact that many Muslims are looking for a just ruler or a caliph who can unite all Muslims and end the conflicts among them.[503] Probably the conflicts and wars in the Muslim world caused them to think more about the notion of caliphate.

For instance, the reformist scholar Abu al-Ala Mawdudi (1903–1979) expressed the need of caliphate to revive the way of Islamic life.[504] However, his call did not attract much attention in the Muslim world for they were struggling with socialism, communism and capitalism. Sayyid Qutb (1906–1966), the Egyptian scholar who spent at least ten long years of his life in prison, believed that the values of the Qur'an are valid for all humanity at all times and that the world must inevitably submit to Islam under a universal caliphate.[505] In 1925, Taqiuddin al-Nabhani (1909–79), established the Hizb ut-Tahrir (Party of Liberation), in the Jordanian land to revitalize the institution of caliphate[506] but he could not succeed it.

In 1996, Mullah Mohammed Omar, the leader of Taliban, announced himself as the Commander of the believers (*Amir al-Mu'minin*) and tried to revitalize caliphate in his personality. His attempt was recognized by Osama bin Laden, pledging his personal loyalty to him as the legitimate ruler of the state of Afghanistan.[507] In 1998, Osama bin Laden and Ayman al-Zawahiri co-signed a *fatwa* in the name of the "World Islamic Front for Jihad against Jews and Crusaders" which declared the killing of Americans and their allies to liberate the al-Aqsa Mosque (in Jerusalem) and the holy mosque (in Mecca).[508] Al-Zawahiri reportedly once declared that terrorist

---

[502] Liebl, Vernie. "The Caliphate," *Middle Eastern Studies* 45 (2009), pp. 373-391.
[503] START: Study of Terrorism and Response to Terrorism (College Park, MD, Program on International Policy Attitudes and University of Maryland), accessed April 20, 2015, http://www.worldpublicopinion.org/pipa/ pdf/apr07/START_Apr07_quaire.pdf.
[504] Mawdudi, *Islamic Way of Life*, (Delhi: Markazi Maktaba Islami, 1967), p. 40.
[505] Qutb, Sayyid, *Social Justice in Islam*, (Beirut: Dār al-Shuruq, 1975), 7.
[506] McQuaid, Julia V. "*The Struggle for Unity and Authority in Islam: Reviving the Caliphate?*" (Alexandria, VA: CNA Center for Strategic Studies, 2007), 21.
[507] Scheuer, Michael. "The Pious Caliphate Will Start From Afghanistan," *Jamestown Global Terrorism Analysis* 2 (2005), p. 12.
[508] Liebl, Vernie. "The Caliphate", *Middle Eastern Studies*, 45 (2009), 3, pp. 373-391.

attacks would be nothing more than disturbing acts, regardless of their magnitude, unless they lead to a caliphate in the heart of the Islamic world.[509] However, all of these terrorist groups failed to revitalize the institution of caliphate for they could not receive support from the majority of Muslims.

The strong view on caliphate is that it cannot be revitalized because of the establishment of nation states and the development of the ideas of independence. Additionally, caliphate has lost its function and effectiveness.

Conclusion

In Islam, Prophet Muhammad, upon whom be peace and blessings, is the Seal of the Prophets and no one can take the place of the Prophet in his position as Messenger of God. However, his position as a ruler can be represented by other Muslims.

Choosing a caliph from outside of the Quraysh bloodline is a controversial issue among Muslim scholars. There are two views on this matter: the Kharijite and Mutazilite sects held that any person who has the necessary qualifications and knows the Islamic principles can be a ruler while many Sunni scholars maintained that a caliph must be from the Quraysh. A marginal group in the Kharijite sect held that Muslims do no longer need the institution of caliphate. Some contemporary scholars hold that Islamic caliphate came to an end after the first four caliphs because it lost its meaning and function. The prominent Islamic scholar Fethullah Gülen, however, holds that the revival of the caliphate would indeed be very difficult and making Muslims accept such a revived caliph would be impossible.[510]

---

[509] McQuaid, Julia. *The Struggle for Unity and Authority in Islam*, p. 16.
[510] Saritoprak, Zeki and Ali Ünal, "An Interview with Fethullah Gülen," *Muslim World* 95 (2005), pp. 465-467.

We see, however, some terrorist organizations that have attempted to revitalize it today. Al-Qaida and ISIS declared some lands in Iraq and Syria as their Islamic state and recognized certain people as their caliph. However, such attempts have not received much attention from the Muslim world. This is mainly because of the fact that terrorist groups cannot represent Muslims nor can they ever provide justice with their rulership. It is just a political trick that they use in an attempt to deceive some ignorant masses and propagate their terrorist agendas.

Chapter 4

AN ANALYSIS OF ISLAM AND ITS PRIMARY SOURCES IN THE CONTEXT OF VIOLENCE AND TERRORISM

INTRODUCTION

The global terror and violence have increased the tension in the world. The conflicts between some Sunni and Shiite groups, brutal violence of ISIS, frequent terrorist attacks in different parts of the world dominate headlines in the mainstream media. The governments in the Muslim majority countries as well as those in the other parts of the world are concerned about their security and are deeply worried about a clash of civilizations. The ongoing terror and violence by the jihadist groups yet again raises questions about Islam and its stance on violence and terrorism. The so-called Muslim terrorist groups (in reality, a terrorist cannot be a Muslim) use some Quranic passages and religious concepts, such as jihad, caliphate and Islamic state, to justify their evil acts. In this section, we will address what the Qur'an and Islamic law have to say about violence, jihad and warfare and what the primary motives of "terrorism in the name of religion" are.

JIHAD AND WAR IN THE QUR'AN

Islam is a religion which aims to address every aspect of life directly (through the Qur'an and the traditions of the Prophet) or indirectly (through the process of *ijtihad* – deriving a legal ruling from the Qur'an and the Sunnah). As a reality of the long course of history, war is one of these aspects of life. Obviously, the notion of war and fighting against the enemy was not introduced by Islam as they can be observed through the course of human history, including the ancient history of the heavenly religions of Judaism and Christianity.[511] Historically, many of the followers of these religious traditions resorted to war for various reasons.

Irrespective of their claim of being Muslims, Christians or Jews, terrorist groups commit terror and violence, usually with the claim of warring in the name of religion. They have been manipulating the religious texts out of their true context in an attempt to justify their evil actions or to cover up their violence. The vast majority of Muslims understand the Quranic verses dealing with the rules of war in their historical contexts; therefore, they hate those "jihadists" who kill innocent people in the name of Islam. Interestingly, some Christian ministers and political commentators often refer to war verses in the Qur'an while they overlook the much greater number of passages that command violence, killings and even genocide in the Bible.[512] The Quranic verses about warfare are an indication of recognizing human nature and setting boundaries, limits and guidelines to prevent violence and unjust murders.

One of the conditions to understand the Quranic verses or interpret the religious text is reading the text within its historical context. The individual verses must be understood in connection with the previous passages and

---

[511] For more information, see: Stark, Rodney. *One True God: Historical Consequences of Monotheism*. (Princeton: Princeton University Press, 2007); Mark Jurgensmeyer. *Terror in the Mind of God: The Global Rise of Religious Violence*. (Los Angeles: University of California Press, 2003); Jessica Stern. *Terror in the Name of God*. (San Francisco: Harper One, 2009).

[512] For mass killings and genocide passages, see, for example, 1 Samuel 15:1–9, Joshua 6:20–21, Deuteronomy 2:32–35 and 3:3–7.

the passages that come after them as well as understanding them in the totality of the Qur'an. Additionally, the subject of Usul at-Tafsir (providing the guidelines, principles and methodology for the Quranic interpreter) must be known well to understand the text properly. Therefore, a sound Quranic commentator takes into account the demands of internal consistency in the Qur'an, the relevance of the occasions of revelation, and distinctions between the kinds of verses, for example between the verses that are explicit and clearly understood and the ones that are allegorical, whose referents are fully known only to God, or between those that are ambiguous in meaning and those that are absolute or restricted in their entail for action, or those abrogating or abrogated.[513]

The Noble Prophet lived in a place where tribal raids and warfare were considered normal and lawful. He had to deal with the bitterly hostile world while conveying the message of God. He faced extreme violence, severe enmity and threat from his own tribe, surrounding tribes and even the Sassanid and the Byzantine Roman emperors. During the first thirteen years of his prophethood, the Noble Prophet and his followers were persecuted and many of them were tortured to death in Makka, but God did not allow them to resort to war right away, even to defend themselves against their relentless enemies. Initially, God commanded His Noble Prophet and the Muslims to immigrate to Medina so that they could freely practice their religion. However, the Quraysh, the Makkan unbelievers of the time, did not stop persecuting and threatening the immigrant Muslims in the city of Medina. In the meantime, the Noble Prophet consolidated his power in the city by unifying all residents of Medina, including the unbelievers, Jews, Christians and Muslims, under the Charter of Medina. According to this charter, all residents of Medina were accepted as equal citizens regardless of their religious background.

As the unbelievers of Makka continued to persecute Muslims although the latter had already left Makka for Medina after having suffered for long from the very hands of the former simply because of their belief in God,

---

[513] Kurucan, Ahmet and Mustafa Kasım Erol, *Dialogue in Islam* (London: Dialogue Society, 2011), p. 44.

the Almighty God allowed His Noble Prophet to resort to war to protect his community of believers. God Almighty revealed war verses to His Prophet to guide him on how to defend Muslims during times of war. We will quote some war verses here which are frequently brought forth by some biased non-Muslims in their effort to prove Islam as "a religion of violence" and then analyze them in their historical context as these verses speak of the events that relate to those relentless enemies of Muslims who actively fought and harmed the believers:

> (1) (While at war) kill them wherever you come upon them, and drive them out from where they drove you out (thus recovering your lands from their usurpation). (Though killing is something you feel aversion to,) disorder (rooted in rebellion against God and recognizing no laws) is worse than killing. Do not fight against them in the vicinities of the Sacred Mosque (and thus violate its sanctity) unless they fight against you there; but if they fight against you (there), kill them – such is the recompense of the (rebellious) unbelievers.[514]

This verse regards the disorder (*fitnah*) as one of the most prominent reasons for war. Although war is something undesired and abhorrent, it becomes inevitable in some situations such as outright hostility and fierce enmity against Muslims, destroying collective security or causing public disorder and oppression. The verse refers explicitly to the unbelievers of Makka for they did not give any freedom to Muslims to practice their religion nor did they recognize their rights. Muslims were persecuted, boycotted, tortured, killed and finally driven out as a whole from their homeland. In the Medinan period, they continued to show their extreme hostilities and acts of war against Muslims. The verse that permitted fighting for Muslims was revealed after the Muslims had suffered nearly fifteen years of persecution. Muslims immigrated to Medina to escape persecution but the unbelievers of Makka did neither give up chasing them

---

[514] Qur'an 2: 191.

nor recognized any space for them to practice their religion; rather they persisted on hostility and openly committed acts of war against them. In these tragic circumstances, God allowed Muslims to fight against those who fought them relentlessly.

Yet, God Almighty reminded Muslims not to exceed the bounds set by Him even during the times of war.[515] In order to deter enemy from their wrongdoings and persecutions, the Almighty used strong language to encourage Muslims in their fight.[516] Finally, He declared His mercy for those who desist from fighting and stop persecuting Muslims.[517] This part of the text indicates that peace is essential in Islam and if the enemy stops fighting Muslims, it is not permissible to fight them. It is important to note that these verses that command fighting against the enemy are related to those who are already engaged in war against the Muslims. Therefore, it is not permissible to wage war without the enemy actually engages in war against Muslims.

> (2) But if they turn on you (with hostility against you), seize them and kill them wherever you find them; and do not take to yourselves any of them as confidant, nor as helper.[518]

This verse refers to those people who belonged to the Ghatafan and Asad tribes. They believed in God, but later turned back to unbelief. Since they cooperated with the unbelievers of Makka in their plot to attack the Muslim community living in Medina, these hypocrites could not be trusted. However, this verse is not restricted to them; rather it presents a typical hypocrisy. When the new Muslim community obtained power in Medina, some groups or tribes worked against them in high treason. These hypocrites pretended to be believers whenever they were together with Muslims but worked against the Noble Prophet in the company of unbelievers. Emigration to Medina was a very important criterion to show

---

[515] Qur'an 2: 190.
[516] Qur'an 2: 191.
[517] Qur'an 2: 192.
[518] Qur'an 4: 89.

one's sincerity in living his or her faith. Instead of staying in Medina with Muslims, hypocrites returned their homelands and cooperated with the unbelievers against the believers. Thus, by revealing the hypocrisy in the hearts and attitudes of such people, the Qur'an warns the believers against them. Because of the flagrant betrayal of hypocrites Muslims had dispute among themselves with regards to how to respond to it; therefore, God revealed:

> (O believers!) How is it with you that you are in two groups regarding the hypocrites (from Makkah and other tribes who claim to be Muslims yet take part in the hostile machinations of their people against you), seeing that God has thrown them back (to unbelief) on account of what they have earned (by their sins)? Do you seek to guide him whom God has led astray? Whoever God has led astray, for him you cannot find a (safe) way (to follow).[519]

After this Divine warning God Almighty instructed Muslims on how to deal with the hypocrites: *"Do not, therefore, take from among them confidants and allies until they emigrate (to Medina and join you) in God's cause."*[520] After these explanations it is clear that Islam never allows Muslims to fight unbelievers who wish to live in peace and observe the conditions of the treaty they make with them. However, betraying the treaty and acting treacherously is a reason for waging a war. In other words, if there is no active hostility and war against Muslims, the verses dealing with war in the Qur'an are not applicable. This is because God Almighty says, *"If they withdraw from you and do not fight against you, and offer you peace, then God allows you no way (to war) against them."*[521]

> (3) When the (four) sacred months (of respite, during which fighting with those who associate partners with God and violate their treaties

---

[519] Qur'an 4: 88.
[520] Qur'an 4: 89.
[521] Qur'an 4: 90.

was prohibited to you,) are over, then (declare war on them and) kill them wherever you may come upon them, and seize them, and confine them, and lie in wait for them at every conceivable place.[522]

This verse above is related to the unbelievers who openly violate treaties. When reading the verse in its own context in the Qur'an, its meaning will be clearer. The Arabs of pre-Islamic age had a custom to refrain from fighting during the months they deemed sacred. First of all, it is worthy of notice here that God encouraged Muslims to be respectful to the culture of polytheists for it only promotes peace. The expression *"kill them wherever you may come upon them, and seize them, and confine them, and lie in wait for them at every conceivable place"* in the verse above is only related to the state of war. If there is no war and Muslims are not threatened, nor their treaty is breached, this verse is not applicable.

In Islam, peace is essential and war is a temporary, last resort. Therefore, if there is no valid reason and an actual threat, it is not permissible to wage war. The hostile, deceitful attitudes and behaviors of unbelievers which Islam deems as the reason for war are explained in the following verses in the same Quranic passage. The hostile or deceitful attitudes and behaviors of the unbelievers are identified as not observing any bond, law, or agreement, being transgressors, breaking the treaties for a trifling price, exceeding all bounds, and pleasing Muslims with their mouths but hating them by heart.[523]

The context of this verse refers to the polytheists of Makka, not to the Jews, Christians, or the followers of other faith traditions. However, medieval exegetes reinterpreted this verse and expanded its meaning to war against all non-Muslims. The meaning of this verse is distorted by the terrorist groups to justify their brutal acts against innocent people. Moreover, some non-Muslim scholars who have prejudice against Islam have often cited this verse to show Islam as a religion of violence. Terrorist groups, such as Al Qaeda, ISIS and Boko Haram, have used this verse to

---

[522] Qur'an 9: 5.
[523] Qur'an 9: 8-10.

justify their killings of all unbelievers and Muslims who do not accept their extreme doctrines. The original and historical context or reason for the revelation of this verse was the permission for the Noble Prophet and the Muslims to fight to defend themselves. They were further commanded by God to cease the fire if the enemy stops its aggression.

God commands Muslims to establish peace and observe justice among people but also warns them against those who are a constant threat to their lives. Although God Almighty encourages Muslims to have peace with all people regardless of their faith, when fighting becomes inevitable, He permits them to fight against those who break their oaths, show hostility to Muslims and attack them.[524] Upon examining these Quranic verses, we can clearly see that if people, regardless of their faith, are not in actual war against Muslims there is no reason to fight them. Historically, the polytheists and hypocrites broke their treaties with the Noble Prophet at various times and threatened the security of all society. According to the customs of the time, this treachery was considered as a reason for war. The hypocrites made secret agreements with the unbelievers against the Muslims and thereby violated their obligations incurred according to the treaties they signed. Therefore, the Qur'an deemed this flagrantly treacherous act as waging war against Muslims.

Waging war or fighting against the enemy is a political decision and it becomes appropriate only when Muslims are persecuted and fought by a persistent enemy. The Divine commands regarding war and its rulings are not to be applied constantly; rather warring is temporary and limited to a real threat. What's more, God commands Muslims to accept the offer of treaty when the enemy ceases fire and makes a treaty request. This shows that the regulations regarding war and military operations are heavily weighted towards mercy and forgiveness and ultimately aim to establish peace.

The Muslim community grew rapidly after the Noble Prophet, and many internal and external problems emerged. Muslims faced many issues such as the following: choosing a ruler (caliph) for the Muslim community,

---

[524] Qur'an 9: 13-15.

the caliph's position and power and whether he has a religious authority besides the political one, the options for an appropriate response to rebellions and civil war, as well as the issue of what is considered jihad and what is terrorism. Muslim scholars, jurists and politicians have developed answers to this kind of questions by interpreting the Qur'an according to their own circumstances and the conditions of time. In order to better understand the discussion the verses dealing with war and its rulings will be provided below:

> Say to those of the dwellers of the desert who stayed behind: Soon you will be called (to fight) against a people of great military power, then either you will fight against them or they will submit to God and become Muslims. If you obey, God will grant you a handsome reward, but if you turn away as you turned away before, He will punish you with a painful punishment. There is no blame on the blind nor any blame on the lame nor any blame on the sick (for staying away from a war in God's cause). Whoever obeys God and His Messenger (in the religious duties he is charged with and can carry out), God will admit him into Gardens through which rivers flow. But whoever turns away, He will punish him with a painful punishment.[525]
>
> (While at war) kill them wherever you come upon them, and drive them out from where they drove you out (thus recovering your lands from their usurpation). (Though killing is something you feel aversion to) disorder (rooted in rebellion against God and recognizing no laws) is worse than killing. Don't fight against them in the vicinities of the Sacred Mosque unless they fight against you there; but if they fight against you (there), kill them – such is the recompense of the (rebellious) unbelievers. Then if they desist (from fighting), surely God is All-Forgiving, All-Compassionate (especially towards those who return to Him in repentance.) (But if they persist in causing disorder, continue to) fight against them until there is no longer disorder rooted in rebellion against God, and the religion (the right for worship and the authority to order the

---

[525] Qur'an 48: 16-17.

way of life is recognized) for God. However, if they desist, then there is no hostility except to the wrongdoers.[526]

And if they (the enemies) incline to peace, incline to it also, and put your trust in God. Surely, He is the All-Hearing, the All-Knowing. And if they seek (thereby only) to deceive you (O Messenger), surely God is sufficient for you. He it is Who has strengthened you with His help and with the believers.[527]

They yearn that you should disbelieve just as they disbelieved so that you might be all alike. Do not, therefore, take from among them confidants and allies until they emigrate (to Medina and join you) in God's cause. But if they turn away (from this call and continue their hostility against you), seize them and kill them wherever you find them; and do not take to yourselves any of them as confidant, nor as helper. Except those who seek refuge in a people between whom and you there is a treaty (of peace or alliance), or (those who) come to you with hearts shrinking from fighting against you as well as fighting against their own people. Had God willed, He would certainly have given them power over you and they would have fought against you. If they withdraw from you and do not fight against you, and offer you peace, then God allows you no way (to war) against them.[528]

In Islam, it is not permissible to kill civilian men, women, children and the clergy. The main position in jihad is stopping the transgressing and protecting the citizens. Whenever soldiers deviate from the main goal of Islam and harm civilians and noncombatants, they are punished by Islamic government. The soldiers were promised war booty and the promise of reward in heaven in case of martyrdom. However, if they killed innocent people and violated Islamic rulings, they were punished instead.

Muslim community expanded their territories with these strict religious guidelines on war. In addition, Muslim rulers did not force people from other faiths to convert Islam whenever they conquered new lands because

---

[526] Qur'an 2: 191-193.
[527] Qur'an 8: 61-62.
[528] Qur'an 4: 89-90.

there is no compulsion in religion.[529] Islam encourages interfaith dialogue, respect for the sacred and creating a peaceful environment among people from different faiths, nations and races so that everyone can practice their religion freely. Actually, promoting good and preventing evil is the main mission in jihad.[530] Establishing justice for God on the earth and protecting the rights of all human beings is the higher objective that Islam aims to achieve.[531]

It must be noted that there is no single doctrine of jihad which is universal and accepted by all Muslims. Nevertheless, jihad in Islamic history can be analyzed within the framework of what the Qur'an teaches about jihad. As discussed earlier in detail, jihad is a broad concept and it has many meanings, but the discussion here is focused on its usage in the military sense. Muslims interpreted the verses dealing with the rules of war according to their own perspectives; therefore, it can be said that there have been various interpretations of jihad in Islamic history as a result of different authorities interpreting and applying the Quranic principles in specific historical and political contexts. The radical terrorists have hijacked Islam and its principle of jihad much as those Christian and Jewish extremists who have committed their acts of terrorism in their own unholy wars in the name of Christianity or Judaism.[532]

It is to be noted that there are a number of reasons for why God commanded Muslims to struggle on His way (*jihad*). The important ones are struggling against evil, carnal desires to live a moral and virtuous life, preventing injustice and oppression, and creating a just society.[533] Jihad in the military sense can be analyzed in two categories: defensive jihad which is fighting against aggression, and offensive jihad which is fighting

---

[529] Qur'an 2: 256.
[530] Qur'an 3: 104.
[531] Qur'an 3: 110.
[532] Esposito, John L. "Islam and Political Violence" *Religions* 6 (2015), p. 1067–1081.
[533] For more details see, *Asma Asfaruddin. Striving in the Path of God: Jihad and Martyrdom in Islamic Thought.* (New York: Oxford University Press, 2013).

adversaries to be able to convey the message of Islam.[534] Even in the case of offensive jihad, Islam never legitimizes violence or terrorism. Jihad is done to protect the community and religion for the sake of God.

It is important here to point to the fact that during his twenty-three year long Prophethood, the Noble Prophet and the early Muslims were persecuted in the first fifteen years of this entire twenty-three year period. Then, God Almighty permitted them to respond to aggression and oppression with the revelation of the following verse:

> The believers against whom war is waged are given permission to fight in response, for they have been wronged. Surely, God has full power to help them to victory those who have been driven from their homeland against all right, for no other reason than that they say, "Our Lord is God." Were it not for God's repelling some people by means of others, monasteries and churches and synagogues and mosques, where God is regularly worshipped and His Name is much mentioned, would surely have been pulled down (with the result that God is no longer worshipped and the earth becomes uninhabitable). God most certainly helps whoever helps His cause. Surely, God is All-Strong, All-Glorious with irresistible might.[535]

In order to stop injustice, persecution and oppression God Almighty encouraged Muslims to fight with great commitment:

> "If you meet them in war, deal with them in such a manner as to deter those behind them (who follow them and those who will come after them), so that they may reflect and be mindful."[536]

Since peace is essential and universal, if the enemy proposes peace, then the fighting must end.[537] Unfortunately, those "scholars" who do not

---

[534] Bassiouni, M. Cherif. "Evolving Approaches to Jihad: From Self-Defense to Revolutionary Regime-Change Political Violence." *Chicago Journal of International Law* 2007 (8), p. 119.
[535] Qur'an 22: 39-40.
[536] Qur'an 8: 57.
[537] Qur'an 8: 61.

understand the higher objectives in the Qur'an have interpreted the verses on war as if they are permanent and universal, and legitimated attacking against other nations in the name of spreading Islam.

IS THERE A RELIGIOUS BASIS FOR TERRORISM OR VIOLENCE?

It is a fact that religious beliefs and values motivate human action. The extremist groups, however, often refer to them to express their identity. In order to create a common bond between their members they make use of this power of religion and put their strong emphasis on religious concepts.

The meaning of terrorism is related to the use of violence against innocent people to achieve some political, social, economical or religious aims. Although the violent approach in obtaining such objectives seems to be appealing for adventurous minds, the majority of people in every culture and nation disagree with them. Therefore, terrorist groups remain as marginal and extreme. Unfortunately, there are no internationally accepted criteria to designate any organization as terrorists. Nevertheless, it can be said that the only common theme among different variants of terrorism is the use of deadly violence against civilians.[538] Terrorists threaten and violate the rights of human beings such as life, liberty and security.

Interpreting the religious sources in extreme ways has caused many violent and terrorist groups to emerge throughout the long Islamic history. They have used the Qur'an and the prophetic traditions to justify their violence and legitimize their terrorist acts. It is, therefore, a duty upon moderate scholars to produce counter arguments to refute their claims and protect young Muslims from their evil agenda. The Qur'an is the primary source for Muslims to understand Islam and practice it in every aspect of

---

[538] Security Council Foreign Ministers Discuss Counter-terrorism, US Department of State, International Information Programs, http://usinfo.state.gov/topical/pol/terror/01111206.htm.

life. Unfortunately, it is also a source for the terrorist groups to interpret in extreme ways, thus using it as a pretext for justifying their violence.

The terrorist groups highlight only those verses which allow Muslims to defend their country and people while ignoring many more verses which command peace, harmony and good relations with others. Such partial approach to the Qur'an ruins the thematic unity among its verses. Using any terrorist activity in the name of religion is the worst method to "serve" (or rather, give harm to) Islam because this extremism harms Muslims more than anyone else. However, the extremist groups try to mask their evil crimes by quoting Quranic verses out of their context and interpreting them in a violent way. They claim that violence is needed to revive Muslim society and bring the divine laws (Sharia) to be implemented. This type of aggressive discourse seems very attractive for the young, ignorant minds for they do not know Islamic principles enough to see that these claims are directly opposite to Islam and its universal message. Therefore, the counter-arguments which aim to stop radicalism and terrorism must be simple and yet very strong in language. This is because the discourse employed on any issue must be precise and better than the language of the competitors though it does not necessarily have to explain all the facts with which it can be confronted.[539]

Terrorism among Muslims occurs when radical groups interpret religious texts fanatically and only in an attempt to justify their extremist ideology. Religious terrorism operates on the basis of some key concepts such as holy war, blind obedience, absolute truth claims and the ideal times.[540] Every terrorist group has its own "absolute truth" and fights for it. This truth is the basis of their ideology. Therefore, terrorist groups use religious traditions and doctrines almost like weapons for their organizations. People who are very brave but lack the comprehensive and authentic knowledge can commit violence easily in the name of religion

---

[539] Huntington, Samuel, *Clash of Civilizations and the Remaking of the World Order*, (New Delhi: Penguin Books, 1996), p. 30.
[540] Kimball, Charles, *When Religion Becomes Evil*, (San Francisco, New York: Harper, 2003), p. 46.

because they are satisfied with and totally convinced of those extreme doctrines.

Using religious concepts to justify violence creates religious terrorism and it is systematized by the extremist interpretations of any religious text.[541] Similarly, some radical groups among Muslims have created religious terrorism by interpreting the Qur'an in extreme ways. When there is a debate over the sacred or whenever any pillar of Islam is violated, the terrorist groups provoke the masses towards committing violence in the name of religion. In this type of terrorism, the participants show unquestioned devotion and blind obedience.

Although Islam does not offer any specific type of governance, it has laid down principles which can be interpreted and implemented according to the conditions of time. However, the radical groups put their mere emphasis upon Islamic government and Islamic law in their classical forms. When examining the Qur'an and the Prophetic traditions, some key concepts can be extracted with regards to politics. In Islam, people are free and no one can usurp their democratic rights. Muslims are required to worship none but God alone; therefore, the ruler is not above the law. In other words, people are equal before law and whoever violates the law he or she is punished regardless of their status and position. The rulers and the government are supposed to provide justice, security and protect their citizens against any kind of aggression. The ruler is not a master of people but a servant and in the service of people. Therefore, if the ruler governs in conformity with the Islamic principles he or she is obeyed.

Muslims who are under persecution and oppression often express their love for an ideal Islamic government which can guarantee their rights and protect them against aggression. Their natural feelings for a just ruler and state are manipulated by terrorist groups and are used as a pretext for violence in the name of religion. Muslims who have been suffering from the internal tyrants or the foreign military occupations have increasingly interpreted their problems from a religious perspective. In the name of

---

[541] Ruf, Werner, *Islam and the West- Judgments, Prejudices, Political Perspectives*, (Munster: Verlag GmbH&Co.Kg, 2002), p. 21.

constituting a force against the oppression the extremists have exploited these feelings and have made use of such Quranic verses as follows: "*The believers against whom war is waged are given permission to fight in response, for they have been wronged. Surely, God has full power to help them to victory.*"[542] What's more, there is a perception among Muslim population that the western world, and especially the US, has political power in Islamic countries through leaders who can be manipulated. In this context, terrorist organizations argue that the Qur'an condemns unsolicited involvement of non-Muslims in Muslim affairs. They also evaluate the US oil-trade in the Middle East from this perspective.

Another argument they use is the existence of the power hungry leaders in the Islamic world who are used by world powers against the interest of Muslims. On the basis of these arguments, the extreme groups interpret the Qur'an in a way which justifies the violence against the west. They often refer to the life of the Prophet and the early Muslims in an effort to revive the pristine form of Islam lived in that age. This manner causes the emergence of fundamentalism, radicalism and religious violence.

Violence and terrorism conducted in the name of Islam is the worst thing that can be done to give harm to Muslims by the extremists. Yet, there have always been some marginal groups that have resorted to violence in the history of Islam. These marginal movements can be categorized into many groups according to their ideology, methodology, targets and religious motives. There is no coherence and integrity between the movements. For example, the Taliban in Afghanistan and the Shia in the Islamic Republic of Iran both wanted to establish Islamic government system by cleansing society from non-religious practices or innovations in religion and correct the wrongs of current regimes. However, they never agree among themselves.

Similarly, Muhammad ibn Abd al-Wahhab, the founder of Wahhabism, emerged with the claim to revive the pristine form of Islam. He used religious texts to establish his way of understanding in contrast to

---

[542] Qur'an 22: 39.

the understandings of the Sunni and Shia Muslims. His followers used violence such as mass-murders, assassinations, abductions and aggressive threats in Saudi Arabia in 1800s with the claim to revive the pristine form of Islam. They claimed that they would continue to do jihad until all the world either adopts the Muslim faith or submits to Islamic rule.[543] In order to recruit new members, they put their strong emphasis on the Prophet's life as a "warrior," the Golden Age he lived in as well as the Crusades and the European colonization. With the "Golden Age," they referred to the age Islam was practiced in its purest form. This understanding is one of the reasons for the use of violence in contemporary times especially when Muslims' independence is threatened.[544]

According to the majority of Muslims, terrorists never represent Islam; they only give harm to it with their violence in the name of religion. However, in order to gain new recruitments from among ignorant masses they have often referred to the Qur'an and the important Islamic concepts. By referring to main religious sources (the Qur'an and the traditions of the Noble Prophet) and interpreting them in an extreme way, they have presented their actions as "struggling for God's cause." They have kept speaking "on behalf of God" and misinterpreting "the divine will." Indeed, any religion can be hijacked and interpreted in extreme ways by some fanatics seeking solutions to problems in a society. Similarly, extremist groups in Islam have used the Qur'an and other important Islamic concepts extensively to legitimate their violence. In this way, they aim to present their actions as something "holy" – the will of God.

According to Muslims, the Qur'an is the Word of God, the last Divine Revelation sent down to humanity. It is an authority and reference point for all Muslims; therefore, it has been interpreted by scholars throughout the Islamic history. The second source of Islam is the Sunnah, the traditions of the Noble Prophet. The biography of the Noble Prophet (*Sirah*) is a criterion on how to understand and implement Islam according to the

---

[543] Lewis, Bernard. *The Crisis of Islam – Holy War and Unholy Terror*, (New York: Modern Library, 2003), p. 31.
[544] Armstrong, Karen. *Holy War – The Crusaders and Their Impact on Today's World*, (New York: Anchor Books, 2001), p. 237.

conditions of time for it provides a contextual framework for the revelation of the Qur'an. The words, the acts and the tacit approvals of the Noble Prophet constitute the Sunnah. Trying to use Sunnah out of its historical context causes many misunderstandings and misinterpretations. This is also true for the Qur'an; therefore, only the well-versed, qualified scholars have the authority to interpret them. Muslims used to consult the scholars more often for guidance rather than trying to interpret these religious sources. For this reason, radical groups have been interpreting the religious sources in an effort to fill this gap and meet the needs of Muslims from their ideologically extremist perspectives.

The scholars have laid down the very conditions to be qualified as a scholar who can interpret the Qur'an and the Sunnah. When it comes to the extreme groups and their so-called scholars, it can clearly be seen that they are not suitably qualified to interpret these sources. Nevertheless, they keep doing so as it is easy for them to convince some ignorant minds. This fact has very important consequences when they turn religious issues into their political ideology. The extremist movements claim that their desire is to return to a purer form of Islam; therefore, they often resort to the Qur'an or the Sunnah although they are not even sufficiently qualified to interpret them. They read and interpret Islamic sources from their radical, political perspective. Unfortunately, there are few contemporary scholars and leaders who are well-versed in classical Islamic disciplines and interpret the Qur'an and the Sunnah in a balanced, moderate way. However, their voice is not loud and strong in media. The extremist movements are good at using social media and conveying their message to everyone globally. In this regard, moderate Muslim scholars and community leaders should discuss the problem among themselves and produce effective methods to refute the arguments of terrorist groups, preventing especially the young, ignorant minds to join them.

The terrorist groups cherrypick certain passages from the Qur'an to justify their extreme views, approaching them ideologically. Indeed, the way they read and interpret the Qur'an is highly political. They never see or refer to the Quranic passages or the traditions of the Noble Prophet that promote peace, mutual respect, interfaith dialogue and coexistence with the members of other religions. They are very rigid and partial in understanding the Qur'an and the Sunnah. They want only to shape the society through violence and terror. This approach definitely contradicts with the life and teachings of the Noble Prophet for he suffered the tortures, persecutions and wrongdoings of his people while educating them and eradicating the evil customs among them. He forgave even his bitterest enemies when he conquered Makka and never forced them to accept Islam. Today, however, the terror groups are aiming to achieve their targets through violence and terror.

The radical movements put their emphasis on social change and the return to the purist form of Islam in their publications. They give new meanings to the quotations from the Qur'an and the Sunnah by taking them out of their original context. With this misinterpretation, they try to legitimatize their ideology through some kind of religious authority. They cherrypick only certain marginal interpretations from the long history of interpretation in an attempt to support their radical views and actions. This approach is a selective, ill-mannered reinterpretation of the history that is favorable to their extreme doctrines. Although the radical movements seek to return to a glorious past, they distort the understandings of the past by their partial and political approach. Thus, their understanding of Islam often presents the controversial nature of their interpretation.

There are some key concepts all radical groups often refer to. The concept of *umma* (Muslim community) is one of them. This concept represents a worldwide Muslim community and embraces all believers regardless of their sectarian disposition. This concept is very appealing for Muslims who have been suffering from disunity. However, this same concept becomes a political tool for the extremist movements to unite Muslims in their formation of an ideal society. They argue that Muslims participation in the struggle to achieve this target is a duty upon them. With this claim, they aim to recreate a single Muslim community, but in reality they disunite and divide it. This is because everyone is considered an infidel if they do not agree with their extreme doctrines. They never respect or tolerate any differences among Muslims; rather, they impose their way of understanding as the only true form of Islam.

Another concept they exploit is the Islamic law (*Sharia*), which refers to the practice of Islam in daily life. The radical groups always manipulate and misinterpret this concept. They argue that in order for the Sharia to prevail in the lives of Muslims there is a necessity for an Islamic government. This is not true because ninety percent of the Islamic rulings, obligations and duties can be practiced individually or collectively without needing an Islamic government. The Islamic law represents a lifestyle accorded with the principles of the Qur'an and the Sunnah. However, the extreme movements put their mere emphasis upon the remaining ten percent of the Islamic Law as if it is the entire Sharia disregarding the fact that it is the manmade law through juristic opinions (*ijtihād*s) and represents very little part of the law. Once examined closely, it will easily be noticed that radical groups do not practice Islam as the Noble Prophet established and taught; rather they just focus on a certain area which is more in line with their ideology. This attitude indicates that they are not sincere in their claim of returning to the pristine of form of Islam.

Moreover, the radical groups label any un-Islamic government as *jahiliyya* which refers to the period before the revelation of the Qur'an. They use the concept of *jahiliyya* in the meaning of a life far from pure form of Islam and the religious values rather than a specific historical period. In other word, *jahiliyya* is the exact opposite of the ideal Islamic society according to the usage of these radical groups. Instead of peaceful coexistence with people from different religions, cultures and nations, they deem the rest of the world in the state of *jahiliyya*, therefore worthy to be killed. For the extreme movements, people are either the Muslims (those who agree to their extreme doctrines) or evil. The radical terrorist groups' perception of a divided world is the starting point to restructure the society through violence and terror.

According to the extreme groups, the "illegitimate governments" represent a threat to the ideal Umma; therefore, they need to be destroyed. Unfortunately, today there are too much disunity, conflicts, disputes and fights among Muslims. The notion of one global Muslim community seems very appealing to the Muslims who have long been suffering from disunity. Therefore, the radical movements often focus on the concept of Umma and the unity of Muslims as political tools.

Sometimes, the terrorist groups draw heavily on the feeling of honor in Muslims and thus try to legitimize their terrorist acts. For example, they put too much emphasis upon the Israeli occupation of Palestine and its control over it. The radical groups have used this situation in their terror propaganda and have brainwashed many individuals for suicide attacks in the region. Therefore, their attempt to restore the honor is one of the bases for radical groups to recruit new members.

THE USAGE OF JIHAD IN MODERN TIMES

Today, there is too much confusion among Muslims about the notion of jihad and its application in accordance with the instructions of the Qur'an and the practice of the Noble Prophet. The issue of how contemporary Muslims understand jihad is recently examined thoroughly through the interviews with open ended questions. The responses can be outlined as follows: "A commitment to hard work," "achieving one's goals in life," "struggling to achieve a noble cause," "promoting peace, harmony and cooperation, and assisting others," "living the principles of Islam," "divine duty," "worship of God," "sacrificing one's life for the sake of Islam, God and/or a just cause," and "fighting against the opponents of Islam."[545]

Looking back upon the political situation of the Muslim world in the second half of the twentieth century, it could clearly be seen that Arabic countries adopted the Arab nationalism/socialism approach in their governance system on the basis of Arab-Islamic roots. They focused on Arab unity and criticized liberal nationalism and the West. However, this approach lost its appeal to people when Arab nations lost the 1967 battle against Israel. When the coalition forces of Egypt, Jordan and Syria lost the

---

[545] Esposito, John L. and Dalia Mogahed. "Battle for Muslims' Hearts and Minds: The Road Not (Yet) Taken," *Middle East Policy* 14 (2007), pp. 27–41.

war, Israel captured the Sinai Peninsula and Gaza Strip from Egypt, the Golan Heights from Syria, and the West Bank and East Jerusalem from Jordan. It was devastating for Arab Muslims. Indeed, it was also disturbing for many other Muslims because Masjid al-Aqsa in Jerusalem, which is the third holiest mosque of Islam, now it fell into the hands of Israel. Muslim world was in shock due to this failure; therefore, they blamed the defeated Arab nations who chose Western political and economic models to progress, saying that this preference caused their economic, political and moral decline. Many Muslims believed that they abandoned the Islamic values and principles and, therefore, God punished them with the hands of their enemy. They further voiced that this failure would continue if they do not turn back to Islamic values and identity. This belief caused some Muslim scholars to interpret the Qur'an in a political sense and to make Islamism dominant in society and the politics across the Muslim world.[546] This belief is still valid in Arab nations and among many other Muslim peoples.

From the 1970s onwards, Islamism and political Islamist movements have become a major force in Muslim politics.[547] Islamism has become the primary language of political discourse in many countries in such a way that Muslim politicians have enhanced their legitimacy, rule, and policies. Irrespective of whether they called themselves Islamist or conservative parties, these political parties have used Islamic concepts in their election campaigns in order to get more votes from public. For example, Turkey's Justice and Development Party (AKP) participated in the 2002 elections as the opposition party within the same year it was established and heavily used Islamic concepts to lure more votes from Muslim population. Even after their massive corruption was exposed to public in December 2013, they have increased their use of religious discourse in an effort to cover it up. They put the blame on the US, Israel and some dissidents in Turkey for undermining their legitimacy and collapsing their government because the long ruling Erdogan government's target was (and still is) to be re-elected.

---

[546] Esposito, *The Future of Islam*. (New York: Oxford University Press, 2010), p. 61.
[547] Esposito, "Islam and Political Violence," *Religions* 6 (2015), pp. 1067–1081.

Indeed, he has long been pursuing his burning ambition for executive presidency rather than working towards the party's so-called aim of "striving to revive religious values in society." Therefore, they have not even hesitated to use un-Islamic methods such as lying blatantly, making certain groups that they deem as dissidents the scapegoats for all their failures, purging, witch-hunting, and arresting tens of thousands of people to cover up their massive corruption scandals and achieve their political goals.

On the other end of the political Islamism spectrum, militant Salafi movements that oppose the existence of political parties have used terror and violence in the name of Islam to achieve their targets. In this regard, the militant terrorist groups such as Al Qaeda, Hamas, Hezbollah and ISIS emerged as a reaction to the western invasion in Muslim lands and the occupation of Palestine. For the militant Shiite groups, the main target is gaining the control and power in the Middle East over the Sunni world.

While the primary meaning of jihad is the non-militant inner struggle for the majority of Muslims, the militant meaning has gained dominancy in the minds of terrorist groups. The extreme groups have hijacked and misused this concept to legitimate, recruit, and motivate their followers. These groups continued to exist as local phenomena until the early 1990s within the national borders. However, Soviet-Afghan war was a turning point for the terrorist groups to transform into global organizations. There were many Muslims from different parts of the world going to Afghanistan to help the Afghan Muslims against the Soviet invasion. At this stage, jihad became a global phenomenon. A global jihad ideology was used by those Muslims to prevent the expansion of communism in Afghanistan. Harsh treatment and rigid policies against the public in many Muslim countries increased the process of radicalization, violence and terrorism, especially among young Muslims. Additionally, the 9/11 attacks by Osama bin Laden and Al-Qaeda became a model for other terror groups that have been trying to achieve their aims through the use of violence and terror in the name of religion. They have adopted the global jihad ideology against the corrupt

Muslim governments and the West.[548] Al Qaeda and other terrorist groups have represented a new form of terrorism, transnational in its identity and recruitment and global in its ideology, strategy, targets, and network of organizations.[549]

In support of Bin Laden, Ayman Al-Zawahiri issued a religious ruling which legitimized, and even encouraged, radical groups to kill the Americans and their allies irrespective of their being civilians or military staff:

> Killing the Americans and their allies is an individual duty for every Muslim who is capable of it and in every country in which it is possible to do so. This will continue until Masjid al-Aqsa and the Holy Mosque in Mecca have been liberated from their grip, and their armies have moved out of all the lands of Islam, being defeated and unable to threaten any Muslim.[550]

Bin Laden declared his fight against the US foreign policy in the Middle East and, in particular, against the American support for the House of Saud and Israel.[551] He aimed to wage a global war against Zionist crusaders of the West and tried to provoke Muslims in this way. However, when Al Qaeda or other terrorist groups are examined, it can be seen that they exceed the boundaries of Islam and violate the Islamic principles by employing any weapons or means to achieve their targets. They do not recognize the Islamic principles with regards to the goals and means of a valid jihad.

In Islam, jihad in the military sense must be for a just cause and it must be declared by the head of state with public consensus. Accordingly, no person or group can declare a war. In addition, Islamic Law explicitly defines the acts that are permissible during peace and wartime. Violence is

---

[548] For more information see, Peter L. Bergen. *Holy War, Inc.: Inside the Secret World of Osama Bin Laden*. (New York: Free Press, 2002).
[549] Esposito, "Islam and Political Violence" *Religions* 6 (2015), pp. 1067–1081.
[550] Esposito, *Unholy War: Terror in the Name of Islam*. (New York: Oxford University Press, 2002), pp. 2–21.
[551] Esposito, "Islam and Political Violence" *Religions* 6 (2015), pp. 1067–1081.

not permitted in a just war, with the exception of repelling the enemy with the necessary amount of force. It is prohibited to kill civilians, including the non-combatant men and women, clergy, children and elders. Muslim soldiers cannot steal, torture, rape, usurp or commit any other immoral behaviors even during the times of war. Any terrorist act towards non-Muslims or Muslims from a different sect is not permissible. However, for terrorist groups it is permissible to employ any weapons or means to achieve their goals, even they excommunicate (*takfir*) other Muslims who do not agree with their extreme doctrines and label them as enemies of God, therefore worthy of killing.

SUICIDE TERRORISM

Radical militant groups from various faith traditions have carried out suicide attacks throughout history mostly to end the occupation of their lands or defend their homeland against the enemy. Secular militant groups such as the Tamil Tigers, ETA or PKK have also used suicide attacks as a means to fight against their stronger enemies. The incidents of suicide bombing have been witnessed globally in various countries and regions, such as Northern Ireland, Sri Lanka, Kashmir and Chechnya.[552] The main idea in suicide bombing is that the enemy is too strong to confront in the battlefield; therefore, the terrorist groups deem their evil attacks legitimate to achieve their targets.

Suicide bombing is not simply driven by blind religious motives; it is mostly a reaction to the occupation of foreign forces. For example, The Tamil Tigers, a non-religious Marxist-Leninist group, whose main tactic was suicide attacks, appealed to Tamil Hindu religious identity in their struggle for independence against Sinhalese Buddhists in Sri Lanka.[553]

---

[552] Pape, Robert. "Why the Bombers are so angry at us." *The Age*, 2005. Available online: http://www.theage.com.au/news/opinion/why-the-bombers-are-so-angry-at-us/2005/07/22/1121539145036.html, accessed on November 28, 2015.

[553] Esposito, "Islam and Political Violence" *Religions* 6 (2015), pp. 1067–1081.

Suicide terrorism was unknown in the Middle East before the US forces occupied various countries in the region. This method is now increasingly used by some Sunni and Shiite militias, to gain the upper hand in sectarian conflicts and to end occupation.

The Muslim scholars have unanimously agreed that the killing of non-combatant men and women, children, elderly people, the clergy, and the pious that are secluded in their places of worship and engaged in worship, is forbidden in Islam.[554] Suicide attacks cannot be accepted as a method of defense in Islam. A Muslim cannot strap a bomb around his or her waist and go into a public space and detonate a bomb killing civilians.

Islam is a system which aims to secure rights and benefits to the individual and the community, and its laws are established to protect these rights and benefits and to facilitate the improvement and perfection of the conditions of human life on earth. Protection of life is the foremost among these essentials; therefore, if a person is attacked or threatened with his life, he is allowed to defense himself. Killing is strongly prohibited in Islam whether a person kills himself or herself or others. Indeed, God considers killing one innocent person as killing the entire humanity:

> It is because of this that We ordained for (all humankind, but particularly for) the Children of Israel: He who kills a soul unless it be (in legal punishment) for murder or for causing disorder and corruption on the earth will be as if he had killed all humankind; and he who saves a life will be as if he had saved the lives of all humankind.[555]

Islam and other monotheistic religions aim to protect the five essential rights: religion, life, property, lineage and intellect.[556] Out of these five inalienable rights, life is the best miracle of God in its every form. Protecting the life of every being is thus a sacred duty upon human beings. Above all, human life is an important trust that each person needs to care about well. Therefore, taking one's own life or others' life is breaching the

---

[554] Tahawi, *Muhtasar al-Ikhtilaf al-Fuqaha*, 3/455-456.
[555] Qur'an 5: 32.
[556] Shāṭibi, *Muwafaqat*, 2/3-5.

divine trust. God has given life to human beings so that they can fulfill the divine missions in the name of God according to the capacity embedded in their nature. Killing one person is like killing all humanity because each individual has a share in completing human mission on earth. All people must live to fulfill their own task so that the desired result is obtained. If some individuals are killed unjustly, this will affect human mission negatively. Additionally, human life is a sacred trust and no one has a right to terminate it; therefore, suicide or murder is strongly prohibited in Islam.

God endowed humankind with great capacity, ability and intellect. People come to this world to undertake a responsibility and they are expected to carry it out until the time God takes their lives. A person who leaves the duty of life without God's invitation (that is, dying naturally) is considered a fugitive deserving punishment because this act is considered as breaching divine trust, wasting one's great abilities, negating all the goods in past, and disobedience to God's will. Indeed, desiring to die (due to some serious sickness, wound, or calamity) is a sin in Islam. Thus, committing suicide is the worst disrespect toward God for it is an attempt to interfere with the time of dismissal from duty without waiting for the command of God.

Although the default religious verdict (*fatwa*) for life is protecting it from all kinds of harm, God legitimized the lawful defense to protect life, religion, property and family. The Noble Prophet said that one who is killed in defense of their property, religion, life, or family is a martyr.[557] In the time of the Noble Prophet, a person named Quzman was wounded during the Battle of Uhud. He was in great pain; therefore, he committed suicide to end his suffering. He placed the blade of the sword on the ground with the tip on his chest and then pressed himself against the sword and killed himself. Thereupon, the Noble Prophet stated that the man is a dweller of the Hellfire.[558] Quzman fought together with the Muslims against the enemy to defend Medina and was expected to receive great reward, but he lost by committing suicide.

---

[557] Tirmidhi, *Sunan*, Diyat, 22; Nesai, *Sunan*, Tahrim al-Dam, 23.
[558] Muslim, *Sahih*, Kitab al-Iman, 1.

Muslims are required to be patient during the times of calamity. They cannot end their life due to the suffering from wound, disease or calamity. God states in the Qur'an: *"O you who believe! Keep from disobedience to God in reverent piety, with all the reverence that is due to Him, and see that you do not die save as Muslims (submitted to Him exclusively)."*[559] This verse alludes that in order to die as Muslim one must not commit suicide because it is an act which ruins one's life in this world and the Hereafter.

After these preliminaries, one would understand that suicide bombing or suicide attack is a multiple murder; therefore, it is a much worse crime in Islam. As mentioned earlier, suicide attack is not limited to Islamic world; rather, it first started in non-Islamic communities and then started to be witnessed in Muslim societies. Suicide attack is a major sin in Islam and it is strongly prohibited. However, the radical criminals try to justify their evil act by some baseless arguments. They argue that with these attacks they sacrifice their lives for the sake of their ideologies. They assume that they do it to protect their religion. However, suicide attack is a criminal act for it is a multiple murder; therefore, it cannot be justified with any reason. The prominent scholar Fethullah Gülen stated this as follows:

> Suicide attack is a form of murder because just as those heedless murderers who have nothing to do with humanity and who have no idea about the true spirit of Islam go to Hell headfirst by killing themselves, they kill so many innocent people as well. Therefore, just as they will be called to account on the Day of Judgment for taking their own lives, they will have the same trouble for the people they killed—for every child, woman, man, Muslim, and non-Muslim victim one by one.[560]

Suicide attacks or any other act of terror is not compatible with Islam. The Noble Prophet stated that a person does not commit murder as a

---

[559] Qur'an 3: 10.
[560] Gülen, "Suicide," June 18, 2012 http://www.herkul.org/tag/suicide-attacks/ (accessed on November 30, 2015).

believer.[561] This tradition explains that a murderer is not a believer while committing murder. This is simply because when committing this crime, the murderer's intentions, acts and case are not Islamic. The psychology of murderer in the time of crime is not the portrait of a Muslim. They cannot be saved in the Hereafter when they will be called to account for killing people. For this reason, Gülen stated as follows:

> A person who acts as a suicide bomber and kills innocent people, no matter what country or religious group they are from, the murder they commit has absolutely nothing to do with being a Muslim. A person taking so many lives cannot be saved in the next world.[562]

Indeed, just like the other forms of terrorist acts, suicide attacks blacken the bright face of Islam. Although the terrorist groups are pretending to commit murder for the sake of religion, they do not know the original teachings of Islam. They manipulate the verses on war by interpreting them out of their historical context and disconnecting them from the totality of the Qur'an and the general principles of Islam. Moreover, they misinterpret the battles during the time of the Noble Prophet by ignoring their historical context.

The Noble Prophet had to deal with the hostile world to protect the city of Medina in which Muslims, Jews, Christians and unbelievers lived. The Noble Prophet and his Companions joined a number of military campaigns, but in none of them they attacked the enemy on the basis of their disbelief. Historically, all of the military engagements during the Prophet's time happened either to stop an enemy attack that had already started or to prevent it while it was at the stage of preparation. This is because peace is the essential and permanent value in Islam while war is temporary and a last resort.

When examining the terrorist groups, we have seen that their acts and the means to achieve their goals are neither legitimate nor Islamic. In

---

[561] Nasāī, *Sunan*, Qasama, 48.
[562] Gülen, "Suicide," June 18, 2012, http://www.herkul.org/tag/suicide-attacks/ (accessed on November 30, 2015).

Islam, it is strongly prohibited to kill the civilians, burn houses, cars, and kidnap people. The Noble Prophet ordered Muslims to be just and merciful even during the times of war:

> It was in the month of Shawwal in the eighth year of the Islamic calendar that the Noble Prophet sent Khalid ibn Walid with a force of 300 men to the tribe of Bani Jadhima. He told Khalid not to wage war against them unless they were attacked first. When the Bani Jadhima saw the Muslim army, they grabbed their weapons to attack and the war started. During battle, a young man was killed by the Muslim forces in front of the woman who loved him so much. She collapsed upon the man and sobbed tears. Then she died due to the deep sorrow she felt. When this incident was later reported to the Noble Prophet, he was saddened deeply, saying: "Was there no one who had mercy among you?" When he was informed that Khalid killed some of the prisoners of war, he raised his two hands and pleaded, "Dear God! I swear to You that I am in no way involved in what Khalid has done. I did not order him to do so!"[563]

At the time, Khalid was a new Muslim who did not know the rules of war in Islam; therefore, he violated them. For this reason, the Noble Prophet rejected his act and blamed him severely. Muslims cannot kill the prisoners nor can they torture them.[564] They are required to show mercy even to their enemy. Thus, the Noble Prophet warned his Companions regarding civilians, women, children and other non-combatants to prevent their murder mistakenly.[565] Since it is forbidden to kill civilians, even during war, it is strongly prohibited to kill them under any circumstances. Terrorists or suicide bombers cannot be considered Muslims for they kill civilians randomly. They torture and kill people that they have kidnapped or taken as hostage. The acts of suicide bombers who kill themselves and the innocent people with explosives can never be seen as jihad. Terrorism and suicide attacks are against the principles of Islam. The rules on war are

---

[563] Ibn Kathir, *Sirah Nabawiyya*, 3/591.
[564] Ibn Hisham, *Sirah*, 2/304.
[565] Wāqidī, *Maghāzī*, 3/117-118.

established by the Qur'an and the Sunnah and a person cannot be considered as a true Muslim if he or she violates these rules.

Martyrdom or Suicide

According to the Qur'an and the Sunnah, the martyr is guaranteed a place in paradise and they will receive provisions even after death:

> And say not of those who are killed in God's cause: 'They are dead.' Rather they are alive, but you are not aware.[566]
>
> Do not think at all of those killed in God's cause as dead. Rather, they are alive; with their Lord they have their sustenance, rejoicing in what God has granted them out of His bounty, and joyful in the glad tidings for those left behind who have not yet joined them, that (in the event of martyrdom) they will have no fear, nor will they grieve. They are joyful in the glad tidings of God's blessing and bounty (that He has prepared for the martyrs), and in (the promise) that God never leaves to waste the reward of the believers.[567]
>
> The Noble Prophet said that the person who participates in battles in God's cause and nothing compels him to do so except belief in God and His Messenger, will be recompensed by God either with a reward, or will be admitted to Paradise (if he is killed in the battle as a martyr).[568]

In order to understand terrorism and suicide attacks better, we will examine the notion of martyrdom as terrorist groups often use this concept to encourage their followers to commit suicide attacks. Indeed, martyrdom is an important "motivational" factor used by these groups as it leads its members to take serious risks or destroy themselves for the cause of their ideology. Muslim jurists, however, discussed how a person achieves a status of martyrdom during the time of war. From the juristic point of view, it is permissible for a soldier to attack a group of enemy combatants

---
[566] Qur'an 2: 154.
[567] Qur'an 3: 169-171.
[568] Bukhari, *Sahih*, Bab al-Jihad Min al-Iman, 26.

in defense for his country, people and/or property in those cases where he hopes that he will be saved in the end.[569] There are three major conditions required for martyrdom to be valid:

- it must be a state of war where two rival armies confront to fight,
- the soldier does not know if he will die when he attacks,
- the soldier is killed by the enemy side.

According to these criteria, suicide attack is not permissible and the doer of this evil act cannot be considered a martyr. However, the terrorist groups try to legitimize their suicide attacks with the argument that the enemy has incomparable advantages in terms of weapons, numbers, logistic support, facilities and military training; there is thus no alternative to suicide attacks. However, this argument is problematic from two points. Firstly, the means (suicide attack) and the goals to attain martyrdom are not legitimate according to Islamic principles. The methods that Muslims employ must be as righteous as their purpose. The Noble Prophet never used any illegitimate means to reach his goals although Muslims were always lesser in number, shorter in weapons and weaker in logistic support in their battles against the enemy. Secondly, if an illegitimate means would be permissible because of the circumstances and the power of enemy, this would then open the door to other illegal and inhumane activities. However, Islam prohibited any illegitimate methods and means even during the times of war.

The Almighty God states: *"Fight for the cause of God those who wage war against you, but do not commit aggression. Indeed, God does not love aggressors."*[570] Egyptian scholar Sayyid Qutb interpreted this verse as follows:

> The Companions knew that they would not prevail as a result of their numerical strength or superior armament; they were hopelessly deficient

---

[569] Shaybani, Muhammad. *Sirah al-Kabir*, 4/1512.
[570] Qur'an 2: 190.

on both counts. The main secret of their victory lay in their faith in, and obedience to, God and the support they received from Him. To ignore God's commands and the Prophet's instructions would have deprived them of the only force that could ensure their victory. These principles had to be strictly observed, even with those enemies who had persecuted them and inflicted unspeakable atrocities on them.[571]

When we examine armed attacks committed around the world, we notice that it is either done by an army against the other army or by individuals and groups against some foreigners or the citizens or soldiers of another country. If the armed attacks are committed by designated persons within the army and they die because they fight in a just war and use legitimate means, they are considered to be martyrs. According to the second scenario where a person or a group of terrorists tie bombs to their bodies, or load the vehicle that they are driving with bombs, and plunge into the midst of foreigners or soldiers of another country, exploding the bombs, such evil acts are not permissible in Islam. Islam prohibits suicide;[572] therefore, those who commit such evil acts can never be considered martyrs. Additionally, in suicide attacks, the committers usually kill many civilians and non-combatants, damage the property and create fear and terror in society; therefore, it is forbidden and must be condemned.

In a just war, Islam recognizes the right of fighting to protect one's religion, life, property, progeny, honor and sacred values and deems a person martyr who dies while defending these rights. However, during times of peace, Islam never allows any type of attack against any target, civilian or military. In the case of suicide attacks, the perpetrators kill many innocent civilians; therefore, they incur God's wrath and a fearful torment is prepared for them in the Afterlife. The Qur'an uses very strong language against killing innocent people:

---

[571] Qutub, Sayyid, *In the Shade of the Qur'an*, 1/236-237.
[572] Qur'an 4: 29; Bukhari, *Sahih*, Janaiz, 84; Muslim, *Sahih*, Iman, 175.

"If a man kills a believer intentionally, his recompense is Hell to abide therein (forever): and the wrath and the curse of God are upon him and a dreadful penalty is prepared for him."[573]

Ibn Abbas, the prominent scholar in the field of Quranic exegesis argues that the repentance of those who killed a believer purposefully will be denied, and they will be doomed to eternal hellfire.[574]

Islam sets guidelines for Muslims so that they live their lives in accordance with these principles. They are required to follow these guidelines at all times and under all circumstances. Terrorism, violence and brutality are in complete contradiction with the fundamental principles of Islam. In Islamic law, attacking the enemy in the time of war is permitted to defend one's country and people. Unfortunately, terrorist organizations have manipulated this religious ruling (*fatwa*) to legitimize their terrorist actions, especially their suicide attacks. However, no person or terrorist organization can declare a war except the head of state. In Islamic law, the religious ruling of attacking the enemy is related and restricted to the time of war and its target is military combatants. However, suicide attacks are committed against civilian targets and innocent people. Therefore, suicide attack is strictly forbidden (*haram*) just as any other terrorist act is forbidden in Islam.

EXPLOITATION OF A QURANIC CONCEPT: "STRIKING FEAR INTO THE HEARTS OF THE ENEMY"

The Qur'an has a special place for Muslims; therefore, terrorist groups often use the Quranic verses that deal with the rules of war, taking them out of their original and historical context, in order to manipulate the young and ignorant minds. One of these verses radical groups use is the

---

[573] Qur'an 4: 93.
[574] Tabari, *Jami' al-Bayan*, 4/295.

verse of *irhāb* (striking fear into the hearts of the enemy). Along with the English translation of this verse, its interpretation will be provided below:

> Against them make ready your strength to the utmost of your power, including steeds of war to strike fear into (the hearts of) the enemies of God, and your enemies and others besides, whom you may not know, but whom God does know. Whatever you shall spend for the sake of God shall be repaid unto you and you shall not be treated unjustly.[575]

Terrorist groups rely on this verse to legitimize their suicide attacks, claiming that they strike fear into the hearts of the enemies of God through such terror attacks. The literal reading of this verse indicates that Muslims should frighten their enemies so they cannot dare to attack against Muslims. In its historical and original context, this verse commands the Noble Prophet and the Muslims to have strong military power to deter their enemies. This power creates a natural fear and acts as a deterring force. However, this verse cannot be the basis for suicide attacks or any other forms of terrorism.

The Quranic exegetes have interpreted this verse "to be equipped with the necessary military means and technological tools against the enemy in order to have a deterring power in accordance with the conditions of the day."[576] The main idea in this verse is protecting peace against any kind of threat. This verse does not engage Muslims to wage a war; rather, it aims to protect society by preventing enemy attacks through the presence of military power.[577]

The Noble Prophet wanted to protect his nascent society against all kinds of threats. In order to have peace the state must have the deterring power against its enemies; therefore, the statement of the Qur'an and the traditions of the Noble Prophet on this topic should be understood as such.[578] Moreover, the word *irhāb* (striking fear into the heart of the

---

[575] Qur'an 8: 60.
[576] Tabari, *Jami al-Bayan*, 6/42; Razi, *Mafātih al-Ghayb*, 15/192; Ālūsī, *Ruh al-Ma'ani*, 10/26.
[577] Ridha, Rashid. *Tafsir al-Manar*, 10/66.
[578] Bazzar, *Musnad*, 6/30; Ahmad ibn Hanbal, *Musnad*, 3/493.

enemy) is understood by early scholars as the state of being so powerful that it is able to deter the enemy altogether from attacking.[579] The Prophet's Companions and the early Muslim generations understood this verse as such and thus possessed a deterring power to keep the peace. For example, in order to be better prepared for an unexpected enemy attack Umar, the second caliph of Islam, detained forty thousand extra horses besides all those horses that were already reserved for active service in the farms near Medina.[580]

The Qur'an sets a goal for Muslims with regards to defending their country, religion, honor, people, property and all sacred values against the enemies who have malicious intentions.[581] Muslim jurists interpreted the word *irhāb* as a deterring force against the enemy[582] but not in the meaning of causing terror and fear in society. Sometimes, having a strong military power is sufficient to discourage the enemy from an attack or finish a war. Historically, Muslim armies used various tactics, such as preparing and training many horses for war, dying gray hair black, decorating the sword and its sheath with gold embroidery and designs, to deter the enemy from an attack against Muslims.[583]

The other meaning the concept of *irhāb* connotes is protecting one's sacred values against transgression and despotism. In this regard, democratic societies aim to protect people's religious identities and sacred values and the word *irhāb* is in line with this goal. It is a grave mistake to interpret the word *irhāb* as killing innocent people in public areas by tying bombs to one's body, shedding of blood, setting fires, causing damage to houses or property, spreading horror in order to introduce chaos into society. All these evil acts are labeled as terrorism and violence and are, therefore, against the essential principles of Islam. Unfortunately, the meaning of *irhāb* was mistakenly given as terrorism in some dictionaries

---

[579] Ibn Athīr, *al-Nihaya fi Gharib al-Hadis*, 2/262.
[580] For more details see, Mawlana Shibli an-Numani, *Bütün Yönleriyle Hazreti Ömer ve Devlet İdaresi*, Istanbul: Hikmet Yayinlari, 1986. Translated by Talip Yasar Alp.
[581] Gülen, Fethullah. *The Messenger of God: Muhammad*, pp. 211-216.
[582] Sarakhsī, *Mabsut*, 10/42; Ibn al-Qudama, *al-Kafi*, 4/264.
[583] Ibn al-Abidin, *Hashiya*, 6/756.

compiled by non-Muslims, especially in the second half of the twentieth century.[584] This meaning is not true for it contradicts with the classical Arabic dictionaries. Therefore, the concept of deterring force cannot be used in the meaning of terrorism.

In suicide attacks, the committers attack shopping malls, restaurants, bus stations, and so on; they kill Muslim and/or non-Muslim civilians. While they claim that they fight with the enemy forces, they really don't have a specific target; rather, they kill innocent civilians randomly. From the standpoint of Islamic law, it is unlawful (*haram*) to attack civilians or any unspecified targets for it clearly violates Islamic boundaries.

One of the principles of Islamic Law is that the penalty can only be applied to the criminals. In other words, the penalty for a crime is given to the committer of that crime. The Qur'an states, "*No soul, as bearer of burden, is made to bear the burden of another.*"[585] Opposing to this principle, the targets of suicide attacks are innocent civilians. Adopting some "un-Islamic" methods and means in the name of "reaching Islamic goals" clearly demonstrates an obvious contradiction in the minds of the bloody terrorists. Thus, their acts result in divine reproach and tremendous punishment in the Hereafter.

Today, we often see the word terrorist being interchangeably used with Muslims. It is, therefore, the duty and responsibility of Muslims to distance themselves as much as possible from any behavior or action that could be used to make such an incorrect and unfair accusation.[586] Unfortunately, terrorist groups use certain Islamic concepts to justify their terror and violence and this causes some ignorant or biased minds to accuse all Muslims as terrorists. In reality, Muslims hate terrorists more than any other people because they are, in most of the cases, the victims of terrorism and they suffer greatly from seeing terrorists tarnishing the image of Islam with their brutal violence. As a matter of fact, any suicide act involving the

---

[584] Oxford Wordpower, New York: Oxford University Press, 1999; English Arabic Glossary; Hans Wehr, A Dictionary of Modern Written Arabic, Beirut: Maktabat al-Lebanon, 1960.
[585] Qur'an 17: 15.
[586] Cevdet, Said. *The Problem of Violence in Islamic Struggle*, pp. 65-67.

use of bombs in any place anywhere in the world brings infamy to the name of Islam and to all Muslims.[587]

In conclusion, terrorism and violence is a crime against all humanity. No religion legitimizes any terrorist act. Terror attacks are strongly prohibited in Islam and the perpetrators of this evil act will end up in Hell. Islamic principles cannot be violated by anyone under any circumstances; therefore, the means that Muslims use must always be legitimate just like their goals. If a person kills innocent people in the name of Islam, he or she is not considered to be a Muslim, but simply a terrorist.

---

[587] Capan, Ergun. "Suicide Attacks and Islam" in *Terror and Suicide Attacks*, edited by Ergun Capan, (New Jersey: Light, 2005), p. 115.

Chapter 5

RESPECT FOR THE SACRED VERSUS FREEDOM OF EXPRESSION: AN ANALYSIS IN THE CONTEXT OF DE-RADICALIZATION

INTRODUCTION

Freedom is the most basic of rights every human being is born with, and freedom of expression is one of the essential elements of a democratic society. On the other hand, all human beings expect respect for their sacred values, regardless of religion, ethnicity or culture, as this is the only way to build peaceful societies in today's globalized world. This section aims to critically examine whether freedom of expression should be compromised when criticizing the sacreds of others, and also seeks to analyze if respecting the sacred can be a solution towards the process of de-radicalization. Finally, it encourages interfaith dialogue among people from different faith traditions to eradicate radicalism globally.

FREEDOM OF EXPRESSION

Freedom is a right that allows people to live however they wish and do whatever they want to do, as long as they do not harm others. True freedom is civilized freedom that is free from all shackles which hinder people from making material and spiritual progress.[588] Human rights are universally accepted and protected by law in the modern world. Moreover, every religion aims to secure these rights through their teachings. For example, preserving freedom of faith, life, reproduction, mental health, and personal property are basic essentials in Islam, and they must be preserved for all people regardless of their nationality or faith.

Freedom of expression is a right of people to think and express themselves freely. This right also includes seeking, receiving, and imparting information and ideas of all kinds either orally, in writing, in various forms of art, in print, or through any other medium of one's choice.[589] Generally, some economic, political, social, and security problems have been used to justify authoritarian worldview and validate the rejection of a pluralistic view of society for which freedom of expression is essential.[590] Freedom of expression is a requirement for a democratic society, but there are some concerns as to whether this freedom could cause harms to others.

Every human being is potentially a vicegerent of God in Islam,[591] and with this paradigm, human rights are higher objectives that Islamic law aims to achieve. According to the Holy Qur'an, everything in the heavens and the earth is created for the benefit of humanity;[592] therefore, Islam gives high importance to human beings and never neglects their rights even if it is about the rights of one person. All people are equal as the teeth of a comb[593] and Islam does never discriminate on the grounds of race, color,

---

[588] Gülen, Fethullah. *Pearls of Wisdom*, (New Jersey: Tughra Books, 2005), pp. 63.
[589] American Convention, supra note 2, art. 13 (1).
[590] Grossman, Claudio. "Challenges to Freedom of Expression within the Inter-American System: A Jurisprudential Analysis", in *Human Rights Quarterly*, Volume 34, Number 2, May 2012, pp. 361-403.
[591] Qur'an 2: 30-33.
[592] Qur'an 45: 13.
[593] Al-Daylami, Abu Shuja'. *Al-Firdaws bi-Ma'thur al-Khitab* (*The Heavenly Garden Made Up of the Selections from the Prophet's Addresses*), (Beirut: Dar al-Kutub al-'Ilmiya, 1986), 4/300.

age, nationality, or physical traits.[594] All rights are equally important for every individual and they cannot be ignored or sacrificed for the benefit of a society. Another key aspect of the freedom of expression is the relation between rights and duties from a legal perspective. People have various responsibilities in a society which is composed of conscious individuals equipped with free will. They cooperate with one another by sharing the duties and establishing the essential foundations of a healthy society.

In democratic societies, people are free to determine how to live their own life. However, they achieve a better existence by living within a society and this requires that they adjust and limit their freedom according to the requirements of social life.[595] The freedom of expression may cause violence if the sacred rights of people are humiliated through media, newspaper articles, or any other means. This perspective may help policy makers to approach it in a more scientifically-grounded way. Freedom of expression is not an absolute right; therefore, the International Covenant on Civil and Political Rights (ICCPR), the American Convention on Human Rights (ACHR) as well as the European Convention on Human Rights (ECHR), include grounds of limitation through which states can legally limit it when it is necessary in a democratic society.[596] For example, according to the ICCPR, any advocacy of national, racial or religious hatred that constitutes incitement to discrimination, hostility or violence is prohibited by law.[597]

The freedom of expression is not an impenetrable fortress but rather a flexible notion that can be balanced according to universal human values and rights. Usually, freedom of expression is conceptualized in the legal agreements linked to duties and responsibilities. In the human rights treaties, the potential dangers of freedom of expression are acknowledged, especially if it has the potential to lead to violence and hatred. However,

---

[594] Bukhari, Abu 'Abdullah Muhammad ibn Ismail. *Saḥīḥ al-Bukhari* (*A Collection of the Prophet's Authentic Traditions*) (Istanbul: al-Maktabat al-Islamiya, n.d.), Kitāb al-Nikāḥ (Book of marriage), 45.
[595] Gülen, Fethullah. *Essays, Perspectives, Opinions*, (New Jersey: Light, 2006), p. 14.
[596] Buyse, Antoine. "Words of Violence: Fear Speech, or How Violent Conflict Escalation Relates to the Freedom of Expression" in *Human Rights Quarterly* 36 (2014), pp. 779–797.
[597] ICCPR, supra note 57, art. 20.

there is no universally accepted criterion that clearly measures and determines whether an expression violates human rights, and leads specific groups or people of certain faiths to violence and hatred.

The relationship between violence and freedom of expression is one of the most difficult topics debated for long. In order to establish the connection between violence and expression, the former must be actual and not imaginable. Additionally, there should be a clear link between how violence is actively framed by the speaker and how the target audience is motivated by this expression. One of the methods that helps us to understand if an expression has caused violence is to examine a text, speech, blog or radio/TV broadcast and see whether a specific group or faith is explicitly blamed and subsequently becomes a target.

Sometimes there may not be a direct link between radicalism and expression but the policies that are produced by states to solve the problem may greatly influence the risk of violence. The stereotype approach to radicalism, including all Muslims as potential radicals, diminishes the chance to resolve the claimed conflict with peaceful methods and provides the golden opportunity to radical terror groups, for them to propagate their agenda among the young and ignorant minds.

The other form of expression that contributes to radicalism is the *fear* speech. In this expression, a certain group is labeled as a threat to a nation or all people, and the instrument of fear is to convince the nation that they would attack them with the aim of extermination. With fear speech violent action against a specific group or faith is legitimized as a form of self-defense against a claimed danger.

In order to bring balance to fear speech expression there should be alternative voices in the debate and their voice should reach their target audience. In this regard, the leading personalities who have great influence on people should express themselves with great caution. Additionally, the leaders who promote world peace and interfaith dialogue should have a voice in media.

Although freedom of expression is a core value of democratic societies, it should be balanced from the human rights perspective to prevent violence and hatred towards certain groups or faiths. The right to life, religion, property and other inalienable rights and universal values are to be protected against the freedom of expression.

CARTOON VIOLENCE AND FREEDOM OF EXPRESSION

Democratic rights are subject to some limitations and the law reflects an equilibrium point (in constant progress) in a trade-off between freedoms to think, act and speak as one wishes and freedoms from the harmful behavior of others. Prevention of harm is the main goal that involves a cost-benefit analysis where different rights, benefits and policy objectives are weighed up against each other.

In a democracy, rights are not divinely bestowed and manifestly inalienable. For a majority of countries, democratic rights and responsibilities are determined by parliaments which are elected by the citizens or residents of a state. The enacted laws are enforced by the executive arm of government and the law and its application is upheld and overseen by courts. This separation of powers is needed due to the risk of potential abuse of power by any governmental institution against citizens. A constitution or a bill of rights affords an additional layer of protection for minorities. Additionally, international law framework serves to set minimum standards to protect universal human rights.

In some cases, basic human rights can be practiced against each other. Debasing religious values or religious leaders through various means of expression may cause violence amongst people in a society. For example, the cartoons of Prophet Muhammad published in the Danish newspaper Jyllands-Posten in 2006 caused an attack on the Danish embassy in Islamabad, Pakistan, in June 2008.[598] Within a year, the Swedish cartoonist Lars Vilks drew a cartoon showing the Noble Prophet's head in a very humiliating way and it was published by Nerikes Allehanda newspaper on

---

[598] Walsh, Declan. Bomb at Danish Embassy Kills Six in Pakistan, *The Guardian* (London), June 3, 2008, available at http://www.guardian.co.uk/world/2008/jun/03/pakistan.terrorism.

August 18, 2007.[599] Upon this, Abu Omar al-Baghdadi, head of Al-Qaida in Iraq, offered a reward of $100,000 to anyone who kills him. Seeing the tension among people from different faiths, the Swedish Prime Minister called for "mutual respect between Muslims, Christians and non-religious groups to try to avert a wider conflict in the country."[600] More recently, the French magazine Charlie Hebdo was attacked by terrorists on January 7, 2015 in Paris upon publishing controversial cartoons depicting the Noble Prophet.[601] Armed with assault rifles and other weapons, the terrorists killed 11 people and injured 11 others in the building.

The use of cartoons for various purposes has a long history. Mostly, it has been employed frequently and effectively as an aid in building up resistance, for instance, to the policies of politicians.[602] We can also see that anti-Semitic cartoons were prevalent throughout the twentieth century and Jews were the victims of ridicule and hatred.[603] Obviously, the conflict between freedom of expression and respect for the sacred appear in different forms in different parts of the world. The champions of freedom of expression, however, argue that demanding respect for the sacred is incompatible with secular democracy, in a democratic society one has to be ready to put up with scorn, mockery and ridicule.[604]

On September 30, 2005, twelve cartoons of the Noble Prophet were published in the Danish newspaper Jyllands-Posten. Although the cartoons were said to be published for the intention to encourage tolerance in Danish children through better understanding of the tenets of Islam,[605] the

---

[599] Swedish Cartoonist Gets Protection, *BBC News*, Sept. 17, 2007, available at http://news.bbc.co.uk/2/hi/middle_east/6999652.stm.
[600] Keane, David. Cartoon Violence and Freedom of Expression, *Human Rights Quarterly*, volume 30, 2008, pp. 845-875.
[601] Silva, Cristina. *Charlie Hebdo Attack: The Prophet Muhammad Cartoons That May Have Caused Paris Magazine Massacre*, available at http://www.ibtimes.com/charlie-hebdo-attack-prophet-muhammad-cartoons-may-have-caused-paris-magazine-1775898.
[602] Keane, David. *Cartoon Violence and Freedom of Expression*, Human Rights Quarterly, volume 30, 2008, pp. 845-875.
[603] Goodwin, George M. *More than a Laughing Matter: Cartoons and Jews*, Judaism, volume 21, 2001, p. 146.
[604] Boyle, Kevin. The Danish Cartoons, *Human Rights Quarterly*, volume 24, 2006, pp. 185-187.
[605] Post, Robert. Religion and Freedom of Speech: Portraits of Muhammad, 14 *Constellations* 2007, p. 76.

cartoons were very offensive to the followers of Islam. The question that needs to be answered here is why someone would deliberately present information to children about another religion in a very offensive way.[606] Initial reaction to the publications was a peaceful protest involving approximately 3,500 protestors in Copenhagen.[607] A group of Muslims requested a meeting with the Danish foreign minister to discuss the issue with the aim of preventing polarization among people in the society, but this request was somehow refused. This lack of official response led Danish Muslim groups to internationalize their protest.[608]

In a meeting of the Organization of the Islamic Conference (OIC) in Mecca, it is stated that Muslims have a great concern at the rising of hatred against Islam by the incident of desecration of the image of the Noble Prophet.[609] The institution called on the United Nations to intervene and apply a binding resolution to prevent contempt of religious beliefs. However, the media in Europe approached the matter reactionary instead of empathizing with the feelings of Muslims towards the published cartoons in various magazines.[610] A strong reaction against cartoonists and magazines appeared in the Muslim world at large.[611] People around the world are puzzled with the madness of the cartoonists. They wonder if it is worthy to plant the seeds of hatred by disrespecting the sacred in the name of "the freedom of expression."

---

[606] Carens, Joseph. Free Speech and Democratic Norms in the Danish Cartoons Controversy, 44, *International Migration*, 2006, pp. 33, 36.

[607] Saloom, Rachel. You Dropped a Bomb on Me, Denmark—A Legal Examination of the Cartoon Controversy and Response as it Relates to the Prophet Muhammad and Islamic Law, 8 *Rutgers J. L. & Religion* 3, 2006, p. 6.

[608] Anderson, Kenneth. Remarks by an Idealist on the Realism of The Limits of International Law, 34 *Georgia J. Int'l & Comp. L.* 2006, p. 235.

[609] Saloom, Rachel. *You Dropped a Bomb on Me, Denmark—A Legal Examination of the Cartoon Controversy and Response as it Relates to the Prophet Muhammad and Islamic Law*, p. 103.

[610] Saloom, *You Dropped a Bomb on Me, Denmark—A Legal Examination of the Cartoon Controversy and Response as it Relates to the Prophet Muhammad and Islamic Law*, p. 103.

[611] In Damascus, Syria, protestors torched the Norwegian Embassy and the Danish embassy; in Lebanon, thousands of protestors burned the Danish consulate; in Tehran, Pakistan and Afghanistan violent protests and riots took place. 139 people have died as a result of the cartoon controversy. (http://web.archive.org/web/20060326071135/http://www.cartoon bodycount.com)

In response to the growing racism many European countries have regulated the elimination of all forms of racial discrimination considering it an offense whereby "a group of people are threatened, insulted or degraded on account of their race, color, national or ethnic origin, religion or sexual orientation."[612] However, they do not consider that the satirical caricatures of the Noble Prophet are an infringement for their constitutions and basic human rights.[613] They argue that the cartoons depicted an individual (the Prophet of Islam); therefore, it could not be taken as degrading or insulting all Muslims! This approach is very absurd, puzzling or offensive for many Muslims around the globe.

Obviously, this disrespect of an individual cartoonist is not something which can be dismissed, disregarded or tolerated by their government since the impact of such disrespect affects all Muslims and many sensitive people all around the world. It should also be kept in mind that Islam encourages its followers to be patient when insults and disrespect are directed toward their person. However, if such insult or disrespect is directed towards God, His Messenger and the Holy Qur'an, it is not the violation of just an individual right; rather, it is the violation of respect for the sacred of all Muslims. Nonetheless, Muslims should show their reaction to such disrespect without resorting to any violence, and in a civilized fashion, by using all lawful means available.

It is also to be noted that Islam forbids any depiction of the Noble Prophet; therefore, the cartoons are considered blasphemous by Muslims. Indeed, there are many evidences in the Holy Qur'an and the Traditions of the Prophet that forbid Muslims from images and paintings:

> Angels of mercy do not enter a house that has a picture in it.[614]
> Aisha, the wife of the Prophet, had a thick curtain, having pictures on it, and she screened the side of her house with it. The Noble Prophet said

---

[612] Boyle, Kevin. The Danish Cartoons, *Human Rights Quarterly*, volume 24, 2006, p. 189.
[613] Keane, David. Cartoon Violence and Freedom of Expression, *Human Rights Quarterly*, volume 30, 2008, pp. 845-875.
[614] Bukhari, *Al-Jāmi' Al-Saḥīḥ*, Beginning of Creation, Riyadh, Saudi Arabia: Darussalam Publishers and Distributors, 1997, 17.

to her, "Remove it from my sight, for its pictures interfere in my prayers."[615]

The makers of pictures of living beings will be punished on the Day of Resurrection, and it will be said to them, "Give life to what you have created."[616]

There is a general consensus among Sunni scholars on the prohibition of the images of the Noble Prophet. Some contemporary intellectuals, mainly the orientalists, argue that there is nothing that prevents Muslims to draw pictures of the Prophet.[617] However, this does not change how Muslims scholars understand and interpret their own religious texts, and how Muslims perceive the cartoons. Indeed, according to Islam, the depiction of any Prophet of God is prohibited because representations of all Prophets are strictly forbidden. In summary, the cartoons are a great insult to Muslims.

Moreover, the UN Special Rapporteur Doudou Diène considers the cartoons as racist. He argues that the cartoons illustrated the increasing emergence of the racist and xenophobic currents in everyday life, and the political atmosphere in some European countries has contributed to a context for the emergence of strong racist and extremist political parties.[618] Previously, he had produced a report on Defamation of Religions and Global Efforts to Combat Racism. In this report, he stated that Islamophobia had two characteristics: "the intellectual legitimization of hostility towards Islam and its followers, and the political tolerance of such hostility in many countries."[619] He believes that persistent Islamophobia in the media causes more radicalization toward Muslims.

---

[615] Bukhārī, *Saḥīḥ*, Dress, 93.
[616] Bukhārī, *Saḥīḥ*, Marriage, 76.
[617] Boyle, Kevin. The Danish Cartoons, *Human Rights Quarterly*, volume 24, 2006, p. 185.
[618] UN News Centre, *Racism and Racial Discrimination on Rise around the World*, UN Expert Warns, Mar. 7, 2006, available at http://www.un.org/apps/news/story.asp?NewsID=17718&Cr=racis&Cr1.
[619] Report Submitted by Mr. Doudou Diène, Special Rapporteur on Contemporary Forms of Racism, Racial Discrimination, Xenophobia and Related Intolerance: Addendum, Defamation of Religions and Global Efforts to Combat Racism: Anti-Semitism,

Combating against the defamation of religions is one of the agendas of the UN Human Rights Commission and their focus has been largely over the negative experience of Muslims in Europe.[620] Doudou Diène focused on the 2006 annual report of "the Situation of Muslims and Arab Peoples in Various Parts of the World," with a section entitled "The Cartoons of the Prophet Muhammad Published in a Danish Newspaper."[621] He strongly criticized the publishers of the Danish cartoons in an international legal document for they practice unlimited freedom of expression which harms international norms that seek an appropriate balance between freedom of expression and religious freedom. He maintains that the publication of the cartoons for the sake of freedom of expression has supported the idea of "clashes among civilizations" in some intellectual, media and political circles.[622]

The report of Doudou Diène, the UN Special Rapporteur, highlights that the underlying causes for increasing Islamophobia can be identified as:

- The political and ideological considerations overshadowed some human rights such as respect for the sacred,
- Defamation of religions or religious leaders only contributes to radicalization in the Muslim world and in turn it causes Islamophobia in the West,
- The inadequacy of international law on human rights and respect for the sacred gave opportunity to some media to feed Islamophobia by criticizing religious values,
- Racism, racial discrimination, xenophobia and related intolerance fuel and promote religious hatred and Islamophobia,
- The combat against terrorism increased levels of racial discrimination and religious intolerance after 9/11 terror attacks.

Christianophobia and Islamophobia, U.N. ESCOR, *Comm'n on Hum. Rts.*, 61st Sess., Provisional Agenda Item 6, U.N. Doc. E/CN.4/2005/18/Add.4 (2004).
[620] Keane, David. Cartoon Violence and Freedom of Expression, *Human Rights Quarterly*, volume 30, 2008, pp. 845-875.
[621] Diène, Doudou. *Special Rapporteur on Contemporary Forms of Racism*, 23-32.
[622] Diène, *Special Rapporteur on Contemporary Forms of Racism*, 28.

The United Nations International Covenant on Civil and Political Rights (ICCPR) states that "any advocacy of national, racial or religious hatred that constitutes incitement to discrimination, hostility or violence shall be prohibited by law."[623] Member States should avoid free speech in defiance of the sensitivities existing in a society. The right to freedom of expression carries special duties and responsibilities. Although it is a democratic right to express ideas, it is a duty to prevent racist ideas targeting certain groups on the basis of their religious or ethnic origins. Cartoons have a special role in forming public opinion because they have stronger impact on the brain than words do. Obviously, the freedom of drawing whatever one wishes does not give cartoonists the right to discriminate or make fun of the sacreds of others and thus offend the feelings of all those who love and revere them. It can be suggested that cartoonists can use their influence to promote peace and understanding among different faiths and cultures.

RESPECT FOR THE SACRED FROM THE ISLAMIC PERSPECTIVE

In Islam, respect for the sacred can be analyzed from two main points: preventing the means that lead to evil results, and promoting the means that contribute to human rights and world peace. Islam aims to establish healthy relations among the members of society irrespective of whether they are from different faiths, cultures or ethnic groups.

When the Noble Prophet emigrated from Mecca to Medina in 622 CE, he signed a pact with the people of Medina ensuring the rights of citizenship for all minority groups in Medina.[624] This constituted an agreement between the Muslim, Jewish, Christian and polytheist groups in

---

[623] International Covenant on Civil and Political Rights, adopted 16 Dec. 1966, G.A. Res. 2200 (XXI), U.N. GAOR, 21st Sess., Supp. No. 16, art. 20, U.N. Doc. A/6316 (1966), 999 U.N.T.S. 171 (entered into force on Mar. 23, 1976).

[624] Ibn Ishaaq, *Sirah al-Rasul al-Allah*, (tr: A. Guillaume, *The Life of Muhammad*), Oxford University Press, Karachi, 1955, pp. 231-233.

Medina, declaring them to constitute one nation and this Charter of Medina formed the basis of a multi-religious Islamic state in Medina.[625]

In order to promote mutual respect and friendship with different religions God commanded His Prophet to engage in interfaith dialogue with the People of the Book in the Qur'an.

> Say (to them, O Messenger): "O People of the Book, come to a word common between us and you, that we worship none but God, and associate none as partner with Him, and that none of us take others for Lords, apart from God."[626]

This call, made by Islam 14 centuries ago to the People of the Book (Christians and Jews), is still valid today, and it shows how various consciences, nations, religions and books can unite on one essential concept and word of truth.[627] In line with this call, the Noble Prophet visited Christian churches and Jewish synagogues in order to foster understanding and put an end to the inter-religious enmity and hatred.[628] Similarly, a group of Christians came and visited the Noble Prophet, and during their stay they requested permission from the Prophet to perform their rituals in the Masjid al-Nabawi (the Mosque of the Prophet) in Medina.[629] The Noble Prophet not only granted them their wish, but also hosted them in a friendly manner. This visit resulted in a peace treaty which contained the following articles:

> Christians have the right to live in safety, their property will be protected, their churches will not be harmed, monasteries will not be closed and priests will not be impeded when performing their duties. Moreover, Christians will not be compelled to provide supplies for

---

[625] Watt, W Montgomery. *Muhammad at Medina*, Oxford: Clarendon Press, 1956, pp. 227-228.
[626] Qur'an 3: 64.
[627] Yazır, Elmalılı Hamdi. *Hak Dini Kur'an Dili*, İstanbul Azim Dağıtım, 2007, vol.2, p. 1131.
[628] Al-Tabarī, Abū Ja'far Muhammad ibn Jarir. *Jami al-Bayan an Ta'wil al-Qur'an*, Beirut: Ālam al-Kutub 1992, vol.3, pp. 162-163.
[629] Al-Tabarī, *Jami al-Bayan*, 3/162-163.

Muslims during times of war and it is not permitted to interfere with or interrupt Christian worship.[630]

On another occasion, at the funeral of a Jew, the Noble Prophet stood up to show his respect to people from other faiths.[631] This example shows that interfaith dialogue is not limited to Arab or non-Arab people; rather, religious progress is possible by expanding universally and in unison, and not by being separate from one another.[632] There is no place for repulsive manners, condemnation or rudeness in Islam when dealing with people from other faiths.[633] Muslims are required to act in a way that is in harmony with their belief and Islamic doctrines. In other words, Muslims should show their reactions within the boundaries of democratic rights without resorting to violence and terror.

Unfortunately, people witness different forms of extreme behaviors triggered by grudge, hatred, and animosity in different parts of the world. Humiliating the sacred of certain groups or faiths through cartoons or media in general is a counter provocative act. This approach causes Islamophobia in the West and, in turn, radicalization in the Muslim world. There are various remarks or acts aiming to degrade the sacred with a grudge and hatred. Contemporary scholar Fethullah Gülen holds that if somebody makes an insult against God, His prophets and angels, he or she is also insulting all of the people who cherish these values.[634] He argues that an insult related to certain issues such as resurrection after death disturbs not only Muslims, but also the followers of other religions because such matters of belief are also accepted by people who follow other faiths.[635] According to his approach, if a common article of faith among Abrahamic religions is humiliated by media or cartoonists, then 4 or 5

---

[630] Al-Tabarī, *Jami al-Bayan*, 3/162-163.
[631] Bukhari, *Saḥīḥ*, Faith, 50.
[632] Dogan, Recep. Conflict Resolution Forms in the Life of Prophet Muhammad, *The International Journal of Religion and Spirituality in Society*, vol. 4(2), 2014, pp. 9-19.
[633] Gülen, M. Fethullah. *Reflections on the Qur'ān: Commentaries on Selected Verses*, New Jersey: Tughra Books Publishing, 2012, p. 68.
[634] Gülen, *Journey to Noble Ideals*, The Broken Jug Series 13, New Jersey: Tughra Books, 2014, p. 184.
[635] Gülen, *Journey to Noble Ideals*, p. 184.

billion people are negatively affected from this disrespect. Therefore, they should expect the same scale of a responsive insult toward themselves. Gülen emphasizes the respect for the sacred and maintains that whenever a person insults another, he or she triggers a relevant response, whereas showing respect towards people will elicit respect towards them.

In general, it is not acceptable for a person to comment on a field in which they have no knowledge. If a layman who never studied science severely criticizes scientific methods and discoveries, he will both expose himself to ridicule and commit disrespect toward scientists. In short, people can become experts in any field after a certain level of effort and relevant study. At this point Gülen draws people's attention to some people who publicly throw terrible insults at the religion of Islam and its followers in their blissful ignorance:

> Today, some people who have no serious knowledge about Islam, a faith that has realized significant transformations and breakthroughs in world history and, at the same time, conduced to a dizzying renaissance that had continued for about five centuries in a vast territory are making insulting remarks about the faith and its followers, and then call it, "freedom of thought and expression."[636]

Showing disrespect for the sacred may elicit certain responses from some inflamed people because the scale of the insult covers millions of people, and it is always possible that some people in such a large population will act upon their emotions. At this point, we will mention about the Islamic principle of "blocking the means to evil" (*sadd al-dharā'ī*) and analyze the topic from this perspective.

BLOCKING THE MEANS TO EVIL (*SADD AL-DHARA'I*)

Respect for the sacred can be analyzed from the perspective of preventing means that lead to evil acts. Blocking the means that leads to

---

[636] Gülen, *Journey to Noble Ideals*, p. 185.

Respect for the Sacred versus Freedom of Expression

evil is a concept which is used by Muslim jurists to prevent harm from people in a society. The juristic definition of the Arabic expression of *sadd al-dharā'ī* is blocking the means which would lead to bad or evil results.[637] The means get the same juristic value with their results; therefore, if a means leads to a forbidden act (*haram*), then it is forbidden; if it leads to a permissible act (*mubah*) then it is also permissible. Both the means and the end may be good or evil, physical or moral, and they may be visible or otherwise, and the two need not necessarily be present simultaneously.[638] The nature and value of the means is determined by the result it leads to and the intention of the perpetrator is not taken into account.

As a main principle of Islam, Muslims are always supposed to be very careful about their words, attitudes, and behaviors. They should consider the consequences of their words and carefully refrain from sudden outbursts of emotion. The Qur'an forbids Muslims from disrespecting the sacred of people from other faiths to avoid conflict and clashes among civilizations:

> Do not (O believers) revile the things or beings that they have, apart from God, deified and invoke, lest (if you do so) they attempt to revile God out of spite and in ignorance.[639]

A means which leads to an evil result acquires the value of the latter. The Quranic text forbids Muslims from insulting idol worshippers to prevent the means to an evil result because the idol worshippers or people from other faiths would insult the sanctity of Muslims in return and this causes enmity, hatred and clashes among people. Insulting the idols and their worshippers is thus forbidden regardless of the actual result that such conduct may lead to. Similarly, the intention of the perpetrator is irrelevant to the prohibition under discussion on an objective basis that it is most

---

[637] Dogan, Recep. *Usul al-Fiqh Methodology of Islamic Jurisprudence*, New Jersey, Tughra Books, 2014, 215.
[638] Kamali, M. Hashim. *Principles of Islamic Jurisprudence*, Cambridge: Islamic Texts Society, 2003. p. 269.
[639] *Qur'an* 6: 108.

likely to invoke the evil result.[640] Imam Shāṭibī (d. 1388 CE), an Andalusian Sunni Islamic scholar holds that if the means violate the basic purpose of religion they must be blocked:

> The Lawgiver (God) has legalized certain forms of conduct and prohibited others in accordance with the benefit or harm that they lead to. When a particular act or form of conduct brings about a result which is contrary to the objectives of the Lawgiver, then it must be prohibited.[641]

According to the principle of "blocking the means that lead to an evil result" Muslims are required to protect the honor of their sacreds by respecting the sacreds of others. If a Muslim insults others' deity, they will do the same. Therefore, Islam never commands or recommends believers to insult the idols and the sacred of others.

Terry Jones, the pastor of Dove World Outreach Center, a small nondenominational Christian church located in Gainesville, Florida, USA,[642] was arrested in Florida after announcing plans to burn nearly 3,000 copies of the Qur'an on the anniversary of the 9/11 attacks.[643] He also authored a book titled "Islam Is of the Devil" but he did not become widely known until after announcing his plan to burn copies of the Qur'an. The then US Secretary of State Hillary Clinton labeled this act as outrageous and disgraceful. The commander of the International Security Assistance Force in Afghanistan, General David Petraeus said, "It is precisely the kind of action the Taliban uses and could cause significant problems."[644] When President Barack Obama was asked on September 9,

---

[640] Abu Zahra, Muhammad. *Usul al-Fiqh* (*Methodology of Islamic Jurisprudence*), Cairo: Dār al-Fikr al-'Arabī, 1958, p. 228.

[641] Shāṭibī, Ibrahim ibn Musa. *Al-Muwafaqat fi Usul al-Shari'a* (The reconciliation of the fundamentals of Islamic law), Egypt: al-Maktabah al-Tijariyah al-Kubra, 1975, vol. 4 p. 194.

[642] Curry, Christopher. *Dove World sold, soon moving to Tampa Bay area*, Gainesville.com. Retrieved 28/07/2015.

[643] http://www.bbc.com/news/world-us-canada-24059408 retrieved 28/07/2015.

[644] Petraeus Condemns U.S. Church's Plan to Burn Qurans - WSJ.com. *The Wall Street Journal*. Retrieved 28/07/2015.

2010, on ABC's Good Morning America about the Qur'an burning controversy he said the following:

> You could have serious violence in places like Pakistan or Afghanistan. This could increase the recruitment of individuals who would be willing to blow themselves up in American cities or European cities. I just want him to understand that this stunt that he is talking about pulling could greatly endanger our young men and women in uniform who are in Iraq, who are in Afghanistan. I hope he listens and understands that this is a destructive act that he is engaging in.[645]

Upon examining the statements of the US administrators, one can see that they act in a responsible way to block the means that would lead to an evil result because they know well that hatred, enmity and disrespect for any specific group will cause them to have the same sort of attitude in response.

Fethullah Gülen states that insulting the sacred hurts Muslims deeply; however, destroying buildings and places of worship, such as churches, in reaction to such insolence is another type of extremism.[646] Before resorting to offensive attitudes, people from any faith need to consider the consequences of their acts. Although insulting faith, religion, and sacred values are seen as a form of freedom of expression, it bears the potential to boost radical terror groups. Gülen suggests that Muslims who are subjected to insults should respond within acceptable limits. They should prefer correcting ugliness through scholarly and legal means, but never resort to violence and terror. He expresses his strong desire upon an international agreement on respecting the sacred to prevent conflicts and clashes among people from different faiths:

---

[645] Alexander, David and Matt Spetalnick, *Obama says planned Koran burning is boosting Qaeda*, http://ca.reuters.com/article/topNews/idCATRE68820G20100909?sp=true retrieved 28/7/2015.

[646] Gülen, *Journey to Noble Ideals*, p. 186.

There is a serious need for making respect for the sacred a thought owned by the entire humanity and for evoking this feeling in everyone. If the principle of respecting others' sacred values—an important component of peaceful coexistence—is not observed, conflicts arising from such incidents of disrespect will make their presence felt as much more horrible and greater problems in today's globalized and shrunken world.[647]

In his life, the Noble Prophet showed respect for all people, Muslim and non-Muslim alike, and encouraged his followers to do the same. Today, however, the extremist groups are misinterpreting religion by being offensive to all "others" who think differently. They are interpreting Islamic sources to suit their political agendas, often resorting to terror to actualize their objectives. Indeed, no period of Islam witnessed the like of today's atrocities committed or so-called *jihadist* acts in the name of religion, including suicide attacks, resulting in a mass murder of women, elderly, children, and all. There is, however, no room for hate and hostility in Islam, nor in the entire life of the Prophet of Islam.

Conclusion

Freedom of expression is an essential right for every individual to think and express themselves freely, while it is the responsibility of all human beings to promote peace by blocking all means that cause enmity, hatred and fight among people.

If freedom of expression is exploited without any limit, it may become a source for provoking violence, especially when the sacred values of people are humiliated through various visual, print and social media or any other means. Such an approach causes Islamophobia in the Western world and, in turn, radicalization in the Muslim world. Therefore, Muslims and non-Muslims should come together to foster mutual understanding and put

---

[647] Gülen, *Journey to Noble Ideals*, p. 186.

an end to hostility and hatred by working collectively for the solution of the problems of the interreligious enmity and violence; otherwise, they will always be under threat.

It is also to be noted that some people from among the western intellectuals and media professionals have failed to question their "problematic" interpretation of Islam and its concepts; yet, it is not wise to put all the blame on them without recognizing the problems within Muslim societies. Therefore, the first step for eliminating extremism and terror in the Muslim world is to recognize ignorance and poverty as the major sources of this extremism and violence in the Muslim world. It is difficult to eliminate terror without solving these problems, especially without educating the young, ignorant minds. The members of the Muslim community, and especially the moderate Muslim scholars, must collaborate to refute the extremist ideologies of radical terrorist groups in order to prevent the potential young recruits to join their ranks and contribute to the education of the youth with the moderate and true Islamic beliefs to eradicate extremism.

REFERENCES

Abbas, T. "The Symbiotic Relationship between Islamophobia and Radicalization." *Critical Studies on Terrorism*, 5 (2012), pp. 345–358.

Abdisaid, M. Ali, *"The Al-Shabaab Al-Mujahidiin – A Profile of the First Somali Terrorist Organization"* [The Al-Shabaab Al-Mujahidiin – A Profile of the First Somali Terrorist Organization"] Institut fur Strategie – Politik–Sicherheits– und Wirtschaftsberatung, June 2, 2008, available at http://www.isn.ethz.ch/isn/Digital-Library/Publications/Detail/? ots591=0C54E3B3-1E9C-BE1E-2C24-A6A8C70 60233&lng=en &id=55851.

Abu Dawud, Sulayman ibn al-Ash'ath. *Sunan Abi Dawud*. Beirut: Dar al-Kutub al-Ilmiyah, 2008.

Abu Ya'la, Ali ibn Muthanna al-Tamimi. *Musnad al-Abu Ya'la al-Mawsili*. [Play Games] Beirut: Dar al-Mamun, 1992.

Abu Yusuf, Yakub ibn Ibrahim al-Ansari. *Kitab al-Kharaj*. [Extern Book] Lahore: Islamic Book Centre, 1993.

Abu Zahra, Muhammad. *Usul al-Fiqh: Methodology of Islamic Jurisprudence*. Cairo: Dār al-Fikr al-'Arabī, 1958.

Acosta, Benjamin. "Assassins" *Cultural Sociology of the Middle East, Asia and Africa: An Encyclopedia*, 2012.

Albert, Isaac Olawale. "Explaining Godfatherism in Nigerian politics," *African Sociological Review*, vol. 9: 2, 2005.

Alia Brahimi, *The Taliban's Evolving Ideology*, LSE Global Governance Working Paper WP 02/2010, July 2010.

Ālūsī, Muhammad ibn Abd Allah. *Ruh al-Ma'ani fi Tafsir al-Qur'an al-Azim*. [The spirit of Alma is in the interpretation of the Great Qur'an.] Beirut: Dar al-Fikr, 1994.

Asfaruddin, Asma. *Striving in the Path of God: Jihad and Martyrdom in Islamic Thought*. New York: Oxford University Press, 2013.

Ash'ari, Abu al-Hasan Ali ibn Ismail. *Maqalat al-Islamiyyin wa Ikhtilah al-Musallin*. [Articles Islamists and the disobedience of worshipers.] Cairo: Maktaba al-Nahdiyya al-Misriyya, 1950.

'Asqalani, Ibn Hajar. *al-Isaba Fi Tamyiz al-Sahaba*. [Injury in the discrimination of companions.] Egypt: Dar Naḥḍat, 1970.

Ansary, F. A. "Combating Extremism: A Brief Overview of Saudi Arabia's Approach." *Middle East Policy* 15 (2008), pp. 111–142.

Antúneza, Juan Carlos and Tellidisb Ioannis. "The Power of Words: The Deficient Terminology Surrounding Islam-Related Terrorism." *Critical Studies on Terrorism* 6 (2013), pp. 118–139.

Arberry, A. J. *Aspects of Islamic Civilization*. Ann Arbor: University of Michigan Press, 1967.

Armajani, Jon. *Modern Islamist Movements: History, Religion, and Politics*. Wiley-Blackwell, 2012.

Armstrong, Karen. *The Battle for God: Fundamentalism in Judaism, Christianity and Islam*. Glasgow: Harper Collins, 2001.

—— *Holy War: The Crusaders and Their Impact on Today's World*. New York: Anchor Books, 2001.

Anderson, Kenneth, *Remarks by an Idealist on the Realism of the Limits of International Law*. Georgia: School of Law, University of Georgia, 2006.

Atwan, Abdel Bari. *The Secret History of Al Qaeda*, University of California Press, 2006.

Ayni, Badr al-Din. *Umda al-Qari Sharh Sahih al-Bukhari*. Beirut: Dar Ihya Turath al-Arabi, n.d.

Azami, Dawood. "*Why are the Taliban resurgent in Afghanistan?*" BBC News, retrieved on January 5, 2016.

Baghawi, Abu Muhammad Husayn ibn Masud, *Maalim al-Tanzil*. Beirut: Dar al-Marifa, 1987.

Baghdadi, Abd al-Qāhir. *Al-Farq Bayn al-Firaq*. Cairo: Muessasat Ibn Sina, n.d.

────── *Usul al-Din*. Beirut, 1981.

Bahgat, Gawdat. 2004. *Saudi Arabia and the War on Terrorism*. Arab Studies Quarterly, 26.

Baladhuri, Ahmad ibn Yahya. *Futuh al-Buldan*, trans. by P. K. Hitti and F. C. Murgotten, Studies in History, Economics and Public Law, New York: Columbia University Press,1916.

Baker, Aryn. "Is the Assad Regime in League with al-Qaeda?" *Time*, January 27, 2014, http://world.time.com/2014/01/27/syria-assad-geneva-al-qaeda/

Barth, Hans. *Le Droit du Croissant*. [The Right of the Crescent.] Paris: H.C. Wolf, 1898.

Bassiouni M. Cherif. "Evolving Approaches to Jihad: From Self-Defense to Revolutionary Regime-Change Political Violence." *Chicago Journal of International Law* 2007 (8): 119.

Baqillani, Abu Bakr Muhammad. *Kitab al-Tamhid*, Beirut: al-Maktabah al-Sharqiyah, 1957.

Bayhaqi, Ahmad ibn Husayn. *Sunan al-Kubra*. Makkah: Maktaba Dar al-Baz, 1994.

Bazzar, Ahmad ibn Amr. *Musnad*. Beirut: Muassasa Ulum al-Qur'an, 1994.

Beauchamp, Zack. "ISIS, Islamic State or ISIL? What to call the group the U.S. is bombing in Iraq." *OSINT Journal Review*, September 17, 2014.

Bergen, Peter L. *Holy War, Inc.: Inside the Secret World of Osama Bin Laden*. New York: Free Press, 2002.

Blanchard, Christopher M. *"The Islamic Traditions of Wahhabism and Salafiyya"* (PDF). Updated January 24, 2008. Congressional Research Service. Retrieved February 26, 2016.

Blitz, James (January 19, 2010). "A threat transformed." *Financial Times*. Retrieved March 24, 2016. http://www.ft.com/cms/s/af31e344-0499-11df-8603-00144feabdc0,Authorised=false.html?siteedition=uk&

_i_location=http%3A%2F%2Fwww.ft.com%2Fcms%2Fs%2F0%2Faf31e344-0499-11df-8603-00144feabdc0.html%3Fsiteedition%3Duk&_i_referer=https%3A%2F%2Fen.wikipedia.org%2Fd41d8cd98f00b204e9800998ecf8427e&classification=conditional_standard&iab=barrier-app#axzz43 m3opdZp.

Boyle, Kevin. The Danish Cartoons. *Human Rights Quarterly*, volume 24, 2006, pp. 185-187.

Burke Jason and Allen Paddy. (September 10, 2009). "The five ages of al-Qaida," *The Guardian* http://www.theguardian.com/world/interactive/2009/sep/10/al-qaida-five-ages-terror-attacks.

Bukhari, Muhammad ibn Ismail. *al-Jami' al-Sahih*. Beirut: Dar Ibn Kathir, 1987.

Bulac, Ali. "*Jihad*," in *An Islamic Perspective: Terror and Suicide Attacks*, ed. Ergun Capan New Jersey: Light, 2004.

Buyse, Antoine. "Words of Violence: Fear Speech, or How Violent Conflict Escalation Relates to the Freedom of Expression" in *Human Rights Quarterly* 36 (2014), pp. 779–797.

Brown, C. *Religion and state: the Muslim Approach to Politics*. New York: Columbia University Press, 2000.

Brockelmann, Carl. *History of the Islamic Peoples*. New York: Capricorn Books, 1960.

Buruni, Abu al-Rayyan. *al-Athar al-Baqiya An al-Ghurun al-Haliya*, [The remaining effect is that of the current] Leipzig, 1923.

Carens, Joseph. Free Speech and Democratic Norms in the Danish Cartoons Controversy, 44 *International Migration*, 2006, 33, 36.

Capan, Ergun. "Suicide Attacks and Islam," in *An Islamic Perspective: Terror and Suicide Attacks*, ed. Ergun Capan, New Jersey: Light, 2004.

Celso, Anthony N. "Zarqawi's Legacy: Al Qaeda's ISIS Renegade." *Mediterranean Quarterly*, 26, 2015.

Chailand, Gerard and Blin Arnaud. *The History of Terrorism from Antiquity to Al Qaeda*. Trans. Edward Schneider, Kathryn Pulver, and Jesse Browner, Los Angeles: University of California Press, 2007.

Claudio Grossman. "Challenges to Freedom of Expression within the Inter-American System: A Jurisprudential Analysis," in *Human Rights Quarterly*, 34: 2 (2012), pp. 361-403.

Combs, Cindy C. *Terrorism in the Twenty-First Century*. New Jersey: Pearson Prentice Hall, 1997, pp. 10-18.

Commins, David. *The Wahhabi Mission and Saudi Arabia*. I.B. Tauris, 2006.

Cook, David. *Martyrdom in Islam*. Cambridge: Cambridge University Press, 2007.

Crisis Group Middle East/North Africa Report N°37, *Understanding Islamism*, March 2, 2005.

Crone, Patricia and Martin Hinds. *God's Caliph: Religious Authority in the First Centuries of Islam*. Cambridge and New York: Cambridge University Press, 1986.

Constable, Pamela "Afghanistan: Arena for a New Rivalry", *The Washington Post*, Jan 9, 1998. http://pqasb.pqarchiver.com/washingtonpost/doc/408407755.html?FMT=ABS&FMTS=ABS:FT&type=current&date=Sep%2016,%201998&author=Pamela%20Constable&pub=The%20Washington%20Post&edition=&startpage=&desc=Afghanistan:%20Arena%20for%20a%20New%20Rivalry.

Dallal, A. "The Origins and Objectives of Islamic Revivalist Thought 1750-1850." *Journal of the American Oriental Society*, 113 (3), 1993.

Darimi, Abd Allah. *Sunan*. Beirut: Dar al-Kitab al-Arabi, 1987.

Daylami, Abu Shuja. *Al-Firdaws bi-Ma'thur al-Khitab* (*The Heavenly Garden Made Up of the Selections from the Prophet's Addresses*). Beirut: Dar al-Kutub al-'Ilmiya, 1986.

DeLong-Bas, Natana J. *Wahhabi Islam: From Revival and Reform to Global Jihad*. Oxford: Oxford University Press, 2004.

Dallal, Ahmad. The origins and objectives of Islamic revivalist thought, 1750-1850. *The Journal of the American Oriental Society*, 113, (1993).

Dogan, Recep. *Usul al-Fiqh Methodology of Islamic Jurisprudence*. New Jersey, Tughra Books, 2014.

—— "Conflict Resolution Forms in the Life of Prophet Muhammad." *The International Journal of Religion and Spirituality in Society*, vol. 4(2), 2014, pp. 9-19.

—— "Contributing to World Peace: An Examination of the Life of Prophet Muhammad as a Leader" *Sociology and Anthropology* 3 (2015), pp. 37-44.

Doudou Diène. *Special Rapporteur on Contemporary Forms of Racism, Racial Discrimination, Xenophobia and Related Intolerance: Addendum, Defamation of Religions and Global Efforts to Combat Racism: Anti-Semitism, Christianophobia and Islamophobia*. U.N. ESCOR, Comm'n on Hum. Rts., 61st Sess., Provisional Agenda Item 6, U.N. Doc. E/CN.4/2005/18/Add.4 (2004).

Doorn-Harder, Nelly Van. *Progressive Muslims. On Justice, Gender and Pluralism*. Theological Studies, 2004, 65.

Duhul, Salad. "Suicide bombs kill 22 in northern Somalia, UN hit." *San Diego Union Tribune*, Oct. 29, 2008. http://legacy.sandiegouniontribune.com/news/world/ 20081029-0635-af-somalia.html.

Duruji, Moses Metumara. "Social Inequity, Democratic Transition and the Igbo Nationalism Resurgence in Nigeria." *African Journal of Political Science and International Relations*. 2009, 3:1. pp. 54-65.

Dupree Hatch, Nancy. "Afghan Women under the Taliban" in Maley, William. *Fundamentalism Reborn? Afghanistan and the Taliban*. London: Hurst and Company, 2001.

Elgood, C. *Tibb ul-Nabi or Medicine of the Prophet*. Osiris, 14, (1962), pp. 33-192.

Erwin, Michael. "Key Factors for the Recent Growth of the Afghan Insurgency," *CTC Sentinel*, 1:9, August 2008.

Ergil, Dogu. *Fethullah Gülen and The Gülen Movement in 100 Questions*. New York: Blue Dome Press, 2012.

Esposito, John. *What Everyone Needs to Know about Islam*. Oxford: Oxford University Press, 2002.

—— *The Oxford Dictionary of Islam*. Oxford: Oxford University, 2003.

—— *Unholy War: Terror in the Name of Islam*. New York: Oxford University Press, 2002.

―――― "Islam and Political Violence." *Religions* 6 (2015), pp. 1067–1081.
―――― *The Future of Islam*. New York: Oxford University Press, 2010.
―――― and Mogahed. Dalia. "Battle for Muslims' Hearts and Minds: The Road Not (Yet) Taken." *Middle East Policy* 14 (2007), pp. 27–41.
Euben, Roxanne I. and Muhammad Qasim Zaman, *Princeton Readings in Islamic Thought: Texts and Contexts from al-Banna to Bin Laden*. New Jersey: Princeton University Press, 2009.
Evans, Jonathan. "Speech delivered by Jonathan Evans, head of MI5 to the Worshipful Company of Security Professionals." Sept. 17, 2010, London: *The Daily Telegraph*. Retrieved on April 4, 2016. http://www.telegraph.co.uk/news/uknews/terrorism-in-the-uk/8008252/Jonathan-Evans-terrorism-speech.html.
Falola, Tayin and Heaton Matthew M. *A History of Nigeria*. Cambridge, 2008.
Farwell, James P. "The Media Strategy of ISIS" *Survival* (56) 2015, pp. 49–55.
Fazlur Rahman. *Islam*. Chicago: University of Chicago Press, 1979.
Felbab-Brow, Vanda. *Shooting Up: Counterinsurgency and the War on Drugs*. Brookings Institution Press, 2010.
Fletcher, M. "How Life Returned to the Streets in a Showpiece City that Drove out Al Qaeda." UK, *London Times*, Aug. 31, 2007.
Frampton, John. *The Most Noble and Famous Travels of Marco Polo*. London: The Argonaut Press, 1929.
Fuller, Graham. *A World, Without Islam*. New York: Little, Brown and Co., 2010.
Gall, Carlotta. "*At Border, Signs of Pakistani Role in Taliban Surge*" http://www.nytimes.com/2007/01/21/world/asia/21quetta.html?_r=0 *New York Times*, retrieved on Jan. 21, 2007.
Garlow, James. *A Christian's Response to Islam*. Oklahoma: River Oak Publishing, 2002.
Geltzer, Joshua A. *US Counter-Terrorism Strategy and al-Qaeda: Signalling and the Terrorist World-View*. Routledge, 2011.
Gerges, Fawaz A. *The Far Enemy: Why Jihad Went Global*. Cambridge University Press, 2005.

Ghani, Ashraf. "Afghanistan: Islam and Counterrevolutionary Movements," in John Esposito (ed), *Islam in Asia: Religion, Politics and Society*. New York: Oxford University Press, 1987.

Ghazali, Abu Hamid Muhammad. *Ihya al-Ulum al-Din*. Lahore: Islamic Book Foundation, 1983.

Giustozzi, Antonio. *Koran, Kalashnikov and Laptop: The Neo-Taliban Insurgency in Afghanistan*. London: Hurst & Co., 2007.

Giraldo, Jeanne K. *Terrorism Financing and State Responses: A Comparative Perspective*. Stanford University Press, 2007.

Girardet, Edward. *Killing the Cranes: A Reporter's Journey through Three Decades of War in Afghanistan*. Chelsea Green Publishing, 2011.

Glasse, Cyril. *The New Encyclopedia of Islam*. Alta Mira Press, 2001.

Goldziher, Ignaz. *Al-Aqida wa al-Shariah fi al-Islam*. [Creed and Poeticism in Islam.] Egypt, n.d.

Goodluck, I. and Juliana, J. "Provision of Formal Education to Almajiris: Role of Libraries." *European Scientific Journal*, 8/15.

Goodwin, George M. More than a Laughing Matter: Cartoons and Jews. *Judaism*, volume 21, 2001.

Gülen, Fethullah. *Endeavor for Renewal*. New Jersey: Tughra Books, 2015.

—— *Journey to Noble Ideals, The Broken Jug Series, 13*. New Jersey: Tughra Books, 2014.

—— *Reflections on the Qur'ān: Commentaries on Selected Verses*. New Jersey: Tughra Books, 2012.

—— *Toward a Global Civilization of Love and Tolerance*. New Jersey: The Light, 2006.

—— *Essays, Perspectives, Opinions*. New Jersey: The Light, 2006.

—— *Advocate of Dialogue*. Fairfax, VA: Fountain Press, 2000.

—— *Pearls of Wisdom*, New Jersey: Tughra Books, 2005.

—— *Messenger of God: Muhammad*. New Jersey: The Light, 2005.

—— *Asrın Getirdiği Tereddütler* (*Questions and Answers about Islam*) (Izmir: Nil Yayınları, 1998.

—— *Kirik Testi (Broken Jug), Vol. 4, Umit Burcu*. Istanbul: Gazeteciler ve Yazarlar Vakfi, 2005.

References

───── "*Anarşist Ruhlar ve Modern Karmatîler*" (*The Anarchic Souls and the Modern Qarmatians*), Weekly Sermons at herkul.ord, last modified 1/11/2004 http://www.herkul.org/kirik-testi/anarsist-ruhlar-ve-modern-karmatiler/

───── "*The Grave Consequence of Murders Committed under the Guise of Religion*," accessed on February 24, 2015. http://www.herkul.org/weekly-sermons/the-grave-consequence-of-murders-committed-under-the-guise-of-religion-1/

───── "*The Grave Consequence of Murders Committed under the Guise of Religion*," accessed on February 24, 2015. http://www.herkul.org/weekly-sermons/the-grave-consequence-of-murders-committed-under-the-guise-of-religion-2/

───── "Three Groups Opposing Dialogue: Kharijites, Qarmatians, Anarchists," last modified on June 14, 2006. http://en.fgulen.com/recent-articles/1878-three-groups-opposing-dialogue-kharijites-karmatis-anarchists.

───── "*ISIS Cruelty Deserves Our Strongest Condemnation*," accessed on February 24, 2015. http://www.fethullah-gulen.org/news/gulen-isis.html.

───── "*Fethullah Gülen's statement on Paris attacks*," accessed on February 24, 2015. http://fgulen.com/en/press/messages/47207-fethullah-gulen-statement-on-paris-attacks.

───── "*Suicide*," June 18 2012 http://www.herkul.org/tag/suicide-attacks/, accessed on November 30 2015.

Guparatma, Rohan. *Inside Al Qaeda. Columbia University Press*, 2002.

Hakim, Muhammad ibn Abd Allah. *Mustadrak Ala al-Sahihayn*. Beirut: Dar al-Kutub al-Ilmiya, 1990.

Hammadi, Khalid. "The Inside Story of al-Qa'ida," part 4, *Al-Quds al-Arabi*, March 22, 2005.

Hashim, Ahmed S. "The Islamic State: From al-Qaeda Affiliate to Caliphate." *Middle East Policy*, 11/4, 69-82, 2014.

Herriott, Peter. *Religious Fundamentalism and Social Identity*. London: Routledge, 2007.

Higgins, Annie C. "Kharijites, Khawarij." In Martin, Richard C. *Encyclopedia of Islam and the Muslim World,* vol. 1. Macmillan, 2004.

Hindi, Ala al-Din Ali al-Muttaqi. *Kanz al-Ummal.* Beirut: Dar al-Fikr, 1986.

Horowitz, Alana (July 27, 2011). "Al Qaeda Group Al Shabaab Recruited Muslims Americans: U.S. Report." *Huffington Post.* Retrieved April 4, 2016. http://www.huffingtonpost.com/2011/07/27/al-qaeda-american-recruits_n_911432.html.

Hoyle, Carolyn et al. *Becoming Mulan?* Institute for Strategic Dialogue, London (2015). Available at http://www.al-monitor.com/pulse/originals/2014/12/european-women-joinjihad-motives.html.

Iraqi, Abd al-Rahim. *al-Mughni an Haml al-Asfar.* [Singer that carry yellow] Beirut: Dar al-Kitab al-'Arabi, 2011.

Ian Black et al. "The Terrifying Rise of Isis." *The Guardian,* 16 June 2014, accessed on September 30, 2015, http://www.theguardian.com/world/2014/jun/16/terrifying-rise-of-isis-iraq-executions.

Ibn Abidin, Muhammad. *Radd al-Mukhtar.* Beirut: Dar al-Fikr, 1987.

Ibn Abi Shayba, Abd Allah ibn Muhammad. *Musannaf.* Riyadh: Maktaba al-Rushd, 1980.

Ibn Athir, Ali ibn Muhammad. *Al-Kāmil Fi Al-Tārikh.* Beirut: Dar Sadir, 1979.

―――― *Usd al-Ghaba.* [Lion Forest.] Beirut: Dār Iḥyā' al-Turāth al-'Arabi, 1968.

―――― *al-Nihaya fi Gharib al-Hadith.* [The end in a strange talk.] Cairo, 1904.

Ibn Hanbal, Ahmad. *Musnad al-Imam Ahmad ibn Hanbal.* Beirut: Dar al-Kutub al-'Ilmiyya, 1993.

Ibn Hajar al-Asqalani, Ahmad ibn Ali. *Fath al-Bari Sharh Sahih al-Bukhari.* Beirut: Dar al-Marifa, n.d.

Ibn Hazm, Abu Muhammad Ali ibn Ahmad. *al-Fasl Fi al-Milal wa Ahwa al-Nihal.* Baghdad: Maktabat al-Muthanna, 1964.

Ibn Hisham, Abu Muhammad Abd al-Malik. *Sirah.* Beirut: Muasasa al-Risala, 1993.

Ibn Humam, Kamal al-Din. *Fath al-Qadir.* [Open the Almighty.] Quetta: Maktaba Rashidiyya, n.d.

Ibn Kathīr, Ismail Abu al-Fida. *Al-Bidāya wa'l-Nihāya.* Beirut: Dar al-Kutub al-Ilmiyya, 2003.

Ibn Kathīr, Ismail Abu al-Fida. *A compilation of the Abridged Tafsir Ibn Kathir.* (Riyadh: Darussalam, 2000.

Ibn Khaldun, Muhammad. *Kitab al-Ibar.* [Book of needles.] Egypt: 1863.

────── *Muqaddima.* [Introduction.] Princeton, NJ: Princeton University Press, 2005.

Ibn Majah, Muhammad ibn Yazid. *Sunan Ibn Majah.* Beirut: Dar Al-Kutub al-Ilmiyah, 2008.

Ibn Manzur, Muhammad Ibn Mukarram. *Lisan al-Arab.* Beirut: Dār Ṣādir, 2000.

Ibn Ishaq, Muhammad. *Sirah al-Rasul al-Allah,* (tr: A. Guillaume, *The Life of Muhammad*), Karachi: Oxford University Press, 1955.

Ibn Sa'd, Muhammad. *Kitab al-Tabaqat al-Kabir.* [Great Layers Book] London: Ta-Ha Publishers Ltd, 2012.

Ibn Sallam, Abu Ubayda al-Qasim. *Kitab al-Amwal.* [Book money.] Beirut: Dar al-Fikr, 1980.

Ibn Taymiyya, Ahmad ibn Abd al-Halim. *Al-Nubuwwat.* Beirut: Dar al-Kitab al-Arabi, 1985.

────── *Majmua al-Fatawa.* Beirut: Maktaba Ibn Taymiyya, n.d.

Ibn Qayyim, Muhammad ibn Abi Bakr. *Ahkam al-Dhimma.* Beirut: Dar Ibn Hazm, 1997.

Ibn Qudama, Abd Allah ibn Ahmad. *al- Kafi fi Fiqh al-Imam Ahmad Ibn-Hanbal.* [Enough in the jurisprudence of Imam Ahmad Ibn Hanbal.] Beirut: Dar al-Kutub al-Ilmiya, 1994.

Ingram, Haroro J. "The strategic logic of Islamic State information operations." *Australian Journal of International Affairs* 69 2015.

International Covenant on Civil and Political Rights, adopted 16 Dec. 1966, G.A. Res. 2200 (XXI), U.N. GAOR, 21st Sess., Supp. No. 16, art. 20, U.N. Doc. A/6316 (1966), 999 U.N.T.S. 171 (entered into force Mar. 23, 1976).

Isfahani, Raghib. *Mu'jam Mufradat Alfaz al-Qur'an*. Beirut: Dar al-Kutub al-Ilmiyya, 1997.

Jassās, Abu Bakr. *Kitāb al-Aḥkām al-Qur'an*. Beirut: Dār al-Kitāb al-'Arabī, 1978.

Jocelyn, Thomas. "Al Qaeda's Chief Representative in Syria Killed in Suicide Attack," *Long War Journal*, February 23, 2014, www.longwarjournal.org/archives/2014/ 02/zawahiris_chief_repr.php.

John Pike (2001-10-07). "Intentions of U.S. military operation." *Globalsecurity.org*. Retrieved on Mar 11, 2016.

Iornongu Ker, David. "Diagnostic Review of Insurgency in Nigeria: The Cultural Dimension", *CCT Research Paper*, October 2013 http://www.icct.nl/download/file/ICCT-Olojo-Nigerias-Troubled-North-October-2013.pdf.

Judit Barna, *Insecurity in context: The rise of Boko Haram in Nigeria* Policy Department, Directorate-General for External Policies, July 2014, 3.

Jurgensmeyer, Mark. *Terror in the Mind of God: The Global Rise of Religious Violence*. Los Angeles: University of California Press, 2003.

Kasani, Ala al-Din. *Badai al-Sanai*. [Hurricane al-Sanai.] Beirut: Dar al-Kitab al-Arabi, 1982.

Karawan, I. (1992). Monarchs, Mullas, and Marshals: Islamic Regimes? *Annals AAPSS*, 524, pp. 103-119.

Karliga, Bekir. "Religion, Terror, War, and the Need for Global Ethics." in *An Islamic Perspective: Terror and Suicide Attacks*, ed. Ergun Capan. New Jersey: Light, 2004.

Kamali, M. Hashim. *Principles of Islamic Jurisprudence*. Cambridge: Islamic Texts Society, 2003.

Kayaoglu, Turan. "Constructing the Dialogue of Civilizations in World Politics: A Case of Global Islamic Activism." *Islam and Christian–Muslim Relations* 23 (2012), pp. 129-147.

Keane, David. Cartoon Violence and Freedom of Expression, *Human Rights Quarterly*, volume 30, 2008, pp. 845-875.

Kechichian, J. The role of the Ulema in the politics of an Islamic state: the case of Saudi Arabia. *International Journal of Middle East Studies*, 18, 55. 1986.

Kenney, Jeffrey T. *Heterodoxy and Culture: The Legacy of the Khawarij in Islamic History*. PhD Dissertation, 1991.

Kepel, Gilles. *The War for Muslim Minds*. Belknap: Press of Harvard University Press, 2004.

—— *Jihad: The Trail of Political Islam*. London: I.B. Tauris, 2006.

Kimball, Charles. *When Religion Becomes Evil*. San Francisco, New York: Harper, 2003.

Kirmani, Ahmad. *Kitab al-Riyad*. [Book of Riyadh.] Beirut: 1960.

Kron, Josh (October 21, 2011). "African Union Peacekeepers Killed in Somalia Battle." *The New York Times*. Retrieved April 4, 2016. http://www.nytimes.com/2011/10/22/ world/africa/african-union-takes-casualties-in-somalia-but-numbers-vary.html?_r=0.

Kurucan, Ahmet and Kose, Erol. *Dialogue in Islam*. London: Great Britain, 2012.

Lacey, Robert. *Inside the Kingdom: Kings, Clerics, Modernists, Terrorists, and the Struggle for Saudi Arabia*. Viking: 2009.

Larsen, Curtis. *Life and Land Use on the Bahrain Islands: The Geoarchaeology of an Ancient Society*. Chicago: University of Chicago Press, 1984.

Leeuwen, Van T. *Discourse and Practice*. Oxford: Oxford University Press, 2008.

Lentini, Pete. (2015), "Demonizing ISIL and Defending Muslims: Australian Muslim Citizenship and Tony Abbott's "Death Cult" Rhetoric." *Islam and Christian–Muslim Relations*, 26:2, pp. 237-252.

Lewis, Bernard. *The Arabs in History*. New York: Harper Torchbooks, 1966.

—— *The Origins of Ismailism*. Cambridge: 1940.

—— *The Assassins: A Radical Sect of Islam*. Oxford: Oxford University Press, 1967.

—— *On the evolution of early Islam*. Studa Islamica, 1970, (32), pp. 215-231.

―――― *The Political Language of Islam*. Chicago, IL: University of Chicago Press, 1998.

―――― *The Crisis of Islam – Holy War and Unholy Terror*. New York: Modern Library, 2003.

Ling, Trevor. *A History of Religion*. New York: Harper & Row, 1970.

Litwak, Robert. *Regime change: U.S. strategy through the prism of 9/11*. Johns Hopkins University Press, 2007.

Loimeier, R. "Boko Haram: The Development of a Militant Religious Movement in Nigeria." *Africa Spectrum*. 47/2-3, 2012.

Maqrizi, Ahmad ibn Ali. *Kitab al-Muqaffa al-Kabir*. [Great book attitude.] Riyadh, 1989.

Maqrizi, Ahmad ibn Ali. *Ittiaz al-Hunafa, bi Zikri Aimma al-Khulafa*. Cairo, 1948.

Masudi, Husayin ibn Ali. *al-Tanbih wa al-Ishraf*. [Alert and supervision.] Beirut: 1981.

Marayati, S. 2014. *Islam's Theology of Life Is Stronger than ISIS' Cult of Death*. September 5. Accessed September 15, 2015. http://religion.blogs.cnn.com/2014/09/05/islams-theology-of-life-is-strongerthan-isis-cult-of-death/

Marcela Grad. *Massoud: An Intimate Portrait of the Legendary Afghan Leader*. Webster University Press, 2009.

Marghinani, Abū Bakr. *Al-Hidaya*. Karachi: Darul Ishaat, 2007.

Matinuddin, Kamal. *The Taliban Phenomenon, Afghanistan 1994–1997*. Oxford University Press, 1999.

Matroudi, Abdul Hakim. *The Hanbali School of Law and Ibn Taymiyyah*. London: Routledge, 2006.

Maturidi, Abu Mansur Muhammad ibn Muhammad. *Tawilat Ahl al-Sunnah*. Beirut: Muassasa al-Risala, 2004.

Maura Conway. "From al-Zarqawi to al-Awlaki: The Emergence and Development of an Online Radical Milieu." *CTX Journal* 2, 4 (2012): pp. 12 – 2.

Mawdudi, Abu al-Ala. *Islamic Way of Life*. Delhi: Markazi Maktaba Islami, 1967.

Mehmed, Seyyid. *Usul-i Fıkıh: Medhal*. Istanbul: Kitap Yurdu, 2011.

McGrath, Kevin. *Confronting Al-Qaeda*. Naval Institute Press, 2011.
McQuaid, Julia V. *"The Struggle for Unity and Authority in Islam: Reviving the Caliphate?"* Alexandria, VA: CNA Center for Strategic Studies, 2007.
Morony, Michael G. *Iraq after the Muslim Conquest*. Princeton, New Jersey: Princeton University Press, 1984.
Moussalli, Ahmad. "Wahhabism, Salafism and Islamism: Who Is The Enemy?" (PDF). (January 2009), *Conflicts Forum Monograph*. Retrieved February 26, 2016.
Mubarrad, Abu Al-'Abbas Muhammad ibn Yazid. *Al-Kamil*. Cairo: al-Istiqama Publishing, 1951.
Mullins, W. A. (1972). On the concept of ideology in political science. *The American Political Science Review*, 66(2), pp. 498-510.
Muslim, Muslim ibn al-Hajjaj al-Qushayri. *Sahih al-Muslim*. [True Muslim.] Lahore: Muhammad Ashraf, 1972.
Naím, Moisés (January–February 2003). "The Five Wars of Globalization." *Foreign Policy* (134), pp. 28–37.
Nakash, Yitzhak. *Reaching for Power: The Shia in the Modern Arab World*. Princeton, 2007.
Nasafi, Abul Mu'in Muhammad. *Tabsirat'ul Adilla*. [Look at the evidence.] Ankara: Diyanet Isleri Baskanligi Yayinlari, 1993.
Nasai, Aḥmad ibn Shu'ayb. *Sunan Nasai*. Riyadh: Darussalam, 2007.
Natana J. Delong-Bas. *Wahhabi Islam*. Oxford: Oxford University Press, 2004.
Nowell, Charles E. "The Old Man of the Mountain" *Speculum* 22 (4) 1947.
Nir Rosen. "In the Lair of the Taliban," *The Sunday Times*, December 7, 2008.
Nuwayri, Ahmad. *Nihaya al-Ereb Fi Funun al-Adab*. [The end of the Arabs in the arts of literature.] Cairo, 1984.
Orhan, Mehmet. "Al-Qaeda: Analysis of the Emergence, Radicalism, and Violence of a Jihadist Action Group in Turkey." *Turkish Studies* 11 (2010), pp.143-161.
Ostebo. "Islamic Militancy in Africa", *Africa Security Brief*, No. 23, November 2012.

Pate, Amy. *Boko Haram: An Assessment of Strengths, Vulnerabilities, and Policy Options*. Report to the Strategic Multilayer Assessment Office, Department of Defense, and the Office of University Programs, Department of Homeland Security. College Park MD: START, January 2014.

Peresin, Anita and Alberto Cervone. "The Western Muhajirat of ISIS." *Studies in Conflict & Terrorism*, (38) 2015, pp. 495-509.

Philby, S. *Saudi Arabia*. London: Ernest Benn Limited, 1955.

Post, Robert. *Religion and Freedom of Speech: Portraits of Muhammad*, 14 Constellations, 2007.

Qadi Iyad, *Al-Shifa*. [Newspaper.] Damascus: Dar al-Wafa lil-Ṭibaʻah wa-'al-Nashr, 1972.

Qarafi, Shihab al-Din. *Al-Furuq*. Beirut: Dar al-Kutub al-Ilmiya, 1998.

Qanta Ahmed. "Who are the Invisible Women Joining ISIS?" *Fox News*, September 19, 2014. Available at http://www.foxnews.com/opinion/2014/09/18/unveiling-invisible-women-joining-isis/

Qutub, Sayyid. *Social Justice in Islam*. Beirut: Dār al-Shuruq, 1975.

—— *In the Shade of the Qur'an*. Leicester: Islamic Foundation, 1999.

Ramsbotham O. et al. *Contemporary Conflict Resolution: The Prevention, Management and Transformation of Deadly Conflicts,* Malden, MA: Polity Press, 2011.

Rashid, Ahmed. *Taliban: Islam, Oil and the New Great Game in Central Asia*. I.B.Tauris: 2002.

Razi, Abu Hatim. *Kitab al-Zinah* [Book of decoration], Baghdad, 1988.

Razi, Fakhr al-Din. *I'tiqadat al-Firaq al-Muslimin wa al-Mushrikin*. [The Muslim and polytheistic sects are complicated.] Cairo: Maktaba al-Nahda al-Misriyya, 1938.

—— *Mafatih al-Ghayb*. [Keys of the eyebrow.]Beirut: Dar al-kutub al-ilmiyyah, 1990.

Ridha, Rashid. *Tafsir al-Manar*. [Interpretation of Manar.] Jakarta: Pen. Erlangga, 2006.

Robinson, Chase F. *Empire and Elites after the Muslim Conquest*. Cambridge: Cambridge University Press, 2000.

Roggio, Bill. "Al Nusrah Front Emir Issues Ultimatum to ISIS," *Long War Journal*, February 25, 2014, www.longwarjournal.org/archives/2014/02/al_nusrah_front_emir_1.php.

Rosenthal, Erwin Isak Jakob. *Political Thought in Medieval Islam*. Cambridge: University Press, 1958.

Sabri, Mustafa. *Hilafet ve Kemalizm*. [Caliphate and Kemalism.] Istanbul: Arastırma Yayınları 1992.

Saeed, Amir. "Media, Racism and Islamophobia: The Representation of Islam and Muslims in the Media." *Sociology Compass* 2 (2007), pp. 443-463.

Samuel, Huntington. *Clash of Civilizations and the Remaking of the World Order*. New Delhi: Penguin Books, 1996.

Salem, Elie Adib. *Political Theory and Institutions of the Khawarij*. Baltimore: The John Hopkins Press, 1956.

Saloom, Rachel. You Dropped a Bomb on Me, Denmark—A Legal Examination of the Cartoon Controversy and Response as It Relates to the Prophet Muhammad and Islamic Law. *Rutgers J. L. & Religion* 3, 2006.

Sarakhsī, Shams al-Din. *Mabsut*. Beirut: Dar al-Marifa, 1978.

Saidu, Mahmud Sakah. *Sharia or Shura: Contending Approaches to Muslim Politics in Nigeria and Senegal*. New York: Lexington Books, 2013.

Saikal, Amin. *Modern Afghanistan: A History of Struggle and Survival*. London, New York: I.B. Tauris & Co, 2006.

Saritoprak, Zeki. "Fethullah Gülen's Thoughts on State, Democracy, Politics, Terrorism," *The Muslim World*, 95 (2005), pp. 325–471.

Saritoprak, Zeki, Ali Unal. "An Interview with Fethullah Gülen," *Muslim World* 95 (2005), pp. 465-467.

San'ani, Abd al-Razzaq. *Musannaf*. Riyadh: Al-Maktaba al-Islami, 1982.

Saunders, John J. *A History of Medieval Islam*. Routledge, 1978.

Schacht, Joseph. *An Introduction to Islamic Law*. Oxford: Oxford University Press, 1964.

Scheuer, Michael. "The Pious Caliphate Will Start From Afghanistan." *Jamestown Global Terrorism Analysis*, Vol. 2, No. 12, June 24, 2005.

Shane, Scott and Hubbard, Ben. "ISIS Displaying a Deft Command of Varied Media." *New York Times*, August 31, 2014, accessed September 30, 2015, http://www.nytimes.com/2014/08/31/world/middleeast/isis-displaying-a-deft-command-ofvariedmedia.html?_r=0.

Shaybani, Muhammad. *Sirah al-Kabir*. Baltimore: John Hopkins Press, 1965.

—— *Al-Mabsut*. Karachi: Idara al-Qur'an wa Ulum al-Islamiyya, n.d.

Shaban, M. A. *Islamic History, A. D. 600-750 (A.H. 132): A New Interpretation*. Cambridge: Cambridge University Press, 1971.

Shafi'i, Muhammad ibn Idris. *Al-Umm*. [Nations.] Beirut: Dar al-Marifa, 1973.

Shahristani, Muhammad ibn Abd al-Karim. *Al-Milal Wa'n-Nihal*. [Boredom and 'well.] Beirut: Dar al-Ma'rifa, 1993.

Shatibi, Abu Ishaq Ibrahim ibn Musa. *Muwafaqat fi Uṣul al-Shari'ah*. Egypt: Yuṭlabu min al-Maktabah al-Tijariyah al-Kubra, 1975.

Shaybani, Abd al-Karim ibn Abd al-Wahid. *Al-Kāmil fi al-Tārikh*. Beirut: Dar al-Kutub al-Ilmiyya, 1987.

Sherwood, Harriet et al., "Schoolgirl Jihadis: The Female Islamists Leaving Home to Join ISIS Fighters." *The Guardian*, September 29, 2014. Available at http://www. theguardian.com/world/2014/sep/29/schoolgirl-jihadis-female-islamists-leaving-home-join-isis-iraq-syria.

Shepard, William E. "Sayyid Qutb's Doctrine of Jahiliyya," *International Journal of Middle East Studies*, 35 (2003): 524.

Shibli, Mawlana. *Bütün Yönleriyle Hazreti Ömer ve Devlet Idaresi [All aspects of the Prophet Ömer and the State Administration]*, Translated by Talip Yasar Alp, Istanbul: Hikmet Yayinlari, 1986.

Sevindi, Nevval. *Fethullah Gülen'le Global Hosgoru ve New York Sohbetleri*. [Global Hosgoru and New York Conversations with Fethullah Gülen.] Istanbul: Timas, 2002.

Sijistani, Abu Ya'qub Ishaq ibn Ahmad. *Kitab-Al-Iftikhar*. [I wrote a book.] Beirut: Kutub, 2000.

Sirriyeh, E. (1989). *Wahhabis, Unbelievers, and Problems of Exclusivism*. British Society for Middle Eastern Studies, 16(2), pp. 123-132.

Sivan, Emmanuel. *Radical Islam, Medieval Theology, and Modern Politics*. New Haven: Yale University Press. 1985.

Skain, Rosemarie. *The women of Afghanistan under the Taliban*. McFarland, 2002.

Stark, Rodney. *One True God: Historical Consequences of Monotheism*. Princeton: Princeton University Press, 2007.

Stern, Jessica. *Terror in the Name of God*. San Francisco: Harper One, 2009.

Tabarani, Sulayman ibn Ahmad. *Musnad al-Shamiyyin*. Beirut: Muassasa al-Risala. 1985.

Tabari, Abu Ja'far Muhammad ibn Jarir. *Tārikh al-Umam wa al-Muluk*. Cairo: Dar al-Maarif, n.d.

—— *Jami al-Bayan an Ta'wil al-Qur'an*. Beirut: Ālam al-Kutub, 1992.

Tahawi, Abu Ja'far Ahmad ibn Muhammad. *Mukhtasar al-Ikhtilaf al-Fuqaha*. [Summary of the difference in jurisprudence.] Beirut: Dar al-Basha'ir al-Islamiyya, 1995.

The Amman Message, *Jordan: The Royal Al-Bayt Institute for Islamic Thought,* 2009.

Tirmidhi, Abu Isa Muhammad ibn Isa. *Sunan*. Beirut: Dar Ihya Turath al-Arabi, n.d.

Touati, Houari. *Islam and Travel in the Middle Ages*. Chicago: University of Chicago Press, 2010.

Toynbee, Arnold. *An Historian Approach to Religion*. New York: Oxford University Press, 1956.

Unal, Ali. *The Quran with Annotated Interpretation in Modern English*. New Jersey: Tughra Books, 2007.

Ula, Abdul. "Deobandi" in M. J. Gohari, *The Taliban: Ascent to Power*. Karachi: Oxford University Press, 1999.

Vernie Liebl, "The Caliphate," *Middle Eastern Studies*, 45 (2009), 3, pp. 373-391.

Wagemakers, Joas. "Protecting Jihad: The Sharia Council of the Minbar Al-Tawhid Wa-L-Jihad." *Middle East Policy* 18 (2011), pp. 148–162.

Walsh, Declan. Bomb at Danish Embassy Kills Six in Pakistan, *The Guardian* (London), June 3, 2008, available at http://www.guardian.co.uk/world/2008/jun/03/pakistan. terrorism.

Walker, Andrew. *What is Boko Haram?* U.S. Institute of Peace (USIP), June 2012.

Watt, W. Montgomery. *Islam and the Integration of Society*. London: Routledge & Kegan Paul, 1961.

—— *Muhammad at Medina*. Oxford: Clarendon Press, 1956.

—— *Islamic Political Thought: The Basic Concepts*. Edinburgh: University Press, 1968.

Wāqidī, Abu Abdallah Muhammad ibn Umar. *Kitāb al-Maghāzī*. London: Oxford Univ. Press, 1966.

Weaver, Matthew. Isis declares caliphate in Iraq and Syria. *The Guardian*, July 1, 2014. http://www.theguardian.com/world/2014/jun/30/isis-announces-islamic-caliphate-iraq-syria.

Wehr, Hans. *A Dictionary of Modern Written Arabic*. Beirut: Maktabat al-Lebanon, 1960.

Wellhausen, Julius. *Die Religios-Politischen Oppositionspartein im Alten Islam* [The Religious-Political Opposition Parties in Ancient Islam], Berlin: n.p., 1901.

Werner, Ruf. *Islam and the West- Judgments, Prejudices, Political Perspectives*. Munster: Verlag GmbH&Co.Kg, 2002.

White, Jeffery. "Assad's Indispensable Foreign Legions." *Policy Watch* 2196, January 22, 2014, Washington Institute, www.washingtoninstitute.org/policy-analysis/view/assads-indispensable-foreign-legions.

Wilfer, Madelung. *The Succession to Muhammad, a Study of the Early Caliphate*. Cambridge: Cambridge University Press, 1997.

Wright, Lawrence. *The Looming Tower: Al-Qaeda and the Road to 9/11*. Knopf, 2006.

Yaman, Mansur. *Kitab al-Rushd wa al-Hidaya*. [Book of Ridth and Gifts.] Leiden, 1948.

Yazir, Hamdi. *Hak Dini Kur'an Dili* [The religious right of Kor'an Dili], İstanbul: Azim Dağıtım, 2007.

Yushau, Sodiq. "A History of Islamic Law in Nigeria: Past and Present." *Islamic Studies*. 1992, 31:1, pp. 85-108.

Zelin, Aaron Y. "Up to 11,000 Fighters in Syria: Steep Rise in West Europeans," *ICSR Insight*, December 17, 2013, Washington Institute, www.washingtoninstitute.org/policy-analysis/view/up-to-11000-foreign-fighters-in-syria-steep-rise-among-western-europeans.

WEB PAGES

"A Message to the Mujahidin and the Muslim Ummah in the Month of Ramadan," *Abu Bakr Al-Baghdadi*, 2014. Al Hayat Media Centre. http://www.gatestoneinstitute.org/ documents/baghdadicaliph. Pdf.

"Al-Shabaab joining al Qaeda, monitor group says." *CNN*, February 9, 2012, retrieved April 4, 2016. http://edition.cnn.com/2012/02/09/world/africa/somalia-shabaab-qaeda/.

Country Reports on Terrorism 2013, U.S. Department of State, Bureau of Counterterrorism, retrieved April 14, 2016. http://www.state.gov/j/ct/rls/crt/2013/ 224829.htm.

Country Reports on Terrorism: Annex of Statistical Information, NCTC (National Counterterrorism Center), accessed June 15, 2015. http://www.nctc.gov/docs/ir-of-the-9-11-comm-act-of-2007.pdf.

"*Social inequity, democratic transition and the Igbo nationalism resurgence in Nigeria.*" Duruji, Moses Metumara, accessed April 15, 2016 available at http://www.academicjournals.org/article/article 13797591 06_Duruji.pdf.

Charlie Hebdo Attack: The Prophet Muhammad Cartoons That May Have Caused Paris Magazine Massacre, Cristina Silva, available at http://www.ibtimes.com/charlie-hebdo-attack-prophet-muhammad-cartoons-may-have-caused-paris-magazine-1775898.

Free speech Rally and Anti Cartoon Counter-Protest in UK accessed April 15, 2016 available at http://web.archive.org/web/20060326071135/ http://www. cartoonbodycount.com.

Dove World sold, soon moving to Tampa Bay area, Curry, Christopher, Gainesville. com.

US pastor Terry Jones held after threats to burn Korans, accessed April 15, 2016 available at http://www.bbc.com/news/world-us-canada-240 59408.

Global Terrorism Index 2015 (PDF). Institute for Economics and Peace, November 2015, p. 41, retrieved April 14, 2016. http://economics andpeace.org/wp-content/ uploads/2015/11/Global-Terrorism-Index-2015.pdf.

"Jihadist groups across globe vying for terror spotlight." *Fox News*, July 10, 2014, retrieved April 4, 2016. http://www.foxnews.com/world/2014/07/10/world-worst-jihadist-groups-across-globe-vie-for-terror-spotlight.html.

"Is Islamic State shaping Boko Haram media," *BBC*, March 4, 2015, retrieved April 14, 2016. http://www.bbc.com/news/world-africa-31522469.

Definitions for radicalization. accessed April 15, 2016 available at http://www. definitions.net/definition/radicalization.

Iraq in Crisis, Anthony Cordesman and Sam Khazai, (Washington, DC: Center for Strategic and International Studies, 2014), csis.org/files/publication/140513_ Cordesman_IraqInCrisis_Web.pdf.

Obama says planned Koran burning is boosting Qaeda, David Alexander and Matt Spetalnick, http://ca.reuters.com/article/topNews/idCATRE6 8820G20100909?sp= true.

Racism and Racial Discrimination on Rise around the World, UN Expert Warns, UN News Centre, Mar. 7, 2006, available at http://www. un.org/apps/news/story.asp? NewsID=17718&Cr=racis&Cr1.

START: Study of Terrorism and Response to Terrorism (College Park, MD, Program on International Policy Attitudes and University of Maryland), http://www.worldpublicopinion.org/pipa/pdf/apr07/STAR T_Apr07_quaire.pdf.

"Swedish Cartoonist Gets Protection," *BBC News*, Sept. 17, 2007, available at http:// news.bbc.co.uk/2/hi/middle_east/6999652.stm.

Terrorism 2002–2005, U.S. Department of Justice Federal Bureau of Investigation, accessed June 20, 2015. https://www.fbi.gov/stats-services/publications/terrorism-2002-2005.

"UN Points to Progress in Battling Al-Shabab in Somalia." *VOA*, January 3, 2015, retrieved April 4, 2016. http://www.voanews.com/articleprint view/2584631.html.

"Understanding Al-Shabaab," Daveed Gartenstein-Ross and Madeleine Gruen, *CTR Vantage*, (Foundation for the Defense of Democracies), November 4, 2009, available at http://www.defenddemocracy.org/images/stories/Al-Shabaabs_ Recruiting_ Efforts_in_the_West.pdf.

ABOUT THE AUTHOR

Dr. Recep Dogan is a prominent Muslim scholar, prolific author and a respected community activist in Australia. He completed his Bachelor of Divinity (Islamic Theology) at Ankara University, Turkey. He then continued on at Ankara University to complete a Master of Islamic Studies and later a PhD in the Islamic Studies Department, Philosophy of Religion. Dr Dogan gives lectures on various Islamic disciplines such as Qur'anic Exegesis, Prophetic Traditions, The Methodology of Qur'anic Exegeses, Core Islamic Sciences, Islamic Jurisprudence, The Methodology of Islamic Law, The Methodology of Prophetic Traditions, Islamic Theology, the life of the Prophet Muhammad and Prophetic History

INDEX

#

2010 Erbil Agreement, 162
72 virgins, 141

A

Abbasid Caliphate, 69
Abd al-Aziz, Umar ibn, 32, 51
Abd al-Wahhab, Muhammad ibn, 92, 93, 94, 98, 99, 107, 191, 248
Abdillahi, Hassan, 137
Abdirahman Abu Zubayr, Sheikh Mukhtar, 136
Abdul Rahman, Atiyya, 133
Abi Tālib, Ali ibn, 43, 48, 75
Afghanistan, 108, 109, 110, 111, 112, 113, 114, 115, 116, 117, 118, 119, 121, 123, 124, 128, 129, 132, 133, 137, 143, 155, 159, 230, 248, 255, 277, 286, 287, 292, 295, 296, 297, 298, 304, 307, 308
African Union Mission, 136
Age of Bliss, 62
Age of Ignorance, 7
Aisha, 47, 57, 63, 216, 278
al Ittihad al Islamiya, 138
al Khidamat, Maktab, 128
Al Qaeda, viii, 51, 66, 93, 109, 113, 124, 125, 127, 128, 129, 130, 131, 132, 133, 134, 137, 140, 143, 159, 162, 164, 182, 227, 239, 255, 256, 292, 294, 297, 299, 300, 301
al Salafiya al Jadid, 138
al-Ahwazi, Husayin, 71
Alamut, 79, 80, 82, 83, 84, 89, 92
Alamut Castle, 81, 90
al-Aqsa, Masjid, 254, 256
al-Ash'ari, Abu Musa, 44, 63
al-Aswad, Hajar, 72
al-Baghdadi, Abu Bakr, 159, 162, 163, 172, 182, 229
Aleppo, 166
al-Hasa, 64, 67, 71, 292
Ali, Caliph, 17, 18, 39, 40, 42, 43, 44, 48, 49, 50, 52, 55, 57, 58, 59, 65, 82, 190, 218
al-Islam, Ansar, 160
al-Jawlani, Abu Muhammad, 163
al-Khudrī, Abu Sa`id, 41
al-Libi, Abu Yahya, 133
al-Mahdi, Ubaydullah, 68

al-Maliki, Nouri, 172
al-Muhajir, Abu Hamza, 161
al-Mulk, Nizam, 83, 91
al-Muntasir, Imam, 79
al-Nabhani, Taqiuddin, 158, 230
al-Nusra, Jabhat, 163
Al-Shabab, 135, 136, 138, 139, 312
al-Shabab al-Mujahidin, Harakat, 135
al-Zarqawi, Abu Musab, 159, 166
al-Zawahiri, Ayman, 113, 126, 127, 129, 132, 137, 144, 163, 230
ambassador, 27
America, 33, 130, 131, 170, 172, 173, 287
Amman Message, 16, 181, 308
anarchists, 76, 77, 299
anarchy, 12, 13, 22, 111, 123, 205
ancient times, vii
anti-Christ, 166
anti-west, 5
apocalyptic message, ix, 169
apostasy, 4, 18, 27, 101, 105, 159, 179, 180, 196
Arabian Peninsula, 72, 92, 100, 127, 134, 157, 181, 220, 225
Arabic letters, 86, 87
Arabs, viii, 7, 54, 59, 101, 114, 156, 211, 216, 224, 225, 226, 239, 303
Arbitration Incident, 42, 45, 46, 47, 50, 52, 57, 58, 63, 65, 220
arguments of terrorists, 21
armed struggle, 21, 32, 136
Ashura massacre, 125
assassins, viii, 78, 79, 80, 81, 82, 83, 84, 85, 86, 87, 88, 89, 90, 91, 92, 291, 303
Assyrians, viii
Australia, 136, 144, 172, 313
awaited Mahdi, 68
'Ayro, Aadan Haashi, 139
Ayrow, Adan Hashi, 136
Azariqa, 50
Azzam, Abdullah, 124, 144
Azzam, Abdullah Yusuf, 128

B

Baathist insurgents, 164
Baghdad, 71, 73, 78, 99, 125, 157, 182, 221, 300, 306
baghy, 7
Bahrain, 71, 72, 73, 78, 303
Bakool regions, 137
Bakr, 55, 59, 156, 157, 208, 217, 223, 224, 225, 226, 301, 304
Bakr, Abu, 30, 42, 46, 54, 55, 63, 156, 159, 162, 163, 170, 172, 182, 205, 217, 220, 221, 223, 225, 226, 229, 293, 301, 310
Bamyan, 118
Bangladesh, 110, 137
Bani Tamim, 41, 92
barbaric doctrines, 2
barbarism, 5, 9, 181
Basra, 42, 43, 68, 71, 78, 99
Battle of Camel, 42, 57, 58
Battle of Siffin, 39, 42, 43, 52, 54, 58
battlefield, 2, 3, 257
Baz, Ibn, 105
beautiful wives, 9
Bedouin, 51, 52, 55, 59, 104
Bedouin Arabs, 55, 59
beheading, 165, 171, 229
Belgium, 178
belief system, viii, 12, 86, 180
best art of God, 33
Billah, Abdullah al-Mahdi, 68
bin Laden, Osama, 113, 116, 124, 126, 128, 159, 160, 230, 255
Black Stone, 68, 72, 76, 78
blocking the means to evil, 284
Borno, 145, 147, 149
Bosnia Herzegovina, 115
brainwash, 21, 35, 36
brainwashing, 9, 144
British Colonial Office, 98
British colonial rule, 151

brotherhood, 89
Brussels, 114
Buddha statues, 117
Buddhism, 3, 210
Buddhists, 257
burqa, 116
Byzantine, 28, 51, 214, 217, 235

C

Cairo, 40, 42, 45, 60, 61, 64, 66, 75, 82, 84, 94, 157, 216, 220, 221, 286, 291, 292, 293, 300, 304, 305, 306, 308
Caliph of Umar, 27
caliphate, ix, x, 3, 28, 31, 42, 43, 45, 46, 49, 51, 57, 63, 67, 68, 69, 71, 105, 126, 130, 141, 147, 152, 153, 155, 157, 158, 159, 160, 161, 166, 168, 169, 172, 175, 179, 182, 183, 184, 185, 190, 192, 215, 216, 217, 218, 219, 220, 221, 222, 224, 225, 226, 227, 229, 230, 231, 233, 299, 304, 307, 309, 310
Caliphate, Fatimid, 68
caliphs, 18, 62, 68, 69, 79, 156, 157, 175, 193, 217, 218, 222
Cameroon, 145
Canada, 144
Carmathians, 66
cartoons, 275, 276, 277, 278, 279, 280, 281, 283, 298, 311
Caucasus, 163
Chad, 145
chaos, 12, 13, 22, 75, 77, 90, 111, 123, 138, 165, 171, 268
Charter of Medina, 176, 211, 228, 235, 282
Chechnya, 257
cherry-picking, 9, 17
Christianity, viii, 3, 69, 85, 88, 143, 154, 181, 197, 198, 199, 209, 211, 234, 243, 292
Christian–Jewish alliance, 126

Church of Damascus, 32
churches, 3, 25, 26, 29, 31, 154, 161, 177, 229, 244, 282, 287
city of Hims, 28, 214
clashes among civilizations, 210, 280, 285
clergy, 12, 24, 96, 242, 257, 258
Clinton, Hillary, 286
Code of Federal Regulations, 188
colonialism, 98, 192
concept of emanation, 88
concubines, 168
constitution of the state, 54
corruption, 1, 5, 6, 7, 8, 14, 19, 21, 22, 23, 24, 26, 33, 36, 108, 111, 116, 121, 132, 145, 147, 148, 150, 154, 174, 194, 203, 218, 254, 258
counter-terrorism policies, 37
cover up, 7, 57, 63, 234, 255
criminal mentality, 6
crusader, 131

D

Dabig, ix
Daesh, 172
Dahir Aweis, Hassan, 139
Dajjal, 166
Damascus, 18, 43, 44, 45, 49, 58, 94, 209, 277, 305
dangerous doctrines, 7
Danish cartoons, 276, 277, 278, 279, 280, 294
Danish newspaper, 275, 276, 280
Day of Resurrection, 2, 279
deadly weapon, 3, 98
death cult, 171, 173, 303
defamation of religions, 279, 280, 296
deficient scholarship, 10
Deobandi, 110, 117, 121, 309
Deobandi fundamentalism, 110
destruction, 12, 30, 201, 207

deviant sect, 9
deviant thinker, 94
deviated leaders, 35
deviated sect, 8
Diène, Doudou, 279, 280, 296
dignity of human life, 12
diplomats, 27, 114, 140
disbeliever, 7, 8, 9, 18, 19, 188, 208
disorder, 1, 4, 5, 6, 14, 19, 22, 26, 33, 36, 47, 56, 99, 100, 119, 174, 194, 203, 205, 212, 218, 236, 241, 258
divine, ix, 15, 33, 59, 71, 73, 74, 77, 87, 88, 89, 105, 122, 205, 209, 210, 238, 240, 246, 249, 253, 259, 269
divine trust, 33, 259

E

early Islamic period, 7, 14, 39, 51
early period of Islam, vii, 211
Eastern Arabia, 67, 95
Efendi, Mustafa Sabri, 158
Egypt, 27, 43, 49, 57, 69, 98, 129, 132, 204, 225, 253, 286, 292, 298, 300, 307
elimination of polytheism, 161
embassy, 27, 125, 275, 277, 309
End of Times, viii, 70, 75
enemies of God, 167, 257, 267
enemy combatants, 2, 30, 263
enjoining good, 16, 22, 205
envoys, 24, 27
esoteric knowledge, 71, 75, 81, 89
esoteric teachings, 67, 86
Esposito, John, 121, 165, 297
Ethiopia, 139, 140
Europe, 33, 96, 128, 163, 168, 200, 277, 280
European people, 33
European Union, 125
evangelical, viii

evidence, 14, 37, 58, 61, 120, 127, 194, 196, 224
evidences from the Qur'an, 21, 36
extreme ideas, vii, 15, 95, 195
extremist ideology, ix, x, 37, 50, 53, 65, 74, 78, 97, 116, 129, 145, 246

F

faith traditions, vii, 3, 23, 24, 29, 70, 88, 89, 90, 176, 178, 197, 198, 212, 213, 239, 257, 271
Fallujah, 172
fanatic rebels, 11
Farewell Pilgrimage, 4
Farrah Aidid, Mohamed, 138
Fatima, 82
Fatimid caliph, 79, 84
fatwa, ix, 16, 35, 190, 202, 210, 230, 259, 266
fearsome warriors, 167
Federal Government of Somalia, 136
first caliph of Islam, 30
first communists, 76
forbidding evil, 16, 53
foreign forces, 30, 119, 120, 121, 141, 143, 161, 257
foreign representatives, 27
four caliphs, ix, 142, 156, 157, 217, 220, 222, 226, 227, 231
four levels of meaning, 86, 87
fourth caliph of Islam, 18, 158
France, 144, 178, 201
fundamental Islamic teachings, 12

G

Gaza, 254
Ghana, 144
Global Terrorism Index, 146, 311
Gnosticism, 67, 71, 74

Index

God Almighty, 1, 3, 4, 5, 6, 11, 13, 14, 25, 29, 32, 33, 100, 103, 160, 174, 206, 218, 236, 237, 238, 240, 244
Golan Heights, 254
Golden Age of Islam, 217
good orators, 15
Grand Master, 84
Grand Temple, 89
Great King, vii
Group of the People of Sunnah for Preaching and Jihad, 145
guerrilla war, 115, 143

H

Habbab ibn Arat, Abdullah ibn, 46
hadith, 8, 10, 42, 46, 61, 77, 223, 300
Haji Muhammadu Ndimi Mosque, 149
Hajr, 71
Hamadan, 59
Hamas, 255
Hanafi school of thought, 208
Hanifa, Abu, 208
Haram, Boko, 136, 143, 145, 146, 147, 148, 149, 150, 151, 152, 153, 154, 239, 302, 303, 305, 309, 311
Harura, 40, 46, 47
Haruriyya, 40
Hashashīn, 78, 82, 87
Hekmatyar, Gulbuddin, 111
Hell, 1, 4, 6, 7, 13, 14, 34, 35, 56, 69, 74, 143, 203, 204, 207, 210, 260, 266, 270
Hempher, Mr., 98
Herat, 159
Hereafter, 4, 19, 34, 203, 260, 261, 269
heretic sect, 78
heretical movement, 71, 78
heroism, 9, 84
Hezbollah, x, 164, 255
Hinduism, 3, 209
Hizb ut-Tahrir, 158, 230

Hizbul-Wahdat, Hazara, 111
Holy Book, 9, 142, 182
holy war, 5, 56, 94, 107, 139, 140, 142, 192, 198, 207, 246, 249, 256, 292, 293, 303
Horn of Africa, 134, 138, 141
House of God, 2, 225
Hudaybiya Treaty, 48
hujjah, 85

I

ibn al-Ash'as, Hamdan, 68
ibn As, Amr, 44, 63
ibn Hanbal, Ahmad, 30, 93, 103, 156, 216, 267, 300
ibn Hassan al-Qurmuti, Abu Taher, 76
ibn Ismail, Qaim al-Zaman Muhammad, 75
ibn Muljam al-Muradi, Abd al-Rahman ibn Amr, 50
ibn Saud, Abd al-Aziz, 96
ibn Saud, Muhammad, 93, 102
ibn Shaddad, Abdullah, 47
ibn Ubayda, Urwa, 45
ibn Yusuf, Hajjaj, 55
ibn Zuhayr al-Sādi, Hurkus, 42
ICCPR, 273, 281
idolatry, 92, 106, 117
imamate, 67, 68, 69, 75, 83, 89
imperialism, ix, 192
in the name of religion, vii, 3, 9, 50, 60, 66, 77, 78, 91, 189, 208, 233, 234, 246, 247, 249, 255, 288
India, 95, 110, 180, 225
inevitable victory, 167
injunctions of the Qur'an, 13
injustice, 8, 13, 17, 22, 23, 28, 29, 33, 34, 52, 70, 152, 174, 194, 205, 211, 212, 243, 244
innovators, 7, 105
interfaith dialogue, 24, 176, 177, 209, 210, 243, 250, 271, 274, 282, 283

interfaith harmony, 24
International Security Assistance Force, 286
Iran, x, 68, 69, 85, 94, 111, 113, 165, 171
irhāb, 267, 268
IS, ix, 161, 162, 163, 168, 172
ISIL, ix, 146, 155, 159, 167, 171, 173, 182, 293, 303
ISIS, ix, 46, 51, 66, 93, 135, 146, 155, 159, 162, 163, 164, 165, 166, 167, 168, 169, 170, 171, 172, 173, 174, 175, 176, 178, 179, 181, 182, 183, 184, 185, 188, 191, 192, 193, 195, 198, 199, 200, 201, 202, 209, 229, 232, 233, 239, 255, 293, 294, 297, 299, 304, 305, 306, 307, 308
Islamic Courts Union, 136, 139, 140
Islamic disciplines, 10, 250, 313
Islamic Emirate of Afghanistan, 109, 113
Islamic eschatological literature, 166
Islamic history, 1, 3, v, ix, 8, 17, 18, 23, 32, 39, 43, 51, 52, 54, 55, 56, 66, 82, 95, 122, 134, 152, 156, 157, 176, 185, 189, 215, 216, 227, 243, 245, 249, 302, 307
Islamic lands, 23, 31, 50, 51, 129, 175, 193
Islamic law, 28, 33, 72, 74, 101, 102, 103, 106, 110, 112, 116, 119, 122, 126, 130, 131, 135, 138, 141, 142, 145, 147, 148, 149, 150, 151, 154, 155, 166, 190, 204, 222, 233, 247, 252, 256, 266, 269, 272, 277, 286, 307, 310, 313
Islamic regimes, 101, 129, 302
Islamic Republic of Iran, x, 248
Islamic revivalism, 154
Islamic sects, 16, 29, 168
Islamic state, 43, 50, 54, 96, 100, 129, 132, 142, 145, 147, 148, 149, 150, 152, 154, 155, 157, 160, 163, 166, 173, 176, 182, 184, 185, 223, 227, 232, 233, 282, 302
Islamic State, x, 111, 112, 133, 135, 138, 141, 142, 145, 155, 159, 160, 161, 163, 164, 166, 168, 169, 170, 171, 172, 182, 217, 293, 299, 301, 311
Islamic State in Iraq and the Levant, 171

Islamic State in West African Province, 145
Islamic State of Afghanistan, 111, 112
Islamic State of Iraq and Syria, 171
Islamic symbols, 12
Islamic system, 115, 124
Islamic teachings, 3, 5, 12, 16, 25, 30, 72, 75, 154, 174, 179, 213
Islamic terminology, 36, 193
Israel, viii, 131, 168, 253, 254, 256, 258
Israeli occupation, 253

J

jahiliyya, 105, 181, 252
Jama al-Tawhid wa'l-Jihad, 159
Jamiat Ulema-e-Islam, 111
Jerusalem, 31, 230, 254
Jesus, viii, 75, 88, 166, 210
Jewish Zealots, viii
jihad, ix, 3, 5, 6, 7, 9, 12, 17, 18, 20, 21, 22, 30, 56, 94, 95, 120, 121, 124, 127, 129, 130, 131, 132, 133, 134, 141, 144, 149, 152, 153, 155, 160, 175, 179, 187, 190, 192, 193, 195, 198, 199, 200, 202, 204, 205, 207, 209, 230, 233, 234, 241, 242, 243, 244, 249, 253, 255, 256, 262, 263, 292, 293, 294, 295, 297, 302, 309
jihadist ideology, x, 195
jihadist struggles, 152
Jordan, 159, 168, 181, 253, 308
judgment belongs to God alone, 40
Judgment Day, 1, 13, 26, 28, 35, 36, 194
Jurist, 28
just cause, 121, 123, 134, 174, 194, 212, 214, 253, 256
just war, 2, 3, 257, 265

K

Kabul, 111, 112, 121, 123
Kampala, 140

Index 323

Kandahar, 108, 112, 118
Karmathians, 66
Kashmir, 257
Kenya, 139, 140, 143
Khaldun, Ibn, 69, 70, 157, 158, 222, 300
Khan, Möngke, 92
Kharijite, vii, 8, 39, 40, 42, 45, 46, 50, 51, 52, 53, 54, 55, 56, 57, 58, 59, 61, 62, 63, 65, 77, 157, 199, 220, 221, 231
Khaybar, 31
khilāfa, 155, 218, 219
Khuwaysira, Dhul, 41
Kingdom of Saudi Arabia, 93, 97
Kufa, 43, 44, 45, 49, 50, 70, 71, 78
Kufa Mosque, 50

L

last sermon, 4
lawful, 1, 3, 5, 7, 9, 17, 19, 26, 28, 30, 46, 57, 74, 116, 208, 235, 259, 278

M

madrasa students, 111, 118, 123
Maghreb countries, 134, 136
Mahdi, viii, 69, 70, 75, 76
Maiduguri, 145, 147, 149
major sins, 8, 9, 42, 190
Makkah, 4, 30, 156, 216, 223, 225, 228, 238, 293
Malaysia, 137
Maliki, Prime Minister, 162
malls, 3, 143, 269
Mansur, Akhtar, 109
Mariqa, 40
martyrdom, x, 9, 35, 61, 120, 141, 148, 161, 174, 190, 242, 243, 263, 264, 292, 295
Masjid al-Nabawi, 282
Massoud, Ahmad Shah, 112, 113, 120

media, 5, 16, 119, 127, 133, 134, 140, 141, 145, 166, 167, 169, 170, 171, 172, 193, 195, 196, 201, 233, 250, 273, 274, 277, 279, 280, 283, 288, 289, 297, 306, 307, 310, 311
mediation techniques, 81
Medina, 24, 35, 43, 44, 50, 58, 72, 78, 97, 98, 154, 156, 176, 177, 211, 216, 223, 226, 227, 228, 235, 236, 237, 238, 242, 259, 261, 268, 281, 282, 309
megalomania, 89
Mesopotamian region, 134, 171
Messiah, viii, 69
messianic movements, viii
messianic sects, viii
Middle East, 23, 33, 79, 98, 99, 100, 101, 104, 138, 149, 158, 160, 168, 171, 175, 178, 181, 189, 198, 217, 230, 248, 253, 255, 256, 258, 291, 292, 295, 296, 299, 302, 308, 309
militant radical Islamic view, 128
militant Salafi movements, 255
misinterpretation of the religious texts, 19
misinterpreting the Holy Qur'an, 3
moderate Muslim scholars, 37, 97, 135, 136, 144, 200, 209, 250, 289
Mogadishu, 136
monasteries, 25, 30, 175, 177, 194, 244, 282
Mongol attacks, 79
Mongol emperor, 92
Mongols, 82, 92, 131
monks, 24
moral guidelines, 12
mosques, 3, 4, 25, 26, 106, 161, 244
Mosul, 165, 172
Movement of Warrior Youth, 135
Mu'āwiya, Yazid ibn, 56
Muawiya, 18
Mubarakiyya, 69
Mudar, 59
Muhakkima, 40
*mullah*s, 123

Index

Musaylama, 27
Muslim army, 29, 30, 223, 225, 262
Muslim Brotherhood, 105
Muslim ruler, ix, 18, 29, 31, 53, 61, 83, 104, 132, 156, 213, 220, 242
Muslim youth, 5
Mutazilate, 157
mystical interpretations of the Qur'an, 67

N

Nahrawan, 46, 49
Nairobi, 143
Najd, 92, 95, 101
NATO, 114, 125
Neo-Platonism, 67, 85, 87
New Zealand, 144
Niger, 145
Nigeria, 143, 145, 146, 147, 148, 149, 151, 152, 153, 154, 155, 296, 297, 302, 303, 307, 310
Nizari Isma'ili state, 79
Nizari-Isma'ilism, 79, 82
noble goal, 7
nomads, 51, 54, 61, 94
North Africa, 51, 102, 149, 163, 168, 217, 295
North Atlantic Treaty Organization, 125
Northern Ireland, 257
notion of piety, 53, 60
notion of *takfir*, 134, 161

O

Obama, Barack, 286
Oman, 51, 72
Omar, Mohammed, 108, 159, 230
only true Muslims, 19, 20, 32
Operation Desert Storm, 129
Operation Enduring Freedom, 109, 129
oppression, 5, 8, 17, 22, 23, 24, 26, 29, 32, 33, 76, 128, 152, 205, 214, 236, 243, 244, 247
oppressive, 15, 22, 138
Ottoman Caliphate, 94, 95, 105

P

Pakistan, 109, 110, 111, 112, 113, 116, 128, 137, 171, 275, 277, 287, 309
Palestine, 253, 255
paradise, 9, 21, 26, 35, 55, 79, 84, 90, 203, 208, 263
partial approach, 9, 10, 12, 17, 60, 195, 246
Party of God, x
Pashtun tribes, 109
peaceful coexistence, 24, 252, 288
People of the Book, 27, 31, 47, 65, 176, 177, 213, 282
Persian Gulf, 72
Persian language, 81, 98
Person of God, 73
Petraeus, General David, 286
PKK, 257
places of disbelief, 23
political assassinations, 79, 140
political Islam, 130, 149, 190, 198, 200, 254, 255, 302
political Islamist movements, 130, 254
political power, x, 53, 90, 92, 97, 106, 141, 152, 248
Polo, Marco, 80, 84, 90, 297
polytheist, 7, 94, 156, 211, 216, 281
Practice of the Prophet, 47, 48
pre-Islamic Age of Ignorance, 133
priests, 24, 29, 30, 177, 282
primary Islamic sources, ix, 102, 179, 187, 196, 198, 200, 201, 227
pristine form of Islam, 92, 118, 132, 142, 176, 248

Index

prophetic traditions, 1, 10, 11, 15, 35, 41, 158, 180, 188, 197, 198, 199, 227, 230, 245, 247, 313
protector of Islam, 166
pro-Western regimes, 131
psychologically, 23, 178
pure form of Islam, 96, 107, 118, 133, 252
purification of Islam, 54
puritanical Islamic movement, 96

Q

Qarafi, 28, 306
Qarāmita, 66
Qarmat, Hamdan, 67, 68, 69, 70, 71
Qarmathians, 66
Qarmatians, 66, 67, 68, 69, 70, 71, 72, 73, 74, 75, 76, 77, 78, 298, 299
qisas, 7
Quetta, 110, 300
Qur'an, 1, 44, 52, 117, 155, 218, 219, 272, 278
Quranic verse, 4, 11, 18, 35, 36, 41, 45, 48, 52, 60, 63, 64, 65, 75, 117, 189, 211, 212, 234, 240, 246, 248, 266
qurra, 48, 52, 61

R

rabbis, 24, 29, 30, 64
racist tendencies, 81
radical interpretation, vii, 135, 199
radical Islamists, ix
Rahman, Omar Abdel, ix
Ramadi, 159, 172, 227
Raziq, Ali Abdur, 158
rebellion, 17, 18, 32, 53, 54, 56, 62, 78, 236, 241
rebellions, 50, 55, 70, 241
rebellious attacks, 83

reform, 6, 7, 16, 17, 22, 32, 37, 95, 146, 151, 154, 205, 295
religious arguments, ix, 36, 95, 160
religious concepts, 3, 4, 5, 7, 36, 53, 101, 108, 120, 134, 141, 143, 144, 148, 152, 153, 175, 179, 189, 233, 245, 247
religious garb, 9, 12
religious police force, 117
religious propaganda, 133
religious rituals, 9, 10, 13, 15, 17, 19, 20, 24, 60, 86, 103
religious ruling, ix, 16, 47, 127, 190, 256, 266
religious verdicts, 34
religious zealot, 9, 55, 162
religious zealotry, 9, 162
respect for the sacred, v, 200, 203, 243, 271, 276, 278, 280, 281, 284, 288
resurrection, 75, 82, 89, 283
revivalist movements, 149, 152
revolt, 17, 23, 39, 40, 54, 55, 59, 70, 78, 83, 105
Rightly Guided Caliphs, 55, 217
rights of minority groups, 31
rights of non-Muslims, 24, 27, 28
Riyadh, 66, 92, 102, 199, 224, 226, 229, 278, 300, 303, 305, 307
Roman Emperor, 28
Roobow, Mukhtar, 137, 141
Ruler of Believers, 118
Russians, 115, 214

S

Sabbah, Hassan, 78, 79, 80, 81, 83, 84, 85, 90, 91
sacred, 1, 4, 7, 25, 29, 33, 34, 76, 97, 129, 158, 174, 176, 192, 200, 203, 215, 236, 238, 239, 241, 247, 258, 265, 268, 271, 273, 276, 277, 283, 284, 285, 286, 287, 288

sacred trust, 29, 34, 203, 259
sacrifice, ix, x, 80, 260
sadd al-dharā'ī, 284, 285
Sadr City, 125
salaf, 105
Salafism, 95, 96, 176, 190, 191, 304
Salafists, x, 92, 104, 138
sanctity, 1, 7, 12, 25, 30, 34, 236, 285
sanctity of life, 1, 34
Sargon of Akkad, vii, viii
Sargon the Great, vii
Sargonic dynasty, viii
Saudis, x
Sawad, 66
Sayyaf, Abdul Rasul, 111
schools, 3, 102, 104, 108, 111, 119, 145, 146, 150, 154
second coming of Jesus, viii
Second Gulf War, 105
secret cells, 83
sectarian bigotry, 175
sectarian disputes, 151
secular Arab regimes, 131
sedition, 18, 23
self-sacrificing agents, 90, 91
Seljuk State, 79
Semitic Akkadian, vii
September 11, 2001, 96, 109, 110, 113, 114, 124, 125, 126, 127, 128, 130, 173, 200, 202, 255, 280, 286, 303, 310
set things right, 6, 48
seven speakers, 74
seveners, 67
Sharia, 23, 75, 95, 101, 104, 109, 127, 133, 139, 152, 161, 166, 170, 179, 191, 198, 222, 246, 252, 307, 309
Sharia committee, 127
Sharia courts, 139
Sharia law, 95, 170
Sharif, Mazar-i, 113
Shāṭibī, Imam, 286
Sheikh, ix, 136, 138, 139, 141, 158

Sheikh al-Islam, 158
Shekau, Abubakar, 146
Shia groups, 67
Shia sect, 66, 78, 99
Shiite, viii, x, 69, 80, 82, 83, 87, 94, 99, 111, 117, 133, 159, 162, 164, 167, 172, 185, 189, 233, 255, 258
Shiite creed, 83
Shiite extremism, x
Shurat, 41
Siad Barre, General Mohamed, 138
Sinai Peninsula, 254
Singesar, 112
Six-Day War, viii
slave girls, 168
Smokers of hashish, 78
Somalia, 127, 135, 136, 137, 138, 139, 140, 141, 142, 143, 144, 296, 303, 312
Somalian Islamic scholars, 136
Soviet occupation, 108, 132
Soviet Union, 111, 128
spoils of war, 41, 50, 94, 178
Sri Lanka, 257
strict interpretation of religious texts, 96
strike fear upon society, 19
striking fear into the hearts of the enemy, 266, 267
Sudan, 129, 137
suicide attacks, 34, 115, 120, 125, 140, 143, 148, 167, 199, 207, 208, 253, 257, 258, 260, 261, 262, 263, 264, 265, 266, 267, 269, 270, 288, 294, 302
suicide bombers, 25, 120, 148, 160, 164, 181, 197, 262
suicide bombing, 8, 12, 30, 34, 35, 120, 137, 140, 161, 210, 257, 260
suicide jacket, 120
Sumerian, vii
Sunnah, 14, 21, 22, 27, 35, 36, 37, 42, 47, 49, 60, 66, 102, 106, 117, 118, 134, 136, 142, 145, 152, 153, 158, 185, 188, 190,

Index

191, 195, 198, 224, 227, 228, 234, 249, 250, 251, 252, 263, 304
Sunni Muslims, 68, 73, 78, 82, 83, 99, 156, 189, 217
Sunni scholars, 56, 85, 91, 157, 223, 231, 279
Supreme Gathering, 13
supreme leader, 122
Swahili Coast, 137
synagogues, 3, 25, 26, 29, 177, 229, 244, 282
syncretic religious group, 67
Syria, 30, 50, 68, 69, 79, 81, 100, 127, 159, 162, 163, 164, 165, 166, 169, 171, 172, 182, 183, 184, 229, 232, 253, 277, 301, 309, 310
Syrian regime, 163, 165
Syrian region, 28
Syrian town, ix, 169

T

taking arms against a state, 17
Talha, 57, 63
talib, 108
taliban, 108, 109, 110, 111, 112, 113, 114, 115, 116, 117, 118, 119, 120, 121, 122, 123, 124, 129, 143, 154, 155, 159, 230, 248, 286, 292, 296, 297, 298, 304, 305, 306, 308, 309
Taliban state, 113
Tamil Tigers, 257
Tamim, 59
Tamim, Bani, 41, 92
tawhid, 92, 95, 104, 105, 161, 179, 184
Tay, 59
Taymiyya, Ibn, 9, 93, 94, 98, 101, 103, 104, 131, 190, 191, 301, 304
Temple of Light, 89
terrorist groups, vii, viii, ix, x, 5, 37, 51, 56, 66, 93, 95, 96, 100, 124, 125, 126, 127,

130, 131, 132, 134, 135, 144, 148, 150, 153, 155, 162, 168, 174, 176, 178, 181, 183, 184, 188, 192, 193, 195, 197, 199, 202, 207, 209, 210, 214, 227, 229, 231, 232, 233, 234, 239, 245, 246, 247, 250, 252, 253, 255, 256, 257, 261, 263, 264, 266, 267, 269, 289
the act of Satan, 8
The African Union, 135, 136, 137, 303
The United Nations International Covenant on Civil and Political Rights, 281
theological responses, 1, 3, v, ix, 187
Tigris, 46
traditions of the Noble Prophet, vii, 182, 249, 250, 267
trials, 18
tribal fanaticism, 59
true Muslims, 16, 23, 103, 133, 206
twelve imams, 67, 83
twelve zodiacal constellations, 74
twisted ideology, 10
tyrants, viii, 22, 76, 247
Tyre, William, 80

U

'Ubayda, Abu, 28, 224
Uganda, 140
UK, 110, 137, 144, 151, 159, 297, 311
Umayyad, 32, 42, 50, 51, 62, 189, 218
Umayyad caliphs, 50, 51
Umayyad period, 50, 51
un-Islamic customs, 100, 101, 102
United Arab Emirates, 109
United Front, 113
United Kingdom, 144, 151
United Nations Security Council, 125
United States, ix, 125, 126, 128, 129, 130, 131, 132, 135, 141, 144, 161, 163, 209
unlawful, 3, 5, 7, 143, 154, 188, 269
unlawful means, 5

Index

US citizens, 33, 167
Usama, 2, 229
utopian state, 76

V

value of human life, 2
vehicles loaded with bombs, 25, 208
vicegerency, 155, 218
violence, 1, 3, v, vii, viii, ix, x, 3, 4, 5, 6, 7, 8, 9, 10, 12, 13, 15, 16, 17, 19, 20, 21, 22, 23, 26, 30, 33, 34, 35, 36, 37, 39, 40, 50, 51, 53, 54, 55, 56, 58, 60, 63, 65, 66, 68, 71, 76, 77, 78, 79, 81, 82, 84, 90, 91, 95, 106, 107, 108, 120, 121, 123, 124, 125, 128, 130, 131, 132, 134, 135, 141, 142, 144, 148, 150, 153, 154, 161, 165, 168, 173, 174, 175, 178, 179, 183, 185, 188, 191, 193, 195, 198, 199, 200, 202, 204, 207, 215, 233, 234, 235, 236, 239, 243, 244, 245, 246, 247, 248, 249, 251, 252, 254, 255, 256, 257, 266, 268, 269, 270, 273, 274, 275, 276, 278, 280, 281, 283, 287, 288, 289, 293, 294, 296, 302, 305
visiting tombs, 95, 100, 101
von Hammer Purgstall, Joseph, 79

W

Wahhabi ideology, 92, 94, 97, 98, 99, 101, 103, 105, 106, 107, 108, 142, 154
Wahhabism, 92, 93, 95, 96, 97, 98, 99, 100, 101, 102, 103, 104, 105, 106, 107, 108, 124, 136, 176, 190, 191, 248, 293, 304
West Bank, 254
western countries, 5, 110, 136, 137, 172, 191, 192, 195, 196, 200, 211
western culture, 131, 153
western education is forbidden, 145
western imperialism, 144
Word of God, 19, 47, 249
World Trade Centre, ix, 124

X

xenophobia, 169, 279, 280, 296

Y

Yazidi community, 125
Yemen, 50, 66, 137, 226
young Muslims, 5, 124, 149, 185, 191, 245, 255
Yusuf, Mohammed, 145, 147, 148, 149, 154, 155

Z

Zamzam Well, 72
Zoroastrian temple, 32
Zoroastrianism, 67, 72
Zubayr, 57, 63
Zubayr, Mukhtar Abu, 140